Lincoln's Tragic Admiral

A NATION DIVIDED:
NEW STUDIES IN CIVIL WAR HISTORY

James I. Robertson Jr., *Editor*

LINCOLN'S TRAGIC ADMIRAL

The Life of Samuel Francis Du Pont

Kevin J. Weddle

UNIVERSITY OF VIRGINIA PRESS

Charlottesville and London

UNIVERSITY OF VIRGINIA PRESS
© 2005 by the Rector and Visitors of the University of Virginia
All rights reserved
Printed in the United States of America on acid-free paper

First published 2005

9 8 7 6 5 4 3 2 1

Library of Congress Cataloging-in-Publication Data
Weddle, Kevin John,
Lincoln's tragic admiral : the life of Samuel Francis Du Pont /
Kevin J. Weddle.
p. cm.—(A nation divided)
Includes bibliographical references and index.
ISBN 0-8139-2332-8 (cloth : alk. paper)
1. Du Pont, Samuel Francis, 1803–1865. 2. Admirals—United
States—Biography. 3. United States. Navy—Biography. 4. United
States—History—Civil War, 1861–1865—Naval operations. 5. United
States—History, Naval—To 1900. I. Title. II. Series.
E467.1.D9W43 2005
359′.0092—dc22
2004022258

For Jeanie and Anne

Contents

Illustrations

MAPS

Acknowledgments

I would like to thank everyone who contributed to the successful completion of this book, but limited space renders that goal impossible. So with sin-
cere apologies to those I have omitted, I will try my best. Since this biography started out as a dissertation, thanks go first to my adviser, Professor
James M. McPherson. I am fortunate indeed to be able to call Jim, a highly
acclaimed Civil War historian, my friend. Always cheerful and positive, Professor McPherson's advice and guidance always provided the right motiva-
tion. Professors John Murrin and Mike Mahoney, members of my dissertation committee and distinguished professors, friends, and mentors, are
perfect examples of the kind of professionals all historians should aspire to
be. Without their patience, encouragement, and guidance, I would never
have come this far. Dean of American military historians, the late Temple
University professor emeritus Russell F. Weigley also rendered great service. I am grateful that he agreed to give early versions of the book a very
close reading. Special thanks go to my friend, professional colleague, men-
tor, and former boss, Colonel (Retired) Paul L. Miles. A remarkably talented
army officer, historian, and engineer, Paul has been a role model for me
since we met at West Point nineteen years ago.

Other distinguished historians graciously agreed to read the manuscript,
including Craig L. Symonds, Eliot A. Cohen, and Robert M. Browning Jr.
They saved me from making several embarrassing errors of fact and inter-
pretation. The final product is much better due to their efforts. I can never
repay their kindness. Dr. Michael Oplinger, a very talented surgeon and an
enthusiastic history buff, helped me understand the medical issues associated
with Du Pont's final illness and death. My colleagues and students at the
United States Army War College were always supportive and enthusiastic
about the book, if perhaps a bit dubious about the nautical subject matter.
Particularly helpful were Frank Hancock, Dave Brooks, Len Fullencamp,

Williamson "Wick" Murray, Mike Matheny, Dan Klippstein, Al Lord, Paul Jussel, and Jim Johnsen. It is a privilege and an honor to serve with these outstanding soldier-scholars.

Many people at dozens of libraries and repositories have helped make this project possible. Jon Williams, Barb Hall, and Lynn Catanese of the Hagley Library and Museum were very helpful. Chief among those from the Hagley who deserve special mention is Marge McNinch, who never balked at any request or question no matter how obscure or difficult. Her amazing ability to guide me through the massive Du Pont collection ensured that each visit to the archives was productive. The interlibrary loan staffs at Princeton's Firestone Library and the Army War College, especially Patsy Meyers and Nancy Baylor, were always friendly, accommodating, and efficient. The superb and knowledgeable staff of the Army Heritage and Education Center (formerly the Military History Institute) was indispensable. Dr. Conrad Crane, Dr. Dick Sommers, and Jay Graybeal were instrumental in suggesting sources and finding photographs. The Naval Historical Center staff was equally impressive. Dr. Ed Marolda provided useful suggestions, and the expert staff at the center's photo archives were helpful and efficient. Thanks also go to the staffs at the National Archives, Library of Congress, and the Nimitz Library, United States Naval Academy.

In addition, this project benefited from timely financial support provided by the United States Naval Historical Center and the Hagley Museum and Library. Portions of chapter 4 first appeared as " 'The Magic Touch of Reform': Samuel Francis Du Pont and the Efficiency Board of 1855," *Journal of Military History* 68 (2) (April 2004): 471–504. Portions of chapter 6 first appeared as "The Blockade Board of 1861 and Union Naval Strategy," *Civil War History* 48 (2) (June 2002): 123–42, and are reprinted with permission of The Kent State University Press. All of the maps are reprinted, by permission, from Craig L. Symonds, *The Naval Historical Atlas of the U.S. Navy.* Cartography by William J. Clipson. (Annapolis, Md.: Naval Institute Press, © 1995), pp. 70, 80, 84, 96. My sister-in-law and a very talented artist, Aimee Falk of Albarella Design in South Saint Paul, Minnesota, made some necessary changes and prepared the maps for publication.

The friendly and talented staff at the University of Virginia Press made this, my first book, an enjoyable experience. My editor, Dick Holway, showed initial interest in Du Pont and provided timely encouragement along the way. The rest of the staff was equally supportive and without their considerable efforts and talents, this book would have never been born.

Thanks also to my parents, Betty and Ernie Weddle, who passed on to me their fondness for history and provided a loving home not unlike that enjoyed by Frank Du Pont. Finally, the most heartfelt love, thanks, and appreciation go to the two most important women in my life: my wife, Jeanie, and our beautiful daughter, Anne. Jeanie spent countless hours reading chapter drafts, producing the index, and providing nothing but the most helpful criticism. For this and all the separations, challenges, and hardships she has endured during twenty-five years of life as an army spouse, I have incurred a debt I can never repay. Anne is simply the best daughter anyone could ever have.

Lincoln's Tragic Admiral

Introduction

T HE CEREMONY took place in the morning of 6 July 1863. It was a typical summer day in coastal South Carolina, and the heat and humidity had already enveloped Port Royal Sound like an oppressive blanket. Officers and sailors stood at rigid attention, suffering in their best uniforms as rivers of sweat ran down their backs. Despite the ongoing war with the South, the crews had worked hard to prepare for the day's special event. The deck and rigging of the steam frigate *Wabash*, flagship of the Union's South Atlantic Blockading Squadron, looked as good as could be expected from a ship that had undergone months of combat duty. Crews of ships anchored nearby manned the rails and yards and prepared to render a salute to their new commander and to cheer the old. As Rear Admiral Samuel Francis Du Pont hauled down his flag, took the eighteen-gun salute, and prepared to hand over command of the squadron to his replacement, Rear Admiral John A. Dahlgren, he was at the end of almost half a century of naval service. It was a great career by almost any objective measure, but Du Pont was leaving the *Wabash* and the squadron under a cloud. In merely twenty months he had gone from being the toast of the Union, receiving the Thanks of Congress, and being among the first men in the history of the United States to achieve the rank of rear admiral to this melancholy summer day on the *Wabash*'s quarterdeck when he was relieved of command and castigated in the press and his own service as an incompetent and worse. In part, Du Pont's downfall was the result of his own excessive pride and stubbornness. Du Pont's career, which had been so full of promise and accomplishment, had in its last two years displayed all the elements of a classical Greek tragedy: the noble hero suffering a fall from his lofty perch due at least in part to his own personal character flaws. Du Pont's distinguished career had slowly but inexorably been reduced to a Civil War tragedy.[1]

The North had rejoiced on 7 November 1861 when Du Pont won the first major Union victory of the Civil War at Port Royal, South Carolina. With this achievement the Union gained a vital foothold deep in enemy territory from which to sustain its naval blockade and to conduct future joint operations that directly threatened Confederate forces. For a few brief weeks, Du Pont, an ambitious and capable officer, found himself the favorite of the Lincoln administration and the entire North. His achievement appeared to be the culmination of an eventful antebellum career that was virtually unprecedented in its scope and influence. On the eve of the war, Du Pont was arguably the most capable, most experienced, and best-known officer in the United States Navy. Superiors, peers, and subordinates all recognized his considerable talents, and all fully expected Du Pont to rise to the pinnacle of his profession. His victory at Port Royal seemed to confirm this conventional wisdom. Yet less than two years later Du Pont would leave his flagship for the last time, relieved of his command, disgraced, and struggling to retrieve his career and reputation.

Du Pont entered the United States Navy in 1817 and served continuously on active duty for forty-eight years, nineteen of them at sea. During this time the United States underwent a remarkable transformation from a localized agricultural society to an industrializing and market-based system. The navy also experienced epochal changes from sail to steam, from wood to iron, and from paddle wheels to propellers. Samuel Francis Du Pont was at the center of these and many other extraordinary events during this transforming period in the navy's history.

This book encompasses three major themes: Du Pont's role in the development of United States naval strategy before and during the Civil War, his push to reform and transform the navy between the Mexican War and the Civil War, and his place at the nexus of the navy's technological transition from wood to iron. Du Pont's most recent biographer, James M. Merrill, argued that the most significant thing about Du Pont is how his remarkably varied experiences shaped his ability to lead and influenced his preparation to assume high flag rank. It is hard to dispute Merrill's thesis. This book argues, however, that the true significance of Du Pont's naval career is not in how he was affected by his experiences but in the tremendous and positive influence he exerted on the transformation of the United States Navy structurally, technologically, and strategically from the Mexican War through the Civil War.

Du Pont's natural leadership skills, his superb seamanship, and his conduct in combat during the Mexican War, as well as his impeccable pedigree, marked him as one of the navy's brightest talents. By the start of the 1850s, although only a commander, Du Pont had emerged as a highly influential officer whose professional opinion and advice were often sought by the navy's top military and civilian leadership. This position was shared by only a small coterie of widely respected and trusted naval officers; it allowed Du Pont to advance his ideas on the service's—and the nation's—strategic direction and on how to reform the navy.

This book is largely based on the voluminous Du Pont papers. Du Pont's handwriting is notoriously illegible at times, and his punctuation can best be described as imaginative. For this reason I have made some minor changes in punctuation to clarify quotations from his writings when necessary.

1

The Early Years

To do my duty wherever it may lie.
—Samuel Francis Du Pont

After enduring a horrifying three-month winter passage across the Atlantic, Pierre Samuel DuPont de Nemours and his two sons, Victor and Eleuthère Irénée, and their families landed in the Newport, Rhode Island, on New Year's Day 1800. Leaving behind most of their possessions and property in the wake of the political turbulence of revolutionary France, the Du Ponts found it providential that they had started their new life on the first day of a new century. Du Ponts ever after (even to this day) would celebrate New Year's Day as the anniversary of the family's escape from France, its deliverance from the violent sea, and its acceptance by its adopted country. Although Victor had grown to love the United States while serving as French consul in Charleston, South Carolina, from 1795 to 1798, Pierre had to convince his reluctant sons to leave their ancestral home for the New World.

The three Du Ponts and their families initially settled in Bergen Point (now Bayonne), New Jersey. Pierre and Victor had already established friendships with many prominent Americans, the most helpful of whom was the newly elected president, Thomas Jefferson. Soon Victor's brother, Eleuthère Irénée, left New Jersey to build a gunpowder mill on the banks of the Brandywine River in Delaware; these were the mills that would ultimately develop into the immense DuPont Chemical Corporation. Victor and his family stayed on in New Jersey where on 27 September 1803 Gabrielle Josephine du Pont gave birth to a son, Samuel Francis—called Frank by his family and closest friends—the first Du Pont born in the New World.

Frank joined an already tight-knit family that included an older sister, Amelie Elizabeth, and a brother, Charles. Three years later another sister, Julia Sophia, joined the children. The Roman Catholic Gabrielle and the Protestant Victor agreed to raise their sons in Victor's faith and their daughters in Gabrielle's. After several unsuccessful business ventures and the failure of Pierre's land company, Victor decided to move his family. He joined his brother on the Brandywine and there built and ran a successful woolen mill. Soon the family moved into Louviers, a new Regency-style house across the river from the gunpowder works of his soon-to-be-famous brother.[1]

Because both Pierre and his two sons were well connected socially and through business ties to prominent Americans, young Frank was treated to an exciting and stimulating childhood. Discussions of literature, politics, foreign affairs, and other interesting topics were commonplace in the Du Pont home. These childhood experiences undoubtedly contributed to his lifelong love of books, lively and intelligent conversation, and political debate. Although his parents quickly embraced the American way of life, they retained many reminders and customs of their native country and ensured that all of the children maintained fluency in French. His heritage was French, but Du Pont was an American through and through. Life on the Brandywine was idyllic for a young boy. Du Pont was blessed with a loving extended family that stretched from one side of the river to the other. Indeed, he addressed some of his early letters home after entering the navy to his "dear parents on both sides of the Brandywine." Determined to educate their children in the best schools in the area, Victor and Gabrielle sent Frank to the Mount Airy Academy, a military prep school in Germantown, Pennsylvania, to ready him for a future profession in the armed forces of the United States. Academies—as opposed to many colleges and universities of the period—played a key role in preparing future sea officers by concentrating on practical instruction.[2] In one of his reports on Frank's conduct and bearing, the headmaster provided a hint of the boy's future occupation: "Francis continues to be the best of children and a most exemplary scholar. To the gentleness and obedience of a girl, he adds the energy of a boy. I have to correct in him only his inclination to swear."[3]

Du Pont spent five years at Mount Airy Academy, and like many boys of his age, he fell in love with the United States Navy during the War of 1812. As the nation's only military service to achieve some spectacular victories throughout that conflict, the navy lured many young men into its ranks immediately after the war. Looking to further strengthen his family's ties to his new country, Pierre sought assistance from Jefferson and secured for his grandson appointments as a naval midshipman and a West Pont cadet.

Du Pont would recall that his parents, then experiencing financial hardships, wanted him to join the military and there receive practical (and free) training for an "honorable profession." It is unclear whether young Frank actually wanted to join the military or if he succumbed to parental pressure, but it is known that he chose the sea and officially joined the United States Navy on 19 December 1815.[4] Thus started a career that lasted almost fifty years.

His family later wrote a colorful description of Du Pont as the fourteen-year-old midshipman prepared to depart on his first cruise in November 1817. Young Frank was "very short of stature and small." His large blue eyes were penetrating, and his curly dark brown hair contrasted with a light complexion "that flushed like a girl's with modesty or pleasure." It is striking that observers of the young Du Pont usually commented on feminine traits that may partially explain his sensitive nature. But even at this tender age, Du Pont did not hesitate to voice his opinion on the issues of the day, situations, or individuals he encountered. "Frank by name, and frank by nature," his relatives observed.[5]

His first cruise aboard the ship of the line *Franklin* brought Du Pont into direct contact with the first of many famous naval leaders, Commodore Charles Stewart, and with the Mediterranean Squadron. The young midshipman was responsible for the ship's gig and thus had many opportunities to observe some of the great naval heroes of the day. The life of a midshipman aboard a man-of-war in the early nineteenth century was difficult at best. Working twelve to sixteen hours a day was the usual lot for a midshipman at sea, as well as keeping pace with demanding practical academic work in navigation. Off duty he had no privacy, as Du Pont related in a letter home from his shared berth in the forecastle: "I am at present writing with an old lantern at my desk and a half dozen of intolerable noisy midshipmen around me."[6] Along with extra pay and increased responsibility and prestige, promotion promised at least a modicum of privacy in the tiny cabins authorized for commissioned officer and warrant ranks. For Du Pont and most of his contemporaries, the midshipmen's berth was something to get out of as soon as possible.

After a rough voyage from New York to the Mediterranean, the enthusiastic youngster reported to his parents that "I pride myself with saying that I was not sea sick at all," unlike many of his messmates. This first voyage exposed the fifteen-year-old officer to many wondrous sights and sounds of such places as Gibraltar and the catacombs and caves of Syracuse where he experienced an earthquake. At Pisa he climbed to the top of the tower, telling his parents, "I have no doubt you have heard of it," and described the town's cathedral as "the most beautiful place I ever was in."[7] It was also on

Samuel Francis Du Pont as a midshipman, at about fifteen. Painting by unknown artist. (Courtesy of Hagley Museum and Library)

this cruise that Du Pont first served with lifelong friends Franklin Buchanan and Garrett Pendergrast.

After nine months on the *Franklin*, Du Pont transferred to the smaller sloop of war *Erie*. Du Pont loved the smaller ship, much to the consternation of his parents who thought it unsafe. In the *Erie* and *Franklin*, Du Pont took every opportunity to go ashore, visited many famous places throughout the Mediterranean, and met a number of prominent people. Du Pont

spent much of his early sea experience in this part of the world. When he returned after almost three years away from the Brandywine, Du Pont had
reached his full adult height. A passport issued to Du Pont in 1840 when he
was thirty-six listed his height as 6 feet, 4½ inches and noted his high fore-
head, oval face, straight nose, small mouth, dark brown hair, and dark complexion. Observers would often remark about Du Pont's imposing stature.
Years later family members would recall that the gangly seventeen-year-old
midshipman bounded up the banks of the Brandywine upon his return from
his first and very important cruise shouting, "I'm home, again! I'm home!
Yes, I'm home at last!"[8]

After another brief stint at Mount Airy in preparation for his lieutenant
examination, Du Pont embarked on the venerable frigate *Constitution* for another trip to the Mediterranean. After this trip Du Pont confronted the
navy's notoriously poor promotion prospects as he prepared for his examination for promotion from midshipman to sailing master and ultimately the
coveted rank of lieutenant. Fewer vacancies due to naval reductions following the Treaty of Ghent denied him advancement during this period, as they
would throughout his career, creating in him a lifelong passion for personnel reform. A trip to the West Indies in the USS *Congress* preceded yet another Mediterranean cruise in 1824, this time in the newly launched *North
Carolina*, a beautiful vessel designated the flagship of Commodore John
Rodgers's Mediterranean squadron. Du Pont gained additional and critical
practical experience in seamanship and leading sailors by serving under
Rodgers, the senior officer in the navy, who was an exceedingly strict disciplinarian. Calling the *North Carolina* a "hard ship," Du Pont nevertheless approved many of Rodgers's methods and became himself a believer in strict
(but not harsh) leadership. On the *North Carolina* Du Pont became acquainted with Matthew C. Perry, the first lieutenant of the ship. As a midshipman the harried Du Pont was under Perry's intense scrutiny at all times.
He wrote home that he was "employed from daylight until 8 [P.M.] without
the least interruption. I can scarcely get my meals, and indeed, I am never
seated at the table more than two minutes, without hearing myself repeat-
edly called by the first lieutenant with some new order to execute."[9] The
practical experience he gained aboard ship and in the classroom at Mount
Airy enabled Du Pont to pass his lieutenant's examination with ease. However, because of the navy's seniority system, he would have to wait several
months before advancing in rank. As he awaited a lieutenant's vacancy, he
was advanced to the position of master's mate, enabling the ecstatic Du Pont
to "bid adieu to steerage, which very name has disgusted me for the last two
or three years."[10] Finally, in April 1826 the twenty-three-year-old Du Pont
was promoted to lieutenant after eleven years of service, most of them at sea.

While Du Pont was at sea aboard the *North Carolina*, his father, Victor, died. The young man was devastated and turned increasingly to his uncle, Eleuthère Irénée, as a surrogate father figure. After a short time at home, Du Pont received orders for the USS *Ontario*, bound once more for the Mediterranean. He was not pleased at the prospect of leaving his mother so soon after his father's death but tried to put the best face on a tough situation. Before departing, Du Pont met and after a whirlwind courtship became engaged to Catherine Morris, daughter of a wealthy Philadelphia businessman. Once at sea he confided in a letter to a cousin that his fiancée possessed the "mildest of dispositions [and] the proper solidity of character."[11] This less-than-passionate description of Catherine demonstrates Du Pont's lack of enthusiasm toward the engagement. It was not a good match, and the three-year cruise did not help the relationship.

The voyage of the *Ontario* gave the young officer valuable experience leading sailors and enabled him to visit many famous sites including his ancestral homeland. But France was not as impressive as Constantinople. After a shore excursion to the exotic city, Du Pont would write, "If I had but one city to see, that city would be Constantinople."[12] However, the wonders of the Mediterranean were no match for the feminine charms that Du Pont would experience upon his return home in May 1832.

Upon his homecoming for an extended leave, the popular twenty-eight-year-old officer cut a dashing figure on the Brandywine as he fielded numerous invitations to social events in Delaware and nearby Philadelphia. As he enjoyed his time at home, Du Pont spent more and more time with his relatives across the creek, including his twenty-two-year-old cousin, Sophie Madeline du Pont. She was the fifth of seven children from the union of Du Pont's uncle, Eleuthère Irénée du Pont, and Sophie Madeline Dalmas. A painting of Sophie in her early twenties by Rembrandt Peale portrays a beautiful, refined, poised, and intelligent, if reserved, young woman. Although often dominated by her older sisters, Sophie could be very independent on issues such as politics and religion. Like all of the Du Pont women, Sophie was highly educated in the arts, literature, and domestic sciences. As they grew up in the early nineteenth century, the fervor of the Second Great Awakening engulfed the Du Pont sisters; as a result, Sophie developed a lifelong commitment to the evangelical wing of the Protestant Episcopal Church. Although religion was probably the most important thing in Sophie's life, she could and often did demonstrate a whimsical sense of humor. A talented caricaturist, Sophie portrayed life on the Brandywine through a delightful series of primitive drawings. Her "carics," as she called them, depicted the day-to-day life and adventures of a very close-knit extended family.[13]

Du Pont began to spend even more time than usual in Sophie's home. He

Sophie Madeline du Pont only months before her wedding to her first cousin Frank in June 1833. Painting by Rembrandt Peale. (Courtesy of Hagley Museum and Library)

regaled the family and their friends and visitors with descriptions of his travels and naval adventures. After one successful evening Sophie wrote that "Cousin Frank entertained us with accounts of foreign countries, naval adventures, etc etc etc all most intensely interesting—He describes everything and relates anecdotes so well that it is more delightful to hear him than to read an amusing book." In Sophie's company Du Pont quickly forgot his

Philadelphia debutante—much to Sophie's somewhat guilty delight—and was soon captivated by his cousin's physical and intellectual charms. Sophie struggled with her feelings for her cousin while trying to maintain some emotional distance between them. She chided herself for disliking Catherine Morris but rationalized in her diary that "*My only motive* [for opposing Du Pont's engagement] is the idea that Frank was unacquainted with the lady, and that neither she nor her family are calculated to make him happy."[14]

Sophie's image of the gallant naval officer was enhanced when Du Pont rushed headlong into flaming debris to rescue injured workers in the aftermath of an explosion at the Du Pont gunpowder works in August 1832. Despite the growing romantic attraction between the two, Sophie engaged in a private battle with her thoughts toward her cousin, thoughts that she tried to repress. "Oh how different my feelings are from what I know they should be, so wild and deep and passionate, so hard to control! And yet, so invisible as to make others think me unfeeling!"[15] Although Sophie clearly was in love with Du Pont, she was frustrated by her social awkwardness and inability to demonstrate or articulate her feelings. She continued to wrestle with her romantic awkwardness even after the couple was married.

For his part, Du Pont had less trouble expressing his feelings toward Sophie. Du Pont described his cousin as a "woman of sound sense and education, but an angel of purity and of sensibility. She is pretty too!" He continued to spend more and more time on the other side of the creek and in Sophie's company throughout the fall of 1832 and into 1833. Finally, on an unchaperoned sledding trip to Newcastle, Delaware, on Washington's Birthday in February 1833, Du Pont proposed and Sophie accepted. Although they had been growing ever closer since Du Pont's return from the Mediterranean, their engagement seemed to surprise them both. In 1810 the family's patriarch, Pierre Samuel du Pont, had urged his sons to encourage their children to marry cousins to ensure "honesty of soul and purity of blood," but there is no evidence that Frank and Sophie had Pierre's admonition in mind when they became engaged. Breaking the news to her brother, Henry, and a bit shocked that Du Pont had not formally asked her father for her hand, Sophie wrote that "for the first time in my life I am at a loss how to write to you my dearest Harry. . . . I wrote to you dear brother that Frank and I paid a visit to Newcastle last Friday week. It was not until our ride home that I had the least idea that our cousin's regard for me was *more* than that of a *cousin*."[16]

Sophie's astonishment was probably due, in part, to her regret at the thought of leaving behind the "*serene corps* of Tabbies," a group of close female friends in the Brandywine neighborhood who had vowed never to marry. She admitted to one of her best friends that "in truth I feel a little *awkward* at confessing my treason *against the sisterhood*." She went on to beg her friends to love Du Pont as she did and not to think less of her. She had resolved many months before never to marry but to devote herself to her family and to God; thus she had to come to grips with a future she never dreamed would occur.[17]

Although Sophie may have felt guilt at the thought of abandoning her female friends for the joys of domestic bliss, she expressed great happiness over her engagement and a certain resolve. A month after the sleigh ride to Newcastle, the previously timid bride-to-be hinted to Du Pont that she intended to be an equal partner in the upcoming marriage. She gently scolded Du Pont when he took it for granted that he was constantly on her mind: "I should like to know what makes you suppose *I think of you?* Is it not great vanity in you to imagine I have *nothing better* to do with my thoughts?" While confessing that she did think of him quite often, she could not resist a little teasing: "The truth is I am beginning to lose my *great awe* of you very fast, at least when I am not in your presence."[18]

An ecstatic Du Pont quickly informed his friends of the upcoming match. To Garrett Pendergrast he wrote "to inform you that I expect to be married in June to a fair cousin of mine; a woman of education, refinement, beauty and angelic purity of mind—altogether too good for me, but as she does not think so, why I have not disputed her." Excitement soon gave way to mild frustration as Sophie and her father refused to set a date for the wedding and the young couple dealt with the changing nature of their relationship. They had long discussions on religion, children, and Sophie's role in family decision making.[19] Sophie may have been shy and retiring in public, but this well-educated and strong-willed young woman did not intend to let Du Pont run roughshod over her opinions and was determined to have him follow her own religious path.

Finally, after several delays to accommodate Henry du Pont's graduation from West Point, the wedding took place on a cool and bright June day in the parlor of Eleuthère Irénée's home overlooking the DuPont gunpowder mills. Family, neighbors, friends, and several of Du Pont's fellow officers attended the ceremony. Following an August honeymoon trip to West Point, New York City, and upstate New York, the newlyweds settled down to domestic life on the Brandywine in Du Pont's family home, Louviers. After their marriage the young couple began to capitalize the particle of their name, unlike the rest of the family, probably in an effort to distinguish them from the other two families. Du Pont and Sophie lived at Louviers for about four years, and then upon his mother's death, the young couple moved to a farmhouse about a quarter of a mile up the hill in 1837 that they christened Upper Louviers.[20]

Louviers may have been merely a stone's throw across the Brandywine from Sophie's childhood home, but it often seemed like another world to the young bride. While both families were very close, Sophie often remarked at how uncomfortable she felt in the company of Du Pont's Roman Catholic mother and sisters. After their marriage and when Du Pont was at sea, Sophie often divided her time between the two Du Pont families along the Brandywine.[21] For Sophie religion was thicker than blood. Although raised as a nominal Protestant, Du Pont was not particularly religious. However, through his wife's gentle but persistent prodding, Du Pont gradually adopted his wife's devout Episcopalianism and later became a nationally prominent member of the church. These fervent religious convictions helped guide his actions and personal relationships the rest of his life. Sophie also became his best friend and closest confidante. Endowed with an engaging and vibrant personality and great curiosity, Sophie was intensely interested and well versed in national politics, literature, foreign affairs, and her husband's career. Du Pont and Sophie shared almost everything with each other; Du Pont seldom made a major career decision without first running his options past Sophie's discerning eye. Indeed, Sophie often restrained the hot-tempered and impulsive Du Pont. They rapidly became true partners.

Sophie injured her back sometime after they returned from New York. The chronic condition that resulted coupled with the medical advice of the day sent Sophie to her bed for extended periods. Over the years the couple would seek relief from specialists, medication, and water cures with mixed and usually disappointing results. One of Sophie's most delightful "carics" depicts Frank tenderly carrying her in his arms at Warm Springs, Virginia, where they went vainly seeking relief. For the rest of her life, Sophie endured many months as a near invalid. For a woman who had been physically active, this was extremely frustrating. Although by any objective measure the union between Du Pont and Sophie was a great success, the relationship that developed between the two young people was complex and enigmatic and is difficult to penetrate. While hundreds of letters exist between Sophie and Du Pont, they reveal little about their intimate private life.[22]

What is clear is that Du Pont and Sophie were devoted to one another as their loving, affectionate, yet almost platonic letters attest. There is little evidence of a passionate and physical relationship despite Sophie's injury. Tantalizing hints of such a bond exist in some of the correspondence—particularly Du Pont's—but nothing concrete. Sophie's accident probably ended or at least drastically curtailed the couple's intimate relations and probably explains, at least in part, why the marriage produced no children. To treat the pain in her back, Sophie's doctors often prescribed laudanum and morphine, and she may have developed a mild addiction to these powerful drugs. Sophie seems to have experienced other health problems—the nature of which is unclear, but it may have been a miscarriage—in the spring of 1834, about ten months after their wedding date.[23] Sophie either destroyed or altered many of the more personal letters and diary entries after Du Pont's death, obscuring many of the details behind this most intimate part of their relationship.

By the summer of 1835, Du Pont had been home for over three years. A shortage of active-duty positions ensured that officers during this period could expect months and sometimes years to pass without employment either ashore or at sea. Perhaps because of Sophie's status as an invalid, or due to simple wedded bliss, or just the fact that he had spent an extended period at home, Du Pont began to have second thoughts about a naval career. To a close friend Du Pont confessed that "one of my castles in utopia has been a farmer's life: to kill my own mutton, and raise my own turnips has been one of my dreams of future happiness in this world of trials and vicissitudes." Indeed, wrote Du Pont, he had been testing his agricultural skills throughout that summer and was pleased to report that "what was a preference, has grown with a passion, and my mind for the future is fully made up." Unlike many of his fellow officers, Du Pont had this kind of career flexibility because his and Sophie's investments in the DuPont Gunpowder Company allowed them to live very comfortably without relying on navy pay. The life of a gentleman farmer had more appeal than another trip. But he owed the navy another active assignment. Du Pont lamented: "A bitter pill must be swallowed. I have determined to go soon, that I may be back soon."[24]

After marveling at the appearance of Halley's comet in October 1835, Du Pont received orders to the sloop *Warren* in the West Indies as her first lieutenant. Although he had hoped for a Pacific cruise, the cruise aboard the *Warren* would lead to Du Pont's first command. Once at Pensacola, Du Pont was detached to join Commodore John Rodgers's flagship the USS *Constellation* as the first lieutenant. Excited at his lofty station in an important ship, Du Pont became enthusiastic once more for the navy life. "Tell Sophie," he wrote his cousin Henry, "she may be a *Captain's lady yet.*" Six weeks after Du Pont moved to the *Constellation*, the captain of the schooner *Grampus* became ill; Rodgers appointed Du Pont to take over. Although only a temporary command, Du Pont made the best of it and happily wrote Sophie from the spacious captain's cabin that for the first time in his career "it will take me some time to accustom myself to *being alone.*" Days later he was moved yet again, back to the *Warren*, this time as captain. A brief but very successful cruise throughout the Gulf of Mexico followed, during which Du Pont helped protect United States commerce with Mexico. He returned home in September 1836 in part because of Sophie's health. With this brief but important assignment, Du Pont abandoned all thoughts of exchanging the thrill of naval life for a farmer's plow. Command of the *Warren* proved to be exciting and highly gratifying, and he gained tremendous self-confidence in his ability to manage and lead a ship's company, particularly in the areas of seamanship and discipline. To his great friend Alexander Slidell Mackenzie, Du Pont explained his theory of naval leadership: "Consistency, no favoritism, a great firmness and severity at times—enough to convince them you can use the lash and that most soundly, but would infinitely prefer not being compelled to resort to it, will readily effect all you may wish."[25] The young Du Pont was rapidly making a name for himself.

Shortly after his marriage, Du Pont joined the newly established Navy Lyceum founded by his old shipmate, Commander Matthew C. Perry. The lyceum acted as a clearinghouse for the exchange of ideas in the absence of an officially sanctioned professional organization. It sponsored lectures and papers on various professional topics. The lyceum stood at the center of the navy's intellectual life and formed an integral part of what Samuel P. Huntington has called "the American Military Enlightenment of the 1830s and 1840s."[26] The lyceum also served as a central forwarding post office for officers serving at sea. Besides Du Pont and Perry, the lyceum's membership also boasted officers who would play key roles in the modernization and reform of the navy including Matthew F. Maury and John A. Dahlgren. Du Pont's relationships with the navy's intellectual giants paid great dividends as he developed his own ideas for how the navy could and should be improved.

During the early years of his career, Du Pont made numerous lifelong friendships with fellow officers such as Charles Henry Davis, Louis M. Goldsborough, and Alexander Slidell Mackenzie. Extremely popular throughout the service among officers and sailors alike, Du Pont exhibited a warm, easy manner toward his friends and colleagues. Fellow officers (even seniors) routinely sought his advice on technical, service, career, and even personal issues; throughout his life, he maintained a lively correspondence with dozens of his fellow officers discussing all aspects of their personal and professional lives. However, he was also a proud man who seldom strayed from the ordered social stratum dictated by his naval rank. To outsiders, or those lacking close contact with Du Pont, he could appear aloof and arrogant as he behaved with reserved but polite correctness toward others while demanding to be treated in return with respect and dignity. He could take offense very easily; his most precious possession was clearly his reputation. Once he suffered an offense or insult, whether actual or imagined, he could be an implacable enemy who would go to any length to right a perceived slight, often to his further detriment. To Du Pont a naval career was not merely an occupation, it was his reason for being. His personal wealth meant that he could afford to decline some assignments (although unless he was ill, he never declined sea duty), especially shore positions that would take him away from Sophie, who was often in frail health; it also meant that he felt few constraints concerning controversial subjects such as transforming the navy. His popularity, outspoken nature, influence, spotless reputation, and professional competence gained from years at sea ensured that fellow officers and the navy's civilian leadership were compelled to pay attention to his arguments for service reform. By the early 1840s he was an acknowledged leader in the service despite his relatively low rank.

An incident aboard Commodore Isaac Hull's Mediterranean Squadron flagship *Ohio* in 1839 helped reinforce Du Pont's ardent desire for reform. Although the cruise had many pleasant and interesting aspects, including an audience with the pope in Rome, Du Pont came into direct conflict with the hero of the War of 1812, who had commanded the frigate *Constitution* in her victorious battle over the HMS *Guerriere* on 19 August 1812. In a direct violation of naval regulations, Hull evicted Du Pont and three other officers from their wardroom cabins to provide quarters for his wife, sister, and other long-term visitors. The four officers—Du Pont and Lieutenants Garrett J. Pendergrast, John S. Missroon, and Sylvanus W. Godon—bitterly protested this cavalier treatment by their superior. The men were great friends, and all four were to serve together again on several occasions.

The resulting clash between Hull and the officers led by Du Pont resulted in a reprimand by the secretary of the navy against the rebels for disrespect to a superior officer. Angrily, Du Pont wrote, "I am one of those Sir who believe, that a Lieutenant is as much entitled by regulation, usage, and propriety to a permanent and fixed apartment, suitable to his rank . . . as the captain of a ship is to his cabin."[27] Du Pont saw this clash as another example of a senior officer promoted or retained beyond his capabilities based only on seniority, one who had stayed too long in the service, while displaying little respect for his subordinates. A disgusted Du Pont requested to be relieved of his duties and traveled to Washington, D.C., to present his case directly to the secretary. Once Secretary of the Navy James K. Paulding heard Du Pont's side of the story, he immediately cleared all four lieutenants of any wrongdoing.[28]

After a short leave at home and after visiting England, Holland, and France, Du Pont rejoined the *Ohio* and finished the cruise in July 1841. This seemingly minor incident had a profound impact on Du Pont. It illustrated his willingness to fight for what he believed, even at the cost of his career; it showed how angry and determined Du Pont could get when confronted with an affront to his rank and dignity; and it demonstrated that Du Pont would not tolerate any affront to his reputation or an assault on the perquisites of his rank. From this point on, Du Pont saw personnel reform as his special crusade.

Important as the *Ohio* cruise was in shaping Du Pont's reformist tendencies, it also marked an important milestone in his personal life: the first extended separation from his wife. Despite Sophie's medical problems, seven years of marriage had strengthened and defined their relationship. Although Sophie exerted profound influence on Du Pont in many ways, religion was the most significant. Writing from the Mediterranean, Du Pont, at best a tepid Protestant in his bachelor days, assured Sophie, "I have read dearest a good deal in my bible, I know this will please you and I like it better and better, what was rather a task or done as a duty, is now from inclination." They discussed intelligently and at length the controversy over the tenets of the Oxford movement, an effort by Anglican clergy to adopt many of the customs and ceremonies of the Roman Catholic Church. He also wrote long love letters to Sophie on a daily basis. A lonely Du Pont declared, "Oh Sophie how much I would give to see you and be with you again, there are times when I can hardly restrain that desire within proper bounds—this day is one of them." Sophie responded in kind. The once reticent Sophie now had little difficulty expressing herself to Du Pont on a wide range of topics. Upon hearing of his indignant reaction to Commodore Hull's actions on the *Ohio*, Sophie unhesitantly offered some mild criticism and sound advice. "I do not wonder you were so indignant. I only wish my love, I could have been there that night you wrote, to put my arms around you, and tell you how I shared in all your feelings, and to calm and sooth them! Oh my dearest, *do be prudent* as you so kindly promise me. Do nothing rashly, or while under exasperation. Resolutions formed, words spoken, under excited feeling, are not those we can best uphold afterwards. Whenever you can, try to have a good night's sleep before you act in any important matter."[29] More often than not, Du Pont took Sophie's counsel to heart. He usually asked her advice on all important decisions, both personal and professional. Sophie quickly became his most important confidante and adviser. In only two areas did Sophie's influence have little or no effect: anything to do with Du Pont's reputation and the subject of slavery after the start of the Civil War. Du Pont's failure to heed Sophie's advice concerning the former would prove disastrous.

The cruise of the *Ohio* marked the end of one phase in Du Pont's life and the beginning of another. Professionally, Du Pont was now more than capable of assuming greater responsibilities. He was a superbly competent and confident seaman and leader. Du Pont was well liked and well respected by superiors, peers, and subordinates alike. He was ready for command. Personally, their marriage emerged from the separation even better than it had been, and from the experience of this cruise both Sophie and Du Pont learned how to handle even longer deployments.

2

The Mexican War

I have never been so happy in my life.

— SAMUEL FRANCIS DU PONT

ALWAYS INTENSELY interested in politics, Du Pont was particularly pleased with the outcome of the 1840 election when the Whig candidate, William Henry Harrison, defeated Andrew Jackson's handpicked successor, Martin Van Buren. As the son and nephew of manufacturers, Du Pont had always been anti-Jackson and anti-Democrat and was now a confirmed and enthusiastic Whig. A gleeful Du Pont wrote, "I am happy to tell you that Old Harrison is sweeping everything."[1] A Whig he would remain until that party's collapse in the early 1850s when he became a reluctant Republican.

Politics were important, but for Du Pont the navy came first. Du Pont's major concerns included the promotion system. His upper-class heritage and upbringing left him thoroughly comfortable in the navy's hierarchical structure. He enjoyed being an officer with all the perquisites that rank bestowed. But he was also adamant that an officer must earn advancement and not rely on simple seniority. It took but a few years in the navy for Du Pont to become an outspoken advocate of promotion by merit. The young officer also advocated major organizational reform including replacement of the cumbersome and ineffective Board of Navy Commissioners with a bureau system similar to the army's. Moreover, Du Pont, a strict disciplinarian, was concerned about the overall state of order in the service. In addition to his experience on the *Ohio*, the aftermath of the United States Exploring Expedition's voyage of discovery and the infamous *Somers* incident convinced Du Pont that the navy needed to change and change soon.[2]

From 1838 to 1842 Lieutenant Charles Wilkes led the largest federally funded scientific exploring project since the Lewis and Clark expedition. During the voyage in which the squadron circumnavigated the globe, Wilkes's overbearing personality and his penchant for strict discipline inevitably led to tensions between the commander and his officers and men. When the expedition finally returned to New York in June 1842, the squadron's considerable scientific achievements were overshadowed—at least temporarily—by the charges and countercharges that flew between Wilkes and many of his men. The navy was forced to convene a series of courts-martial to answer these complaints including allegations that Wilkes exceeded his authority, abused his men, and illegally discharged sailors during the cruise. To Du Pont's considerable dismay, the secretary of the navy appointed him as the junior member of the court that would hear the evidence and decide the fate of the officers involved. "It is a hard pill to swallow," Du Pont complained to a close friend, but he also recognized the implied compliment in being ordered to carry out such sensitive duties in the company of such eminent officers as Commodores Matthew C. Perry and Charles Stewart. He did not relish the prospect of summertime travel to the sweltering city from the relative comfort of his home on the Brandywine. In addition, the thought of enduring weeks of acrimonious testimony was thoroughly disagreeable. Despite his protestations, Du Pont was sitting in his designated place when the first court martial began on board the USS *North Carolina* in the Brooklyn Navy Yard on 25 July 1842.[3]

After his experience on the *Ohio* less than two years before, Du Pont's first tendency was to favor Wilkes's subordinates. But on observing that Wilkes was always "perfectly self possessed" amid the sensational and, Du Pont believed, largely overblown accusations of his former shipmates, Du Pont developed a grudging admiration for the tough officer. Du Pont's final verdict on Wilkes was that "he was a disagreeable, overbearing and disgusting commander, but I don't think he has transcended his authority." A firm disciplinarian himself, Du Pont faulted both Wilkes and his officers: the conflict never should have gone as far as it did. In the end, the court acquitted Wilkes on all counts except that of illegal punishment, a relatively minor charge for which he received a reprimand. Du Pont's experience on the Wilkes court-martial reinforced his firm belief that too many undeserving officers reached high rank and responsibility and were too quick to abuse their authority. The sordid episode also convinced him that somehow the navy must improve the overall quality of its junior officers. Du Pont had hardly returned home when another shocking episode brought the navy unwanted publicity and highlighted its personnel deficiencies.[4]

In a sensational and highly controversial incident in 1842, Du Pont's closest friend, Alexander Slidell Mackenzie, while in command of the training brig *Somers* had hanged three sailors for mutiny. One of the condemned men was a midshipman who also happened to be the son of the secretary of war. Du Pont, like most naval officers, strongly supported Mackenzie's actions. To Du Pont discipline was critically important on board a man-of-war, and captains of ships had to be given the latitude to maintain order as they saw fit. However, the public and the press greeted Mackenzie with almost universal condemnation upon his return to the United States. Du Pont stood by his old friend, tirelessly writing letters and lobbying the department and senior officers on Mackenzie's behalf. Although Mackenzie was acquitted by a court of inquiry and then a full court-martial for his actions aboard the *Somers*, Du Pont was shocked at the official treatment his friend received; a service that could censure a fine officer like Mackenzie for doing his duty had to be changed.[5] The *Somers* episode, following so closely on the heels of the Wilkes court-martial, only reemphasized Du Pont's desire for significant naval reform.

In January 1843 Du Pont was finally promoted to commander after twenty-eight years of service; he was forty years old. Having served on multiple cruises to the Mediterranean and the Caribbean, Du Pont longed to make a voyage around Cape Horn into the Pacific. The department granted his request in 1843 when he received his first real command, the newly constructed brig *Perry*. Du Pont sailed in November 1843 for the Pacific and the Orient. Stopping at Rio de Janeiro, the new commander was stricken with a gastrointestinal illness that forced him ashore. In the space of a few weeks, Du Pont lost over forty pounds as he struggled to recover. Prematurely relinquishing his new command devastated Du Pont. He was particularly disappointed at missing the chance to circumnavigate the globe and to round Cape Horn for the first time in his career.[6] He would get another chance soon enough.

By the mid-1840s the newly promoted commander attracted the attention of Secretary of the Navy George Bancroft. Bancroft named Du Pont to a board of officers convened to establish and organize the United States Naval Academy. Du Pont happily served on this board along with Franklin Buchanan and William McKean, for he saw the creation of a naval academy organized along the same lines as West Point as the best way to ensure professionalism and competence throughout the entire officer corps.[7]

Here was a chance to prevent or at least reduce the chances of a reoccurrence of another Wilkes court-martial or *Somers* incident. Despite the obvious advantages that a naval academy would bring to the service, Du Pont's position in support of an academy was not universal in the navy at the time. Many, if not most, officers felt strongly that the only place a young midshipman could learn his profession was at sea; most officers believed that midshipmen should go to sea early and that they could learn their trade only on board a warship. Naval officers were not the only ones who thought this way. Congressman John Reynolds exclaimed: "What? Educate a sailor in a cloister! Set a man down in a dark retreat of a college cell to learn how to manage a ship in a storm! No Sir!"[8]

However, as Du Pont and others observed, a midshipman's training and development were uneven at best; Charles Wilkes's experience and the unfortunate *Somers* incident certainly demonstrated that. Many ship captains and their officers viewed a midshipman as just another crew member. Few officers were suited by temperament or inclination to provide quality instruction to these young men. Thus to reform minded officers like Du Pont, the navy needed a reliable source of uniformly high-quality midshipmen. A naval academy equipped with a curriculum that included both classroom and hands-on training on board ship could go a long way toward ensuring a steady flow of fresh, well-trained leaders to the navy. Although Annapolis, like West Point, endured a fitful start, its graduates slowly began to contribute at sea. Several new academy graduates served under Du Pont in later assignments including the cruise of the USS *Minnesota* to China in 1857 and during the Civil War. Notable among these young officers was the future influential naval historian and strategist Alfred Thayer Mahan. Two of Du Pont's closest friends, Franklin Buchanan and Louis Goldsborough, served as superintendents of the academy. The Navy Department twice offered the superintendency to Du Pont, but he declined due to Sophie's ill health. Du Pont was always proud of his role in founding the academy and went out of his way to support both the institution and its graduates.[9] Du Pont's role in the academy's founding may have led to his next assignment.

When the Democrat James K. Polk defeated the Whig candidate, and Du Pont's political idol, Henry Clay in the 1844 presidential election, the resulting political and foreign policy crisis over Mexico led to another important episode in Du Pont's career. Skillfully avoiding war with Great Britain over the Oregon boundary, the proslavery and expansionist Polk turned to Texas and California. Although already annexed and admitted as the fifteenth slave state in December 1845 through the machinations of the outgoing president John Tyler, Texas still had a disputed border with Mexico. Polk was determined to seize California and the disputed border territories of Texas. But to do so he had to provoke war with Mexico. Polk sent reinforced naval forces into the Gulf of Mexico and troops into the disputed areas along the Texas border and attempted to convince Californians to support annexation. These provocations brought to power a Mexican anti-American government. War between the two neighbors was now a matter of time. Polk hurried the inevitable by ordering General Zachary Taylor and his force of 4,000 soldiers to advance to the Rio Grande River. When Mexican troops attacked some of Taylor's men on the north side of the river, Polk had his war. On 11 May 1846 Congress voted overwhelmingly to declare war.[10]

As relations with Mexico began to deteriorate in the mid-1840s because of Polk's avowed desire to annex Texas, the navy looked to reinforce its Pacific and Gulf squadrons. As Commodore Robert F. Stockton prepared to assume command of the Pacific Squadron, he asked Bancroft to assign Du Pont to command his flagship, the frigate *Congress*, on the long voyage around Cape Horn to California. Bancroft quickly agreed, and Du Pont assumed command of the frigate on 1 September 1845 with the understanding that he would get an independent command once the ship arrived on station. This came as something of a shock to Sophie, who had expected Du Pont to be assigned to the Gulf. She had reconciled herself to a separation of some months, but a voyage to the Pacific could last years.[11] She was right, but during this cruise Du Pont would gain valuable experience both in independent command and in combat. A photograph taken of Du Pont around the time of his departure for the Pacific shows a man who looks younger than his forty-two years. Du Pont exuded enthusiasm, pride, and confidence as he made final preparations for the most important cruise of his career.

The *Congress* sailed from Norfolk on 30 October 1845, and for the first time Du Pont was faced with the awesome responsibility of a major command and leading a crew of "so many men, composed of the usual diversity of character." Two weeks into the cruise, Du Pont wrote Sophie about the critical importance of maintaining strict discipline while being scrupulously fair. Too many officers saw corporal punishment as "the grand panacea for all evils in a man of war." This attitude was not only wrong, Du Pont explained, it demonstrated poor leadership. "Watchful supervision and zeal," he argued, were the key to being an effective naval officer.[12] Although Du Pont was not shy about using the lash when necessary, he saw it as a tool of last resort.

Despite being under the constant watchful eye of Commodore Stockton—a man described as "vain, tactless . . . and glory thirsty"—Du Pont flourished under the pressure and responsibility. The last time Du Pont was in Rio de Janeiro he had almost died, but when the *Congress* called at the port on 21 December 1845, he enjoyed excellent health and the company of con-

Du Pont in his early forties, soon to sail for California and the Mexican War. (Courtesy of Hagley Museum and Library)

genial officers and passengers. The days were long and his duties numerous and often complex, but most evenings were spent in agreeable conversation with fellow officers or games of whist with the passengers. One observer described the *Congress*'s captain as "tall, straight, handsome, with brilliant, yet mild brown eyes, commanding figure, and a strong, clear voice. He is dignified, amiable, exceedingly winning in manners, and . . . he is considered in the Navy a perfect model of an officer."[13] Less than two months after its short stay in Rio, the *Congress* neared the waters surrounding Cape Horn, among the most treacherous seas in the world.

"My most laborious professional service" is how Du Pont described the rounding of Cape Horn in the huge frigate. Negotiating the transit around the Horn was always problematic in the age of sail, and Du Pont's experience was no different. Contrary winds, foul weather, and towering seas forced the *Congress* to beat back and forth until she had sailed a total of 1,500 miles while only moving 450 miles west into the Pacific. After three weeks during which he almost never left the quarterdeck, Du Pont sat down to describe the harrowing ordeal to Sophie: "Clouds rolled up in huge masses, black and threatening, the thermometer began to fall, gusts of wind and cold drizzling rains followed, the ship was soon rolling and pitching, with everything straining and creaking." The young daughter of the general consul of Hawaii who was an official passenger aboard the *Congress* wrote vividly of one night of the passage: "The whole ocean is white with foam which falls in cataracts from the crest of rolling waves. It is terrible and sublime to watch one of these huge combers heaving up within the horizon, and rolling mast-high upon you." Yet the passengers were heartened to have "Captain Du Pont, with his thorough experience and sound judgment," on the *Congress*'s quarterdeck.[14] Despite the trials of the cruise, Du Pont was proud of the way his ship and crew performed on the passage; there was no damage or casualties during the journey. The *Congress* flourished under his direction.

During the eight-month voyage of the *Congress* to California, the Mexican War began. Both Sophie and Frank were opposed to a war they viewed as a naked and immoral Democratic power grab by President Polk rather than preordained "manifest destiny." However, Du Pont as a career military officer did not let his personal feelings interfere with his duties. After a short stop in Hawaii to disembark his passengers, the *Congress* arrived in Monterey, California, on 14 July 1846, only one week after American forces seized the town. Stockton honored his promise and assigned Du Pont to command the eighteen-gun sloop of war *Cyane*. One of Du Pont's officers on the *Congress* noted the occasion of the captain's departure with sadness. "We part with him with much regret; he has been with us in gale and calm, amidst the ice of the Cape and on the burning Line, and cheerfully shared, in his own person, every hardship and peril. His professional knowledge and efficiency, with his social qualities and unblemished character, have won our unmeasured confidence and esteem."[15]

Du Pont, too, had some pangs of regret as he left the *Congress*, but his new command more than made up for any sorrow he felt at leaving the flagship. "I am ordered to the *Cyane*," he wrote Sophie. "The ship is all I could wish for—a fine sea vessel." The *Cyane* was a perfect ship for a captain looking to distinguish himself. Although small in comparison to the *Congress*, the *Cyane* was more than a match for any Mexican warships she might en-

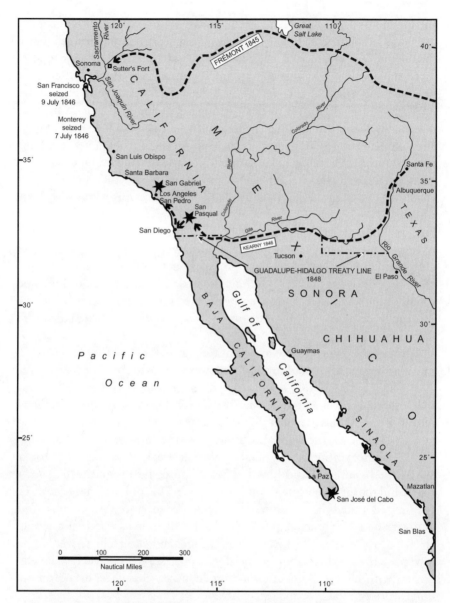

California theater of operations during the Mexican War. Du Pont and the *Cyane* conducted blockading and joint operations with the army from San Francisco in the north to San Blas in the south.

counter. Her speed, agility, and relatively shallow draft made her a perfect blockading vessel, and Stockton (and his replacement, Commodore William B. Shubrick) dispatched Du Pont on many independent missions.[16]

In a war dominated by ground forces, Du Pont's operations in Mexican waters were exceptionally active, and the commander and crew of the *Cyane* distinguished themselves on many occasions. The ship ferried Major John C. Frémont and sixty troops to San Diego. Frémont with a small party had been on a mapping expedition in Upper California in late 1845 when the Mexican authorities tried to drive out all foreigners including Americans. Frémont provided advice and support to the Americans who staged the "Bear Flag" revolt that declared California a republic, and he raised a unit made up of his men and some Bear Flaggers. Upon Stockton's arrival, Frémont's California Battalion was received into the United States Army, and its commander was promoted to major. During the short voyage the famous Pathfinder and most of his men suffered badly from seasickness, much to the amusement of the sailors. On arrival at San Diego a reconnaissance party made up of *Cyane* crew members cleared the way for Frémont's men to land and capture the city, Du Pont's first experience with joint operations. Stockton then declared a blockade of Mexico, but he did not have the force to back it up. Still, the commodore ordered Du Pont to establish a blockade of coastal towns in Lower California (present-day Baja Peninsula and the west coat of Mexico) with special emphasis on San Blas. Another sloop, the *Warren*, was ordered to cover Mazatlán. On 2 September 1846 the *Cyane* arrived off San Blas and established a very porous blockade. Du Pont seized a number of vessels, and on several occasions, taking a page from the great British naval hero Horatio Nelson's book, landing parties from the *Cyane* staged hit-and-run attacks on Mexican shore fortifications and batteries, destroying numerous guns. Du Pont and the commander of the *Warren* were essentially on their own and acted as the only United States presence in Lower California. After a consultation at Mazatlán, the officers decided that they should establish a series of temporary blockades outside several Mexican ports. The *Cyane* moved on to La Paz on 14 September 1846, seizing more ships in that port, and then sailed to Guaymas, arriving on 6 October 1846. During a brief bombardment of the town that destroyed several of the ships in the harbor, Du Pont sent a landing party ashore that captured another. After this action the *Cyane* returned to Mazatlán. The *Warren* and the *Cyane* did as much as they could with their limited resources, but by mid-November, Du Pont was forced to leave station to resupply in San Francisco after only a few weeks of active blockading. As a result of Stockton's inability to send reinforcements and the need for constant replenishment, the blockade was not successful

The sloop of war USS *Cyane* under the command of Commander Du Pont landing John Charles Frémont's troops at San Diego on 29 July 1846. Painting by Carlton Chapman. (Courtesy of the Maritime Museum of San Diego, California; photograph courtesy of the United States Naval Historical Center)

and clearly violated the provision of international law that demanded that a blockade be effective before it can be legal.[17] However, the experience provided Du Pont with valuable insights on conducting a blockade. Two key lessons immediately occurred to him: first, a blockading force must have enough ships to adequately cover all ports, and, second, blockading ships had to be sustained with supplies and maintenance facilities to enable them to remain on station for extended periods. These experiences would serve him well during the Civil War.

In the months that followed the initial blockade, Du Pont and the *Cyane* would take part in a wide variety of operations including additional blockading, seizing fourteen Mexican ships, and participating in several joint operations with army forces led by Brigadier General Stephen W. Kearney. Kearney had arrived in California in December 1846 with a force of about 1,600 troops after a punishing march from Santa Fe. During this period the Mexicans in Upper California rebelled against United States occupying forces. Kearney and Stockton soon began to argue over who should be in charge, hampering the American response. As a result—after the disastrous Battle of San Pasqual near San Diego on 6 December 1846—both men were

on the field at the Battle of San Gabriel, 8–9 January 1847, outside Los Angeles. Du Pont provided officers and men to fight in the battle but had been
ordered by Stockton to remain on his ship. Despite the confused chain of
command, the Americans achieved a victory that cleared the way for the capture of Los Angeles and completed the seizure of Upper California.[18] Du
Pont deeply regretted not being present at San Gabriel with his men, writing to Sophie that "I should have liked to have witnessed a battle. . . . But if
I could not be there I am not the less proud of the Cyanes who behaved as I
knew they would." However, as captain of the *Cyane*, Du Pont was in his element and loved every minute of it. He commanded a fast ship manned by
a happy and well-disciplined crew and led by competent and congenial officers. And he served under commanders who gave him the latitude to make
independent decisions. "I have never been so happy in my life," he wrote to
his friend Garrett Pendergrast.[19]

Happy he may have been in the company of his comrades, but Du Pont
missed Sophie, his family, and friends terribly, and the glacial pace of communications did not help. A letter sent by Du Pont in California to Sophie
in Delaware would take anywhere from three to eight months to reach its
destination. Correspondence traveling in the opposite direction could take
even longer if the winds were contrary at Cape Horn. In a letter to Alexander Slidell Mackenzie in which he apologized for not writing more, Du Pont
lamented, "The immense distance between the dates sent and their reception, the uncertainty of the opportunities offered [to send letters], the difficulty in choosing subjects that will not be very flat if they should ever reach,
I have found a great bar to the pleasure of correspondence."[20] The sporadic
receipt of mail was a constant leadership challenge for officers on the Pacific
station.

Soon after the Battle of San Gabriel, with operations in Upper California completed, Commodore William B. Shubrick replaced Stockton. The
newly arrived Commodore James Biddle, who was the senior officer, in turn
superseded Shubrick. Du Pont was pleased to see Shubrick, an officer he respected (and to whom he was related by marriage) and a pleasant change
from the imperious Stockton. Shubrick would regain overall command
when Biddle sailed home in July 1847; in the interim the two men were able
to forge a good working relationship with each other and, more importantly,
with army commanders in the region. In April 1847 Biddle reestablished the
blockade of the Lower California ports as a preliminary move toward the ultimate goal of seizing a foothold on the Baja Peninsula and Lower California to use as a bargaining chip during peace negotiations. The *Cyane* was ordered to join several other vessels at Mazatlán to participate in the blockade.

Soon the other ships departed for San Francisco, and Du Pont was once again on his own to enforce an unenforceable blockade. In a vain effort to cover several ports at once, Du Pont sailed the *Cyane* from San José del Cabo to La Paz and then back to Mazatlán. This was completely ineffective, and Du Pont knew it. Finally, in late June 1847, after several weeks of fruitless activity, Du Pont was ordered to resupply in Hawaii. Once again the naval commanders did not devote the resources necessary for an effective and legal blockade.[21]

After a short stay in Monterey upon its return from Hawaii, the *Cyane* sailed south, once more bound for Mazatlán, and rendezvoused off the tip of the Baja Peninsula with the rest of a squadron of ships led by Shubrick on 28 October 1847. Before departing for Mazatlán, Shubrick issued a proclamation that was bound to incite die-hard Mexican resistance: "The flag of the United States is destined to wave forever over the Californias. No contingency can be seen in which the United States will ever surrender or relinquish the possession of the Californias." As an exclamation point to the proclamation, Shubrick seized San José del Cabo on the tip of the peninsula and left behind a small occupation force of marines and sailors under the command of Marine Lieutenant Charles Heywood. On 11 November, Shubrick's squadron with the *Cyane* seized Mazatlán without incident. Du Pont acted as the senior occupation officer at Mazatlán and helped reestablish its municipal government. Nation building was also an important mission during the Mexican War.[22]

Shubrick's actions set the stage for Du Pont's first combat experience. Although he missed the action of San Gabriel, Du Pont finally experienced a battle in February 1848. Faced with increased resistance throughout the region, several American garrisons came under attack. Lieutenant Heywood's small band repulsed a Mexican counterattack in November 1847. The small American force—now numbering sixty-three marines, sailors, and California volunteers—was attacked again in January 1848 and besieged in an old barracks building. By mid-February the prospects for the meager garrison's relief were bleak indeed. Fortunately, Shubrick received word of Heywood's plight and immediately dispatched the *Cyane* to lift the siege.[23]

Du Pont arrived in the harbor of San José del Cabo late in the day on 14 February 1848. Although tempted to land immediately, Du Pont prudently decided not to conduct a night attack with sailors unaccustomed to such actions and instead carefully planned a relief operation for first light. The morning dawned calm and cloudy with mild temperatures in the mid-70s. Du Pont handpicked a force of 89 sailors, 5 marines, and 8 officers and at dawn successfully landed them one mile from Heywood's position. After accounting for all of his men, Du Pont led them to the barracks. The *Cyane's* first lieutenant remained on board the ship to provide fire support for the landing party; however, he could not distinguish friend from foe through the dense vegetation along the route. Thus, Du Pont and his men endured a one-mile march during which they were under constant fire from an enemy force that probably exceeded 400 men. "Our general procedure was: when the glimpse of an enemy was caught by anyone in the file, he would step out a pace, fire and fall in again. When the fire upon us seemed concentrated and was specially annoying, the two companies would face alternatively to the right or left and pour in a volley." As the rescue party neared the town, the Mexican force attacked them from the rear where, Du Pont recalled, the fire "was rather hot." Fortunately, Du Pont was able to swing his men around to unleash volleys that dispersed the enemy. To the observers on the *Cyane* and to Heywood in the barracks, however, the smoke-obscured battlefield surely concealed the destruction of Du Pont's small band by the numerically superior Mexican force. As the *Cyane's* landing party neared the barracks, Heywood and his men broke out and linked up with Du Pont. The lieutenant was astonished to discover that the landing party had suffered only 4 wounded during their march to the town. As Heywood and Du Pont met, the Mexicans attacked again, but they were quickly routed by a combination of the *Cyane's* guns and a coordinated counterattack by the combined force of sailors and marines. The *Cyane's* log noted that "at 11:30 [A.M.] . . . white flags were displayed at the village." Du Pont had lifted the siege and saved Heywood and his men. American casualties for the entire siege and rescue totaled 3 killed and 4 wounded; Mexican losses are less certain: estimates range from 13 to 35 killed. In his official report on the action, Du Pont proudly but modestly described the discipline and courage of his men and the bravery of his officers.[24] Du Pont had gotten his wish: he had seen combat close up and had performed coolly and capably while under fire. The officers and men he had trained and led for so long exceeded his wildest expectations. San José, without a doubt, was the pinnacle of Du Pont's career to this point and established him as one of the best talents in the navy.

The sensational news of the relief of the San José garrison spread rapidly from ship to ship as Du Pont and the crew of the *Cyane* became the toast of the squadron. Commodore Shubrick personally commended the *Cyane's* actions and made a special point to visit the ship to congratulate Du Pont and his men. Two weeks after the action, Du Pont finally had a chance to write Sophie. "My beloved," the new combat veteran wrote, "when you receive this, get upon your knees and thank our most merciful Father for my preservation—I have done so again and again. We had a very *short conflict*, suc-

USS *Cyane* at sea in a storm off the coast of California during the Mexican War. Drawing by *Cyane* crewman William Meyers. (Courtesy of the Bancroft Library, University of California, Berkeley)

ceeded in our undertaking, relieved a band of brave men . . . from approaching misery beyond description, and pending capture." When Sophie received Du Pont's description of the battle, he had already been gone for over two and a half years. Her reply hints at the frustration and despair she felt at his absence coupled with his brush with death and her disapproval of the war. "I hastened to my room and threw myself on my knees to thank God for his infinite mercies to us both, before I read any more. I could not frame a prayer of thanksgiving in my extreme agitation, but He read it in my soul! . . . Miserable war! Well you may exclaim, when precious lives are being sacrificed thus, and for what?"[25]

The *Cyane* returned to Mazatlán in April 1848, and there received orders for home. Du Pont departed for Norfolk to the echoes of rousing cheers from the crews of the assembled ships of the squadron on 2 June 1848. Forty-six days later the *Cyane* arrived in Valparaiso to resupply and to give the men a much-needed break. Finally, on 9 October 1848 Du Pont arrived in Norfolk after one of the shortest west-to-east passages around Cape Horn on record and an absence of three years.[26]

Du Pont's experiences in the Mexican War added to his already stellar reputation in the navy and provided him with lessons that he would apply later in his career. Chief among them were how to conduct a successful naval blockade and the vital importance of joint operations. When the *Cyane* arrived in Norfolk, Du Pont had already spent thirty-three years on active duty and fifteen years at sea. The commander, now forty-five, began an extended interval of shore duty that lasted until 1857. For the newly minted combat veteran, this time proved to be one of the most intellectually exciting and fruitful periods of his career.

After a stressful three-year cruise, Du Pont's homecoming did not go as well as he and Sophie had hoped. Although both were overjoyed at his return, the couple apparently had a bitter argument over something. In letters to friends and relatives, Sophie refers to their disagreement in passing but is not explicit. One can only speculate about the cause, but such conflicts are common when military members return home after long deployments. In his absence Sophie had begun to take morphine to relieve her back pain, and she may have become mildly addicted to the drug. In addition, during the voyage home Alexander Slidell Mackenzie, one of Du Pont's best friends, had died suddenly. These things all cast a shadow on Du Pont's return. Even so, Sophie wrote, "Since he came I have been as happy as I suppose it ever falls to the lot of mortals to be."[27]

After a period of readjustment to home life and a long rest, Du Pont spent some months supervising the enlargement and renovation of their home. He also helped establish Christ Church on the Brandywine in 1848, remaining among the most generous of its contributors until his death, and attended the National Episcopal Church Convention in Cincinnati.[28] Sophie had gently lectured and tutored him on religious matters throughout his deployment to the Pacific. At one point during their separation, Du Pont had innocently mentioned in one of his letters that he wanted to be more like his wife and that he hoped he was good enough to deserve God's blessings. Sophie was aghast and replied that his letters "make me fear you do not take an entirely correct view of our position in the sight of God." She proceeded to instruct him on the true meaning of Christianity: God's grace does not come by conduct alone, for "if this were so; if we could by *our goodness merit* these things, where were the need of the Savior?" However, despite this mild rebuke, she did not want to dampen his enthusiasm, "*Far from it!*" Continuing her exhortation, Sophie exclaimed that "it is only when we realize practically our own sinfulness, weakness, helplessness, that we come to Christ with that full faith, and surrender of self, which makes us accept God thro' Him . . . then, we are 'born again.'" Fortunately for their relationship, she closed a letter that must have taken Du Pont aback with a very tender and loving ending. In her long letters and his thoughtful replies, she kindly pushed him to be a thoroughgoing Christian man in every respect: avoid swearing, advice he admitted was very difficult for a man toughened from years at sea; respect himself and his men; and always consider the physical, moral, and religious health of his officers and crew. Although Du Pont would never be as devout as Sophie, and he never pushed his spiritual beliefs on others, their extended separation marked his complete conversion to his wife's religious views. He was now almost as devout as Sophie was.[29]

During the Du Ponts' happy months of reunion, Congress began to debate the oft-discussed, but never acted upon, controversy over corporal punishment in the navy. During his tenure as secretary of the navy, Bancroft had urged naval officers to "cease the casual flogging of sailors." However, the definition of "casual" was in the eye of the beholder, or rather, it was in eye of the captain of each individual ship. Public outrage over flogging had been fueled, in part, by the recent publication of Herman Melville's sensational novel *White Jacket*, which purported to be an accurate account of life aboard an American man-of-war. Joining Melville in the campaign to end corporal punishment in the navy were many opponents of slavery. Prompted by the abolitionist congressman John P. Hale, the House passed a bill outlawing flogging in January 1848. Not until the politically turbulent year of 1850, however, did the Senate, assisted in no small part by Robert F. Stockton, Du Pont's old chief, now a United States senator, enact a complete ban on flogging. This controversy clearly demonstrated the gulf that existed between civilians and professional military during this period. The public almost universally praised the legislation as a long overdue elimination of a barbaric punishment not suited for modern society. Du Pont and many of his fellow officers, on the other hand, were appalled at the passage of this measure.[30]

It was not that naval officers particularly liked the idea of whipping members of their crews, but the bill banning the practice provided no disciplinary alternative. Officers feared that discipline at sea would quickly erode and that captains would have no choice but to impose harsh punishments for relatively minor infractions. Others remarked that the only way a flogging ban could work without harming discipline and order was for the service to seek better recruits. In a response to Secretary of the Navy William A. Graham's request for his views on the controversy, Du Pont tried to defend what was for most Americans an indefensible practice: "The difficulty of finding efficient substitutes consistent with humanity and satisfactory to the seamen themselves for the sharp but prompt punishment of flogging, was the main source of objection to the change." Du Pont assured Graham that every navy officer would rejoice "if any other system can be devised less trying to the feelings and at the same time sufficient to maintain order and efficiency of our ships of war."[31]

Du Pont was particularly disgusted at the impact of Melville's book on Congress and the public. After a thorough reading, he described *White Jacket* as being overly sensationalistic and full of lies and half-truths; he believed the author had tried to demonstrate "every enormity he has ever heard of in the ocean, . . . making the one frigate the stage on which they were exhibited."[32] Some of Du Pont's criticisms were valid. However, Du Pont's reaction to the book—and that of many other naval officers—was overly defensive, for despite his hyperbole, Melville undoubtedly hit the mark in many ways.

While in the capital on other duties, Du Pont wrote Sophie that "I have just heard that on board the *Albany* one of the crew drew a knife on the Captain, with intent to kill; that he was tried by court martial and sentenced to be hung. . . . If this be true . . . doubtless this man's life will be sacrificed to their demagoguery." Du Pont felt that a captain at sea should have been able to resolve such an incident—serious as it was—with a heavy dose of flogging and not by an expensive and time-consuming court martial, and certainly not resulting in the death of the seaman. A friend wrote Du Pont that reports from the fleet indicated that the number of incidents of disobedience and disrespect had skyrocketed. One story making the rounds told of a lieutenant who ordered a cabin boy to stop whistling, "or I'll flog you." The boy gave the officer "a quiet look of cool indifference and said, 'Oh, you can't do that now, Sir', and walked off." Du Pont lobbied against Stockton's bill, and when his efforts failed, he pressed the case with the Navy Department and Congress for a comprehensive punishment bill that would give commanders alternatives to the lash, while maintaining discipline. Not until March 1855 did Congress pass "An Act to Provide a More Efficient Discipline for the Navy."[33]

In the aftermath of the navy's flogging and disciplinary controversies, the service tapped Du Pont to perform two shore duties, one of which turned out to be very important to his future career. He was named commander of the receiving ship *Union* at the Philadelphia Navy Yard, a job that took little of his time. In addition, on 14 April 1851 the secretary of the navy appointed Du Pont to serve on a Lighthouse Board, the purpose of which was to examine all of the lighthouses and other aids to navigation on the eastern seaboard of the United States and to make recommendations for their improvement to the Treasury Department. At this time there was no standardization of lighthouse requirements, design, manning, or maintenance. The lights ran haphazardly and often were poorly supervised and inspected by local politically appointed port collectors under the nominal supervision of the secretary of the treasury. The chaotic state of navigational aids resulted in narrowly averted maritime disasters along many of the nation's treacherous expanses of coastline. Du Pont's appointment to this board reveals just how respected and valued he was in the service despite his rather low rank. It placed him in contact with influential men with whom he would build lifelong friendships and professional associations. Members included the navy's Commodore William B. Shubrick and Lieutenant Thornton A. Jenkins; the army's chief of engineers, Joseph G. Totten; and the head of the United States Coast Survey, Professor Alexander Dallas Bache.[34] Du Pont dutifully accepted this appointment, although he was not pleased with the prospect of spending long weeks in Washington, D.C.[35]

As the spring of 1851 ended, Du Pont was one of the most respected officers in the navy. Thanks to his performance in the Mexican War and his work organizing the Naval Academy, Du Pont's reputation soared throughout the service. Superiors, peers, and subordinates routinely sought him out for his advice, assistance, direct intervention, and support. Although he was still only a commander, for the first time in his career his status and influence would allow him to pursue some of the naval reforms he had advocated for so long. His papers are replete with references to pay issues, disciplinary reform, slow promotion problems, officer retention, the Naval Academy, navy modernization, and strategic subjects. As the summer of 1851 began, the navy gave Du Pont a task that would solidify his reputation as a far-ranging naval thinker, reformer, and strategist.

3

A Strategy for a Modern Navy

To carry the sword of state upon the broad ocean.

—SAMUEL FRANCIS DU PONT

THE NATIONAL defense strategy of the United States had been unchanged since the War of 1812. For many years a combination of coastal fortifications and a small but agile navy had served to defend the North American continent adequately, but the failure of the national strategy to defend Washington, D.C., during the war with Great Britain traumatized the Corps of Engineers and the United States Navy. In the aftermath, a combined Army and Navy Board of Engineers in 1816 developed a new plan for coastal fortifications, what came to be called the "Third System of Fortifications," the first two having proved "haphazard and amateurish." The board—including such talented men as army engineer Joseph G. Totten—considered more than simply building more defensive works and instead conceived a four-part defense strategy consisting of "(1) a strong navy; (2) fortifications at important ports and harbors; (3) improved interior communications; and (4) the regular army and the militia."[1] All four elements should be combined into a reinforcing and interconnected system to produce a defensive posture that would be adequate to protect the United States. The first and foremost layer of defense was the United States Navy, and the board suggested that the service be expanded significantly with additional ships and shore facilities. It was a good plan, and a great start on a unified national strategy, but as historian Russell F. Weigley has noted, it "represented theory rather than practice." Fiscal constraints and an unimpressed Congress combined to thwart many of the board's recommendations and led to fitful appropriations to both services that left the strategy only partially complete by midcentury.[2]

Following up on the work of the Fortifications Board, President James Monroe submitted a report to Congress in 1824 advocating the expansion of the navy because "the great object in the event of war is to stop the enemy at the coast." The president and his secretary of the navy, Samuel Southard, clearly saw the service as a wholly defensive force, and their attitude reflected that of the officer corps as well. Throughout the next three decades, the navy struggled with an identity crisis. During this time it began sporadic and largely uncoordinated experiments with steam propulsion for warships and for floating batteries (believed by many to be more cost-effective than coastal fortifications), starting with the steam frigate *Fulton II* in 1837. Steam enthusiasts such as Matthew C. Perry and Robert F. Stockton performed valuable work designing and perfecting coal-fired warships for the navy, but by the 1850s the United States still lagged far behind most European navies. In 1842 the navy launched four new warships, an occasion that should have markedly improved the navy's capability. However, while two of the new ships were state-of-the-art paddle-wheel steamers, the remaining two were sail frigates designed during the War of 1812. Although forward-thinking secretaries of the navy such as Abel P. Upshur saw the strategic implications of steam propulsion and advocated the expansion of the service, most were content merely to maintain the navy at its historically low levels of ship strength, manning, and technology.[3]

The early 1840s saw a very brief interlude of technological innovation. What would have been the world's first ironclad vessel, the so-called Steven's Battery, was begun in 1841. The design for this strange ship called for a steam-powered bargelike superstructure protected with iron plates with a battery of several large-caliber guns to be used for coastal defense and harbor protection. A novel idea, she was never completed and was finally scrapped in 1885 after huge cost overruns and significant modifications in her design over the years.[4]

In 1843 the influential and politically astute officer Robert F. Stockton and the talented Swedish engineer John Ericsson designed and built the highly advanced steam-powered and propeller-driven sloop of war *Princeton*. Despite the *Princeton*'s impressive technological achievements, she had little influence on the navy at large, especially after a gun explosion killed several dignitaries visiting the ship on 28 February 1844. The eight dead included the secretaries of state and war, and another nine people were injured. President Tyler was also on the ship during the accident but escaped injury.[5] The tragedy shocked the country and stunned the naval community. Du Pont learned of the *Princeton* "catastrophe" on his return to the United States after his illness at Rio de Janeiro in May 1844. When they entered Boston Harbor, "the first news the Pilot gave us was the bursting of Stockton's big gun." As one naval historian has put it, "The explosion . . . gave Congress an excuse to hold up construction of more steam warships, delaying the modernization of the Navy."[6] The disaster set back naval transformation for at least a decade, and the service continued to languish throughout the 1840s and early 1850s.

The memories of the glorious single-ship frigate victories of the War of 1812 were still with the navy in 1850; the navy's prevailing role during that war of commerce raiding and coastal defense still dominated the service's strategic thinking. Although the navy performed well during the Mexican War, it served in a predominantly supporting role, which did little to attract the attention of Congress and successive administrations, despite the addition of thousands of miles of coastline that now required protection. While many officers within the service pushed for a larger and more modern navy, very few bothered to think deeply about how to use this force given the new realities of geography and technology that were becoming increasingly evident by midcentury. In other words, with few exceptions strategic thought was almost nonexistent. Besides Du Pont, Matthew Fontaine Maury, John A. Dahlgren, Franklin Buchanan, Matthew C. Perry, and Robert F. Stockton were all considered reform-minded and farsighted officers in the antebellum navy; but most "reformers" had a very narrow focus. Many of these men belonged to the United States Navy Lyceum, a group formed in 1833 by officers "to promote the diffusion of useful knowledge, [and] foster a harmony and community of spirit in the service."[7]

The result of this inertia both in and out of the service was that the navy went into a precipitous decline after the Mexican War. Weak executive leadership and political infighting caused naval readiness to deteriorate to the point where "the power and efficiency of the Navy steadily declined until, in 1853, the United States possessed not one vessel that could have given battle with prospect of victory against any first-class warship of the major European powers."[8]

With Zachary Taylor's premature death, Millard Fillmore was thrust into the presidency, and William A. Graham became the new secretary of the navy. While the Compromise of 1850 consumed the attention of the Congress, Graham took charge of a navy in considerable disarray. Although hardly a visionary, Graham was a capable administrator, and his tenure was mildly successful as he dealt with the aftermath of the abolition of flogging and the growth of naval exploration, such as Commodore Matthew C.

Perry's trip to Japan. Yet he was opposed to any significant increase in the size or capability of the navy. Graham's tenure proved frustrating to many naval officers such as Du Pont. They lobbied Congress and the administration hard for promotion and rank reform and struggled against the assimilation of officers from the former navy of the Republic of Texas, and most of them argued for the reinstitution of flogging; few of these issues were resolved during Graham's tenure as secretary.[9]

While the navy reeled along after the Mexican War, the army followed suit. Indeed, the fortifications called for by the 1821 Engineer Board were still far from complete by the end of the Mexican War. After the war's successful conclusion, Brigadier General Totten found congressional appropriations hard to come by. The chief of engineers and a succession of secretaries of war found it increasingly difficult to wrest additional appropriations from a skeptical Congress. Indeed, "Totten fairly begged for money to resume work in 1849."[10]

Many in Congress began to wonder if the new technological advances of the age, including steam warships and improved ordnance, made the current—and expensive—system of coastal fortifications obsolete. In March 1851 the House of Representatives directed Secretary of War Charles M. Conrad to report by early December "on the subject of the land defences of the Country" and to review "the general system adopted after the War with Great Britain and since pursued in regard to the permanent fortifications then deemed necessary for the national defence." Congress further instructed Conrad to determine whether it was possible to reduce defense expenditures by scaling back the system of coastal fortifications through an increased reliance on the navy.[11] Conrad turned to the experts to help prepare his response to Congress.

First, he directed several key officers from the Corps of Engineers (including its chief, General Totten) to prepare preliminary reports addressing the House's concerns. Second, he asked Secretary of the Navy Graham to "obtain the opinion of several Naval Officers, combining professional science with experience and practical skill on several points connected with the proposed inquiry." Specifically, Conrad asked Graham to have his officers answer two critical questions: first, how should the current system of coastal fortifications be modified; and, second, could the navy assume a bigger role in the nation's coastal defense.[12]

Graham immediately forwarded this request to some of the leading naval officers of the day: Commodores Charles Stewart, Charles Morris, and Matthew C. Perry; Commanders Du Pont, Franklin Buchanan, and Robert B. Cunningham; and Lieutenants Matthew F. Maury, Joseph Lanman, and

John A. Dahlgren. Graham ordered this distinguished group to "be pleased to give to the subject your best reflections and communicate the result to the Secretary of War."[13] Just as Du Pont's opinion and professional advice had been eagerly sought on such key reform issues as the founding of the United States Naval Academy and the abolition of flogging, he was now asked to comment on a key strategic problem facing the country: What was the best way to defend the shores of the United States? Given the wording of the Conrad's request and the congressional interest in the subject, it is surprising that Graham did not specify that he see his officers' reports before their submission to the secretary of war. The implications for the navy were obvious—if the system of fortifications was changed dramatically, so too would the navy's mission have to change—but because the request came from the secretary of war, Graham probably believed the subject to be of scant importance to his department. Of all the officers requested to answer Conrad's questions, only Du Pont seems to have fully appreciated that the outcome of this congressional inquiry could seriously affect the future of the United States Navy. Du Pont went beyond the narrow bounds of the questions posed by the War Department and seized on the opportunity to develop and put forward his thoughts on not only the efficacy of coastal fortifications but the proper role of the United States Navy as well. For one of the very first times, a serving officer in the United States Navy proposed a coherent, albeit not fully developed, national naval strategy.

Du Pont saw an opportunity to articulate his thoughts on the future course of the navy. A report to the secretary of war would provide him an avenue through which he could communicate his ideas in an official capacity; more importantly, he could reach a large number of influential decision makers both in and out of the military and political professions. He would answer Conrad's questions, but he also would add much more to his report.

Although the Lighthouse Board work was tedious and time-consuming, Du Pont's presence in Washington during the summer and fall of 1851 allowed him to consult with experts and professional colleagues and to collect key documents as he wrote his report. A five-week inspection tour of the lighthouses from North Carolina to Maine allowed him to visit in July 1851 with his friend Lieutenant Charles H. Davis, the head of the Nautical Almanac Office at Cambridge, Massachusetts. Davis agreed to review a draft of Du Pont's work and to provide him any assistance he might require. Du Pont soon wrote to Davis asking for more help in completing his report on the "fortification question." He also noted that he had received a letter from another report writer, Matthew Fontaine Maury, who "gives the opposite view I own."[14] As Du Pont traveled through the beautiful countryside and endured many long, lonely rides out to remote lighthouses on his inspection trips, he began to collect and formulate his thoughts on what the role of the United States Navy should be in peacetime and in war.

Fellow officers responded to Du Pont's queries and inundated him with letters lamenting the sorry state of the navy. Notable among these communications was one from Commander Louis M. Goldsborough: "Our Navy at this moment, is but one degree removed from a disorganized rabble—inefficient from 'title page to colophon'. . . . Still, neither you nor I should dream of abandoning our sinking ship until the flood itself engulfs us. . . . [We must] exert every nerve to keep her afloat, and to get her shattered timbers thoroughly repaired, hopeless as the job may seem." Goldsborough added that he had heard of Du Pont's arguments and efforts on behalf of several other aspects of naval reform and noted that "as a brother-officer, [I] beg to tender you my thanks for the active and efficient part that you played in the controversies they bespeak." Du Pont's correspondence is replete with letters of this sort showcasing his prominence in the reform movement within the United States Navy.[15]

Du Pont's colleagues were quick to answer Conrad, but most of the responses were short, pedestrian, and uninspired. Commodore Morris—a national hero from the war against the Barbary pirates and the most distinguished of the naval officers asked to comment on the fortification issue—submitted a brief report to the secretary less than one month after receiving Graham's letter. Addressing the first question, Morris noted that the application of steam power to warships and the great improvements in ordnance, particularly explosive shells, probably meant that the government would have to make great improvements in the entire system of fortifications. Morris believed that using the navy in lieu of fortifications "would, in my opinion, be highly injudicious." He went on to affirm the belief of most naval officers that the main purpose of the United States Navy was to "afford all protection to our merchant shipping [and] to destroy or harass an enemy's commerce." Morris's report was competent and addressed all of Conrad's questions, but it was also largely a restatement of current and past policy.[16]

Commodore Matthew C. Perry, a leading naval reformer (and the officer who would soon gain fame by opening Japan to the West), recommended that the current system of defenses should be "substantially modified," and he further advocated the "entire abandonment of *exterior* coast fortifications." Perry believed that the fortifications defending the approaches to most of the nation's harbors would be easy prey to a determined enemy force equipped with modern steam warships. Perry instead recommended that a system of interior fortifications be constructed closer to city limits, manned

by "myriads of militia and volunteers" and supported by floating steam batteries to constitute the nation's main line of defense. In answering the secretary's second question, Perry replied that "much reliance could be placed on
all vessels of war, particularly those moved by steam," for coastal defense.
Perry did not elaborate on these ideas in his brief report, nor did he fully develop the rationale behind his recommendations. In the end, Conrad and
Totten virtually ignored Perry's recommendations, and his report was forgotten as he prepared to depart on his epochal voyage to the Pacific.[17]

The reports of Lieutenants Matthew Fontaine Maury and John A.
Dahlgren departed markedly from the others by their length and the depth
and sophistication of their arguments. Maury, director of the United States
Naval Observatory since 1844, responded by arguing for the massive use of
railroads along the coasts to face rapidly any and all enemy threats. He wrote
that technological changes in transportation and ordnance had been so significant that they were "enough to revolutionize the system of coast defence." Railroads, argued Maury in his overly long and sometimes rambling
memorandum, were the key to the defense of the eastern seaboard of the
United States. Indeed, the only fortifications the nation required once railroad access was expanded throughout the country were those that would
"protect our *sea-port* towns from the GREAT GUNS OF BIG SHIPS."[18]

In other words, Maury argued that the invention and perfection of the
locomotive had rendered obsolete the present set of fortifications guarding
the approaches to most of the nation's important waterways, bays, inlets, and
coastal towns. He believed that railroads could transport quickly a massive
mobilization of militia forces to the threatened area in a matter of days and
thus counter any threat of invasion to the United States. Maury also lectured
the secretary of war on the proper placement and disposition of troops and
their command and control structure. For the United States Navy, Maury
proposed no drastic departure from its current role in coastal defense.[19]

Maury's ideas for coastal defense were way of ahead of their time. He was
one of the very first to recognize the vital importance that railroads could
play in the defense of the country. However, his ideas were probably too advanced to have any real impact upon the fortifications debate. Maury apparently circulated his report to many brother officers, but most dismissed it out
of hand. In August 1851 Thornton Jenkins wrote to his friend Du Pont of
"Maury's railroad papers." Jenkins expressed shock that the oceanographer
did not see that "all of the railroads in Christendom could [not] prevent an
intelligent man in command of a fleet from entering a harbor, bay, or port
which are otherwise unfortified."[20]

John A. Dahlgren, like Maury, was working in a scientific capacity when asked to comment on the nation's defenses. Dahlgren was perhaps the navy's foremost inventor and developer of naval ordnance. At the time of Conrad's request, Dahlgren advocated two major changes that were greeted with skepticism by many of his fellow officers: fielding large-caliber guns and recognizing the superiority of shell over shot. These ideas grew out of the theories of French army colonel Henri Paixhans. Dahlgren also advocated a "systems approach" to naval ordnance in which he believed that the best way for the navy to equip its ships was through "a series of complementary weapons: howitzers, IX-inch guns, XI-inch guns."[21] Indeed, Dahlgren was producing the only real technological innovations for the navy during this period. While extolling the advantages of ships equipped with his new shell guns, Dahlgren argued for the deterrence effect of a large number of modern steam warships used specifically for coastal defense that could be concentrated by the use of the telegraph; he was quick to admit, however, that such an expansion of the navy was politically unfeasible. Dahlgren dismissed the utility of the floating battery, which, he perceptively argued, "unites the weak points of both fort and ship."[22]

The wording and tenor of the House of Representatives' directive to the secretary of war and that of the secretary to Graham concerned Du Pont a great deal. He was particularly troubled about the second question posed by Conrad: "What reliance could be placed on vessels of war, or of commerce, floating batteries, gun boats, and other temporary substitutes for permanent fortifications?"[23] It was clear to him that the army (or Congress) might want to push the navy into accepting the responsibility for the defense of America's entire coastline; this, Du Pont believed, was exactly what the navy should try to avoid. His apprehension was alleviated somewhat when he was able to speak with Totten during meetings of the Lighthouse Board. Totten did not want the Corps of Engineers to abandon the lion's share of the coastal defense responsibilities. A much-relieved Du Pont wrote to Charles H. Davis in September 1851, declaring, "I think I know where the case now stands, having got hold of Totten's reports, which eases one's mind a little—at first I felt like a man groping in the dark."[24] This was just the opening Du Pont was looking for. In fact, Du Pont wanted to go much further than simply ensuring that the navy would not take over the sole responsibility for coastal defense; he wanted to free the service from its purely defensive role and build more of an offensive force that could meet an enemy fleet in enemy waters.

Du Pont began his report with a disclaimer. He noted that he might be expected as a naval officer to push the navy's role in the national defense, but he rejected parochialism by noting that "this question is too broad and national to be confined within any such narrow limits, and in examining it an officer should discard from his mind to which arm of the public service he belongs." Yet in the same paragraph he explained that he would make the case for a navy "carried far beyond its present numbers and strength." So, with this somewhat disingenuous introduction, Du Pont claimed his impartiality while also declaring that the navy must expand to ensure adequate defensive capability. Not only must the navy expand, Du Pont argued, but also its role must be redefined. He advocated increasing the number and strength of coastal fortifications to free up the navy for other missions. Without a doubt, said Du Pont, the navy's true mission should be offensive in nature; the navy should not be a passive defensive force tied inexorably to the nation's coast. "Indeed," maintained Du Pont, "this arm [the navy] can only fill its special mission in war, that of *aggression,* by being enabled to *leave* the great seaports and exposed points of maritime frontier to a more certain and economical system of protection, in order to carry the 'sword of the state' upon the broad ocean, sweep from it the enemy's commerce, capture or scatter the vessels of war protecting it, cover and convoy our own to its destined havens, and be ready to meet hostile fleets; in other words, to contend for the mastery of the seas, where alone it can be obtained, on the sea itself."[25]

With these introductory remarks, Du Pont made it clear where he was going with his arguments. The navy must throw off the shackles of coastal defense and be prepared to fight abroad, to fight offensively; maintaining its traditional role of commerce raiding and protection to be sure but also meeting and defeating enemy fleets on the high seas. No longer, argued Du Pont, should the country tie the navy to its homeports for the purpose of coastal defense. Doing so would only eliminate one of the navy's most important attributes, its mobility. The best way to defend the coastline of the United States was to field a large navy that could conduct offensive operations against an enemy fleet. The navy was clearly the main arm, the "sword of the state," and wielding this sword demanded an aggressive not a passive warrior.

Du Pont wrote that he completely agreed with an 1836 report by Secretary of War Lewis Cass, who declared that every city and seaport that might "tempt the cupidity of an enemy should be defended by works . . . suited to its local position." So, in a marked departure from Maury, Du Pont maintained in his report to Conrad that "our principal seaports, naval depots, and all important points on our seaboard, should receive commensurate protection." Du Pont noted that of all the options available to the country for coastline defense, the best was a good system of fixed fortifications. In a particularly prophetic statement, Du Pont observed that "forts can be made impregnable against any naval force that could be brought against them, and are needed for the protection of our own fleets while preparing for hostilities on the ocean." On the other hand, Du Pont viewed other defensive measures such as floating steam batteries to be uneconomical, inefficient, and incapable of providing adequate protection for the cities; these devices should be used only in a very limited support role. Du Pont wrote, "To leave the whole defence of our harbors to such temporary expedients, built of materials as vulnerable and perishable as ships, would be expending enormous sums in order to invite attack."[26]

It is impossible to say whether Du Pont really believed as strongly as he appears to have about the efficacy of fortifications or if he was simply stating what he thought Conrad and Totten would want to hear. Du Pont was an extremely shrewd and politically savvy officer, and he may have simply been trying to gain their support for his naval agenda. Although his correspondence does not reveal extensive writings on fortifications, neither does it indicate anything that would diverge from what he stated in the report.

In response to the argument put forth by some in Congress that the navy should assume the bulk of the responsibility for coastal defense, Du Pont contended that the country's merchant fleet would be unprotected. The navy, claimed Du Pont, was the only mechanism for its protection, "but this is essentially taken away when it [the navy] has assigned to it the defence of our seaports." Some misguided souls claimed that the country could count on the navy to do double duty; it could defend the coasts and the merchant marine. This concept was insane, said Du Pont, and the American people would not stand for it. One of the most important second-order effects of having a viable system of coastal defenses was to maintain public morale; the populations of the key cities of the United States would balk "if [their] approaches were left without forts, equipped and manned." If the navy alone was expected to defend the coastline of the United States, how, asked Du Pont, would one divide the fleet? There would never be enough ships to cover all the key installations. The population would express "endless vexation, dissatisfaction, and dispute."

Du Pont rejected this notion out of hand. Such a course of action "would be to supplant impregnable bulwarks by pregnable ones, a fixed security by a changeable one . . . and would be to ruin our sense of security [and] peace of mind."[27] He recognized one of the key elements of national defense in the mid-nineteenth century: the defenses must be visible and seen as effective by the population. This was not the first time he would instinctively propose a military strategy that was Clausewitzian in nature. He recognized that passion of the people—one leg of the Clausewitzian "remarkable trinity"—had to be considered when developing a national or military strategy. Also, for Clausewitz (and Du Pont), the primacy of political considerations in strategic development was essential.[28] Du Pont instinctively recognized that in a republic such as the United States, the population played a huge role in the military strategy of the country; at a minimum, the civilian and military leaders must consider political issues, or ignore them at their peril.

Not only would the eastern population of the United States reject any major reduction in fortifications in lieu of a purely defensive-minded navy, but also the service would be unable to accomplish its more important tasks. To gear the navy toward defense would divert it "from its highest duty; deprive it of its chief honor and merit, and best claim to the respect and support of the people, that is, the vindication of the national honor, and the maintenance of the national freedom and independence on the high seas." Further, Du Pont maintained, if coastal defense was assigned to the navy instead of the system of fortifications, the country would be forced to raise a large standing army to defend the cities. Depending on the militia, argued Du Pont, was ineffective because of the time it would take to mobilize an adequate force. The American people would surely reject these concepts, too.[29] Once more, Du Pont noted that the main mission for the United States Navy should be on the high seas and not confined to the passive and vulnerable task of coastal defense.

To further bolster his arguments for freeing the navy from a defensive mission, Du Pont cited numerous examples of French and British fortifications. Although blessed with huge fleets and much smaller coastal regions to defend, these countries were continuing to strengthen and increase their coastal fortifications. They did this, Du Pont said, "with a view of making their navies *more efficient* in their share of the national defence."[30] In other words, a workable system of coastal fortifications also served as an economy of force measure, enabling the navy to perform other missions that were more important.

In the remaining pages of his report, Du Pont concentrated on his vision of a naval strategy for the United States. Despite the enduring importance of fixed shore fortifications, the navy would still be responsible for "a large sphere of action in a scheme of national defense." Indeed, argued Du Pont, the navy's importance was "in proportion as it is relieved from harbor defence; and in a war, even defensive in its origin and object, the navy, in almost every case, must assume an offensive attitude. . . . the special function of the navy, in war, is to be aggressive." Du Pont maintained that the navy must take the fight to the enemy and not assume a passive role. He then described what kind of navy the United States should have. He asked some obvious questions: "Now, is our navy, in point of efficiency and numbers, what it should be? . . . [H]as this arm been kept to any degree of vigor commensurate with the work it may have to perform, or in keeping with our position among nations? Is it equal to the ordinary exigencies occurring almost daily?"[31] Du Pont insisted that the answer to all of these questions was a resounding no.

Crises over Cuba, Oregon, France's claims, and other disputes had ended peacefully, declared Du Pont, but what if they had not? All would have ended badly for the United States because it had no formidable naval force with which to impose its will and implement its policies. Du Pont's report anticipated the writings of the late nineteenth-century naval strategist Alfred Thayer Mahan. Although some aspects of Mahan's arguments would not have appealed to Du Pont, such as the requirements for building a large sea-controlling fleet (which he knew the American public would not support) and the seizure of overseas bases, Du Pont's implicit argument suggested something like Mahan's "fleet in being" concept for a smaller mid-nineteenth-century navy.[32] Mahan recognized that Great Britain had "reigned as 'the great commercial nation of the world' through its maritime hegemony."[33] Du Pont was a powerful advocate for a navy strong enough to complement the tremendous capacity of the United States economy.

Assessing the most dangerous potential naval threats to the United States, Du Pont concentrated on Great Britain, noting that the traditional naval power had recently embarked on a major shipbuilding effort. With over 150 steam warships, the Royal Navy dwarfed the United States Navy, and with France building up its already large fleet as well, both countries had "reached the highest state of efficiency, skill, and discipline, and their *morale* never was higher. That of England, roused to the maintenance of its boasted supremacy on the ocean; that of France, burning for the opportunity to show the world that its practical skill is *now* equal to that science and bravery which were ever conspicuous."[34] The United States Navy did not compare favorably to these potential opponents. Dwarfed by European fleets, it included, at best, fewer than ten modern warships. Aside from the unfortunate *Princeton*, the most advanced of these were three paddlewheel frigates, the *Mississippi* and *Missouri*, launched in 1842, and the *Susquehanna*, launched in 1850. These ships "represented a high state of technical proficiency" but had quickly become obsolete.[35]

This disparity, observed Du Pont, "shows the terrible odds against us. It is well to remember this." Still, he did not advocate an all-out attempt to conduct a shipbuilding program to gain naval superiority or even parity with France and Great Britain, for he knew that the American people and the

Congress would not accept the expense of such an immense naval expansion.[36] Du Pont recognized the inviolable link between national commercial success and prosperity and an adequate naval force; he also tended to downplay commerce raiding, while emphasizing commerce protection. Finally, he emphasized fielding a technologically advanced, offensively focused fleet, which would take the battle to the enemy on the high seas.

How then, asked Du Pont, should the United States address the huge discrepancy in numbers and quality between its navy and those of potential adversaries such as Great Britain and France? Du Pont saw the War of 1812 as the model for how the United States should proceed. In a highly flawed historical analysis, he claimed that the United States was able to overcome the British navy during that war because of the morale and skill of its officers and crews and the technological superiority of its warships. Although he was correct in pointing out that the United States Navy was remarkably successful in many ship-on-ship engagements, the navy was hardly able to "overcome" the Royal Navy. But his main point was to highlight the limitless economic and engineering potential of the United States and to promote the rapid buildup of the most technologically advanced warships afloat. If the United States chose this course of action, Du Pont argued, it could "render obsolete one-half or two-thirds of the English and French navies, and compel these powers to remodel their steam as well as sailing vessels." In other words, he called for a kind of a "dreadnought" strategy in which the United States, because of political considerations and expense, would build a relatively small number of highly advanced warships that in one stroke would surpass those of all other fleets.[37]

The fleet that Du Pont envisioned would be large by United States standards, with the most advanced ships that money could buy and that technology could devise. These ships would have the best power plants, superior protection, and the most sophisticated guns available. To increase their survivability, speed, and efficiency, Du Pont insisted that new ships be propelled exclusively by screw propellers. Indeed, a larger, more advanced version of the pathbreaking, if unlucky, *Princeton* should be the model for a modern navy. The fact that the United States Navy was alarmingly small and weak actually worked in its favor, maintained Du Pont. The British and the French had already expended great amounts of capital to build their fleets with only incremental technological improvements; therefore, inevitable technological advances would soon force them to devote even larger expenditures to replace many of their ships. The United States, on the other hand, had very few advanced ships of any kind. Du Pont argued that if the United States implemented such a naval policy, it would "compel these powers [France and

Great Britain], as it were, to start de novo with us, and [would] render comparatively valueless their gigantic naval establishments."[38]

Du Pont's advanced and perceptive strategic recommendations are noteworthy for three reasons. First, Du Pont, unlike many other naval officers of the day, was not afraid and suspicious of the new steam and shell-gun technology; the fact that Du Pont had never commanded or served on a steam warship makes his sophisticated analysis all the more impressive.[39] Second, he advocated the advanced strategy of technological superiority as opposed to numerical supremacy to produce a fleet that would deter the major naval powers of the day. Finally, Du Pont's strategy potentially could catapult a weak American navy ahead of more powerful ones.

He closed his report on coastal fortifications with an ominous warning of the state of naval readiness and an implicit call to action. The ubiquity of steam propulsion meant that "our distance from Europe, measured in time, is now reduced to a brief period of ten days." The United States was a peaceful nation, to be sure, but its expanding interaction with other counties and international "events abroad more and more indicate that we may, at no distant day, be forced, in our own defence, to aid the cause of freedom by an active war." The country had allowed the United States Navy to sink to historic depths, but there was a way out, contended Du Pont. The path to secure commerce, economic self-sufficiency, and a national defense that prevented enemy invasion was a combination of strong coastal fortifications and a sizable and technologically advanced navy that was ready, willing, and capable of offensive operations. If the country failed to adopt his recommendations, Du Pont maintained, "increased expenditure of blood and treasure" would accompany future wars.[40]

Du Pont was the last of the naval officers to submit his report to Secretary Conrad. For a man whose correspondence may be the most voluminous of all antebellum naval officers, writing his *Report on the National Defences* was nevertheless difficult. In September 1851 Du Pont confided to his friend Charles Henry Davis that "I have not the habit for this kind of work." He also agonized over whether he was trying to push the navy too hard; after all, the report was to go to the secretary of war, not the secretary of the navy. He also worried about the quality of his writing and the coherence of his arguments. Sending a draft copy to Davis, he included a note: "I send you . . . a rough sketch of my report—it is poor enough. . . . Remember you promised to be a 'merciless critic'—cut, hack, recast, correct, verbally and in every other way." Davis was quick to respond with enthusiastic praise. "Love your report exceedingly," declared Davis when he returned the draft to Du Pont with only minor grammatical corrections; Du Pont was pleased. Not only was Davis a good friend, but he was also known to possess one of the sharpest minds in the service.[41]

Du Pont discussed his views on naval strategy and the report with Davis and many others. Writing to Davis early in November, he noted that Totten (who with Du Pont had been meeting off and on throughout the preceding months with the Lighthouse Board) had written him urging a swift completion of his report: "Do not delay . . . dear captain, this at any rate is a case where one word for the navy is worth a whole broadside for fortifications." This was a great relief to Du Pont. Clearly, Totten believed strongly that the system of national defense must include a strong navy in conjunction with fortifications, and he encouraged Du Pont to be explicit in his arguments and recommendations; Totten also hinted that this report, if convincing, could be very influential. Still, Du Pont was uncertain how Conrad and his colleagues within naval circles would receive his report. He need not have worried. On 14 December 1851 Du Pont jubilantly wrote Davis: "I am pleased to tell you . . . our report has been well received. The Secretary of War . . . happened to mention my name" and said, "I know Cap. D[u Pont] through a very able report he has made to my Dept. I wish he would call and see me. All the naval reports were able, but I liked his best."[42]

To Du Pont's immense relief, the reports of both Secretary Conrad and General Totten reflected his own. In fact, it appears that they drew most of the navy portion of their reports from Du Pont's paper. Conrad's report to the Speaker of the House, published on 8 December 1851, echoed many of Du Pont's arguments and conclusions. Conrad told the Speaker that the navy should not substitute for coastal fortifications. Indeed, "the navy could not, and if it could, ought not, to be relied on for this purpose." This was not to say, however, that Conrad meant any negative reflection on the navy. Indeed, Du Pont himself could have written parts of Conrad's report. The navy, Conrad argued, should remain as the nation's main defensive force. But the navy should not be shackled to the ports. Instead, it must go "abroad on the wide ocean, protecting her commerce and harassing that of the enemy; hovering on his coast and compelling him, instead of attacking our cities, to look to defence of his own."[43]

Totten's lengthy and detailed supporting paper also echoed Du Pont.[44] Maury's and Dahlgren's papers, and those of the other naval officers, seem to have made no impact on the secretary or the chief of engineers. Du Pont's report, in contrast, presented an excellent example of clearly written, well-supported, and logical arguments that would appeal to other members of the military, and it was free from the scientific and military jargon that was anathema to politicians. Du Pont's report was the product of a combat veteran and line naval officer with years of experience at sea. Maury's and Dahlgren's reports were technical treatises written by men who were, in many ways, more scientists than naval officers. Du Pont succeeded in convincing important and influential military leaders that the navy should not take on the sole responsibility for the nation's coastal defense and that it must expand into a modern force and assume an offensive role; only in this way could the navy ensure the country's protection. Once Du Pont submitted his paper and it appeared in published form as part of the secretary's reply to Congress, accolades lauding Du Pont and his report starting flowing in from all parts of the army and navy communities.

Shortly after Conrad prepared and submitted the final report to Congress, Du Pont was surprised and gratified to learn that a number of army officers were so impressed with the quality of his report that they decided to fund a private printing of the document. Du Pont was touched and wrote a friend, "This is no small compliment, for the Corps of Engineers in the Army to adopt and publish a report on the art of National Defences—their particular field—by a naval officer." Alexander D. Bache, the superintendent of the Coast Survey and a fellow Lighthouse Board member, expressed his complete approval of Du Pont's report. While visiting Washington, D.C., for another round of Lighthouse Board meetings in February 1852, Du Pont received almost universal praise for his report. Henry Winter Davis, his friend and an influential future congressman, declared, "It is a comprehensive and masterly summary of the principles of national defense worthy of the Duke of Wellington, and I cannot tell you how much instruction and delight I derived from it."[45]

At one point, on the urging of his friend Charles Henry Davis, Du Pont considered expanding the report to book length. This was a tempting proposition for an ambitious officer, but Sophie quickly and wisely counseled against it. She recognized that Du Pont's writing style was not suited to long expositions, the fortification report's "very *condensedness* being in my opinion one of its chief merits." For every person that would read a book "such as Mr. C. Davis would have you write," she argued, "99 would read the report as it now stands. . . . 'Tis the ideas people want, and not the words." After all, she wrote, "the defect in Mr. C. Davis's writing is too much diffuseness."[46] Du Pont prudently accepted Sophie's advice and made no more revisions to the report.

To Sophie, a delighted and somewhat embarrassed Du Pont wrote that while he was attending a dinner party, several of the guests had mentioned the overwhelming response to his report. "I am ashamed to speak again of my fortification report even to *you*. But it has had a very remarkable *success*."

A naval officer and acquaintance of Du Pont's wrote that he felt a great deal of "pride that the Honorable Secretary of War and Congress are indebted to a Naval officer for the best and ablest report that has been written on the subject." Another friend and brother officer wrote from the Boston Navy Yard that he was gratified that Du Pont had taken the "opportunity afforded you of bringing the Navy before the public; for many persons, of sense in other matters . . . are particularly obtuse in regard to the Navy." Another officer noted that Du Pont's report was all the more significant because it "is highly creditable to you [and] decidedly the best report made on the defences of the country." Spurred on by the popularity and acceptance of the report among the military community, Du Pont began to distribute copies to a wider audience. He asked Charles Henry Davis to distribute copies to influential persons; Du Pont himself sent a copy to his acquaintance Franklin Pierce, the future president, whom he had first met when Pierce represented a defendant at a court martial on which Du Pont was a member. Other prominent men who received copies included the former attorney general of the United States, Henry D. Gilpin, and prominent ex-congressman Samuel Breck of Pennsylvania. Breck noted that he felt certain that the report would "bring about a *brilliant* and *enlightened* result."[47]

Du Pont's report had succeeded beyond his wildest expectations. His arguments and ideas—some commonly held but most quite original and forward thinking—had gained widespread acceptance within the military community of army and navy officers; so too, due to Du Pont's determination and shrewd political acumen, were his thoughts gaining extensive credence and approval among key civilian leaders. Indeed, perhaps the most remarkable aspect of his fortifications report of 1851 is the fact that it was so widely disseminated to such a varied audience. Du Pont himself was amazed and gratified at his increased celebrity. Using a seemingly innocuous request for comments on coastal fortifications, he seized the opportunity to advance his ideas on the proper role and structure for the navy, and he made sure they reached key decision makers. Du Pont had taken a calculated risk and emerged with his reputation intact. Indeed, this episode further enhanced his standing as one of the foremost thinkers in the United States Navy. He was also willing to conduct an end run around the secretary of the navy, who was uninterested in naval expansion and showed little regard for those who advocated building a modernized fleet. Du Pont certainly was aware of Graham's attitude and felt no apprehension in circumventing his prerogatives.[48]

Reputation was all-important for Du Pont; next to Sophie, it was probably the most important thing in his life. Du Pont's quest for reform was not driven by rank, pay, or overriding ambition but by reputation—both to maintain and enhance his reputation—and an honest desire to improve the service. This is not to say that he did not seek promotion and was not ambitious; he did and he was. But Du Pont was obsessed with his reputation, making his willingness to take on controversial and thankless reform issues—the abolition of flogging and the overhaul of the promotion system—all the more impressive.

Although his report received almost universal praise both in and out of the military establishment, it is difficult to assess fully the impact of Du Pont's efforts. Still, the implementation of two major defense policy decisions within two years of the report's publication and distribution to a wide audience was undoubtedly, at least in part, the result of Du Pont's strategic insights and recommendations. The War Department, after a lengthy period with no congressional appropriations for fixed defenses, resumed construction and improvement of fortifications along the nation's entire coastline in 1853.

When Franklin Pierce's secretary of the navy, James C. Dobbin, assumed office in March 1853, he championed policies that were far different from those of his recent predecessors. In his annual report of 1853, Dobbin "charged that the fleet was unworthy of its name" and that the "nation had not one steam man of war to match any first-class European warship."[49] Dobbin promoted the building of a modern naval force that would protect the national interests and commerce abroad; he also advocated the design and procurement of the most advanced warships possible. As part of President Pierce's new naval policy, Dobbin pushed Congress to authorize six first-class, well-armed, screw-driven, steam-propelled frigates in April 1854 (*Merrimack* class); authorizations for five steam sloops followed (*Hartford* class). These ships were the most advanced in the world at the time of their launching and fulfilled at least part of Du Pont's vision for a navy that was technologically second to none. Just as Du Pont predicted, the new ships forced European rivals to reconsider the United States Navy, and they formed the nucleus of the vast navy the United States would need to fight the Civil War. Although not all of these ships proved effective in the shallow waters that dominated that war's naval operations, many of them performed superb combat service. The steam frigates *Minnesota* and *Wabash* (of the *Merrimack* class) served as flagships for the North Atlantic and South Atlantic blockading squadrons, respectively; the *Hartford* served as Admiral David G. Farragut's flagship at New Orleans and the Battle of Mobile Bay.[50]

Russell Weigley has written that the "surge of naval interest and construction in the 1850s remains surprising and not altogether accountable." Du Pont's paper undoubtedly contributed, at least in part, to this trend. Du Pont's *Report on the National Defences* and the accolades and support it received, combined with his close relationship with influential military and civilian leaders, was unquestionably a factor in the acceptance of a more vigorous and healthy naval policy.[51]

Du Pont spent the rest of 1852 attending the Democratic National Convention in Baltimore as the guest of Henry Winter Davis, publicizing his fortifications report, and putting in arduous hours with the Lighthouse Board. Du Pont was not thrilled about his continued duty with the Lighthouse Board because it required frequent absences away from Louviers and Sophie. Still, the success of his fortifications report and Congress's acceptance of the Lighthouse Board's recommendations later in the year filled him with optimism. "I hope in three or four years," he proclaimed to Henry Winter Davis, "that we may be able to speak of reform no. 2," that is, doing something about the dismal navy personnel and promotion system.[52] The success his report achieved and the praise and notoriety he received from superiors and peers led him to take on what was for Du Pont the most important and necessary change. But before he could turn his sights on "reform no. 2," other duties intervened.

During the summer of 1852, while Congress debated the lighthouse bill, Du Pont received a letter from an acquaintance. Theodore Sedgwick, prominent New York attorney and businessman, was the president of the Crystal Palace Association. In his letter he asked that the commander visit New York as quickly as possible to help examine the plans for an American exposition envisioned by its backers to rival that of Great Britain's Great Exhibition of 1851 in the Crystal Palace. Viewing the great success and international renown earned by the London exhibition, several prominent New Yorkers—Sedgwick included—planned an American version magnificently dubbed the Exhibition of the Industry of All Nations. Sedgwick, referring to Du Pont as an "eminent . . . scientific gentleman," appealed to his patriotism. "Trusting that you will appreciate the important and beneficial objects that this association has in view, and that you will sympathize with the Directors in the feeling that renders them desirous to a consummation that shall be Nationally Creditable, I beg leave to solicit your cooperation."[53] Refusing Sedgwick's initial appeal for assistance, Du Pont would later succumb to patriotic appeals and his own desire to push the navy into the forefront of American consciousness in any way he could. Before long, Du Pont would wish he had never received Sedgwick's letter.

London's hugely successful exhibition provided the inspiration and the model for the American version of what one historian has called the "first American World's Fair." A number of prominent New York City businessmen formed an association to oversee its planning and organization that included such leading citizens as Theodore Sedgwick (elected president),

William Whetten (association secretary), Alfred S. Pell, and August Belmont. The architectural competition for the design of the exhibition's building prompted Sedgwick's first communication with Du Pont; the final choice was a scaled-down version of the British Crystal Palace—an iron and glass structure with a central dome and four equal wings laid out in a cross pattern. Serious problems arose immediately in almost all elements of the project from the engineer's lack of experience and expertise in building such a complicated structure, to the wildly optimistic timelines, to contractual management, to a lack of interest from other countries, to the treasurer's balance sheet; in short, the members of the association realized quickly that they had gotten in over their heads. By Christmas 1852 they understood that to have any chance of meeting their proposed May opening—or to open at all—they had to find someone to take charge of the overall management of the exhibition. To accomplish this, they turned to Du Pont.[54]

Du Pont spent much of the fall working with his colleagues on the permanent Lighthouse Board to implement the recently adopted legislation. He also found time during this period to represent his fellow commanders in an effort to wrest a pay raise from a penurious Congress.[55] When Du Pont received another letter from Sedgwick, asking him to accept the position of general superintendent of the entire Crystal Palace project, he was surprised though understandably pleased that his name had surfaced to head such a prestigious and highly visible undertaking. As Sedgwick explained, the man who held the general superintendency would have to manage and ensure the success of the entire enterprise. Disregarding Du Pont's polite refusal, Sedgwick replied, "I cannot give up hopes of you." Sedgwick was not the only member of the board who had his heart set on Du Pont. Pell wrote Du Pont that "you are the person we want—and I will cut your head off the first time that I see you, if you decline unless you give me a good reason for refusing."[56]

The onslaught of requests from the board continued, and Du Pont quickly began to soften his stance on the directorship despite premonitions that the entire enterprise would be nothing but trouble. He sought out the advice and counsel of his friends such as Charles Henry Davis and Henry Winter Davis. This episode provides insight into Du Pont's deliberate style of decision making and his susceptibility to flattery. He collected all of the available information, analyzed the situation fully, and sought expert advice and counsel from friends and superiors before coming to a conclusion. As it turned out, Du Pont's final analysis was incorrect, and his misgivings were well founded. At any other time he might have resisted the temptation to participate in a scheme that was clearly outside his experience and expertise, but if Du Pont was vulnerable to one thing, it was flattery. The Crystal Palace request came just as his career was soaring: he had just finished a highly successful report outlining a new American naval strategy, and his work with the Lighthouse Board had been universally praised. Finally, after much agonizing, on 9 February 1853 Du Pont and the association reached agreement, and he accepted the position of director and governor of the New York Exhibition of the Industry of All Nations with Charles Davis as his assistant.[57]

It is somewhat surprising, given Du Pont's efforts to learn as much as possible about the position, that he was blindsided immediately after arriving in New York when he discovered the extent of the exhibition's mismanagement. So far, he observed to Sophie, the management of the entire exhibition had been by committee. Already he noted that "if the thing fails, it will rest on two things, want of time, and want of space." The building was far from complete, and haphazard management was the norm. But Du Pont was optimistic that he and Davis could restore order to the chaos: the current standing committees of businessmen, complained Du Pont, "understand nothing of the demarcation between different authorities and managers which is our a-b-c." It quickly became obvious to Du Pont and Davis that they would face considerable challenges, but once the exhibition kicked off, it probably would run by itself. Despite his anxieties, Du Pont was excited by the prospect of the organizational and leadership challenges ahead and exhilarated at the thought of being associated with the most advanced science and technology that the nation—and the world—had to offer. He wrote home that "the more I think of this the more I like it. . . . The advance of art, knowledge and science are so great, that it is of service to have an offer to bring more of their application to society. Information and new ideas meet you at every turn in a duty like this. . . . I feel already my mental vigor stimulated."[58]

In the spring of 1853, Sophie felt well enough to travel, and she joined Du Pont in New York City for several months. The couple set up temporary quarters in a very comfortable lodging house on 7 Waverly Place only blocks from Du Pont's Crystal Palace office. Sophie loved her time in "this modern Babylon," as she called the bustling city, and later described this period as the most exciting in her life. Despite the fact that Du Pont was "immersed in ten thousand cares and perplexities" with his duties, Sophie shopped, saw the sights, and entertained many of the couple's naval and civilian friends. Not the least important aspect of her presence in the city was her moral support to Du Pont as the frustrations associated with the Crystal Palace began to mount. Their time together in the great city was one of the most idyllic periods of their marriage.[59]

Du Pont's considerable efforts getting the building ready despite unscrupulous contractors and the board's reluctance to make decisions probably saved the exhibition—if not from financial disaster, then at least from a public relations debacle. At last the Crystal Palace Exhibition of the Indus-try of All Nations opened to considerable fanfare and with the new presi-dent, Franklin Pierce, as the keynote speaker and guest of honor. Still, the building leaked when it rained before the ceremonies. Writing from the ex-hibition building, Du Pont proudly informed Sophie, who did not attend the opening ceremonies, that he saved the day by ordering the purchase of India rubber blankets to cover the precious exhibits.[60] Despite the puddles and dripping tarps, the opening was hailed as a great success.

By September, the exhibition was running well due in large part to Du Pont's and Davis's efforts. One of Du Pont's decisions caused something of a sensation when he insisted that African-American visitors should be able to attend the exhibition at any time.[61] But there were ominous signs that the board was mismanaging the entire affair. Attendance started to slip, some exhibits were still not in place, and there were rumors of financial troubles. It was time for Du Pont and Davis to make a graceful exit. Du Pont wrote to Sophie that "I would give a good deal to be out of this I must say." The two men drafted a carefully worded letter of resignation regretting the fact that "the affairs of the Association" had required a "greater engrossment in our time and thoughts . . . than was ever anticipated." The board begged them to stay on for a while longer, but the officers were adamant that they would have to rejoin the navy by November. The board finally relented and sent Du Pont off with a ringing testimonial and the gift of a sterling silver tea service but, he lamented, "very little else, except vexation." Indeed, he would later tell a friend that he "bitterly regretted" his association with the Palace.[62]

Their work on the Crystal Palace had not lived up to their expectations. Still, without the tremendous exertions and managerial skills of Du Pont, the exhibition might never have opened, let alone be declared a success—scientifically and technologically if not financially. Regardless of Du Pont's misgivings, their reputations and that of the navy did not suffer any last-ing stain. Indeed, most in the service understood that Du Pont and Davis had come to the rescue of the exhibition, preventing disaster and national disgrace.

After the Crystal Palace ordeal, Du Pont and Sophie settled into a com-fortable routine. Except for his short visits to Washington on Lighthouse Board duties, the couple lived quietly at Louviers throughout 1854. Du Pont finally had time to fulfill his horticultural ambitions. He happily immersed himself in the house's landscape, planting dogwoods and flowers throughout the expansive grounds. Most importantly, however, Du Pont decided that the time was right to pursue his second major reform goal.

4

The Efficiency Board of 1855

The magic touch of reform.

—SECRETARY OF THE NAVY JAMES C. DOBBIN

T HE STATE of the promotion system in the United States Navy at midcentury was appalling. Because it was a personnel structure based solely on seniority, with no provision for retirement, paths to advancement for young officers became accessible only when death or an infrequent resignation left a vacancy. Consequently, many old, infirm, untrustworthy, alcoholic, and immoral men held key positions in the navy and prevented younger and more able and competent officers from taking their place. Samuel Huntington has noted that this system "caused officers to hang on to their posts until they died in their boots, holding up the advancement of juniors."[1] The only way the navy could remove an officer from active duty was by court-martial, and there were many: "From 1841 to 1854, 114 officers were court-martialed on charges ranging from drunkenness to scandalous conduct." However, the navy removed few of the officers sentenced to dismissal because many if not most "turned to their political friends to have their sentences remitted or greatly mitigated."[2] The result was an officer system bloated with deadwood and filled with officers who languished for years in low ranks. In 1854 the navy had 68 captains, the youngest of whom was fifty-eight years old; of 97 commanders, 74 were between the ages of fifty and fifty-five years old; all 327 lieutenants were between the ages of thirty and fifty. In contrast, three decades earlier Stephen Decatur had been promoted to captain at age twenty-four; two of the great naval heroes of the War of 1812, Commodores Oliver Hazard Perry and Thomas Macdonough, were twenty-eight and thirty-one years old, respectively, at the time of their famous actions. Du Pont, one of the most respected officers in the navy, was already fifty-one years old; he had served for thirty-nine years yet was still a commander. One scholar has observed, "This meant that a lieutenant could expect to be promoted to commander at age fifty-three, and a commander could expect to reach captain at age seventy-four."[3] The obvious result of such a system was poor morale and frustration in the lower ranks.

Lieutenant Seth Ledyard Phelps, an officer who would serve with distinction as a captain in combat during the Civil War, flirted with resigning his commission to join the merchant marine where his skills would be recognized and compensated adequately. Returning from a cruise in 1852, he observed that he had a "very fair prospect of command soon with a salary far better than that of a Commodore in the Navy."[4] Phelps was but one of many officers whose disgust with the system forced them to consider strongly whether or not the navy was the best career choice for themselves and their families. Historian Spencer C. Tucker notes that the navy suffered badly from morale problems during this period because "there was a great divide in the navy between the senior officers, many of whom fought in the War of 1812, and younger lieutenants, who advocated change." Early in 1855 the superintendent of the Naval Academy complained that "the general sentiment of the pupils of the Institution, [is] not to devote themselves to the Naval Service, unless some degree of encouragement is held out to them, to remain in it, far exceeding anything which present appearances indicate on the part of Congress."[5] The prevailing attitude among most junior officers—junior, yet of increasingly advanced age—was that they would be old and infirm by the time they had any chance at all of gaining higher rank and responsibilities.

The Navy Efficiency Board of 1855 that attempted to address these problems was one of the most controversial episodes in United States antebellum naval history. In an effort to address the lack of opportunities for competent officers in a personnel system based entirely on seniority, the Navy Department and the United States Senate directed that a board of officers examine the records of hundreds of officers and recommend those who, for one reason or another, should no longer serve on active duty. The controversy that surrounded the board, its proceedings, and its results was intense; indeed, so passionate was the criticism of the board that some of the overheated rhetoric still clouds historians' assessments of the board and its legacy. Though others laid claim to the lead role in this movement, both at the time and later, in fact Du Pont was the driving force behind the reform. Moreover, despite assertions to the contrary, the deliberations were fair, and the board was an important contributor to the overall health of the navy's officer corps on the eve of the Civil War.[6]

As his role in the reformulation of United States naval strategy showed, Du Pont was one of the most dedicated antebellum reformers in the United States Navy. By 1855 Du Pont had built an enviable reputation as one of the best officers in the service. However, his most important contribution to the antebellum navy was his advocacy of personnel reform. For years Du Pont and others had railed against the outmoded promotion system of the navy that rewarded seniority rather than merit. Finally, by the mid-1850s the time was right for reform. Although officers and other senior civilian leaders had advocated reform in the previous decade, the conditions were never right. One problem was the turnover of service secretaries: in one eight-year period, there were five secretaries of the navy. In addition, some secretaries were more concerned with reform than others. Also, naval promotion and personnel improvement did not receive impetus from reform movements in society at large, such as temperance. Fortunately for Du Pont and the service, the right combination of key civilian leaders and active naval support came together in the mid-1850s. Secretary of the Navy James C. Dobbin, arguably the most activist navy secretary in the nineteenth century; President Franklin Pierce; and several important congressmen and senators were willing to act on promotion reform.[7] Although many in the service advocated promotion reform of one kind or another and had been doing so for many years, Du Pont convinced the secretary of the navy to push for this critical legislation. Dobbin had spent considerable effort in 1853 and 1854 modernizing and expanding the navy, and now devoted his full attention to personnel issues. Dobbin had written as early as 1853 that "the great evil in our present system is, that neither merit, nor service, nor gallantry, nor capacity, *but mere seniority of commission, regulates promotion and pay.* The gallant, chivalrous men of the navy feel subdued, dispirited, discouraged; their ardor is chilled; the fire of their young ambition and pride is well nigh extinguished."[8] Du Pont could not have put it better.

During the summer of 1854, Du Pont worked with Dobbin and reform-minded Florida senator Stephen R. Mallory on legislation that would change promotion standards and establish a retirement system of sorts. As part of this effort, Du Pont wrote and distributed a "circular letter" calling for personnel reform among his fellow officers, which he then presented to the secretary. Du Pont advocated retiring older officers, establishing large numbers of officers in the higher ranks to provide adequate promotion opportunities for juniors, and providing for the immediate promotion of officers based on large-scale retirements. His efforts paid off, and in July 1854 Dobbin, impressed by Du Pont's arguments as presented in the circular letter, scheduled meetings with Senator Mallory and Virginia congressman Thomas S. Bocock to sponsor appropriate legislation. Mallory wrote a biting report to the full Senate demanding action to redress the fact that the current system was "a mockery, a delusion, and a snare." The sea was a young man's element, argued the senator, yet the present system was certain to "check the ardor and to deaden the ambition of the whole corps, by sustaining and perpetuating injustice," and it ensured that men were not "employed in responsible positions" while they were in the prime of their lives. Mallory finished his report by demanding a system of retirement to break the logjam.[9]

But the bill that followed Mallory's report failed that summer. Dobbin echoed Mallory in his own 1854 annual report and challenged Congress by declaring that "the magic touch of reform is needed, and if skillfully applied will impart to the now drooping body of the Navy a robust health and a new life."[10] A close study of Du Pont's papers and the language of Mallory's report and the circular letter suggest strongly that Du Pont was the primary author of both documents.

As 1854 ended, neither Dobbin nor Du Pont had given up on promotion reform. Both men, buoyed by Mallory's report and Bocock's highly visible and vocal support, believed it was finally time to push such controversial legislation through Congress. Dobbin asked Du Pont—in Washington, D.C., for Lighthouse Board duties—to draft formal legislation that would establish a system of retirement and furlough and thus make way for large numbers of promotions. In addition, he directed Du Pont to write a lengthy paper justifying the legislation. This Du Pont did between December 1854 and January 1855.[11] Earlier bills had failed in the Senate and the House over objections to a retired list, the method by which an officer could be forced into retirement, how those retired officers would be selected, and the huge expense that mass promotions would cause following wholesale retirements.[12] Du Pont's legislation and his paper attempted to address many of these objections.

Lieutenant Thornton Jenkins, a friend and fellow Lighthouse Board member, judged Du Pont's paper to be a "pretty good resume of the stagnant condition of the Navy."[13] Du Pont's report provided a comprehensive summary of the problems facing the naval officer corps, the history of failed past reform measures, and his proposed remedy. "The clogging up of the lower grades," Du Pont wrote, prevented officers from "reaching responsible stations and responsible commands during the period of their greatest professional efficiency and intellectual rigor—an evil greatly on the increase." Although Chairman Mallory and others had tried to fix the system over the years, Congress always fell short because the "task seems to possess inherent difficulties." A new midshipman, fresh from the United States Naval Academy, argued Du Pont, could expect to be promoted to lieutenant in fifteen years, put in another twenty-five years to become a commander, and might have to wait until he turned eighty to be promoted to commodore, "and the evil is increasing." Du Pont then proceeded to make a case for promotion targets by age and regulated appointments to the Naval Academy.[14] He went on:

> To obviate these objections and yet promote the efficiency of the service, it is now proposed that those officers in the different grades, who from advanced age, disability, or other causes, are no longer available for the efficient discharge of their duties, shall be placed on a *Reserve* list, on their leave of absence pay, subject to the orders of the Navy Department, but to be considered out of the line of promotion. When all such officers have been carefully selected, their places will be supplied by promotion in the order of seniority, but the officers so promoted must remain on their present leave of absence pay until ordered upon duty.

Those placed on the reserve list need suffer no disgrace, Du Pont reasoned; indeed, such an action recognized the long and faithful service of those retired and reserved. With this proposal Du Pont tried to appeal to a frugal Congress by assuring it that the cost for the promotions would be small: there would be no pay increases for promoted officers unless they were serving on active duty with the fleet. He also established that there must be some mechanism to select those officers for retirement or for the reserve list.

This proposal constituted a considerable savings because the active rolls contained many more officers than there were available active billets. Thus many unemployed officers were placed on leave-of-absence status when not actively employed. Du Pont's compromise proposal meant that those promoted due to the retirement or "reserve" of others would receive the leave-of-absence pay of their previous grade until actually employed on active service, when they would then receive the full pay of their new rank. This caused some grumbling by those promoted as a result of the Efficiency Board's findings. But in sum, concluded Du Pont, the action would "put aside those who are incapable of performing the duties of their stations," and it "relieves the Navy from an evil—the want of sufficiently rapid promotion, which is destroying its usefulness."[15]

Du Pont followed the congressional proceedings closely in the weeks that followed. Mallory sponsored Dobbin's (Du Pont's) version of a reform bill on 29 January 1855. Previous bills had described a "retired list," but this bill mentioned only a "reserved" list—Du Pont's adjective. This wordplay was designed to lessen the blow to those officers selected for the "reserved" category. A board of officers would be chosen to select those for the reserve list at either leave-of-absence or furlough pay; furlough pay was less than leave-of-absence pay, and those placed on the former list undoubtedly would suffer some stigma. However, as Du Pont argued, such an officer would always be subject to recall to active duty by the government to "have a bullet put through his head at the shortest notice," and therefore, men so selected would still be honored members of the profession. Aided in part by Du Pont's pay scheme, the bill passed the Senate without objection on 2 February 1855. Bocock pushed the bill through the House with an amendment adding a "third category of inefficient officers" that would include those simply dropped from the rolls with no pay. This category was set aside for those whose "incompetency has arisen from any cause implying blame on the part of the officer."[16] In other words, the House added a provision for the board of officers to drop those who were criminal, immoral, incompetent, or untrustworthy.

As Du Pont sensed final victory for a reform measure that he had advocated for years, he urged his brother officers to besiege members of the House to vote for the bill. Du Pont worked tirelessly throughout the process; he wrote memos and newspaper articles, he lobbied congressmen and senators, and he urged other officers to push the bill with their own colleagues and representatives. He urged Commander Charles Davis to "write to all your delegation and to any others you know" and to do so before 13 February when the "struggle" would culminate in the final House debate. Others wrote to Du Pont to spur him on. Fellow officer Edward W. Carpender wrote glowingly of Du Pont's bill, praising him as the "greatest man in the Navy" and declaring, "I pay court accordingly." Writing from the Brooklyn Navy Yard, Lieutenant William L. Hudson confirmed that "all the officers on this station have written to members of Congress in relation to the Navy bill." Dobbin kept Du Pont constantly moving from House delegation to delegation in close cooperation with Bocock. Indeed, it is likely that Du Pont was the author of the House amendment.[17]

Finally, on 13 February 1855, the House passed "An Act to Promote the Efficiency of the Navy" by the sizable margin of 116 to 46. "The Bill has passed," telegraphed a triumphant Du Pont to his wife. Sophie was equally thrilled: "So it has passed! I can scarcely believe it—I dared so little hope it would, after the experience of past years." This was undoubtedly the most significant act of reform ever passed to improve the personnel condition and officer morale in the history of the navy to that time. For the first time the navy would eliminate the huge logjam of "deadwood" or "inefficient" officers, and scores of deserving junior officers—many of whom had waited for years—would see promotion. The morale problem and the exodus of scores of outstanding officers each year would decrease; the hemorrhaging of the navy would stop. Robert Albion, in *Makers of Naval Policy*, wrote that the three most significant policy initiatives that took place between 1839 and the Civil War were steam propulsion, the bureau system, and the Naval Academy. It is hard to argue with any of Albion's conclusions, but to his three should be added one more: the Efficiency Act of 1855.[18]

Signed into law on 28 February 1855, the act called for the president to "cause a board of naval officers to be assembled" who were to "make a careful examination into the efficiency of the officers" in the grades of master, midshipmen, passed midshipmen, lieutenants, commanders, and captains. Further, the board was to identify "the names and ranks of all officers of the said grades who, in the judgment of said board, shall be incapable of performing promptly and efficiently all their duty both ashore and afloat." Those officers whom the board determined could not fulfill their duties would be "dropped from the rolls" or placed on a "reserved list" to receive either leave-of-absence pay or furlough pay. Most important for Du Pont and his supporters was the provision that "vacancies created in the active-service list by placing officers on the reserve list shall be filled by regular promotion in the order of rank and seniority."[19] In other words, the bill did not eliminate the seniority system, but those unfit for service both "ashore and afloat" would be eliminated in all grades, finally making room for the advancement of those in lower grades in the order of their precedence on the active list.

The secretary learned of the bill's passage from Du Pont, and soon accolades began to pour in from all directions. "You have no idea of the shout of triumph and congratulation yesterday among officers and even members of Congress . . . and you would have been pleased to see that at the moment of success those who brought about this measure were not as usual forgotten," declared Du Pont proudly to his wife. In a single stroke Du Pont became the toast of the service. Charles Davis wrote happily, "The passage of the Reform Bill filled my heart with joy." If the bill had not passed, claimed Davis, the service would have continued in a state "so gloomy that the profession had lost all its usual attractions, and even the life of a Navy officer had become a life without stimulus and almost without hope." But now "the scene before us is made cheerful by the promise of promotion." "*To you,* the whole Navy owes its profoundest thanks," declared Commander Louis M. Goldsborough. Du Pont wrote his wife that "congratulations on the passage of the Navy Bill continue to pour in" and that even army officers praised him for his success.[20]

Time to savor the triumph was short; Dobbin directed Du Pont to prepare the board's instructions and assist in choosing the members. From the beginning Du Pont and many others within the service recognized that the board's makeup would be critical; fulfilling the bill's intent required that the members be highly experienced within their respective grades; they had to be fair and honorable and have impeccable professional and personal reputations to eliminate any perception of favoritism or personal gain; finally, they had to be willing to dismiss or place on the reserved list former shipmates and friends. The members' work required "more *moral courage* than any task an officer could be called upon to perform," declared Du Pont. Goldsborough agreed: "Let the Board be *out and out* of the right stuff! Let every member of it be an officer of admitted intelligence, and known for his sense of justice, good judgment, sound integrity, and thorough knowledge of the Navy from 'title page to colophon.'" Commander Thomas Turner advised: "You must not leave Washington until this [board membership] is decided. If this duty is left to the clerks better would it have been never to have passed the bill." Charles Davis noted wisely that they had but one chance at making this reform work, and "everything depends on the selection of officers who are to constitute the Board." Davis observed ominously that Du Pont's reputation, "whether justly or not," depended on how the board was able to execute the selection process. Du Pont must ensure that the secretary did not make a "fatal mistake" by appointing an "unsuitable Board," counseled another friend. Finally, most of his correspondents urged Du Pont to accept a position on the board. Lieutenant John Missroon wrote: "You are *expected* and *desired* by the entire Navy, so far as I know and hear, to be a member. It is desired, because *all* believe in your honor and fairness of intentions, and all confide so fully in your judgment." "As the *author* of the measure," argued Davis, "you stand in the front rank of danger and responsibility." Because his name was so closely tied to the legislation, Du Pont knew that if its provisions failed, he would be the focus of criticism. He was reluctant to risk his unblemished reputation to be a member of the board, "but," he declared, "I shrink from nothing connected with the work."[21]

Dobbin and Du Pont worked closely over the next several weeks to finalize the board's membership. In the end the board comprised the following officers: Captains William B. Shubrick, Matthew C. Perry, Charles S. McCauley, Cornelius K. Stribling, and Abraham Bigelow; Commanders Garrett J. Pendergrast, Franklin Buchanan, Samuel F. Du Pont, Samuel Barron, and Andrew H. Foote; and Lieutenants John S. Missroon, Richard L. Page, Sylvanus W. Godon, William L. Maury, and James S. Biddle.[22] The commanders and lieutenants were all senior in their grades, which was important because they were being asked to decide the fate of officers based largely on their own personal knowledge. While the department provided the board with files on every officer, the official record was meager. If an officer had been court-martialed or had written letters to the secretary, these records were on hand. Also available to the board was the record of assignments and time at sea for each man. However, the board was forced to rely primarily on its members' personal knowledge of each man to render a just decision.

The membership reflected a compromise between Dobbin and Du Pont. Pleased with the younger officers—he knew them all and was a close friend to many—Du Pont was concerned about the captains; many of these senior officers were either lukewarm or opposed to promotion reform. If the captains did not remove enough senior officers—their peers—the board could never fulfill the legislation's intent. Perry was an obvious choice because of the nationwide acclaim he received after his recently concluded mission to Japan; an officer of his prestige was invaluable to establish the board's legitimacy.[23] Still, Du Pont worried that Perry "will embroil everything" and Shubrick was "opposed to the law"; however, McCauley was "good and amiable." Du Pont was particularly wary of these senior officers because Attorney General Caleb Cushing advised Dobbin—against the counsel of Du Pont—that he could shield himself and the service from criticism if he directed the board to judge only officers who were the same rank or below each group of members. In other words, the entire board could consider lieutenants, midshipmen, and masters, but only commanders and captains could judge commanders, and only the captains on the board could assess captains. Despite Du Pont's objections, this provision was critically important because it ensured that no junior officer could profit himself directly by voting to dismiss a senior. Nevertheless, Du Pont hoped that "the moral influence of the commanders and lieutenants" on their seniors, if used "honorably and kindly," would force the captains to do their duty.[24]

Du Pont was well aware that a barrage of criticism would likely result when the navy released the board's results to the public. Dismissed and "reserved" officers and their friends and political allies would undoubtedly use every weapon available to discredit the board and the act. Dobbin, always optimistic and probably misled by the relative ease of the bill's passage, felt that the entire process would go "as smooth as oil." Du Pont, always attuned to the views of the officer corps and Congress, was less sanguine and envisioned a "fight afterwards upon the issue of which, the final results will depend."[25] He was right.

The provision eliminating those unfit for service "ashore and afloat" was the most important part of the act for many of the board members, including Du Pont. Du Pont interpreted it to go beyond physical infirmity and age; he strongly believed that the role of the board was to weed out those officers who were drunkards and who had engaged in criminal activities without having been charged by court-martial. The requirement also reflected the feelings of the navy's line officers. Du Pont and most of his colleagues believed strongly that an officer's place was at sea. Officers who were incapable, unable, or unwilling to serve at sea were simply not worth keeping on the rolls and should make room for those who could. Du Pont and others argued that those who sought or did not avoid this challenging and hazardous service should receive the lion's share of promotions and rewards from the navy. As Du Pont labored with the secretary on the composition of the board and its instructions, he told a friend that as far as he was concerned, the most important criterion for the board was an officer's ability to serve at sea. He noted this emphasis probably would come as a shock to many officers who have refused to "wet [their] commission[s] . . . yet look to promotion."[26] This attitude alarmed many officers who had served for extended periods in nonstandard billets including scientific postings. It was not that the board dismissed these types of assignments out of hand; indeed, most believed that such assignments were acceptable if they provided a direct benefit to the navy, but many members became suspicious whenever an officer had served for long periods without going to sea.

During a short stay at his home in Delaware in May, Du Pont made final changes on the secretary's instructions to the board and prepared to join the other members in this "most important work" to "eliminate the Navy of some of its worthy but worn out material." The instructions Du Pont drafted for Dobbin's signature sought to clarify the act and to provide guidance to the board for its deliberations. Emphasizing the importance of efficiency to the combat readiness of the service, the instructions noted that the law required that officers of the navy must have a "capacity to perform 'all duty'—'ashore and afloat.'" It is important to note that both the instructions and the act call for duty ashore and afloat, not ashore or afloat. This distinction would later surface as a major point of controversy. Not only that, but an officer had to be able to perform all duties "efficiently." Dobbin's instructions declared that "efficiency, efficiency—*that* is what is required. Inefficiency, inefficiency—*that* is what is to be withdrawn in order to 'promote' the efficient."[27]

But how should the board determine "efficiency"? The secretary (using Du Pont's words) provided the answer: the board was to review an officer's mental, physical, and moral state. Although an officer may possess a strong mind and body, if "his moral perception of right and wrong be so blunted and debased as to render him unreliable, he could hardly be ranked as a capable officer." The instructions also emphasized that placement on the reserved list was "no degradation" but in fact was "a high compliment" and would be a tribute to long and faithful service. For all practical purposes, leave of absence or furlough was roughly equivalent to retirement, as we understand the term today. Left unsaid was that shame could be attributed to those who were actually dismissed. The secretary stressed that the board was but advisory in nature and the final responsibility for approving the findings rested with the president. Dobbin was counting on the board's "intelligence and integrity," its "capacity to discriminate with justice," and the members' intimate "personal and official association with your brother officers" to enable them to make the right decisions. Finally, Dobbin ordered Du Pont and the rest of the board to convene in Washington, D.C., on 20 June 1855 to begin their deliberations.[28]

What Dobbin failed to do, however, was set the conditions for acceptance within the navy. He did not inform the officer corps why he had convened the board, how it would conduct its deliberations, and, most importantly, how its findings would affect those officers reserved and those left on the active list. The onslaught of censure that followed the adjournment of the board would certainly have been muted or perhaps eliminated altogether, and the prospects for future reform would have been brighter, had Dobbin better prepared the navy. Harold D. Langley notes that Dobbin may "have feared that too much advance information might lead to another postponement" in personnel reform.[29] But Congress had overwhelmingly passed the act, the president had signed it, the board members were chosen, and the board's instructions written; Dobbin could have easily sent explanatory circulars throughout the service and in the press or, better yet, letters to each officer on the active list outlining the board's mission and the expected outcome of the proceedings. Du Pont, too, clearly failed to consider the groundwork needed for the board's success, in spite of his prediction of trouble ahead. In particular, he did not advise the secretary to prepare the naval officer corps for the board. Dobbin failed to exercise effective foresight and leadership in this instance, and Du Pont failed to encourage him to act.

It is difficult today to appreciate how momentous this act was, and how important were Dobbin's instructions. For the first time the navy had established criteria—though highly subjective, to be sure—to determine who should earn promotion; or, more accurately, the criteria eliminated those officers who should not be promoted. The legislation and the actions of the board did not eliminate promotion by seniority, but they greatly mitigated the pernicious aspects of the system. Also put into place was a mechanism to assess the officer corps by applying departmental standards. Finally, the navy established an administrative process to dismiss officers without the inconvenience, expense, and stigma of a court-martial and to retire those who could no longer function at the level required for active service. This precedent was critical for enduring personnel reform. The vision and convictions of mid-grade officers, led by Du Pont, provided the intellectual weight behind one of the most important personnel transformations in the history of the navy.

The board met each weekday from 10 A.M. to 3 P.M. from 20 June to 26 July 1855. In the evenings and on weekends, Du Pont often gathered some of his colleagues together for informal discussions of some of the toughest cases; all five commanders stayed together at the same Washington boardinghouse. In his usual methodical fashion, Du Pont drafted procedures that the board should follow throughout its deliberations. The board began by examining the lowest ranks and worked upwards. Each board member came into the meetings with a list of officers he believed the body should consider. Most historians have assumed that the board scrutinized all 712 officers on the active list; this was not the case.[30] This point is significant, however, for it became the basis for severe criticism against the board and especially Du Pont in the months after adjournment. From Du Pont's meticulous notes on the main discussion points on each officer, the vote results, and final disposition of each case—the only existing account of the board's deliberations—it is clear that the board looked at only about 250 officers. Although technically all 712 officers were eligible for review, the rest of the officer corps was deemed efficient in the absence of evidence to the contrary.[31]

The members reviewed all pertinent records provided by the department, thoroughly discussed each case, voted on whether or not an officer should be dropped, and if so, into which category—dismissed, leave of absence, or furlough—the man should be placed. In some instances cases were tabled until the board could gather additional information. In very unusual circumstances—most of them controversial and contentious—the board reopened cases for further discussion and a second vote if necessary. Finally, the board reviewed every list once more, consolidated all the cases, and forwarded them to the secretary of the navy for his review and approval on 26 July 1855. In the end the board recommended 201 officers for removal from the active list. Of these, 159 vacancies were in the ranks of lieutenant to captain.[32]

It is remarkable how closely the Efficiency Board resembles a modern military promotion board. Today's boards are temporary organizations formed to provide specific recommendations to the service leadership, in most cases for promotion or command selections. The service secretaries provide the members with detailed and specific instructions to guide the deliberations. Members of modern boards deliberate in private and must ground their recommendations on a subjective evaluation of an officer's career based on his or her efficiency reports. Finally, the service secretaries can accept or reject their findings, which have been controversial at times. Although the current system of officer promotions and selections is not based on the 1855 navy board, the parallels demonstrate that Du Pont's instincts were remarkably prophetic in that he developed a personnel reform methodology that closely anticipated the one in use 150 years later.

As the board members met in the capital and began their work, the group received letters from officers who feared that their careers might be at risk.[33] This correspondence only made a tough job even more difficult. Du Pont wrote that the entire experience was distasteful because the members had to judge and recommend for dismissal officers with whom they had served for years; in a very small navy, there were few officers whom the board members did not know personally. "I felt awful," and "it is a most trying duty," protested Du Pont, when he wrote his wife about the debate over a particularly difficult case; agony over some cases reduced the members to tears. Making their work more painful yet was the fact that one of the senior captains—probably Perry—went out of his way to disparage the board's work by declaring that "the law is an outrage" in front of all the members. Du Pont wrote to Dobbin that as the board discussed the merits of each case, "there is comparatively speaking no difficulty in determining who should be removed from the active list; but the proper classification of those removed is not so easy." Despite the anguish arising from its onerous labors, most members believed strongly that they were being "equitable" and "just."[34]

Du Pont's document chronicling the deliberations of the board provides a fascinating glimpse into the state of the naval officer corps in the mid-nineteenth century and into the minds of experienced line officers. Because Du Pont's notes are the only written record of the board's deliberations in existence, they must be used with caution. However, given the veracity of Du Pont's public and private correspondence and his desire from the start to keep the proceedings secret, there is little doubt that his notes provide an accurate record of the board's deliberations. Comprising over 300 handwritten pages, Du Pont's notebooks recount officers' career highlights, sea duty, and moral or physical misfortunes. It is clear from the notes that the board conducted this distasteful business with dispatch and compassion. If an officer had overcome physical, mental, or moral problems such as drinking or gambling, despite previous actions he probably would be retained on active duty. When in doubt over an officer's health or willingness to go to sea, the board tabled the case until it could review additional information; on more than one occasion, the board requested supplementary facts from the officers themselves and other relevant witnesses. As Du Pont wrote many months after the board concluded its work, "[We] were giving an opinion as to efficiency, and all elements to come to a right judgment were open to [us]." This kind of reexamination happened on many occasions, and updated information led several cases to be resolved favorably for the officer. The board appears to have gone out of its way to be fair and to give each officer the benefit of the doubt.[35]

Several cases were highly controversial and especially painful. The first difficult case involved that of Lieutenant Matthew C. Perry Jr., son of board member Commodore Perry. This officer was in most respects excellent, but he, like so many others, had a serious drinking problem. At first, the board recoiled from making this decision—particularly after the commodore made an impassioned and understandable, though arguably improper, plea to save his son's career—but Du Pont among others urged the members to "not fall short" of their responsibilities. The board voted thirteen to one for removal from the active list and fourteen to zero for furlough. This stringent decision demonstrates that the board was able to resist pressure exerted by one of the most powerful and best-known officers in the service; it speaks volumes about the quality of the board's makeup and Du Pont's informal moral leadership. Although the board removed many officers who were close friends to board members, the Perry case provides the best evidence that it executed its duties in a responsible and impartial manner.[36]

Evidence of drunkenness and gambling was particularly troubling to the members. An officer with a drinking problem was a danger to himself, his shipmates, and his vessel; a gambler tended to disrupt order on board ship and was prone to other disciplinary problems. The case of Lieutenant James M. Watson is a good example. Although Watson was popular, "an officer of fine abilities," and also an excellent "seaman and navigator," he "gave himself up to intemperance." Despite taking the pledge and upholding it for over two years, Watson "broke down again" and on one occasion "fell overboard" while drunk. Even though he had seventeen years at sea, the board voted unanimously to remove him from the list and place him on furlough pay. Commander James Glynn "runs his ship boldly—very boldly," but he had "been known to be drunk often"; Glynn was removed by a close vote of seven to three and placed on leave pay. Lieutenant Foxhall A. Parker's situation was "a painful case of extreme drunkenness, with intervals of reform."

Although described as having "many accomplishments," when Parker drank, he "behaved in a beastly manner." The board voted fifteen to zero to remove him from the active list and placed him on furlough; once again, previous accomplishments were no protection from a negative recommendation.[37]

General misconduct occurred far more often than the board would have hoped. The case of Lieutenant William D. Porter is a good example. Du Pont's notes describe Porter as "an officer of general notoriety as worthless, considered very deficient in veracity." Porter was also rumored to have abused his own mother and in "1841 was tried by Court Martial and found guilty of scandalous conduct, neglect of duty, and contempt of a superior officer." Porter's case was tailor-made for the Efficiency Board, which did not hesitate to vote unanimously for his removal from the active list. Porter's case was unusual, however. With the exception of an alleged embezzlement of navy funds and a few other suspected criminal cases, drunkenness and gambling represented the great bulk of the "moral" failures that concerned the board. Nothing in Du Pont's notes indicates suspicion or accusations of other failings among those examined such as adultery (although there was at least one case of an officer's unwanted advances toward a young lady), homosexuality, or other offenses then considered serious.[38]

Health was another discriminator for the board. Even extreme physical disability incurred in the line of duty offered no protection. John I. Young lost both arms in action against pirates in 1829 and was the senior commander on the active list; he had already been promoted at least once after receiving his disabling wounds. As Du Pont recorded, successive secretaries of the navy kept Young on active duty due to "great consideration of his misfortunes." The board voted fifteen to zero to remove him, but because his wounds had been "incurred in the performance of active service [and] he is entitled to a liberal provision," by the same vote the board placed him in the highest pay category. Lieutenant James S. Palmer, a superb officer by all accounts, had returned from his most recent cruise suffering from a serious illness. After much anguished discussion, the board voted to furlough Palmer because of his poor health. Commander Edward W. Carpender, although a man of "great integrity of character and benevolence of disposition," was removed and placed on leave by a vote of ten to zero, because the members thought he had been broken by a court-martial for losing his ship and was insane. Du Pont wrote that this case was "a painful one" for the commanders on the board because four of the five men were great friends of Carpender.[39]

Cases of extreme drunkenness and physical disability were easy for the board, but assessing the ability and willingness of an officer to serve at sea was difficult. All of these cases generated much debate and argument among the board members. The board carefully examined the case of Lieutenant Raphael Semmes—later commander of the CSS *Alabama*—because his time at sea appeared too short for some members. However, the board unanimously voted to retain Semmes because "Commodore Perry testified to his gallant services in Mexico."[40]

Lieutenant Matthew Fontaine Maury would prove to be the most controversial of all the cases the board considered. Maury was a distinguished scientist and the internationally celebrated head of the United States Naval Observatory. He had conducted impressive though controversial work on improvements in ocean navigation based on currents and tides. However, despite Maury's reputation and considerable influence in and out of the service, the board decided to consider him for removal due to a severe, prolonged leg injury and his seeming unwillingness to serve at sea. Du Pont described the debate over Maury as "long, very animated and very able." Captain Stribling set the stage when he recognized Maury as "a meritorious and distinguished man, but . . . not able to perform all his duties ashore and afloat." The first vote tied seven to seven with Maury's cousin Lieutenant William Maury abstaining. William Maury then broke the tie in his cousin's favor, allowing the scientist to "escape by the skin of his teeth." Du Pont expressed disappointment that the board did not have the moral courage to make tough decisions; if it had, "Maury would have been retired." Although Du Pont was against reopening cases once decided, the members reconsidered Maury six days later at the urging of Commodore McCauley. The commodore expressed concern over news that Maury was still reluctant to serve at sea. McCauley argued that "it should not be just [that Maury] should prevent the promotion of a seagoing officer." The senior officer's reasoning swayed his peers and the junior members, who then voted eleven to four for removal; it was unanimous to place him on leave status, which allowed him to continue on as observatory director.[41]

In a related case the board considered the career of Lieutenant John A. Dahlgren, the navy's ablest ordnance expert. Like Maury, Dahlgren spent much of his career in the pursuit of scientific goals rather than at sea. Once again, an "animated debate arose." Several members questioned Dahlgren's apparent avoidance of sea duty. Others, such as Foote and Pendergrast, spoke of "his capacity on board ship" and his excellent work with the Coast Survey. It was Du Pont who turned the tide for Dahlgren when he made an important distinction between Maury and the ordnance specialist. Du Pont argued, "If LT D. had not done his share of duty at sea and it was clear he had not, that while on shore of late years, his talents and service had been applied in the direct line of his profession, and the service had been benefited by his labors, investigations and experiments in the Department of Ordnance." In other words, Maury's work had been almost wholly in the area of pure science, important but, as many on the board believed, with little direct benefit to the navy. However, Dahlgren's work, even though scientifically related, was applied science and provided a distinct payoff to the navy; thus most believed he should be retained. Dahlgren's proponents prevailed, and after the board confirmed that the ordnance expert was more than willing to accept his share of sea duty, he was retained in a thirteen-to-two decision.[42] Here once more is evidence that Du Pont had little time for pure science but instead celebrated the practitioner who could provide direct benefit to the navy: men like Dahlgren and Charles Henry Davis.

As the board's work wound down in late July 1855, the members and the department braced for the onslaught of disapproval they knew would come. Never before had officers been eliminated from the service through a wholly administrative process without benefit of trial by court-martial. Also, never before had a board of officers pronounced judgment on their peers outside of a court-martial. Du Pont, sensing that the secretary was starting to feel the heat, wrote a letter intended to strengthen Dobbin's resolve. He noted that the deep cuts made by the board might seem draconian, but "every step in advance in our labors has revealed more and more the necessity for this great reform." Indeed, claimed Du Pont, after examining all the cases of inefficiency, he was amazed that the navy "existed with the amount of dead wood fastened to it." He finished by reassuring the secretary that the "sound part of Navy" would support his efforts.[43]

Still, he knew that Dobbin probably would be surprised at the number of dismissals and furloughs and most likely would take exception to some individual cases such as Maury's and the fact that the captains did not remove seventy-one-year-old Commodore Charles Morris. Wild speculation about the board's procedures and findings flew about in the service and in the public as the anticipated release date of the board's findings crept closer. One officer wrote from the Brooklyn Navy Yard, "Excitement here is *intense*, and becoming more so every day, to know the action of the Board." Dobbin was not the only man who needed encouragement; Foote wrote to Du Pont warning that he could expect to receive much grief because "your agency in framing and getting the Bill through Congress naturally identifies you with it."[44] Foote's prediction would prove to be accurate.

In general, Du Pont was pleased with the results of the board, although he had hoped that the captains would be tougher. Of the 159 lieutenants, commanders, and captains recommended for retirement or dismissal, the most prominent were Maury and Commodore Charles Stewart (age seventy-seven), the navy's senior captain and hero of the War of 1812. In a letter to Henry Winter Davis after the board adjourned, Du Pont declared sadly that while the process was "most necessary and wise," the large number of officers recommended for removal was "perfectly awful to think of." Still, he wrote with pride that the board was entirely fair. "No friendships, however strong, were permitted to weigh a feather, if the individual came under the law."[45] Because of this impartiality, the Maury case had been reopened, Commodore Perry's son had been removed, and many other friends, former shipmates, and even relatives were considered for dismissal. He also believed, a little naively, that in the controversial cases such as Stewart's and Maury's, explanations "will doubtless have to be given, but I think when given they will be satisfactory, though I may be mistaken."[46]

President Pierce met with Dobbin; Commodore Shubrick, the board's chairman; and Du Pont on 7 September 1855 to review the findings. Du Pont reported that the meeting went well and that he thought the president would approve their work. "I liked the bearing of the president amazingly." Du Pont's presence at this meeting, although he was a junior member of the board, is clear evidence of the centrality of his efforts in the process of this reform. Finally, after weeks of rumors and gossip, the president released the board's results to the public on 12 September, affirming his "approval of the 'finding' of the board as set forth in their report." The president's endorsement paved the way for the largest wholesale promotion of officers in the navy's history to that time. On 25 September newspapers published the roll of those reserved and dismissed. With a remarkable lack of discretion and sensitivity, the list of those promoted in consequence of the board's work was released soon after, on 1 October. At the stroke of Pierce's pen, 201 officers were freed—at least temporarily—from a system that had offered them little promise and even fewer rewards.[47]

As expected, release of the promotion list and the names of those reserved and dismissed launched a firestorm of protest aimed at Dobbin, the president, and, most especially, Du Pont.[48] The New York Herald saw a conspiracy in the board's closed proceedings. Under the blaring headline "The Report of the Navy Board Is Kept Secret," the Herald's reporter claimed that the administration was deliberately concealing sinister activities and called for a congressional investigation to "expose the operations of the 'Star Chamber.'" One acquaintance wrote Du Pont that at the Philadelphia Navy Yard "the storm is rising, the peals of thunder are already heard, and the rain of public indignation seems to descend in torrents" in the press. He hoped that the board members "are all provided with coats of impregnable mail" to resist the uproar.[49]

The secretary received dozens of letters from dismissed or retired officers demanding explanations and threatening legal or political retaliation.[50] Most troubling to the members was that at least one of the captains, Matthew C. Perry, had begun to disavow the board's work, probably because his son was removed. Perry, always a reluctant participant, was saying that he was only "responsible for his own votes" and that Du Pont was guilty of "villainy" for pushing so ruthlessly for deep cuts. Du Pont and Buchanan believed that Perry's postboard actions were "traitorous" and "cowardly."[51] Du Pont and other members began to receive protest letters as well. Commander John S. Nicholas, a great friend of Du Pont's who was nonetheless furloughed for drunkenness—although the reason for his removal was not announced—protested bitterly "that I [was] placed in the most degraded position" by the board's action. Maury wrote Dobbin and every member of the "*cowardly* inquisition" demanding to see the "accusation[s] against me." He was particularly upset that "the Board held its sittings in secret . . . [and] it kept no records of proceedings."[52]

The latter point was to become a major issue in the months to come. Du Pont, however, was adamant that he would never allow his notes to become public and that neither the navy nor Congress should force the board to reveal the contents of its deliberations. This, he argued, was imperative to protect the integrity of the board members and the process and to safeguard the reputations of those officers removed and reserved. Many officers, he observed, probably should not demand the specific reasons why they were removed; they might not like what would come out.[53]

The barrage of negative publicity hounded the president and Dobbin almost continuously after the results hit the newspapers. Many in and out of the service protested the findings and sought redress for the individuals dropped from active duty. The Senate, which had passed the bill by acclamation in February 1855, acutely felt the political heat and began to backpedal, threatening to hold up confirmation of the promotions that resulted from the actions of the board.[54]

In the weeks that followed the release of the Efficiency Board's findings and the new promotion list, the lion's share of criticism fell on Du Pont. Charles Davis, writing to his wife, complained that "the feeling against the board is, I may almost say, concentrated upon him. . . . I have never had more cause to admire his courage and strength of character than now, when he is beset with enemies and difficulties." This firestorm was understandable. Du Pont was the act's author and the primary force behind the reform. He was a principal player on the board, and he advanced to the rank of captain as a direct result of the act. Even so, the condemnation was undeserved: as

K. Jack Bauer has written, Du Pont was "incorrectly portrayed as a ruthless assassin of the character of men who had devoted their lives to the service of their country."[55] Indeed, Du Pont had gone out of his way to fill the board with honest, respected, and experienced officers, and he had prepared its instructions and procedures with a view toward fairness and impartiality.

Maury continued his attack on the board, supported by several newspapers. He missed the entire point of the act when he complained that the department did not give him "due process."[56] Of course, the primary reason for convening a body like the Efficiency Board was to avoid the complexities and time-consuming character of a trial-like proceeding and to make the process of "reserving" an administrative action. In other words, the act was designed to cut through red tape to excise the navy's deadwood. Another Maury criticism was that the board did not make a "*careful* examination" of every officer.[57] Given the number of hours the board met, Maury calculated that members spent only ten minutes deciding each officer's fate, but Maury assumed incorrectly that the members examined all 712 officers on the active list. Dividing Maury's own figure for the number of hours by the 250 men the board actually examined indicates that it spent an average of thirty-three minutes on each officer, a much more reasonable figure. In addition, many cases were pro forma and merely required a vote with little or no discussion; other cases took more time and debate. For comparative purposes, it is interesting to note that a military promotion board today spends an average of only three to five minutes reviewing the entire career of each officer.[58]

The board's lack of record keeping was proof, claimed Maury, that the members harbored hidden "grudges" that had festered for "25 and 50 years against their brother officers." But Du Pont's notes and the board members' correspondence show that they saw their duty as a painful, difficult, emotional, but necessary evil. Indeed, because each member had but one vote and because most of the votes were overwhelming, secret grudges and resentments, assuming they did exist, had little or no impact on outcomes. As an example, fifty-seven of the eighty-six votes on lieutenants were unanimous; of the remaining twenty-nine, eleven cases were decided by fourteen to one or thirteen to two, four by less than a two-thirds vote, and only two cases by one vote. Of the thirty-nine commanders removed, twenty-eight were unanimous, and only three were decided by one vote. Of the 201 total cases, 150 were unanimous. In other words, the degree of harmony among the members was remarkable.[59]

Maury also accused the board members of cutting as many officers as they could to advance themselves.[60] Yet because members could only pass judgment on those of equal or lower rank, their decisions had only an indirect bearing on their future prospects. In the end, Maury began to insult board members; at one time, he even began to spread the rumor that Du Pont was descended from slaves.[61]

The increasing tensions between North and South in the United States at the time led some critics of the board to accuse its members of sectional bias. A perplexed John S. Missroon complained in late December: "All sorts of reasons are attributed for my *motives*. The last one is politics!! And I have just heard, of 'Sectional Feeling'!!!" Du Pont's board notes reveal that of the 119 lieutenants and commanders who were removed, 58 were from the South and 61 from northern states.[62] Moreover, there is no evidence that the members consciously tried to achieve this sectional equality among the dismissed officers.

The tremendous pressure exerted on the administration, the department, and Congress by the press and influential individuals placed Senate confirmation of the new promotions in jeopardy. The *Scientific American*, the *New York Herald*, and the *National Intelligencer* in particular questioned Maury's case. The Navy Department and Dobbin added to the controversy by botching any attempt to explain the board's mission and procedures and by failing to provide the public and the affected officers with a full explanation of the "reserve" categories. In his December 1855 annual report, Dobbin wrote with breathtaking understatement that "perhaps no event, either legislative or executive, touching the history of the Navy, has attracted more earnest attention" and that while some have "hailed [reform] with enthusiasm," others "received [it] with undisguised discontent and dissatisfaction."[63] Thus, most officers reserved by the board understandably believed that their service had been dismissed and degraded and felt that they had been humiliated.

To Du Pont's disgust, Dobbin began to search for a solution to the Maury controversy and suggested the formation of a navy "scientific corps"—a proposal never implemented—for officers such as Maury, so that they would not have to compete directly against line officers for promotions. Du Pont traveled to the capital to see the secretary: "I went to Washington to strengthen up Dobbin—politicians are singularly afraid of newspapers—I want him to endure to the end as he has done like a man." Goldsborough believed that the secretary could calm the tempest by "exercising a little tone of authority," for only in this way could he "avoid the fuss and feathers which he seems to dread." Perhaps due to Du Pont's visit in late November, Dobbin expressed strong support for the members in his annual report. Indeed, the secretary wrote, "I have already witnessed [the board's] happy effect in the new impulse and readiness for duty seen and felt at the Department."[64]

For Du Pont the storm climaxed in two ways: the first took place when he ran into a retired officer on the street, the second during the Senate debates over the new promotions.

One day during one of his many trips to Washington, Du Pont was confronted on the street by Commander Robert Ritchie, a veteran of the War of 1812 and an old friend who had been placed on leave by the board for health reasons. Du Pont and Sophie had known Ritchie for many years; he even attended their wedding. Ritchie threatened Du Pont and publicly insulted him, calling him a "liar, scoundrel, and coward." Du Pont let Ritchie vent his frustration and anger, but later lamented that he should "have *whipped* him on the spot," and reluctantly preferred charges against the commander when he heard that the insults were being spread around the capital. Dobbin accordingly referred the case to court-martial.[65] Du Pont reported to the secretary that Ritchie had publicly uttered "certain insulting and contemptuous words relative to my conduct towards him on the naval board." To Du Pont the threat posed by Ritchie and others to his reputation was very real, but he believed strongly that the real defendants on trial were the board and the act itself. The court did not allow Du Pont to testify fully at Ritchie's trial; still, Ritchie was found guilty of misconduct that "tend[ed] . . . to impair the efficiency and independence of tribunals . . . from the conscientious discharge of their duties." Despite the apparent vindication, Du Pont was furious that the court did not find Ritchie guilty of publicly using insulting language. Dobbin agreed and disapproved the court-martial findings because he thought Du Pont should have testified and because the evidence showed that Ritchie had indeed insulted Du Pont in public. Inexplicably, Dobbin set aside the court's findings, and yet he did not order a new trial.[66]

This result was a mixed bag for Du Pont and the board. It was a partial vindication, to be sure, but Dobbin hardly went out of his way to support the primary architect of reform fully. His disapproval of the court's findings did little more than obscure the trial's real issues and did nothing to clarify and champion the purpose of the act and the work of the board. Dobbin's behavior demonstrated an absence of strong and decisive leadership. He failed not only to prepare the service for the efficiency process but also to back the board and the act fully after negative publicity surfaced. Indeed, at times he seemed to have abandoned the members to the mercies of the press and Congress. His inaction may well have resulted from the tuberculosis that would kill him several months after he left office.[67]

The first four months of 1856 were probably the most trying of Du Pont's career to date. His reputation and integrity were under assault from the public, the press, Congress, and, most importantly, many of his brother officers. After the Ritchie court-martial, he began to despair about his life and career. Fortunately, Sophie once again was able to place his troubles into perspective, writing him, "I have been thinking very much of your naval affairs—do not let them discourage you—even should all seem to go most adversely, there is a Guiding hand to bring out all Good for you." Concerns for his trials and well-being "haunt my mind." She cautioned him not to be "angry and vengeful" toward those who attacked him and advised him that when feeling down, he must think of Christ and his ordeals. Despite her admonition that Du Pont trust in God and turn the other cheek, Sophie could not resist a swipe at Congress: "It is a *cruel wrong* to have placed 15 honorable men in the position the Board was placed, by official authority, and then with official authority turn around and blight them with implied censures for performing their duty to the best of their abilities."[68]

Most observers viewed debate in the Senate over the new promotions as a virtual referendum on the board. Senator Sam Houston of Texas was the most vocal in his condemnation of the board's work and of Du Pont personally. Probably still harboring a grudge against Du Pont for fighting the incorporation of Texas naval officers into the United States Navy, Houston delivered a three-hour speech in March 1856 assaulting Du Pont for his "criminal part" with the board. Houston dredged up the old dispute between Du Pont and Commodore Isaac Hull and all the arguments against the act and the board that Maury had previously raised. Joining Houston were fellow senators Robert Toombs of Georgia, John J. Crittenden of Kentucky, and Robert Hale of New Hampshire, as well as delegations representing states of prominent "retired" officers. Senators Mallory of Florida, John M. Clayton and James A. Bayard of Delaware, Albert G. Brown of Mississippi, and Judah P. Benjamin of Louisiana defended the bill—and Du Pont. Clayton was particularly eloquent on Du Pont's behalf. He carefully refuted every one of Houston's charges against Du Pont in a two-hour speech on the floor of the Senate, noting that "no man is more beloved or honored by his brother officers in the Navy, or more respected as an accomplished officer, sailor, and gentleman. No man living stands in higher repute wherever he is known."[69]

Throughout the spring and early summer of 1856, the senators fought over the promotions and a number of competing proposals to amend the original act. Indeed, the Senate debates over the Efficiency Board were almost as long and contentious as those over the sectional issues of the era. Finally, on 15 July 1856, the Senate voted to amend the original act to allow those removed to be granted a court of inquiry that could reinstate officers if warranted (the House did not pass the bill until January 1857). Two days later, and one year after the board adjourned, the Senate voted to confirm the promotions. The navy ultimately reinstated 62 (31 percent) of the original 201 officers removed by the Efficiency Board, including Maury and Ritchie.[70] Du Pont was at sea when the department made public the list of those restored. He found it "a painful sight" when he first saw the list during a port call in Bombay. He was thankful that he had been at sea and thus did not "witness . . . the ignorant and reactionary process."[71] Du Pont's quest for significant naval reform was over.

Some of the restored officers ultimately validated the wisdom of the board's actions. When Lieutenant Seth Phelps went to sea in February 1859, he served with several of these men, including his commanding officer, Commander Robert Thornburn, and found them wanting. After only a few days, Phelps remarked angrily, "Heaven have pity on the men who could in sober state find conscience to reverse the dictums of the immortal 15!" Thornburn, Phelps wrote, was a "damned fool" whose total incompetence demonstrated daily that the board's original verdict would before long "be vindicated." And, indeed, Thornburn was soon court-martialed for drunkenness and relieved of his command, much to Phelps's satisfaction. Despite this small victory, Phelps observed sorrowfully that "Our poor Navy will be long in recovering from the effects of the restorations and the foolish and unwise laws of Congress."[72]

Most historians have emphasized the negative repercussions that resulted from the board, and surely there were some. Donald Chisholm notes that the board produced negative short-term consequences for the navy, but that long-term impacts are difficult to determine. One author noted that the "law of 1855 created a Dreyfus-like atmosphere within the service." Another wrote that an "uproar ensued" and that "a residue of bitter feeling" resulted within the navy.[73] Certainly there was some grumbling, but most of the protests were limited to those officers directly affected by the board and their close friends. Moreover, the positive outcomes for the navy far outweighed the negative ramifications of the act. Geoffrey Smith has observed that because the board paved the way for the promotion of so many younger officers, it "accomplished for the navy what the Mexican War achieved for the army."[74]

Despite the detractors, many officers voiced unqualified support for the board and its work. The superintendent of the Naval Academy, Louis M. Goldsborough, with his unique style and enthusiasm wrote that if the board had not cut those it did, nothing could have "kept the craft [navy] from whirling over and sinking, engulfing all hands." To Du Pont, maintained Goldsborough, "your brother officers owe . . . a debt of gratitude which no mere expression of words can repay." Another praised the board for its courage "under the most trying circumstances." Charles Davis wrote to Dobbin offering his congratulations for boldly embarking on the path to reform and expressing assurance that the act "will occupy a conspicuous place in the future histories of the Naval service." One young officer, although not immediately promoted, recognized the importance of the act for the future and noted that the list "far outreached my wildest anticipations." He went on to say that the board's work "is a great good to the service" because "men of character see now that they are reaping the benefit of their energy and attention to the duties assigned them. Now will be revived the zeal which had nearly disappeared in the general downward tendency of this chief arm of defense and now 'going to sea' will again become tolerable." No less a naval luminary than Alfred Thayer Mahan wrote many years later that "it would be difficult to exaggerate the benefit of this measure to the nation . . . despite the subsequent reactionary legislation." Indeed, argued Mahan, many outstanding officers who languished in low ranks "were thus rescued for the commands and responsibilities of the War of Secession."[75]

Did the Efficiency Board make some mistakes? Of course it did. It inevitably "retired" a few worthy men and retained some poor officers. Even today, military boards fail to promote officers or select them for key command positions because of oversights and administrative errors. Although many safeguards are built into the selection system to ensure fairness, the overall health of the entire officer corps is more important than the fate of one or two individuals. Nevertheless, Mahan, Phelps, and the others were right. Of the five commanders who served on the board, four were duly promoted to captain because of the vacancies: Pendergrast, Buchanan, Du Pont, and Barron. Of the five lieutenants who were members, three advanced immediately to the next rank: Missroon, Page, and Godon. The list of those promoted due to the action of the board reads like a *Who's Who* of outstanding Union and Confederate naval officers. Besides Du Pont and Buchanan, other officers promoted to captain included David G. Farragut, Robert B. Cunningham, Samuel Mercer, Louis M. Goldsborough, Duncan N. Ingraham, George A. Magruder, Thomas O. Selfridge, William W. McKean, George S. Blake, and Andrew A. Harwood. Among commanders the list included Joseph Lanman, Thomas Turner, Samuel Phillips Lee, John P. Gillis, Raphael Semmes, John A. Dahlgren, Percival Drayton, John A. Winslow, Thornton A. Jenkins, John Rodgers, John B. Marchand, and Charles Steedman.

In a navy where many junior officers had resigned their commissions in disgust over lack of opportunities, the Efficiency Board temporarily destroyed the logjam of seniority and freed vacancies for deserving younger men who would lead the service into and through the most challenging war it had ever faced. Perhaps the most important thing the board did was to restore hope in those who had nowhere to go in the service regardless of ability and accomplishment. Finally, the act marked the first step toward true personnel reform in the navy; not until after the Civil War would the personnel situation be as grave as it was in 1855, but reform was easier to undertake the second time around at the start of the Civil War. The courageous junior members of the Efficiency Board paved the way for similar legislation governing the Union navy, which passed with little comment in August 1861.[76] Du Pont's vision of a naval meritocracy, although not fully realized due to the failure of the service to prepare the officer corps, the timidity and frail health of the secretary of the navy, and the apprehension of the Senate, came a step closer to reality through the actions of the Efficiency Board. The Union navy that entered the Civil War in 1861 was qualitatively a better force thanks to Du Pont's vision and perseverance and the actions of the "immortal fifteen."

Eighteen months of grief associated with the Efficiency Board took its toll on Du Pont's physical and mental health. He was exhausted and sick at heart. His vision had been watered down by Congress, but what troubled and upset him even more was the fact that his character and personal honor had been publicly attacked. Although he took solace in the fact that many— probably most—fellow officers supported his conduct and that of the board, he was disturbed that he had received so little support from the service. The personal attacks on his character and motives by Congress and some officers altered his attitude on the whole notion of naval reform. Before the last act of the Efficiency Board played out, Du Pont was one of the navy's most vigorous, articulate, and influential voices for reform on a wide variety of issues. But his experience on the board changed all that. With the exception of naval technology, Du Pont would never again actively challenge the status quo. The critics had been cruel and unjust, and Du Pont would carry those scars for the rest of his life.

5

≈

From China to the Philadelphia Navy Yard

I stick by the flag and the national government.

—Samuel Francis Du Pont

Throughout the early summer of 1856, Du Pont lobbied the Senate against any weakening of the original Efficiency Act with little success, although Congress finally approved the promotions in mid-July. Many reform-minded officers saw the promotions as the best measure of success, but Du Pont knew better. George S. Blake congratulated Du Pont on securing them : "I can hardly express to you my satisfaction at the confirmation of the nominations, for now the whole thing is clinched, and most beautifully. What a change in the Navy in little more than one short year! And little did I think in the 14th of Jan 1855, when you gave Pendergrast and myself in our little dining room at Washington an outline of your plan, what a year would bring forth."[1] Du Pont understood, however, that confirmation of the promotions was a partial victory at best. He knew that the courts of inquiry provided for in the Senate modification of the original act could roll back much of what the board had accomplished. Still, the fifty-two-year-old Du Pont must have been pleased when his captain's commission in the United States Navy finally arrived in August 1856 after forty-one years of service.

Three days after receipt of his commission, Du Pont sent the first of a series of requests for sea duty to the secretary. He did not hesitate to tout his work with the Efficiency Board in his attempt to get a ship: "Aside from my natural desire for sea service, I am persuaded, Sir, you will appreciate the motives which compel me to press for early employment afloat, growing out of circumstances connected with the faithful discharge of an onerous duty, and which no one hereafter at the head of the Department can so well understand as yourself."[2] After the trials associated with the board, he wanted nothing more than to get back to sea and leave his professional troubles behind. Du Pont did not want just any ship; he wanted one of the new *Merrimack*-class steam frigates.

Surprisingly, given the general deterioration of political discourse in the United States and the increase in sectional tensions in 1856, Du Pont made almost no mention of politics during this period, except as it related directly to naval policy and naval reform. This silence is particularly unexpected given his normally intense interest in the American political scene and his close friendship with a political figure of national repute, Henry Winter Davis. Du Pont's unusual indifference to the world around him was probably due to his work and ultimate disappointment over personnel reform and his quest for sea duty. If the political agenda included naval issues, Du Pont was interested and engaged; if not, he remained aloof.

The United States at the time sought to improve its diplomatic and economic position in the Far East in the wake of the first Opium War between Great Britain and China. James Buchanan, inaugurated as president in March 1857, was determined not to assume a backseat to the European powers that were vying for unrestricted economic access to China. As part of this effort and to demonstrate United States resolve and military might, Buchanan decided to send a prominent Philadelphia lawyer, William B. Reed, to the region on board the navy's newest frigate, the USS *Minnesota*, as envoy extraordinary and minister plenipotentiary. Reed's mission was to conclude a new treaty with China, and the navy, including the entire East India Squadron, was ordered to cooperate fully with the minister.[3]

Du Pont continued his Lighthouse Board duties and shuttled back and forth between Louviers and Washington, D.C. His disgust with Dobbin's failure to back reform once the going got tough was evident when he wrote to Sophie with the hope that the new secretary of the navy, Isaac Toucey, would have more fortitude. It was now up to Toucey "to put us on a proper footing," for "Dobbin was literally afraid to do so."[4] Du Pont let the one issue of personnel reform and the Efficiency Board color his assessment of Dobbin, who was actually "one of the best nineteenth-century secretaries."[5]

Early in April Du Pont learned of the *Minnesota*'s impending diplomatic voyage to China. In a letter to one of his best friends who had just returned from command of the *Merrimack*, Du Pont demonstrated that despite his frustration over the "half a loaf" reform victory, he continued the good fight as he attempted to save personnel reform. He reported: "I have lived in railroad cars and in bad boarding houses most of my time since you left in Feb

'56. I do not grumble at this though it has been trying, because I have the comfort to think that I never once went down to Washington that I did not assist in doing some good or staving off some evil. . . . I have changed my application [for sea duty] and am going strong for the *Minnesota*."[6]

After years of selflessly assisting friends and colleagues secure choice assignments, Du Pont asked for help in securing a coveted command for himself. "I am making a desperate effort for the *Minnesota*," he proclaimed to another friend, George S. Blake, a Toucey acquaintance, making what was for him an unusual request by asking Blake to "drop him [Toucey] a line and mention me for this special service." The next day Du Pont, realizing that his letter was not appropriate, apologized to Blake for placing him in an awkward position and asked him to forget the request; but he did not forget the *Minnesota*. In an official letter to Toucey, Du Pont asked "to be considered an applicant for duty, in the Expedition announced as fitting out for China."[7]

As Minister Reed and his entourage prepared for their trip, Toucey compiled a list of fifteen captains who had applied for the command; Du Pont was at the bottom of this list because of his recent promotion. This was perhaps one of the most coveted commands in the navy; the voyage promised to be highly visible and extraordinarily important, and it would employ the newest and most advanced ship in the navy's inventory. Searching for any edge in the competition, Du Pont appealed directly to Reed, a longtime acquaintance who, when showed the list, endorsed Du Pont. Toucey was not thrilled about giving this critical command to such a junior captain, but he bowed to Reed's request and appointed Du Pont to command his first steam warship on 18 April 1857. Although he did not exceed the bounds of professionalism as the mid-nineteenth-century officer corps understood it, Du Pont nonetheless had actively and aggressively pursued the *Minnesota* position.

Du Pont's joy at receiving this prize was tempered by his knowledge that he probably would be gone for up to two years, leaving a wife in "delicate" health behind. He gently but also somewhat disingenuously broke the news to Sophie: "Please prepare yourself for very painful news, but at the same time in another sense very gratifying as an officer . . . *I have the Minnesota*, without any action on my part." Du Pont knew that Sophie would not be pleased to learn that he had actively lobbied for what promised to be a very long cruise. Sophie, like countless military spouses before and since, was torn, at once happy for his professional success while at the same time distraught and not a little resentful over the prospects of another long absence. "God has enabled me to bear my share of this news with courage," she replied. "I am glad my dear husband your professional feelings are gratified, and I trust our Heavenly Father has granted your wishes for some good purpose. I am willing to leave *all* in His hands." After the trials and frustrations over reform and the assaults on his reputation, Du Pont understandably took the opportunity to gloat a little, writing to Charles Davis, "I am heading for China in the *Minnesota* an appointment which was very gratifying to my navy friends and I suppose a bitter pill to the retired gentlemen, [and] Houston, Toombs, etc."[8] This was the crowning professional achievement of Du Pont's career. To be named the first captain of the largest and most powerful ship in the fleet—a ship that he had done much to conceive—on a challenging and important mission was vindication at least in part of his past performance and his efforts to reform the navy.

The *Minnesota* was the newest of the first-class propeller steam frigates authorized by Congress in 1854 and the longest and heaviest of her class. She was a beautiful ship of 4,833 tons, 265 feet long with a 50-foot beam. Like all her sisters, the *Minnesota* was ship-rigged with the latest model steam engines that could drive her through the water at eight knots without sail assistance. Although the *Minnesota* did not have her full ordnance complement during the maiden voyage to China, when fully armed she carried twenty-four to twenty-eight eight- and nine-inch shell guns on each of her two gun decks and a XI-inch Dahlgren gun forward. She was the most powerful United States warship built to that point. Criticized by some historians as too slow and not particularly technically advanced, the *Merrimack*-class frigates "were actually trendsetters for the mid-1850s."[9] Writing many years later, Alfred Thayer Mahan described the *Merrimack* frigates as "much the most formidable ships of their class afloat, or as yet designed." The ships lived up to Du Pont's 1851 expectations when the Royal Navy emulated their design and built eleven propeller frigates to answer this new American threat. "The best compliment was paid to them," observed Mahan, "by the imitations of other navies."[10] It is true that with their large dimensions and deep drafts, they were not the most useful vessels to fight the Civil War, but the navy did not conceive them for that war; they were designed for a bluewater conflict with a major maritime power. By fielding the most technologically advanced ships in the world—even if they were not perfect—the United States Navy forced its main competitors to react, thus giving the nation the initiative on the high seas, if only temporarily.

Securing his release from Lighthouse Board duties, Du Pont spent much of his remaining weeks ashore at home on the Brandywine before officially taking command of the ship at the Philadelphia Navy Yard on 21 May 1857. As anyone who has commanded a military organization knows, Du Pont must have felt some apprehension when he took the *Minnesota* out for the first time under steam alone on 30 May 1857. This initial trip down the Del-

The first-class screw frigate USS *Minnesota* in Boston ca. 1861. Du Pont commanded the *Minnesota* during her successful maiden voyage to China from 1857 to 1859, his first service on a steam-powered warship. (National Archives; photograph courtesy of the United States Naval Historical Center)

aware River to Norfolk, Virginia, to pick up her ordnance and to complete fitting out was the first time the ship had been to sea. Sea trials, which normally precede commissioning, were not conducted, probably due to time constraints. The service was taking a large risk, however, because sea trials provide critical training for the crew and tend to reveal handling idiosyncrasies and any mechanical problems not discovered during construction. In addition, without these trials her new captain had no opportunity to familiarize himself with the ship and her crew, armament, and power plant. This did not seem to bother Du Pont, as his first letter under way reveals: "The ship is admirable under steam—the sails we had no opportunity of trying— indeed this steam is a great thing, and it does not add to but diminishes the anxiety of command." During the short passage with the wind blowing from the south, Du Pont wrote Toucey that "the ship easily attained a speed of eight knots" and sometimes more under engine power alone.[11] The ship was a delight to handle, for the engines "can be started, stopped, and reversed" almost at will and she responded crisply when "obeying helm." For an old sailing officer, Du Pont was very pleased with his new charge.[12]

Sophie Du Pont joined her husband at Fort Monroe for the two weeks before the ship departed for China. The couple spent many happy days visiting the ship at the Norfolk Navy Yard and entertaining navy friends. The night before the *Minnesota*'s departure, Du Pont and Sophie sat on the shoreline adjacent to Fort Monroe gazing across the moonlit waters of Hampton Roads. Their melancholy parting was particularly hard on Sophie, but she was a navy wife. On the day he left, Du Pont wrote a friend that although his wife was "surely sad now . . . she bears up well." [13]

A long cruise in a superb warship was exactly what Du Pont needed after the Efficiency Board's tribulations. The last days before departure were frantic as the new captain and his green crew dealt with myriad details, not the least of which was the quartering, feeding, and entertaining of Ambassador Reed and his large party. Du Pont and Reed never quite hit it off during the voyage as they coexisted in the close confines of a navy ship for months at a time. Du Pont described his traveling companion as "a man of *ability, intellect,* of mental & literary culture, of affable manner—and yet we have not the slightest congeniality—an hour with [Henry] Winter Davis leaves more solid & pleasurable impression, than a day or a week with this gentleman." [14] It is a tribute to the professionalism of both men that their mission was as successful as it was in spite of their social incompatibility.

Departing for the Far East on 1 July 1857, the *Minnesota* sailed alone, stopping at Table Bay on the Cape of Good Hope, sailing on to Java, and arriving at Hong Kong on 5 November. The trip was eventful as Du Pont dealt with a deadly typhoon and a sprung rudder and endured challenging navigational problems as he conned the big ship through the dangerous and uncharted shallows en route to China. [15] Despite these trials, the ship reached speeds in excess of sixteen knots and managed not less than six knots during the height of the typhoon, a feat never experienced by Du Pont and unheard of before the steam era. During the long passage Du Pont trained his 600-man crew in gunnery, a difficult task that was often more art than science; after two months he finally could report that the men had started to hit their targets consistently. [16] He also determined how best to handle the ship and her voracious engines: "I never steam when I can help it," Du Pont explained to Sophie in one of his long "journal" letters. [17] Du Pont learned rapidly that the captain of a steam-propelled man-of-war had to husband carefully his most scarce resource: coal. His experience aboard the *Minnesota* would serve him well during the Civil War as he prepared the plans for and executed the Union's naval blockade.

Arriving in Hong Kong on 5 November 1858, the huge frigate caught the attention of everyone who saw her. She was probably the largest ship

ever to visit the waters of the southwest Pacific. Although Du Pont was nom-
inally under the command of Commodore Josiah Tattnall of the East India
Squadron, Reed's diplomatic mission gave him a large degree of independence. The captain proudly showed off his ship, particularly to the European
naval representatives of France and Great Britain. These admirals commanding large British and French fleets expressed great admiration "uttered
without stint" at the "great beauty of her lines [and] the novel theory of her"
construction. If nothing else, Du Pont argued, the *Minnesota* "paid for herself many times over" because of the "moral effect" of her voyage on the nation's naval rivals.[18] In many ways meeting with the leaders of the greatest
maritime powers at the time and judging their reaction to American naval
power and expertise provided vindication of the naval strategic policy that
Du Pont had advocated five years earlier.

While abroad on the *Minnesota*, Du Pont learned from Sophie that the
effects of the Efficiency Board controversy had yet to run their course. The
politically well-connected Lieutenant Thornton Jenkins, a longtime Du
Pont friend and fellow member of the Lighthouse Board, discovered that
another attack on the Efficiency Board members was imminent in Congress.
Jenkins learned that some of the dismissed and retired officers and their
friends were about to accuse Du Pont of being out to get Commodore
Perry's son during the proceedings, and thus invalidating the entire process.
Sophie, who usually counseled moderation when dealing with personal attacks, was furious that her husband's assailants had waited until he could not
defend himself before making their move. The outraged spouse immediately
counterattacked by enlisting the support of Du Pont's navy and political
friends in a spirited defense of both the board and her husband. She assured
Du Pont that she had a handle on the situation. "My chief object in writing
to you now my dearest husband is to let you know that I am cognizant of this
matter; and to entreat you not to let it worry you—and have but me worry
about it."[19] Her efforts paid off as the false accusations never surfaced. Although Sophie often advised Du Pont to turn the other cheek when attacked, she did not hesitate to defend him to the fullest when he could not
defend himself.

Du Pont also, for the first time, had recent Naval Academy graduates on
board his ship. He went to great pains to welcome the new midshipmen and
took special interest in their training and professional development.[20] All
along Du Pont had been concerned over the probability that the young men
would not be accepted by the officers and men in the navy; many still believed that the academy was an unnecessary waste of money and that the only
way to become a competent naval officer was to serve a long apprenticeship

at sea. The midshipmen performed well aboard the *Minnesota* and with their captain's support helped to vindicate the academy. It was a great source of pride throughout his career for Du Pont to see graduates of the institution he promoted and helped to create reach the fleet and perform well.

The *Minnesota* not only impressed the Europeans throughout the region; she also tended to astonish and intimidate the Chinese. Du Pont and Reed both soon learned that the *Minnesota* and her officers and crew were not simply transportation but proved to be an integral part of the mission. On more than one occasion, the ship eased diplomatic activities with her grand and imposing entrance into a harbor and the presence ashore of her magnificently uniformed officers. At one point during tense negotiations with reluctant Chinese officials, in direct competition with European missions, the ship traveled north from Shanghai to the Hai River. Du Pont bragged, "The Chinese were obstinate until overawed by the presence of the *Minnesota*." When the British and the French finally bombarded the Chinese forts at Dagu (several miles up the river, guarding the approaches to Tianjin and ultimately Beijing), forcing the hesitant Chinese to negotiate, Du Pont and his officers were able to observe the battle. He was witness to the destruction and capture of several forts in less than ninety minutes by warships combined with assaulting troops. Impressed as he was by the capabilities displayed by combined European fleets, Du Pont felt certain that the United States Navy could have done as well or better "under like circumstances."[21]

Some historians have viewed this incident as convincing "Du Pont that steamers could successfully attack forts." This judgment is only partly true. In his *Report on the National Defences,* Du Pont had written of the superiority of shore fortifications over the most modern warship; however, he also noted that there had been numerous exceptions where forts had been defeated by ships, but only when the works were improperly sited, poorly constructed and manned, or inadequately maintained. Thus he made the clear distinction between adequate and inadequate fortifications. In the report outlining his observations from the cruise, he reinforced this important difference, noting that the quality of the Chinese forts was uniformly poor and that the Chinese fired "badly at best."[22]

Also, Du Pont was convinced that the allied force was ultimately successful only because it landed a formidable ground force after its short bombardment. Although the Chinese stayed at their guns against the ships, Du Pont observed that once the landings took place, "not a man stood to receive them."[23] In other words, Du Pont understood that the British and French were successful only in part because of their modern steam warships. More importantly, they succeeded due to the poorly constructed and manned Chinese forts and the allied employment of a large landing force in conjunction with the bombardment.

After subduing the forts, the allied fleet proceeded up the river and forced the Chinese officials to negotiate. Du Pont marveled at the unique sight of "English, French and Russian vessels of war, moored in both the river & canal [leading to Beijing], with admirals' flags flying and bands on their decks playing in the evening." The action of the British and French fleets also enabled the Russian and American neutral delegations to conduct their consultations with the demoralized Chinese diplomats. The resulting Treaty of Tientsin (Tianjin), signed on 18 June 1858, was a great diplomatic, economic, and political coup for the United States. Although tensions and conflicts continued, for the first time the Chinese opened (or, were forced to open) eleven ports to American merchants. United States citizens in China were now free to move about the country and were assured "the protection of local authorities," vessels of the United States (merchant and naval) could be freely provisioned in any Chinese port, and the treaty allowed a formal American diplomatic presence in China. The treaty essentially gave the United States most-favored-nation trading status with China. The treaty's provisions were mutually beneficial but were decidedly favorable to America.[24]

The great success of the mission was due in no small part to Du Pont and the crew of the *Minnesota*. Even though Matthew C. Perry's successful expedition to Japan in 1854 overshadowed the Reed mission,[25] the *Minnesota* expedition and the highly favorable treaty that resulted paid great dividends to the United States in its increasingly profitable and strategically important role in the Far East. Treaties such as Reed's and expeditions like Perry's set the necessary conditions for the expansion of the nation at the turn of the century, the global reach of the navy, and its special relationship with China.

The conclusion of negotiations did not mark the end of the voyage. The *Minnesota* continued to make her presence known with two cruises to Japan and visits to several ports along the China coast. Du Pont was particularly struck by the beauty of Japan and the "affability of the people, the order of their towns . . . their inquisitive intelligence, and desire and aptitude to learn languages." He hoped that since the Japanese wisely decided to associate with the world at large, the United States would treat them fairly in all respects. The only negative incident in the cruise occurred before the ship's first trip to Japan in August 1858 when, despite the captain and officers' best efforts, many of the crew contracted cholera. Sailors returning from liberty ashore were the probable source of the disease; eight men died before the epidemic ran its course. Finally, on 8 December 1858, the *Minnesota* departed Hong Kong for home. After stopping at Singapore, Bombay, and

Muscat and seeing Minister Reed off the ship in India, the *Minnesota* made her last port of call—just as she had made her first—at Table Bay at the Cape of Good Hope. At last, after an exciting, eventful, and remarkably success-ful two-year cruise, the ship arrived in Boston on 29 May 1859.[26]

Du Pont wasted no time upon his return renewing his friendships and professional acquaintances. He wrote to Commander Dahlgren at the Washington Navy Yard to tell him "how much I come back wedded to your guns." After enduring a rigorous two-day inspection of his ship, Du Pont wrote Alexander D. Bache that "the last two years, from beginning to end, have been the most instructive and gratifying of my professional life. Besides having a command to be proud of and which I greatly enjoyed, I had the privilege of a very social and unreserved intercourse with all the bright men of the East, whether naval, military, or diplomatic." But even after a lengthy cruise, personnel reform was still near the forefront of Du Pont's thoughts. In an Independence Day letter to Samuel Mercer, Du Pont triumphantly observed that his enemies probably had "anxiously scanned the *Herald* to see if I had not been sunk to the bottom of the China Sea, by giving my ship's name to a sunken rock, or been used up in a Typhoon. To all such, and to Sam Houston and company, my return . . . give[s] no comfort."[27] Until the beginning of the Civil War, no matter what other duties he performed, Du Pont was haunted by the unwarranted assault on his character by a "certain clique of the retired officers and their sympathizers."[28]

For the next year Du Pont enjoyed his time at home and continued his wide and varied correspondence. As the young Naval Academy graduate Alexander Slidell MacKenzie Jr., his best friend's son, prepared for his first cruise, Du Pont dispensed some sage advice, which illuminated his own lead-ership philosophy. "Never swear, or use epithets—a scrupulous avoidance of this will give you immediately the consideration of the men—not to men-tion that by doing so you would violate the divine law and the regulations of the Navy." In the years since his marriage to Sophie, Du Pont had become increasingly religious and more active in the Episcopal Church; this became even more pronounced during the decade of the 1850s. Du Pont became a respected member of the church hierarchy and served as a Delaware dele-gate to the general convention of the Protestant Episcopal Church in Rich-mond, Virginia, in October 1859.[29]

In the aftermath of the John Brown raid on Harpers Ferry that same month, Du Pont reflected on the many political upheavals that plagued the nation. He very seldom discussed slavery, and he was proud that neither he nor his family had ever owned slaves. However, in the wake of John Brown's trial and execution, he wrote that Brown was certainly a "fanatic" who de-

Sophie Du Pont ca. 1860. Daguerreotype by F. Gurney. (Courtesy of Hagley Museum and Library)

served to be executed for "murder and treason." In one of his only antebellum expositions on slavery, written in the aftermath of Brown's raid, he declared to a British acquaintance that he was sick of other countries, especially Great Britain, criticizing the United States for slavery. Du Pont defensively argued that the British did not know what they were talking about and, after all, they had introduced slavery to America in the first place. He declared that he was firmly against slavery in the "abstract" but if the government tried to abolish the institution, it would "immediately destroy . . . our union of states without in any way benefiting the person of the slave himself"; indeed, his statement suggests that he thought secession might succeed.[30] He was half right.

Six months after his trip to Richmond, the navy detailed Du Pont to the

State Department to serve as the chief of the escort for the first Japanese diplomatic delegation to visit the United States. He was the president's obvious choice after the success of his recent voyage and his experiences in China and Japan, but Du Pont wanted no part of it, as he made clear in a letter to Garrett Pendergrast. "I was ordered to report to the State Department—& there was astounded by hearing the object of my summons. I begged off like a hound on the grounds of great personal inconvenience, that I had done my share to establish friendly relations with the Japanese and bring about the preference they had shown to our country. . . . But it seemed to avail nothing. . . . I yielded . . . [and] the President & every member of the Cabinet . . . [gave] me their thanks after I had accepted."[31]

Du Pont's disingenuous and somewhat arrogant attitude was all too common when he was faced with a disagreeable task; Du Pont makes it seem as though it was his decision, when clearly he hardly would have refused the president's request. Du Pont led an escort team consisting of himself, Commander Sydney Smith Lee (brother of Robert E. Lee), and the future Civil War hero Lieutenant David D. Porter, whom Du Pont described as being "worth his weight in gold."[32] Du Pont requested both of these officers by name. Their job was to take charge of the delegation from the moment it landed on United States soil until its departure. The ostensible purpose of the Japanese mission was to hand over a ratified copy of the "Treaty of Amity and Commerce between the United States and the Empire of Japan" signed on 29 July 1858. but the trip turned out to be much more than a simple delivery.

Because it was the first official Japanese visit to the United States, both parties had a great deal to gain or lose during the delegation's stay. Its mission promised to be highly delicate and visible; this was another in a long series of tough assignments for Du Pont. In his characteristic fashion, after some rather unprofessional grumbling, Du Pont accepted his fate and performed well. Not only were Du Pont and his team expected to escort the mission, they were also to arrange the details of protocol and the visitors' transportation, feeding, and lodging throughout their long stay. Du Pont observed that his "Crystal Palace experience" served him well because of the "thousand details" he faced.[33] Distinguished visitor escort duty is one of those military assignments that are completely transparent if done correctly but if not can easily lead to regrettable misunderstandings and even international incidents. This was undoubtedly the concern of both the State and Navy Departments when they selected the courtly, distinguished, and courteous-to-a-fault Du Pont to guide the Japanese embassy through the bewildering and alien customs and mannerisms practiced by Americans.

Du Pont met the delegation at Hampton Roads as it arrived on board the side-wheel frigate *Powhatan* on 12 May 1860. With great pomp and ceremony, Du Pont and Assistant Secretary of State Henry Ledyard welcomed the Japanese. Du Pont stepped forward and was the first to speak: "Ambassadors! I welcome you in the name of the President of the United States, who has anxiously expected your arrival, and will be pleased that you are well." After a tour of the fortifications at Fort Monroe and a display of United States naval might, the party (seventy-seven in total) departed by ship for Washington, D.C. The five senior Japanese diplomats were all gratified by the warmth of their reception but were not particularly impressed with the military show of strength. The second ambassador confided to his diary that "it would be easy for us to win over them."[34]

The Japanese visit was considered a momentous occasion by the government and the public. Congress went so far as to adjourn so members could greet the delegation upon its arrival in the capital on 14 May 1860. That day, reflecting a kind of condescending racism common in his day, Du Pont shared his first impressions of the Japanese delegation to Sophie: "The Japanese are not great looking but have faces of intelligence, bright as they can be. . . . They are quiet, pleasant, authoritative, refined & delightful people." Japan fever swept the country as merchants stocked Japanese items, the press covered all aspects of the visit in minute detail, Walt Whitman wrote a special poem to commemorate the event, and the Japanese were feted everywhere they went. The day after the Republican Party nominated Abraham Lincoln for the presidency, amid the tumult that event caused throughout Washington, D.C., Du Pont formally presented the Japanese to President Buchanan in the East Room of the White House. They had made their way from Willard's Hotel, "Masaoki [the senior minister] with Captain Du Pont riding in the first carriage." The second ambassador reported that "the wide street was literally packed with vehicles, men and women who were eager to get a glimpse of our procession."[35]

Du Pont described the scene as going off with "not a hitch from beginning to end"; to his mind, "I never saw anything handsomer in my life of the kind." Both the president and the senior Japanese diplomat exchanged speeches, and the ministers were then presented to the cabinet and key congressional leaders including the Speaker of the House. The Japanese enjoyed the reception yet expressed some shock but not outrage over the prominent role that women seemed to play in American society; women attended virtually every event in the embassy's honor throughout its visit.[36]

While they never seemed to grasp most of the nuances of American culture and politics, the Japanese did appreciate the work of Du Pont and his team. He advised the embassy on United States customs such as shaking hands—an unheard-of ritual in Japan—gift giving, speech making, and many others. The three naval officers accompanied the embassy throughout its waking hours during the entire visit, attending to a myriad of details of protocol, diplomacy, and administration. Du Pont also endeavored to shield the Japanese from unwarranted attention. Less than three weeks into their visit, Senator Lyman Trumbull tried to force the officers to ask the members of the embassy to read a copy of the Bible translated into Japanese. Du Pont flatly refused and wrote a letter of protest to Secretary of State Lewis Cass in which he castigated the senator for his "want of courtesy." Du Pont, a highly religious yet also politically astute man, assured Cass that "I yield to no one in anxiety for the spread of Christianity in the East," but lest the "delicacy of the relations" between the United States and Japan "be jeopardized," he would allow no verbal or written communications of a religious nature to reach the visitors. Therefore, declared Du Pont, "the book . . . and Senator Trumbull's letter is herewith returned."[37] There is no record that Cass overruled Du Pont in this delicate matter. In many ways Du Pont was setting the agenda for the embassy as he guarded against anything that might disrupt the visit or unwittingly give the Japanese a bad impression. When the Japanese expressed their appreciation to the president for the officers' work, Buchanan replied that he had chosen Du Pont, Porter, and Lee specifically for this duty because they were "the flower of the Navy."[38]

The remaining six weeks included visits to New York, Baltimore, and Philadelphia. Only once did Du Pont come close to losing his temper during this trying duty. While checking the details of the embassy's visit to New York, he argued at length with Mayor Fernando Wood about the location for the first meeting between the embassy and the New York delegation. Du Pont wanted the mayor to meet the Japanese on their ship, and Wood argued that because Governor Edwin D. Morgan would be in attendance, the visitors must come to City Hall. This petty episode was finally resolved in Wood's favor, but it only served to heighten Du Pont's frustration.[39]

At last, on 30 June 1860, Du Pont bade farewell to his charges as they set sail in the *Niagara* for their homeward journey. Although recognizing the importance of his task, Du Pont's predominant emotion on the *Niagara* that day was one of relief, not sorrow. He observed later that the challenges of the "Crystal Palace & a Typhoon in the China Sea were child's play in comparison" to escorting a large foreign delegation throughout the United States for two months.[40]

Although the naval officers played a supporting role in the visit of the first Japanese embassy to the United States, it was a critical one. The escorts had to make all of the logistical arrangements for the delegation, fight off unwanted visitors, decline impossible invitations, and politely refuse a cornucopia of gifts from the Japanese. The impression they made on their guests and, through their constant vigilance, the low number of embarrassing incidents during a trip strewn with opportunities for disaster spoke well of the three officers and especially their leader, Du Pont. The long-term diplomatic results of the mission were mixed but in sum were positive: Japan launched several other embassies to Western countries, Japanese students began to travel and study abroad, importation of Western technology and goods increased, and, in general, their "intercourse with the West . . . flourished."[41] One historian has observed that because of the overwhelming success of the embassy's visit "there unfolded an era of good feeling extending over a period of nearly a half century which was characterized by [a] cordial relationship unprecedented in the annals of diplomacy between an Oriental power and a Western power." Indeed, claims another, "the land of the rising sun was now a full-fledged member of the world."[42]

For the next several months, chaos on the national political scene occupied Du Pont and his fellow officers just as it did most Americans. Writing from Washington, D.C., in November 1860, Du Pont observed that "this is the gloomiest place politically that I have yet been in—everyone believes that the Union is to be dissolved." To Biddle he wrote, "Things look squally in S.C."[43] While sympathetic to his many Southern friends, Du Pont explained to Sophie that he felt strongly that the results of a constitutionally correct presidential election provided "little cause for secession" and that Lincoln's election was merely an excuse for the South to do what they had wanted to do for some time. He was shocked that many of his Southern colleagues would even consider putting allegiance to their state over their country. He told Goldsborough, "I have never considered that I was serving two masters; to my state I owe good citizenship, but the Constitution of the United States I have sworn to support, and with me it is not only paramount, as legally declared to be, but is so morally and ethically."[44]

Still, life and career went on, and when Du Pont learned that his old commander from forty-three years before, Commodore Charles Stewart, had requested relief from his position as commandant of the Philadelphia Navy Yard, he quickly wrote Secretary Toucey, "I beg leave to be considered an applicant for this station." Du Pont had long coveted the Philadelphia assignment. At the time senior officers considered navy yard commands the best shore assignment they could receive, and it was close to the Brandywine and home. He probably assumed that after forty-four years on active duty, this would be his last assignment before retirement. Philadelphia was particularly important because the commandant was responsible for the security of the entire Delaware River and approaches to Baltimore and Washington, D.C. Ten days after his request, Toucey announced that Du Pont was the new commandant of the Philadelphia Navy Yard. Du Pont was in a reflective mood in a letter to his friend Henry Winter Davis: "On the day I received these orders I had been forty-four years in the Navy, twenty-two years at sea, and at twelve years old made my first cruise as a midshipman with Commodore Stewart, who I am to relieve." Du Pont replaced the old War of 1812 hero on 31 December 1860 and celebrated his last New Year's Eve in peacetime. It appears that Buchanan gave Du Pont this plum assignment partly in recognition for his excellent work with the Japanese embassy.[45]

Like many other large cities in the United States, Philadelphia was beleaguered with politically motivated violence in the wake of Lincoln's election. Republican street quarrels with Democrats often deteriorated into open riots. The city fathers considered the Philadelphia Navy Yard and its Marine Corps contingent important assets for the maintenance of law and order. Du Pont assessed the implications of Lincoln's election with his usual perception. "Things strike me in this way—If S.C. is allowed to withdraw, then our nationality has been a fiction, a compact without solid foundation. . . . One thing certain there never was so little call for secession."[46] Du Pont was outraged that the results of a constitutional election in which the Southerners freely participated could precipitate the Union's destruction.

Uncertainty was rampant among navy officers. Southern officers began to resign their commissions, much to Du Pont's dismay. Friend after friend submitted his resignation, but Du Pont remained a steadfast Union man: "I stick by the *flag* and the national government, as long as we have one, whether my state does or not." Du Pont tried his best to convince friends to remain true to their oaths and was unequivocal in his opinion that men who "went south" were traitors of the worst kind. However, always trying to take care of his subordinates, he tried when possible to protect his officers from departmental pressure as they made what was probably the most difficult decision of their lives. To Commodore Hiram Paulding, head of the Bureau of Detail (similar to a personnel department), Du Pont pleaded for more time for a lieutenant whose relatives were pressuring him to resign. "I do not hesitate to ask you as a favor," he wrote Paulding, "to give him more breathing room."[47]

Du Pont and Marylander Franklin Buchanan, a fellow Efficiency Board veteran, had been very close friends for decades, and Du Pont tried his best to convince "Buck" to stay loyal to the Union. Buchanan wavered for weeks but eventually tendered his resignation. Du Pont then wrote him to express his disappointment and to try to convince him not to fight against his country. He began by praising Buchanan's long service and his "integrity of character." But Du Pont also said he would never have written these words of tribute if he thought his friend would actually fight for the Confederacy. Du Pont reasoned, "Resigning of a commission cannot cancel the obligation and sanctity of the oath we took to bear allegiance to the United States and to support the Constitution—the commission may be laid down, for good and sufficient reasons, but the oath is recorded *above*." Buchanan replied some weeks later, insulting the North; Lincoln; Black Republicans; Henry Winter Davis; the new secretary of the navy, Gideon Welles; and a host of others for waging war against the South and for the "rascally Northern interference with the institution of slavery." Upon receipt of this letter, Du Pont cut off all further communications, and the two men never spoke again.[48] Days after Buchanan finally submitted his resignation to Secretary of the Navy Welles, when it became obvious that Maryland was not going to join the Confederacy, he recanted his decision and asked to be reinstated, but his request was refused. Buchanan then decided he had no choice but to join the rebel navy where he went on to great fame. Despite depressing episodes like Buchanan's, Du Pont was proud of the fact that none of his officers at the navy yard resigned even though his men included a number of Southerners including South Carolina native Percival Drayton.

Having friends like the well-known and controversial politician Maryland congressman Henry Winter Davis meant that Du Pont was a keen observer and commentator on the political events of the day. His first written impression of President-elect Abraham Lincoln was favorable. On Lincoln's trip from Springfield to Washington for the inaugural, he stopped overnight in Philadelphia on 21 February 1861 and presided over a flag-raising ceremony at Independence Hall the next day. From Du Pont's comments to Crystal Palace friend William Whetten, it is likely that the senior military officer in the city was there. He described Lincoln as "younger and much finer looking than his portraits" and noted that his appearance "created always at first pleasurable surprise—tall and gaunt like [Henry] Clay and without the latter's grace, he is still very pleasing and evidently self-reliant." He concluded his assessment of the new national leader with guarded approval of his policies.[49] The next most important national figure for a naval officer was, of course, the new secretary of the navy, Gideon Welles. At first Du Pont was not impressed with the new secretary. "There is nothing in him I think—he was in the clothing bureau once [during the Mexican War], made a remarkable contract for cheese, which made a great row, and is now brought back as head of the Department!" Yet, after receiving approving reports from friends in the capital, he sang Welles's praises to Davis only a week later: "Our secretary, I am glad to tell you, is making a most favorable impression upon the officers; he has already done some good things." [50]

As a Delaware native, Du Pont always tended to favor the South in politics and culture. Although Sophie and Du Pont never owned slaves and were morally opposed to the practice, they nonetheless felt that the Constitution allowed it and thus the North had no business trying to limit or abolish it. Indeed, the Du Ponts believed that the secession crisis had little to do with slavery but was the result of ineffective politicians North and South, a corrupt Buchanan administration, and the unlawful machinations of Northern abolitionists. Still, despite their Southern sympathies, they both felt that nothing justified the actions of the seceding states. For this reason, and for their unshakable belief in the Union, both Sophie and Du Pont viewed Abraham Lincoln as the best possible alternative. Indeed, Sophie always referred to Lincoln in her letters as the "Good Old Soul," although not always with affection. Until his assassination, Lincoln would have the Du Ponts' support, albeit reluctantly on occasion. [51]

The Philadelphia Navy Yard had been in the shipbuilding and maintenance business for over sixty years by the time Du Pont became its commandant. But with war imminent, his mission changed. Now Du Pont was more concerned about securing the yard's facilities and other installations such as key bridges and railroad ferries. Although his station was pretty far north, the loss of the Pensacola and Norfolk Navy Yards to the South served as a grim reminder of the vulnerability of Philadelphia. Consequently, Du Pont proceeded to purchase, seize, lease, and solicit donations of suitable vessels to patrol the waterways adjacent to the yard and to perform the blockade work that would soon follow the commencement of outright hostilities. As the navy expanded rapidly, so too did the Philadelphia Navy Yard, and until called to Washington in June 1861, Du Pont played a major role enlarging the yard's facilities and workforce. After the war began the yard became even more important. Percival Drayton, one of Du Pont's officers, observed that because Philadelphia was "so convenient to the scene of operations," if a vessel needed any maintenance or repairs whatever, "she is generally consigned to us which keeps everyone in a state of constant hurry." [52]

Du Pont also played an active part in defending the nation's capital and securing one of the key border states for the Union. One week after the rebel attack on Fort Sumter, rioting broke out in Baltimore when the Sixth Massachusetts Volunteer Infantry Regiment was making its way to Washington. With tensions high and Confederate sympathizers everywhere, Du Pont acted quickly on his own initiative by deploying forces under his command to protect the Naval Academy as it evacuated Annapolis for Newport, Rhode

Island, and to provide transportation and security for other Union regiments as they made their way south. This bold and decisive action was typical of Du Pont. One historian perhaps exaggerated in observing that Du Pont's performance during those tense days "saved the capital and preserved Maryland for the Union,"[53] but clearly his alert and resolute measures were vital in reducing tensions in the state and ensuring that the flow of forces was no longer threatened.

The commandant did not ignore the yard's shipbuilding role, for Du Pont initiated an expanded program for this part of the station. His management of the yard was so skillful that the sloop of war *Tuscarora* was launched only two months after the laying of her keel, a record.[54] Shortly after he assumed command of the yard, he started a lively correspondence with the chief of the Bureau of Construction, Equipment, and Repair, John Lenthall. Lenthall seemed to resist any urge to follow the lead of Great Britain, which had just launched the first seagoing ironclad, the *Warrior*, in late December 1860. On 3 February 1861 Lenthall responded to an enthusiastic letter by Du Pont discussing the merits of ironclads by noting that he was not particularly interested and that ironclads should be built by "some of these young, smart, *modern improvement, spirit of the age fellows*." Du Pont—who embodied everything Lenthall described except youth—was not deterred and replied thirteen days later with a radical suggestion: "Can you not get the seven sloop bill so amended in the House as to permit the dimensions of one of them to be sufficiently extended to make a proper experiment of iron platting?"[55] Lenthall and the navy never acted upon Du Pont's idea, but this letter demonstrates that Du Pont was no hidebound ancient mariner who looked with disdain upon any new idea or technology that did not include sails. Here he advocated experimenting with combinations of armored plating, engines, and ordnance—the three main components of any modern warship. This suggestion was hardly the idea of a staunchly conservative naval officer but came from an innovative thinker tempered by years of seagoing experience. He was no longer the young mid-grade officer railing against the inefficiencies and incompetence of senior officers (although age did not reduce his propensity for criticizing others), but a leader whose expertise and vision historians have largely ignored ever since he was relived of command in 1863. Perhaps if his prewar plea for experimentation in ironclad design had been adopted, the *Passaic*-class monitors he later commanded at Charleston would have been more capable, or the navy's leadership would have better understood their limitations as did Du Pont.

An incident that further exemplifies Du Pont's willingness to give new technologies a fair hearing occurred in May 1861. In an audacious publicity stunt, a French inventor, Brutus de Villeroi, demonstrated a primitive submarine to officers assigned to the navy yard. Local newspapers reported the strange vessel and its amazing underwater feats as "an infernal machine, which was to be used for . . . scuttling and blowing up government men-of-war." One intrepid young reporter enthusiastically described his own undersea excursion in the craft the next day.[56] Villeroi's initial purpose for designing a submersible was to explore and salvage marine wrecks, but Du Pont quickly saw the potential military benefits as the Civil War began. Intrigued, he detailed a three-man commission to check out the vessel and put it through a series of tests to determine its seaworthiness, safety, and reliability and assess its value to the navy. In July while Du Pont was on detached duty in Washington, the officers "proceeded to . . . examine" the submarine and submitted their report.[57]

Although no photograph or drawing of this vessel is extant, descriptions suggest that it was remarkably similar—with some significant exceptions—to the CSS *Hunley*, the first submarine to sink another ship. The board described the submarine as an iron cylinder thirty-three feet in length and four feet wide, bearing a striking resemblance to a whale powered by a crank-driven, stern-mounted propeller. The performance of the sub impressed the board; they observed that its endurance under water was excellent, that "the boat could be sunk or raised at the will of her commander," divers could enter and leave the vessel while it was submerged, and a larger version probably would be able to maintain a submerged speed of one knot. The board cautioned that the type they examined was designed only for salvage work, but they hastened to add that its military potential was obvious and enthusiastically recommended that the submarine "would be very valuable to the Government, and that the possession of his invention would be an acquisition of the greatest importance."[58]

The Navy Department ultimately accepted this recommendation and gave Villeroi a $14,000 contract for the construction of "one submarine" for offensive purposes. The boat was built (at a Philadelphia shipbuilder's yard), tested, and manned and eventually dubbed the *Alligator*. But inexplicably Villeroi changed the simple and efficient propeller crank to a system of underwater oars that never could produce the minimum necessary power or control to make the submarine a viable military weapon. Her first and only naval captain, Lieutenant Thomas O. Selfridge Jr., also listed other problems such as her temperamental trim and inadequate air supply. Welles and Assistant Secretary of the Navy Gustavus V. Fox attempted several times to get the vessel into combat with no success. So desperate were the naval authorities to defeat rebel ironclads that Fox told Selfridge, "If you will take the *Alligator* up the James River and destroy the *Virginia*, I will make you a captain." Ironically, the Union's submarine foundered in a gale while under tow on her way to join Du Pont's blockading fleet at Port Royal as he prepared for the April 1863 attack on Charleston.[59] Even so, just as he suggested to Lenthall that the navy begin an aggressive ironclad experimentation program, so too did Du Pont's vision allow him to see the potential in this invention of an eccentric Frenchman.

The five years between the traumatic 1856 debates in the Senate over the Efficiency Board and the start of the Civil War in 1861 was a professionally satisfying and fulfilling period of Du Pont's career; the only comparable phase was his time in command of the *Cyane* during the Mexican War. Although still bitter over his treatment in the wake of the Efficiency Board, he rose above his exasperation to command the navy's most advanced warship. The ship, crew, and captain performed brilliantly on their voyage to the Far East and ensured the success of a critical foreign policy mission. Continuing his diplomatic activities, he presided over the groundbreaking visit of a Japanese mission to the United States, thus securing favorable relations between the two countries for the next half century. Finally, he assumed command of arguably the navy's most important shore-based installation as the most costly war in United States history began. In the late spring of 1861, Du Pont stood at the pinnacle of his profession, ready to contribute to the defense of his country, with his reputation restored and enhanced and his experience and expertise recognized by the service.

6

The Blockade Board of 1861
and Union Naval Strategy

There should be no bungling about this blockade.

—SAMUEL FRANCIS DU PONT

O NLY DAYS after the first rebel shells crashed into Fort Sumter to begin the bloodiest war in American history, President Abraham Lincoln issued a document that would establish the basis for the first element of Union naval strategy: the Proclamation of Blockade. Essentially a
de facto declaration of war against the Confederacy, the proclamation declared that "a competent force will be posted so as to prevent entrance and
exit of vessels" from the ports of the states in rebellion. During these early
days of the war, it seemed clear to many that the president's first major war
measure could reap great dividends. Du Pont, commandant of the Philadelphia Navy Yard, declared, "I am anxious for the blockade to get established;
that will squeeze the South more than anything." However, the magnitude
of the Union navy's challenge was enormous. The start of the war saw the
navy, like the army, totally unprepared for the task. Of the navy's forty-two
ships in service in April 1861, Secretary Welles had but twelve to call upon
to enforce the blockade of a 3,500-mile coastline; the remaining ships were
either in ordinary (maintenance or overhaul) or in overseas squadrons. In
addition, most of the available ships reflected the strategic needs of the prewar blue-water navy and were wholly unsuited for blockade duty: they
tended to be too large, too slow, with too deep a draft, and too inefficient for
operations in the South's shallow coastal waters. Everyone in Washington
understood that the existing navy was unequal to the task of effective blockade. Welles not only faced inadequate resources and the need to build a
large, modern navy rapidly, but he also lacked an organizational structure to
command and control the blockade.[1]

To solve these and related problems, the navy established a Blockade Board.[2] This board's importance was not as a joint staff or as a group that planned only naval operations, but rather it was an early—and largely successful—attempt by the United States Navy to produce a military (naval) strategy that was fully coordinated with national strategy and government policies. Unlike the Union army, the navy never established positions such as "admiral in chief" or "chief of staff" during the Civil War. Consequently, responsibility for the formulation of Union naval strategy fell to Secretary of the Navy Welles, his senior officers, and these ad hoc boards. Although some might argue that General Winfield Scott's planning for the Vera Cruz and Mexico City campaigns was also such an effort, the Blockade Board's work was much more comprehensive and lasting. While it never fully realized its early promise, the board created a roadmap for the Union navy to conduct a major portion of its early strategic responsibilities and stood as the role model for later naval boards and commissions.

Effectiveness of the blockade would be a sore topic for both the Navy Department and the State Department for some time to come and remains so for historians. In accordance with international law, the nation initiating the blockade had to proclaim it formally and enforce it effectively. As a minimum, the blockading nation had to sustain a permanent force that would maintain a constant patrol off the enemy coastline and ports. The Confederacy vigorously argued that the blockade was not effective and that Lincoln's proclamation violated the neutral rights of their primary trading partners, but it failed to persuade Great Britain, which officially recognized the blockade in February 1862.[3] The task of maintaining an "effective" blockade would prove difficult but not impossible. As naval experts were later to observe, an effective, and therefore legal, blockade required only a blockade of ports and not the entire coast.

Still the length of the southern coast made the enormity of the task virtually unprecedented, and blockading thousands of miles of Confederate coastline was only one part of the challenge. Most of the coast was a warren of tangled channels and numerous inlets and barrier islands, just the thing for hiding blockade-runners. Adding to the Union navy's problems was the close proximity of neutral ports friendly to the Confederates such as Nassau in the Bahamas and Havana, Cuba. Special-purpose, steam-propelled blockade-runners could take on a cargo in Nassau, for example, pick their time based on weather, tides, and other factors, and make a quick dash to a rebel port. Because their run was so short, space on the ships normally allotted for fuel could be used for precious cargo.

Welles and Gustavus V. Fox, chief clerk of the Navy Department and later assistant secretary of the navy, began to take immediate steps to deploy an adequate force to patrol the southern coast. First, Welles recalled most of the overseas squadrons. By June 1861 all but three ships had returned to augment the blockading squadrons.[4] The next step was to procure ships rapidly to augment the blockading force. Welles and Fox issued orders to commandants of various naval yards to lease ships that would be suitable for blockade duties. An example is Welles's note to Du Pont written two days after the initial blockade proclamation: "By order of the president of the United States, you will forthwith procure five staunch steamers of from ten to twelve feet draft, having particular reference to strength and speed and capable of carrying a 9-inch pivot gun." Welles was clearly sanguine about the length of the war when he concluded his message to the commandants with the optimistic directive that the captains should charter the ships for a period of "three months, on the best terms available."[5] Of course, the key to an effective blockade was not merely the number of ships assigned to blockading duty. Naval authorities recognized early on that the most effective blockade-runner would be a small, shallow-draft, and very fast vessel that was lightly armed.

Not only did Welles and Fox direct their officers to purchase and lease ships for use on the blockade, but they also sought to acquire ships from other governmental agencies, among them the United States Coast Survey. As early as late April 1861, Welles accepted the offer of the Coast Survey to transfer research and survey vessels to the Navy Department.[6] Coast Survey ships routinely conducted their investigations in shallow, inland waters and thus were suitable for blockade duty. Welles would take advantage of this source of shipping for many months to come.

Finally, Welles and Fox initiated a building program that was unprecedented in United States naval history. Beginning with the *Unadilla* class of "90 day gunboats," Union shipyards would produce an astounding number of ships for the navy and especially for the blockade, but in May and June 1861 this effort was just getting off the ground.[7]

Welles initially confronted the problem of command and control of the blockade by dividing the responsibility of the awesome task between two squadrons, the Coast (later the Atlantic) and Gulf Blockading Squadrons. The Atlantic Blockading Squadron's area of operations ranged from Alexandria, Virginia, to Key West, Florida. The Gulf Blockading Squadron's responsibility extended from Key West to the Mexican border.[8] The commanders of these squadrons faced challenges that no amount of additional ships could completely solve. To begin with, the commanders had limited local knowledge of coasts, inlets, harbors, river systems, ports, tides, and water depth. Their quarry usually labored under no such handicaps. Second, the commanders quickly recognized that in order to blockade their assigned coasts effectively, they had to establish bases for refueling and reprovision-ing. Initially, the blockading squadrons had but two widely separated bases of operations available to them: Hampton Roads, Virginia, and Key West, Florida. Indeed, in the early days of the war, "some ships spent nearly as much time going to and from these bases for supply and repair as they did on blockade duty."[9] This made it impossible to maintain an effective block-ade. Thus the United States Navy faced the strategic problem that confronts most military forces, especially early in a conflict, the tyranny of logistics. Clearly, the navy would have to establish additional, more convenient bases for the blockade squadrons.

Finally, the commanders of these squadrons were faced with such a large span of control that it was nearly impossible for them to command, control, and communicate adequately with their scattered and overextended forces. The commander of the Atlantic Blockading Squadron, Flag Officer Silas Horton Stringham, initially believed that fifteen ships would be sufficient for him to enforce an effective blockade. The daunting task of shutting down maritime commerce over hundreds of miles of coastline combined with his inability to command and control his forces properly soon caused Stringham to reassess his estimate of the situation.[10] Lack of local knowledge, command and control problems, and logistics became central concerns of the Block-ade Board.

In the early days of the war, Welles and his small force of assistants and clerks were overwhelmed by the "trees" of details and could not see the "for-est" of strategic challenges that had to be surmounted to enforce an effective blockade. Welles personally addressed issues such as promotions, resigna-tions, leaves, recruiting, procurement of equipment, as well as naval opera-tions against the Confederacy. With breathtaking understatement, Welles declared to his wife that "the rebellion has given me labor and trouble and will make more."[11] Indeed, in April and May 1861, Welles and Fox, in an at-tempt to provide better information on local conditions to their blockading squadrons, found themselves personally requesting copies of charts and maps from the superintendent of the Coast Survey, Alexander D. Bache, on an almost daily basis. Bache provided data to the navy for the use of the blockading squadrons including maps and charts of the Chesapeake Bay, Delaware Bay, the Potomac River area, and sources of fresh water in the Gulf Coast region.[12]

The haphazard nature of these requests and Bache's vigorous support of Union military efforts would serendipitously lead to the formation of the Blockade Board. Bache saw the Union in peril and the national crisis as a di-rect threat to the existence of the Coast Survey, an organization he had led for almost twenty years. The political dislocation of secession and the loss of access to thousands of miles of coastline frightened Bache, who lamented to a friend in January 1861 that "the terrible disruption of our country . . . will sweep our organization away entirely, or sadly cripple it."[13] In this respect, Bache was no different from any other government bureaucrat; he was determined to protect his agency from any threat and to do anything to prove that his organization was indispensable.

Within this context of near chaos, Alexander D. Bache first conceived the idea for the Blockade Board, and on 22 May 1861 Fox presented the idea to Du Pont: "It is proposed to have a board of persons, say General Totten, Professor Bache, and Captain Du Pont, meet here and condense all the vast information in the Engineers Department, Coast Survey, and Navy, for the use of the blockading squadron. Professor Bache suggested it in answer to the numerous inquiries I have made of him. The Secretary is willing and . . . I suggested your name. . . . Will you give up the [Philadelphia Navy] Yard and come with us to the bitter end?"[14] That Fox and Welles were willing to pull Du Pont away from his command in Philadelphia demonstrates the importance that the department placed on improving the blockade.

Bache was a close friend and professional colleague of Brigadier General Joseph G. Totten, chief of engineers, United States Army, and Captain Du Pont; therefore, Bache, not Fox, probably recommended the composition of the board. The number of requests for information to the Coast Survey had reached its zenith in May, overwhelming Bache and his meager organization. Any attempt to streamline and consolidate all of the critical information for the navy would be welcome. In addition, the formation of a board composed of such eminent men as General Totten and Captain Du Pont and supported and sponsored by Secretary Welles himself could go a long way toward ensuring the continued importance of the Coast Survey.

In a letter to Bache several days latter, Du Pont enthusiastically endorsed his idea. "I would be ready to serve on [the board] at any moment," proclaimed Du Pont; "moreover I deemed the suggestion a most important one." Clearly, the creation of such a board appealed to Du Pont, who had strong ideas indeed about how to run a blockade. Du Pont wrote Henry Winter Davis the next day that "I replied to Mr. Fox (who asked me what I thought of it) that I deemed it one of the wisest suggestions that could be made on the subject. . . . There should be no bungling about this blockade, and there is some just now."[15]

Bache's reasons for suggesting the board may not have been obvious to Fox or Welles, but his friends were more perceptive. Du Pont noted after the board's first meeting that it "has been instigated by Professor Bache to bring forward the Coast Survey element" and it "is mainly got up to give notoriety to the Coast Survey." Yet Bache also desperately wanted to contribute to the war effort. He would write, "This War has . . . interest[ed] me to such an extent that I would rather die than not do all that opportunity gives me to do & that my education makes me feel that I can do."[16] The Blockade Board enabled Bache to achieve that goal.

Du Pont remained at his post in Philadelphia until 20 June 1861, when he received a letter from Welles ordering him to Washington, D.C., to chair the board. Because General Totten, Du Pont's friend and old Lighthouse Board colleague, was unable to participate because of other responsibilities, Secretary of War Simon Cameron nominated Major John G. Barnard, engineer in charge of the defenses of Washington, as the Corps of Engineers' representative to the board. Welles designated Commander Charles Henry Davis, no stranger to naval boards in the prewar period, as a member and secretary of the board. Finally, Bache himself rounded out the board's membership. Although every member of the board was a friend or professional acquaintance of the Coast Survey superintendent's, Welles could not have appointed a more competent or an abler group.[17]

As chairman of the Blockade Board, Du Pont provided the members with the appropriate amount of strategic direction and insight, drawing on his considerable experience as a blockader during the Mexican War, without stifling creative thought. Two days before he arrived in Washington, Du Pont recalled his previous blockading experience in a letter to a friend: "During the Mexican War I had two hard years' work at it, with endless correspondence with naval and diplomatic functionaries, for I established the first blockade on the western coast."[18] This experience and his service on other boards had produced an officer uniquely qualified for the chairmanship of the Blockade Board. A few short months before Fort Sumter, Du Pont thought his career would end at the Philadelphia Navy Yard, honorable and fruitful but not particularly glorious. Now he led a group of accomplished professionals as they struggled with devising a strategy that would carry the United States Navy and the Union to victory. Du Pont was fortunate that his fellow members were equally capable.[19]

Bache on the eve of the Civil War was one of America's most famous scientists and educators. A great-grandson of Benjamin Franklin and a graduate of West Point, Bache developed an international reputation and ably led the Coast Survey to considerable prominence. A military engineer, professor at the University of Pennsylvania, founder of the National Academy of Sciences, and friend and peer of the preeminent scientific minds of the day, including Joseph Henry, Benjamin A. Gould, and Louis Agassiz, Bache more than anyone else saw the importance of science to the public good. Historian of science Nathan Reingold observes that Bache was "perhaps the most important single person in the evolution of the government's policy toward science and technology in the past century."[20] Bache, like Du Pont, was no stranger to naval boards; he served on the Lighthouse Board and several other ad hoc boards to report on new and promising technology to the secretary of the navy during the Civil War. Despite being the only civilian on the Blockade Board, Bache's contributions proved indispensable.

Another member of the board, Commander Charles Henry Davis, was one of Du Pont's and Bache's closest friends. Davis left his studies at Harvard to join the navy as a midshipman in 1817. A prominent astronomer, Davis served on detached duty with the Coast Survey in the 1850s and on various boards with Bache. As an acknowledged scientific expert, Davis acted as the head of the Naval Almanac in Cambridge, Massachusetts. The almanac, an agency related to but separate from the Naval Observatory, produced navigational and astronomical tables for the navy. Du Pont called Davis "a remarkable clever talker, giving him great personal influence over those he is associated with." The two men had not served with each other since their days with the Crystal Palace, and the commander wrote to his wife that the board would give him the opportunity to "revive my pleasant old companionship with Du Pont." Davis began the war assigned to the Bureau of Detail, a staff job that he did not enjoy: "I don't like the duty, and am not particularly suited for it." What Davis really wanted was to become head of the Naval Observatory, an ambition that would be fulfilled, for as Du Pont observed in a letter to Bache, "Can there be any doubt of Charles Davis getting the Observatory eventually?" Although Davis had some seagoing experience, his selection for membership on the board had more to do with his friendship with Bache and Du Pont, his knowledge of the coasts, his scientific expertise, and his accessibility in Washington, D.C.[21]

The junior member of the Blockade Board was another West Pointer, Major John G. Barnard. Described by Du Pont as "deaf as a post," Barnard had graduated from West Point in 1833 and spent the next twenty-eight years in the Corps of Engineers. In the prewar years he distinguished himself as an expert on the construction of coastal defenses and harbor improvements and as superintendent of the United States Military Academy. Barnard wrote extensively on scientific and engineering subjects during his entire career; because of these writings and his work on coastal defenses, he naturally became familiar with Bache. Barnard and Bache renewed and strengthened their acquaintance in the early weeks of the war when Barnard took charge of constructing the defenses around Washington, D.C. One historian has described Barnard as the "true 'father' of the defenses of Washington." Bache cooperated closely with Barnard in preparing the capital's defenses; thus Barnard was an obvious choice for inclusion in the board when General Totten was unable to attend. Although he was exceptionally qualified for his assignment to the board by virtue of his work on coastal defenses, Barnard was not, as some historians claim, the army's representative to a "joint staff," nor was he the personal emissary of Major General George B. McClellan. Barnard was available, an expert on coast defenses and coastal topography, and General Totten was too busy. Barnard's personality, intelligence, and obvious competency allowed him to fit easily into the already close-knit group of Du Pont, Bache, and Davis.[22]

With the membership of the Blockade Board established, Secretary Welles provided his guidance for the board's deliberations in a directive to Du Pont:

> The Navy Department is desirous to condense all the information in the archives of the Government which may be considered useful to the Blockading Squadrons; and the Board are therefore requested to prepare such matters as in their judgment may seem necessary: first, extending from the Chesapeake to Key West; second, from Key West to the extreme Southern point of Texas. It is imperative that two or more points should be taken possession of on the Atlantic Coast, and Fernandina and Port Royal are spoken of. Perhaps others will occur to the board. All facts bearing on such a contemplated movement are desired at an early moment. Subsequently, similar points in the Gulf of Mexico will be considered. It is also very desirable that the practicability of closing all the Southern ports by mechanical means should be fully discussed and reported upon.[23]

This guidance reflected Bache's more expansive vision of the board and not that described by Fox in his May letter to Du Pont. Not only was the board to gather all pertinent information that might prove "useful" to the blockade, but explicit in Welles's directive was the order to plan for the seizure of additional bases of operations on the Atlantic Coast and lodgments on the Gulf Coast. Therefore, the board was to address two of the key challenges facing the squadrons: lack of local information and logistical installations. Welles took the order one step further with his instruction to examine the "practicability of closing all the Southern ports by mechanical means." In effect, this charged the board with exploring the possibility of blocking channels with sunken vessels as an economy-of-force measure to reduce the number of inlets that had to be covered by the blockading squadrons.

The board met for the first time on 27 June 1861 in Bache's office at the Smithsonian Castle. According to the minutes, Du Pont read and the board

Secretary of the Navy Gideon Welles. (Courtesy of the Massachusetts Commandery of the Military Order of the Loyal Legion of
the United States and the United States Army Military History
Institute)

discussed the secretary's directive. In a letter to his wife, Du Pont noted that
Welles's order did "not cover the whole ground of the question, though it
sets forth the two most important points in it: the selection of two ports, one
in South Carolina, another in the confines of Georgia and Florida (Atlantic
coast) for coal deposits; these will have to be taken and five to ten thousand
men landed, to fortify and entrench. It seems impossible to supply the
blockading fleet with coal without these depots." He also noted that Bache
wanted to expand the board's charter even more to include a "manual" for
blockading.[24] Also in its first meeting, before addressing the blockade itself,
the board discussed troops required to seize and hold key logistical bases. Du

Pont knew that planning and executing large-scale joint operations would not be a simple matter. The original goal of simply gathering information into a nice package for the squadrons was no longer the first priority.

Operationally, Du Pont's goal was twofold: first, he wanted to determine how the blockading squadrons should best execute their mission. Du Pont was appalled at the initial conduct of the blockade. The squadron commanders seemed content to take their few vessels and simply sail—or steam—aimlessly up and down the coast. Second, he wanted to plan several joint expeditions aimed at seizing logistics bases as springboards from which to launch ground operations that could threaten the very heart of the Confederacy. The board's goal, therefore, was nothing less than to provide essential operational and strategic direction for the blockade and its supporting joint operations.

Despite the excitement and constant commotion that swirled around the capital that summer, the board began its work in earnest after the first organizational meeting. Because Du Pont was the only member with no additional duties in Washington, the board was forced to arrange its meetings around the hectic work schedules of Bache, Davis, and Barnard. Convening early in the morning, the board frequently worked until midnight several days a week from late June until early September 1861. "All days are 'working' days here now," Du Pont reported to his wife on Independence Day. The board produced six major reports and four supplementary reports, or memoirs. Bache provided the maps, charts, and other geographical data for the reports, and each member then freely discussed each major topic of the day's meeting. Davis's sparse minutes do show that Du Pont's penchant for stern discipline affected the board's deliberations. The board stuck to one major topic per meeting, and members were encouraged to submit relevant material and opinions in writing. Although the board labored under the steely gaze of Chairman Du Pont, the members quickly bonded into a tight-knit group that routinely dined and socialized together.[25]

One of the most interesting items in the files of the board in the National Archives is an undated and unsigned outline entitled "Memoir of Topics." The outline includes such subjects as: Atlantic, Gulf, places to be blockaded, how to be blockaded, water depots, coal depots, operations in rivers, harbors of refuge, naval and military considerations of a blockade, what is an effective blockade, law of nations, defenses, and related topics. Given Bache's desire to create a manual for blockading, it is surprising that the members crossed out and did not address an elementary topic on the outline: what force of vessels (number and kind) was required for the blockade. Although the members may have known what forces would be available to the blockading squadrons into the fall of 1861, this was a fundamental oversight. While

not directly addressed by the secretary's directive, the determination of required forces is an essential strategic requirement.

It is not clear who deleted the topic or why—the subject's removal must
have been approved by Du Pont—but the board missed an excellent opportunity to provide the secretary with vital recommendations on the number
and type of ships that would be required to make the blockade work. Many
of the reports addressed troop requirements to take and hold various bases,
but there are few shipping recommendations. Several of the memoirs did address ship numbers and types such as "a small number of shallow drafted vessels are required to patrol this area." But there is no systematic or comprehensive set of recommendations for force requirements. This omission may
have been due to Barnard's influence, but more likely it was because Du Pont
recognized the vital importance of joint operations with the army to accomplish any meaningful goals along the enemy coastline. Du Pont's Mexican
War experience taught him not only how to conduct a blockade but how to
plan and execute support operations as well. Because the president approved
every one of the board's reports, a force recommendation by Du Pont could
have given Welles additional justification to expand the navy rapidly and
thus improve the blockade. Even if Du Pont and the board knew the composition of the available forces, they should have made recommendations for
the structure of the various blockading fleets based on the sailing challenges
and enemy forces they might face. This was one of the board's few failures.[26]

On 3 July 1861 Barnard presented a lengthy memorandum to the board
on relevant coastal defenses, and the board in turn presented its first two reports to Secretary Welles on 5 and 13 July 1861. Getting right to the point,
the board began the first report by confirming the need for extra bases: "It
seems to be indispensable that there should exist a convenient coal depot on
the southern extremity of the line of Atlantic blockades . . . [and it] might be
used not only as a coal depot for coal, but as a depot for provisions and common stores, as a harbor of refuge, and as a general rendezvous, or headquarters, for that part of the coast."[27] The best southern base, the board determined, was Fernandina, Florida. As in all the board's reports, the bulk of the
first memoir included exhaustive and detailed geographical data on the harbor, its approaches, water depths, tides, availability of fresh water, and key
transportation facilities such as railroad links.

The second report addressed the need for a second base farther to the
north. First, the members recommended closing the inlets between the Cape
Hatteras barrier islands. Next, they turned to the South Carolina coast. The
board studied three potential bases: Port Royal Sound, Bull's Bay, and Saint
Helena Sound. Although recognizing the superiority of the harbor facilities
and anchorage at Port Royal, the members believed that the enemy would

aggressively defend the port. Thus the members recommended seizing Bull's Bay. As in every report, the board drew heavily on Major Barnard's expertise to scrutinize the current defenses of likely bases and the suitability for additional fortifications. The board's criteria (many of which can be found in the "topic memoir") for a suitable base included: easy approaches, surmountable defenses, fresh water, anchorages, shelter, shore-based facilities, and the ability of an occupying force to hold the base.[28] Seizing a major base deep in the South would entail considerable risk and require a formidable ground and naval force, but Du Pont felt the prize would be well worth the effort. A base in South Carolina would offer the Union a decided strategic advantage. Not only would it be the main headquarters and the logistics and maintenance base for one of the squadrons, but such a base was very close to Charleston, the seat of the rebellion.

Two days before the Union debacle at the First Battle of Bull Run (Manassas), the board submitted its third memoir, followed ten days later by the fourth memoir. The board made several recommendations, one of which had a profound impact on the blockade. It proposed that the blockade "be divided into two sections, one of which will extend from Cape Henry to Cape Romain, about 370 miles, and the other from Cape Romain to St. Augustine, about 220 miles." The board then described the conditions along both sections of coastline: the northern portion had fewer and less complex inlets and thus was more easily blockaded; the southern section, although shorter, was much more difficult to cover. In other words, the board recommended that the current Atlantic Blockading Squadron be broken into two separate and independent squadrons. The members argued that "if this plan is adopted . . . the commander in chief [of each squadron] while at sea within the limits of his command could, so short is the distance, communicate with the whole line of his blockading squadron, either in person or by his tender, every day, or every two days during ordinary weather." It was impossible for one man to effectively exercise command from the mouth of the Chesapeake to Key West and from Key West to Mexico. By dividing the responsibility for the Atlantic blockade between two squadrons, Du Pont advocated a streamlined command and control arrangement that would greatly ease the burdens of the commanders while increasing the blockade's efficiency. Later the board members recommended that responsibility for blockading the Gulf be divided into two separate but cooperating commands.[29]

Confederate victory at Bull Run lent a sense of urgency to the board's proceedings. Welles must have kept Lincoln acquainted with the board's progress, because the president, in his "Memoranda of Military Policy Suggested by the Bull Run Defeat," issued on 23 July 1861, declared, "Let the plan for making the Blockade effective be pushed forward with all possible

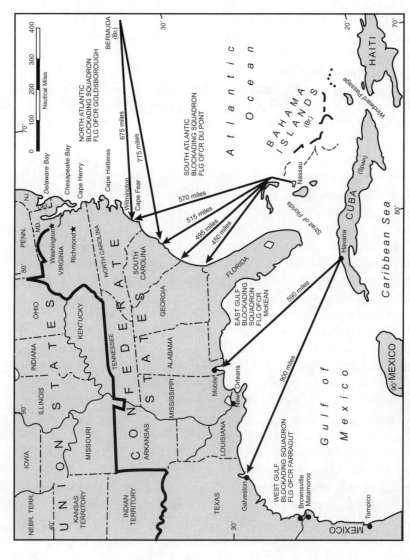

United States Navy blockading squadrons of the Civil War and the distances to ports favored by block-ade-runners

dispatch." Three days later Welles, Fox, and Du Pont presented the board's reports to Lincoln and the rest of the cabinet. Lincoln expressed some misgivings about the risks associated with Du Pont's bold proposals to seize bases deep in the South, but Fox helped Du Pont defend the board's recommendations. "The President," Du Pont reported, "has been told up and down by Mr. Fox . . . that the blockading squadron cannot keep at sea in winter without depots for coal, etc." [30] But it was not simply coaling stations that Du Pont envisioned. He believed that these joint efforts could secure bases from which the army could launch operations that could have significant strategic impact.

The next day Du Pont briefed the board's preliminary recommendations to a group of senior officers including Union general-in-chief General Winfield Scott and the quartermaster general, Montgomery C. Meigs. The rest of the board anxiously awaited Du Pont's return. Fortunately, when Du Pont rejoined the group later that night, he had good news. Davis proudly informed his wife that Du Pont had "just been in to tell me that the general pronounced [the board's reports] to possess high ability, and he said he endorsed every word of them." It is not surprising that the author of the so-called Anaconda Plan, a scheme that, in part, called for a tight blockade, would enthusiastically endorse the board's recommendations. Several days later Lincoln also approved the plans in full. Despite their success, Du Pont and the rest of his team knew that their proposed courses of action were risky. In a display of his rare but excellent dry wit, Du Pont wrote his wife that Welles had "agreed to occupy two of the points recommended, Fernandina and Bull's Bay. . . . I hope it will not be made a 'Bull Run.'" [31]

Did Fox convince the president to act, was Lincoln pleased with Du Pont's memoirs, or did General Scott report favorably to the president? All three are likely true to some extent, but it is clear that Lincoln approved what were the most important recommendations of all: the proposed expeditions to seize two Atlantic coast bases of operations. The ad hoc process that the board followed was remarkably similar to the way modern staff officers conduct theater strategic military planning today: the board members received initial guidance from their civilian leaders, and they conducted an estimate of the situation, developed courses of action, and presented them to the highest levels of military and civilian leadership for approval. This was the essence of military strategy; Lincoln saw that the board's recommendations for the conduct of the blockade campaign well supported his national strategy and war aims. In the summer of 1861, Lincoln had precious few tools with which to take the fight to the Confederacy. The blockade was one of these tools, and the board's proposals promised to make the blockade work.

The board then shifted its attention to improving the Gulf Coast block-

Assistant Secretary of the Navy Gustavus V. Fox. (Courtesy of the Massachusetts Commandery of the Military Order of the Loyal Legion of the United States and the United States Army Military History Institute)

ade, and on 6 August 1861 it submitted its first Gulf report. With complex, tortuous, and constantly shifting channels, the Mississippi Delta region required the longest description among all the coastal regions examined by the board. The members pointed out to "the careful reader of this memoir" that the geographic complexity of this region meant that "the blockade of the river . . . does not close the port [of New Orleans]." They then recommended, due to the prohibitively large naval and military force required, that the capture of New Orleans be placed on the strategic back burner until "we are prepared to ascend the river with vessels of war sufficiently protected to contend with the forts." Another recommendation called for the navy to concentrate on "shutting it up, suspending its trade, and obstructing the freedom of its intercourse with the ocean and with the neighboring coasts, feeling assured that the moral effect of such a course will be quite as striking as that of its possession by the United States." An effective blockade had to be initiated before attempting to seize the great southern port, for the Union lacked the resources in mid-1861 to conduct an expedition directly against the fortifications protecting New Orleans. But the members were exaggerating when they claimed that a blockade would be as effective strategically as Union capture of New Orleans. Instead of seizing New Orleans immediately, the board recommended the capture of Ship Island, a barrier island located midway between the ports of New Orleans and Mobile, as the headquarters and logistical base for the Gulf Blockading Squadron. The seizure of New Orleans, the largest city in the Confederacy, would have a huge strategic impact, and the board clearly recognized this fact. Union operations followed almost exactly the board's recommended course of action, with Flag Officer David G. Farragut using Ship Island as the base of Union operations for his stunning capture of New Orleans in April 1862.[32]

Planning operations is one thing; carrying the plan out is another. Days before the board finished its first Gulf Coast memoir, Du Pont received the most important assignment of his long and colorful career: command of the first major joint operation of the Civil War. The purpose of this expedition was to execute an "invasion and occupation of the sea coast of the states in rebellion." Secretary Welles emphasized that the "importance of this expedition upon the flank of the enemy cannot be overestimated; and in confiding its preparation and organization to your hands, the Department hereby gives you the full authority necessary to ensure success."[33] Du Pont was ordered to wrap up his activities with the board and report to New York to assemble his force, along with Charles Henry Davis, whom Welles designated as the expedition's chief of staff.

Du Pont's new command was the one that would ultimately seize Port Royal, South Carolina; he commanded the naval forces in cooperation with army general Thomas W. Sherman. Du Pont's new assignment was but the first direct consequence of the Blockade Board. Although junior to many officers on the active list, Du Pont was the most intimately familiar with the plan and the risks. Welles later noted in his annual report to Congress that he had chosen Du Pont, in part, because "as chairman of the [blockade] board . . . [he had] special qualifications and thorough preparation for the highly responsible position assigned to him." Du Pont proudly told his wife "the order is in the highest sense complimentary" and "I find myself suddenly thrown up in connection with the most important armament ever made in this country." To his good friend Henry Winter Davis, now a prominent radical Republican in Congress, Du Pont wrote, "The labors of my board produced their effect and I have been selected to carry out the projects."[34]

Several days later Du Pont departed for New York with a brief stop en route to visit his wife in Delaware. Arriving in New York, Du Pont and Sherman began to assemble the assets for America's first major amphibious operation since the Mexican War. Did Du Pont manipulate the board's proceedings to gain the coveted Port Royal command? Looking back on it after their relationship deteriorated, Welles certainly thought so.[35] However, Du Pont did not mention such an ambition in his voluminous correspondence. But given his track record of angling for good jobs, he may indeed have actively sought the Port Royal expedition command. That said, Welles picked the right officer for the job. Du Pont was an experienced blockader, had worked with the army, had developed the basic blockade plan, and was intimately familiar with the geography and the challenges he would face.

With Du Pont's attention divided between his position on the board and his new seagoing command, the board did not complete the second Gulf Coast memoir until 3 September 1861. This report summarized the geographical and topographical characteristics of the rest of the Gulf, including the Florida Keys and the entire coast of Texas. Finally, on 19 September 1861, the board submitted its final memoir. The briefest of all the board's works, this memoir supplemented the first Gulf report by describing the defenses of Ship Island. Now fully engaged in his duties as head of the Port Royal expedition, Du Pont nevertheless requested that the department allow the board to complete one additional memoir "which to us as individuals, and to the Department for convenience, it is most desirable to finish." This report was to be the manual for the conduct of the blockade; it would "furnish the basis of instructions to the different squadrons, while it will be most attractive to the general reader."[36] But Welles and Fox failed to act on Du Pont's request, and this last report was never finished.

The Ship Island memoir marked the end of the board's formal activities, but the experience had strengthened the already close professional bond among its members. They exchanged several letters in the following weeks demonstrating their mutual affection and friendship, which would last the rest of their lives. On 2 October 1861 Du Pont and Davis were painstakingly assembling the Port Royal expedition and wrote Bache informing him that "on closing for the present the labors of the Mixed Conference . . . [we] cannot but express the high opinion [we] have been led to entertain of the usefulness of the Coast Survey to our knowledge of the sea coasts, sounds, and bays of the Atlantic and Gulf borders of the United States, without which the deliberations of the Conference could not have been successfully conducted." Bache thanked his colleagues and stated that it gratified him that although the survey was "primarily designed as an aid to commerce . . . in an emergency it can supply information applicable to the military and naval defense of the coasts." Finally, on the same day, Bache sent a warm note to the newly promoted Barnard: "I have just returned from New York where I had a parting opportunity of a conference with Commodore Du Pont and Commander Davis. We only wanted our general (once our major) to make our quadrilateral complete."[37]

The Navy Department accepted most of board's recommendations. Welles moved rapidly to split the Atlantic Blockading Squadron into the North and South Atlantic Blockading Squadrons under Flag Officers Louis M. Goldsborough and Du Pont, respectively; the Gulf Blockading Squadron was also broken into the East and West Gulf Blockading Squadrons commanded by Flag Officers William W. McKean and David G. Farragut. Second, Lincoln and the War and Navy Departments immediately began to prepare joint operations based on the board's detailed analysis and recommendations: Cape Hatteras in August 1861, Port Royal and Ship Island in November 1861, and Fernandina in March 1862, in many ways the first major Union victories of the war. Third, the success of the Blockade Board led Welles to establish other commissions and boards, including the Board for Purchase of Vessels, the Board of Naval Examiners, the Board on Ironclad Vessels, the Permanent Commission, and the Board on Claims; all of these organizations made significant contributions to the naval war.[38] Finally, the commanders of the blockading squadrons now had at their disposal a thorough, ready-made, and timesaving analysis of their areas of operations along with all applicable charts.

The Lincoln administration did not adopt all of the board's recommendations, and the board addressed only one part of a multifaceted strategic naval problem. However, the Civil War saw no comparable organization, staff, or agency that systematically formulated naval or military strategy, although in early 1865 Du Pont unsuccessfully advocated the establishment of a permanent naval planning staff. Still, the board's most important contribution and its greatest legacy were the determination where and how the Union navy would conduct the blockade campaign, and it provided Lincoln with good strategic options. In the pressure-cooker atmosphere of wartime Washington, D.C., the members of the Blockade Board forged close personal bonds while accomplishing what no other military body would achieve throughout the war: the thoughtful and deliberate gathering and analysis of information to develop a viable, coordinated, and attainable military strategy.

There is plenty of credit to go around for the successes of the Blockade Board. To Bache goes the honor of the initial idea and for selecting—or at least influencing—the board's membership. Welles's vision and administrative abilities allowed him to see the value of Bache's idea and to act upon it, despite the myriad competing demands for his attention and for the experienced officers necessary to man a commission such as the Blockade Board. Welles provided guidance that was clear, concise, and coordinated with Lincoln's national strategic concept. Lincoln and Scott recognized the excellence of the board's work and without exception endorsed its reports. Du Pont directed the board with great skill and professionalism. He instinctively grasped strategist Carl von Clausewitz's admonition that both statesmen and commanders must understand the "kind of war on which they are embarking; neither mistaking it for, nor trying to turn it into, something alien to its nature."[39] Although Du Pont's prewar writings advocated a naval strategy dominated by the decisive battle like that later advocated by Mahan, a viable strategy for the early blockade posed an entirely different set of problems. In the absence of a significant Confederate naval threat, Du Pont directed the board to develop a set of strategic recommendations to identify and take key bases of operations, whose occupation would give the Union a decisive advantage.[40] In this way the strategy Du Pont developed for the campaign of blockade was much closer to that later advocated by the early twentieth-century British naval strategist Julian Corbett. Unlike Mahan (and Du Pont's earlier writings), Corbett echoed Clausewitz in many ways and argued that the most important role for the navy was not as the nation's primary offensive arm but as an adjunct to other arms such as the army and other elements of national power such as diplomatic, economic, and political actions. Du Pont's blockade strategy called for aggressive naval action coupled with extensive joint operations. Once again, his actions anticipated an influential naval strategist.[41]

Du Pont's strategic insight, experience, and leadership ensured that the board would create a quality product that defined the Union blockade for the remainder of the war. No other element of Union military strategy was formulated as early and lasted as long as the Blockade Board's strategic recommendations. It is one of the most interesting historical ironies of the war that the Union army, with a well-developed bureaucracy, a body of strategic writing and theory, and a general-in-chief, was unable to formulate a coherent military strategy until the war was almost three years old. On the other hand, the United States Navy, with none of the army's advantages, developed a superb strategic concept in less than three months that lasted, with few changes, until the end of the war. Du Pont had devised a large portion of the Union's naval strategy; now he was charged with making it work.

7

The Great Southern Expedition

Port Royal is the most important place to strike.

— SAMUEL FRANCIS DU PONT

A S THAT long summer of 1861 wound down and he prepared to conclude his work on the Blockade Board, Du Pont continued to rail against his former navy colleagues who had defected to the South. He must have felt some vindication when his nemesis, Matthew Fontaine Maury, resigned to join the Confederacy. Writing to his friend Louis Goldsborough, who had just returned from a lengthy cruise, Du Pont declared that Maury was a "villain" who had been pressing for secession for the past decade and who wanted nothing less than to "*subjugate* the free states."[1] However, Du Pont had more important things on his mind than the fate of one Southern officer. The problems and challenges that faced the commanders of the blockading squadrons must have appeared daunting indeed in late August 1861. Although the Union navy was expanding rapidly, the blockade was still woefully short of ships, and there were still limited bases for the squadrons. For the next nine months, Du Pont would plan and conduct a series of military operations whose strategic aim was to tighten the blockade. While his plans for both his widely acclaimed victory at Port Royal and for the implementation of the blockade were not executed exactly as Du Pont envisioned, they achieved both objectives.

The Cape Hatteras expedition, led by Commodore Silas H. Stringham, who was then commanding the Atlantic Blockading Squadron, was the first operation undertaken by the United States Navy as a direct result of the Blockade Board's work. As early as 27 July, members of the board met with Stringham to begin planning for this expedition. His joint operation with troops under the command of Major General Benjamin F. Butler was an important, although only partial, success. Stringham's small squadron included two powerful *Merrimack*-class frigates, the *Wabash* and Du Pont's old command, the *Minnesota*. These ships made short work of the partially constructed Confederate fortifications on the barrier island, and the Union had its first victory. The question of using ships against shore-based fortifications was reopened by Stringham's actions. In a letter to Henry Winter Davis, Du Pont suggested that the operation would not even have taken place if he had not personally pushed it with Welles. "The first fruits of the labors of my associates and myself came out on the North Carolina coast," Du Pont proclaimed. "If I had not fairly *insisted* upon the expedition going, and telling the Secretary his Department might as well be shut if he did not compel the flag officer to execute his orders, he would never have sailed."[2]

In making this claim, Du Pont was more than a little disingenuous. In its second memoir the board did state that it would be to the navy's advantage to block the Hatteras and nearby Ocracoke inlets; it did not, however, directly endorse or advocate seizing the barrier islands of the Outer Banks, though it did recommend controlling Pamlico and Albemarle Sounds beyond. These sounds were vitally important because they "served as Richmond's back door to the Atlantic."[3] It is hard to say if Du Pont actually tried to pressure Welles, or if he was merely boasting to his friend and exaggerating his role, something he tended to do. What is clear is that Stringham resisted any attempt by the secretary to encourage offensive operations that would make the blockade more effective. Although Stringham and Butler did not push forward and seize control of Pamlico Sound beyond the Hatteras inlets, they did take a necessary step in the right direction toward improving the blockade. Welles soon forced the flag officer to retire and replaced him with Du Pont's friend Louis M. Goldsborough when he split the Atlantic Blockading Squadron into two separate commands.

Still smarting from the debacle of the First Battle of Bull Run only weeks before, Northern morale received a much-needed boost with the minor success at Hatteras. Soon the navy would produce another victory, one with much greater strategic and operational consequences, with the seizure of Port Royal, South Carolina. The Blockade Board had addressed carefully the area of the South Carolina coast adjacent to Charleston, the seat of the rebellion. Its members closely examined the charts, maps, and characteristics of Port Royal, Bull's Bay, and Saint Helena Sound. Of the three, Du Pont and his associates found Port Royal to have the best harbor, "the finest . . . south of Chesapeake Bay, which it resembles in capacity and extent." Once the bar was passed, "a whole navy can ride at anchor in the bay in uninterrupted health and security." Its other advantages included some existing shore facilities and a bar navigable by large first-class United States Navy steam frigates. But drawbacks included the fact that the bar was a full eight miles from the entrance to the bay, and that entrance was restricted by a channel easily covered by fortifications on either side on Hilton Head and Bay Point Islands. Largely because Port Royal was the most obvious objective for a major Union joint operation, the Blockade Board felt that the area would be much too heavily defended and so recommended seizing the more obscure, if less desirable, anchorages at Bull's Bay and Saint Helena.[4]

Even before the navy named Du Pont commander of the South Atlantic Blockading Squadron on 18 September 1861, he had been dividing his time between the Blockade Board in Washington, D.C., and his nascent fleet in New York harbor. Indeed, by the end of August he had been hard at work overseeing construction of surfboats to be used to land the army contingent of the joint force. With the appointment of Goldsborough and Du Pont to the rank of flag officer and as commanders of arguably the two most important squadrons in the navy, Welles and Lincoln had effectively jettisoned seniority as the driving force of the navy's promotion and assignment system. All four of the blockading squadrons went to officers who had been promoted to captain thanks to the work of the Efficiency Board. Later that day Du Pont rejoiced in a letter to his wife that "seniority . . . has seen its last day. Selection with as much regard to seniority as the good of the service will admit is now the order of the day."[5] The department also allowed Du Pont to handpick most of his staff and the captains of his combatant ships in yet another departure from seniority: Charles Henry Davis became his chief of staff and fleet captain; as commander of the *Wabash*, Christopher Raymond Perry (C. R. P.) Rodgers became flag captain; John Rodgers was named as a special staff officer; and Percival Drayton, the ordnance expert, commanded one of the gunboats. After his protracted campaign against the injustices of the seniority system, it must have been gratifying indeed for Du Pont to be one of the first beneficiaries of the suspension of the old ways, even though it was just a temporary measure dictated by the exigencies of wartime.

Du Pont's painstakingly assembled fleet—the largest fleet in United States history up to that date—sailed from New York harbor in beautiful, clear weather on 16 October 1861. The flagship *Wabash* received and returned the salutes of all the forts ringing the great port. Sophie, Mary Goldsborough, and many other officer wives and well-wishers watched the fleet's departure from the parapet of Fort Hamilton, on the southwestern tip of Brooklyn.[6] None of the thousands of spectators who saw the great amphibious expedition set sail that autumn day knew its objective, nor did many of them care. They simply wanted to strike a blow at the Confederacy.

Designated as the overall commander of the joint expedition to seize a logistical base for the South Atlantic Blockading Squadron and given the latitude to pick his objective by the secretary, Du Pont, understandably, leaned toward Bull's Bay and Saint Helena. While the board had balked at a Port Royal attack as too risky and the port area itself as too costly to consolidate and hold, Assistant Secretary of the Navy Gustavus V. Fox thought otherwise. In an October meeting on board the flagship *Wabash* at Hampton Roads, Fox, again emphasizing that the final decision was Du Pont's, convinced the new flag officer that the objective should be Port Royal. However, Du Pont was beginning to have second thoughts about the conclusions of the board days before meeting with Fox. In a letter to Sophie written on 17 October en route to Hampton Roads, Du Pont declared, "There is no question that Port Royal is the most important point to strike . . . yet we did not think [so] in our conference and I must weigh well before I deviate." He reasoned that Bull's Bay and Saint Helena were still preferable if envisioned as mere coaling depots, but a major staging base for future operations needed to be more substantial, and Port Royal was the only objective of the three that "gives us such a naval position on the seacoast of the enemy."[7] In a series of meetings with the army generals assigned to the expedition and with Fox, Du Pont and Sherman decided to make their objective Port Royal.[8]

Port Royal Sound is one of the most magnificent natural harbors on the east coast of the United States. In 1861 the land neighboring the sound was some of the richest and most productive in South Carolina. The Broad and Beaufort Rivers flow into the sound from the northwest and gave easy ocean access to the small town of Beaufort and the plentiful plantations and farms where wealthy plantation owners amassed fortunes in land and slaves. The vast expanse of the sound promised to provide an unsurpassed anchorage and logistical base for the Union navy, although the bar that guarded its two-mile-wide entrance might deny entry to the largest warships. Du Pont was plagued with doubts about the ability of the *Wabash*, the heaviest of the ships in his fleet, to negotiate the Port Royal bar. To assist the expedition Bache offered the services of one of his best hydrographers, Charles O. Boutelle, for the purposes of identifying the best place and time for the fleet to cross the bar and to survey and mark the main channel into the harbor. When Boutelle was delayed getting to the fleet at Hampton Roads before it departed for its final destination, Du Pont grew increasingly apprehensive. When the coastal expert finally arrived on 24 October, Du Pont felt "a great relief to my mind."[9]

The Blockade Board's planning and gathering of all relevant coastal data proved to be time well spent. In a letter to Bache, Du Pont noted that he and Davis "feel ourselves . . . leaning more and more on the Coast Survey & its marvelous results; no official or other declarations to this effect can convey a little of my estimate of their importance." All the pieces were now in place for the largest joint navy and army operation in the nation's history. Almost 13,000 troops and fifty-one ships (fifteen of them warships) had gathered at Hampton Roads for the move south.[10]

Finally, after several delays caused by threatening weather and breakdowns of important ships, the Port Royal expedition departed the sanctuary of Hampton Roads on 29 October. Flag Officer Louis M. Goldsborough, commanding the North Atlantic Blockading Squadron based at Hampton Roads, marveled at the "grand display" of the largest United States Navy fleet ever assembled, now led by one of his best friends as it departed for its "destiny."[11] Although there would be many turning points during the war, it is hard to underestimate the anxiety of the North's population as it followed the progress of Du Pont's fleet. There had been precious few Union successes and many disappointments. Was Du Pont's expedition destined to join the long string of Northern failures?

From the beginning, this and most other joint operations during the Civil War were plagued by a lack of unity of command, one of the most important principles of war. A military force usually achieves unity of command when there is one officer in charge of the entire joint operation. However, in trying to reduce interservice rivalry, Lincoln hampered unity of command when he announced that although navy flag officers were equivalent in rank to army major generals, neither service could command forces from the other. In a letter to Du Pont, Welles explained that "no officer of the Army or Navy, whatever may be his rank, can assume any direct command, independent of consent, over an officer of the other service, excepting only when land forces are expressly embarked in vessels of war to do the duty of marines."[12] In other words, an army or navy flag officer had to willingly accept direction and command from an officer of another service before unity of command could occur. This did happen on occasion during the Civil War; the relationships of mutual trust, appreciation, and cooperation between General Ulysses Grant and Flag Officer Andrew Foote and Admiral David D. Porter are good examples. Regrettably for Du Pont and a succession of army commanders, such a relationship never evolved in the South Atlantic Blockading Squadron's area of operations, nor did the Navy Department encourage such cooperation.

As Du Pont's fleet—dubbed "The Great Southern Expedition" by Northern newspapers—began to leave the safety of Hampton Roads, it was headed toward an objective for which it had ample data concerning its physical attributes but almost no usable military intelligence. At the same time the Confederate commanders at Port Royal were working feverishly to strengthen the bay's defenses. Although most observers guessed that the huge Union armada was headed for either Charleston or Bull's Bay, efforts to maintain secrecy—including Du Pont's discretionary orders as to the objective—were compromised by the speculation of several Northern newspapers, which caused the Confederate secretary of war to warn Governor Francis Pickens of South Carolina, "I have just received information, which I considered entirely reliable that the enemy's expedition is headed for Port Royal."[13] This and other security leaks would plague Du Pont for the rest of the war.

The rebel commander at Port Royal, Brigadier General Thomas P. Drayton (brother of Du Pont's friend and gunboat captain Percival Drayton) did the best he could in the time he had to fortify the approaches to the bay. Commodore Josiah Tattnall, former United States naval officer and Du Pont's nominal squadron commander during his *Minnesota* cruise, assisted Drayton in Port Royal's defense. Tattnall commanded a small flotilla of modified tugs. Fort Walker on Hilton Head Island mounted twenty-three guns including six 32-pounders and a 10-inch Columbiad. Bay Point Island's Fort Beauregard boasted twenty guns of various types and calibers. It appeared to most observers at the time that the interlocking fields of fire from these formidable works could easily defeat any squadron attempting to force a passage into the inner harbor. However, the fortifications were not as strong as they seemed. The large variety of gun types and calibers—all that the Confederates could scrape together—meant that the rebels faced a difficult logistical challenge to provide enough ammunition of various types and sizes for the guns. In addition, when one gun was disabled, the crews could not in most cases transfer the ammunition to another weapon. Despite General Drayton's best efforts, he was unable to install many of the guns until only days before the Union attack; some of them faced shoreward to guard against an overland assault and so proved useless against an attacking fleet. Thus the gun crews—many of them raw volunteers—had little or no training on their pieces and had no time to register their guns on the areas through which the Union fleet would have to negotiate. In addition, a main channel that was almost three miles wide separated the forts; any warship in the middle of the channel was out of range of much of the Confederate ordnance. Finally, the Confederates packed so many guns into the small forts that the crewmen constantly impeded each other's movements during the loading and aiming processes.[14] Despite Drayton's handicaps, had the largest guns in these forts been well served and sited, they could have done great damage to the attacking fleet, perhaps even repulsing the attack entirely.

However, although the forts at Port Royal achieved far better combat readiness than those at Cape Hatteras, they were still hastily constructed, weakly manned, and poorly outfitted. But contemporary accounts, probably in an attempt to make the Union victory seem more impressive than it was, described the forts as "constructed with great skill" and "beautifully constructed" with formidable armament.[15]

Good weather greeted the fleet as it set sail for Port Royal on 29 October, but then a gale struck almost immediately, followed by a hurricane-like storm that scattered the ships and sank several. By 1 November the flagship's log noted that many ships were in distress; by 3 November only eight vessels were in sight. Although heroic actions by several captains and crews kept the loss of life very low, equipment losses were extremely heavy, including ammunition and many of the surfboats that Du Pont and Sherman had counted on to land the troops. A young officer aboard the *Wabash* vividly described the devastated fleet: "It was very sad to see so many vessels hoisting signals of distress. Some were dismasted some had their engines crippled by the heavy rolling, some sprung a leak until our fleet presented quite a different appearance from what it did when we came out of Hampton Roads; indeed some of the vessels were almost wrecks." The storm only heightened Union apprehension at home. A young army officer spoke for many in the North when he wrote, "I am longing to hear about the naval expedition and whether it suffered from the late storm."[16]

Thus when the *Wabash* arrived off the Port Royal bar on 4 November 1861 with the crippled fleet spread over hundreds of miles of ocean, the commanders were forced to modify their plan. The joint operation now gave way to an all-navy attack to silence the rebel forts; once this objective was achieved, Sherman's troops would land unopposed to expand the beachhead and prepare to conduct future offensives. Charles Henry Davis, John Rodgers, and Charles Boutelle began immediately to sound the entrance and mark a safe channel. Within hours, the fleet—minus the oversized *Wabash* and *Susquehanna*—had crossed the bar. The next day an exuberant Du Pont wrote Sophie: "We are [all] *inside*. . . . One thing is evident, that the Navy has to do the work and the troops can only land after we have silenced the battery on Hilton Head Island."[17]

Later that day Davis, John Rodgers, and Brigadier General Horatio G. Wright conducted a reconnaissance of the inner bay with several gunboats to determine the strength of the fortifications and the small Confederate naval force under Commodore Tattnall. When Rodgers and Wright reported that the "fortifications were works of strength and scientifically constructed," Du Pont anchored the fleet within sight of the forts and prepared to attack the next morning, but poor weather again swept through the area, forcing postponement of the attack until 7 November.[18]

Although Du Pont had counted on a joint operation with the army all along, he; his chief of staff, Charles Henry Davis; and C. R. P. Rodgers devised a modified plan that was communicated to the captains early in the morning of 7 November. Davis later claimed that he alone developed the plan of attack, but Du Pont contradicted this in a 5 May 1862 letter to his wife, stating that the plan "was altogether original to us here—Davis, Raymond Rodgers, and myself—and was one of those maneuvers reached by long and earnest study. The first idea that the ships must not anchor was mine, and I told Davis we might as well be sailing ships if we did, and we threw away the advantage of steam and the locomotion incident to it."[19] Du Pont, normally lavish in his praise of subordinates, did not mention Davis as the lead planner, making it likely that Du Pont and Davis prepared the plan together. Du Pont knew that the key to taking the forts with his warships alone was motion: keep the fleet moving at all times. Moving targets would make life very difficult for the Confederate gunners. Steam power made this possible in the confined channel of Port Royal Sound.

The flag officer's warships were broken into two squadrons: the first, led by the *Wabash*, would reduce Fort Walker on Hilton Head; the mission of the second, led by the gunboat *Bienville*, was to cover the right flank of the main attack against Fort Beauregard and keep an eye out for a sortie by Tattnall's motley force. Du Pont wanted to destroy the stronger Fort Walker first and then turn his full attention to Fort Beauregard. The main force was to steam down the main channel between Hilton Head and Bay Point Islands. The ships were to pass the forts, firing at both, then turn back toward Fort Walker, all the time keeping up a constant fire at close range. It was imperative that the squadron kept moving at all times. If more passes were necessary, Du Pont planned to repeat the original maneuver, steaming in an elliptical pattern as close to Hilton Head as he could, concentrating the fleet's fire on Fort Walker. Once the fleet reduced Fort Walker, the warships would once again repeat the maneuver, directing their fire on Fort Beauregard.[20] Gideon Welles wrote in his diary years later that an officer told him that Du Pont's innovative plan of sailing in a circle was "not part of the original plan but an afterthought, when it was found more convenient to move from under fire than to remain,"[21] but Davis and several of the other captains support Du Pont's account. However, few plans, even the best ones, survive contact with the enemy, and Du Pont's and Davis's design was no exception.

Besides the army's landing craft and other missing equipment, one of Du Pont's warships had not yet arrived after its brush with the storm. Nevertheless, Du Pont decided that to wait for its arrival would only give the enemy more time to prepare. He would have to go with the fourteen warships, most of them small gunboats, on hand.[22]

The battle began at 9:26 A.M. as the *Wabash* neared Fort Walker and began to take fire from both forts. For forty-six years Du Pont had been preparing himself for this moment. He was finally commanding a fleet of ships in his country's service: no naval officer could aspire to do anything more. He was going in harm's way, and he loved every minute of it. His enthusiasm was quickly dampened, however, when he noticed that only the *Susquehanna* had followed the flagship into the correct position. Commander Sylvanus Godon of the *Mohican* "inexplicably led most of the bombardment squadron into an enfilading position off [the northwest corner of] Fort Walker."[23] Commander Charles Steedman of the gunboat *Bienville* saw that the *Wabash* and *Susquehanna* were advancing into the teeth of the enemy fire unsupported and on his own initiative left the flanking squadron to fall in behind the *Susquehanna*. Du Pont's repeated signals from the flagship failed to restore the rest of the fleet to the proper positions, and consequently, as Du Pont would write after the attack, the *Wabash* "did nearly all the work, the *Susquehanna* doing nobly also behind us . . . [and] Steedman who gallantly followed the *Susquehanna*."[24] At the height of the action, a furious and exasperated Du Pont exclaimed, "How is it that I can't get my signal obeyed, and my orders carried out?"[25]

The crew of the gunboat *Seneca* recorded Du Pont's signals in her log: at 10:15 A.M. the flag officer "sent the general signal to close the present order," and from 10:20 A.M. to 11:35 A.M., "he kept signaling for closer action and to follow the movements of the commander in chief." At 12:30 P.M. "he repeated the signal to close the present order." Finally, he signaled cease-fire at 1:55 P.M. One can only imagine the frustration Du Pont must have felt during the battle.[26]

The *Wabash* first passed as close as 800 yards to Fort Walker and on the return trip closed to 600 (some reports claimed as close as 400) yards, almost point-blank range for her modern Dahlgren and Parrott ordnance. Du Pont believed that this maneuver, although risky, was necessary to maximize the effects of his guns on the earthen fortifications. Accurate and intense Union gunnery dismounted the most modern gun in Fort Walker almost immediately, while the poorly trained rebel gunners fired high at the nearby but moving ships, inflicting moderate damage to the rigging and masts of the attacking vessels but causing few casualties. Still, the action was hot, as described by an acting master commanding a division of guns on the flagship: "The whiz and crash of shot and shell being literally incessant. They had very heavy guns. Shell guns, Columbiads and rifled and they cut us up in spars, rigging, and hull pretty severely. There was a perfect thunder from our broadsides which is described by the lookers on in the transports as terrific and which finally silenced their batteries and drove them out in a manner that would have done credit to Bull Run. . . . Part of the time we lay between the two batteries receiving fire from both and giving it to them in return from starboard and port." The enthusiastic young officer described the battle as "the grandest sight I ever saw; the gallant frigate thundering away with both her batteries followed closely by the *Susquehanna* which will ever be dear to all of us for the way she supported us."[27]

Some Confederate gunners fought bravely despite the overwhelming firepower of the Union fleet, but the crews were not to be denied. A sailor on the gunboat *Unadilla* of the flanking squadron wrote that "our vessel was struck seven times but thank God no one was hurt. . . . They fought well while they did fight, giving it to us on both sides at once. But it appeared to me that as if every one in the fleet thought that the country depended on him."[28]

The *Wabash*, *Susquehanna*, and *Bienville* made three full circuits against Fort Walker while the supporting squadron chased Tattnall's diminutive fleet out of the area and the rest of the main squadron joined the bombardment from longer ranges. On the last pass Percival Drayton's gunboat, the *Pocahontas*, having just arrived after her struggle with the storm, sailed to the sound of the flagship's guns and joined the three other ships to deliver the final blows. As Drayton's ship passed the *Wabash*, Du Pont shouted to the South Carolina native, "Captain Drayton, I knew you would be here."[29] After over four hours of intense firing, the garrison at Fort Walker abandoned its positions, and the rebels from Fort Beauregard followed in great haste. Union losses totaled eight killed in action and twenty-eight wounded; Confederate casualties numbered eleven killed and forty-eight wounded.[30]

In the best traditions of the old navy, Du Pont dispatched one of the heroes of the battle, Steedman and the *Bienville*, to Washington with reports and the first American flag flown over South Carolina territory since the fall of Fort Sumter. Port Royal and environs were now in Federal hands, and Du Pont and his fleet handed the North a major success. Union newspapers were ecstatic as the North celebrated its biggest victory of the war so far. "Our Brilliant Naval Victory," trumpeted the *New York Herald;* "a heavy blow for the rebellion," declared the *New York Tribune;* the *New York Times* declared that "now, indeed, Sumter begins to be avenged!" Welles described the Union victory at Port Royal as a "brilliant achievement" in his 1861 annual report and praised Du Pont for his "consummate naval strategic skill."[31]

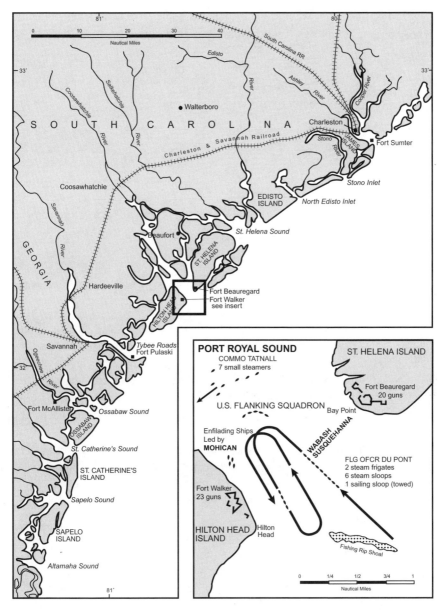

Charleston, South Carolina, and vicinity and the capture of the Port Royal forts, 7 November 1861

Du Pont's victory was even commemorated in verse by Herman Melville whose poem, "Dupont's Round Fight," celebrated the action at Port Royal.

In time and measure perfect moves
All Art whose name is sure;
Evolving rhyme and stars divine
Have rules, and they endure.

Nor less the Fleet that warred for Right,
And, warring so, prevailed,
In geometric beauty curved,
And in an orbit sailed.

The rebel at Port Royal felt
The Unity overawe,
And rued the spell. A type was here,
And victory of LAW.[32]

Naval landing parties supported by platoons of marines led by Commander John Rodgers quickly occupied both forts. The transports then proceeded to land the army's regiments, starting with General Wright's brigade followed in rapid succession by the rest of Sherman's forces. The day after the victory, Du Pont issued a congratulatory note to the fleet in which he acknowledged "the coolness, discipline, skill, and gallantry displayed by the officers and men under his command in the capture of the batteries on Hilton Head and Bay Point." It was a significant and emotional victory because for the first time since the war began "the ensign of the Union [was] flying once more in the State of South Carolina, which has been the chief promoter of the wicked and unprovoked rebellion [we] have been called upon to suppress."[33]

Du Pont went out of his way to praise the *Susquehanna*'s actions during the battle with a special message to Captain James L. Lardner, which read in part: "Your noble ship throughout the whole of the battle was precisely where I wanted her to be, and doing precisely what I wanted her to do, and . . . your close support of this ship was a very gallant thing." The senior Royal Navy officer in the area, Captain George Hancock, was impressed. He wrote that the attack was planned in a "bold and able manner, and that it was carried out with much Gallantry and Skill."[34] Du Pont and the local Royal Navy commanders established cordial relationships despite heightened diplomatic tensions between the two countries. This was due in large part to the personal friendships and acquaintances that Du Pont had developed with the Royal Navy during his many years at sea.

Consolidating their gains, Union forces moved to occupy Hilton Head Island—described by one participant as having "few inhabitants being principally Negroes and mosquitoes (the latter not few however)"—and two days later the town of Beaufort, South Carolina. Not only did Port Royal harbor provide a sanctuary and logistical base for the South Atlantic Blockading Squadron, but the occupation of the surrounding area placed a large Union ground force in a central position where it could threaten Charleston, Savannah, and the strategically vital Charleston and Savannah Railroad only twenty miles inland. While the loss of Port Royal was a major strategic setback for the Confederacy, it was also a huge economic disaster, for the populous area was one of the South's most agriculturally fertile regions, producing sea island cotton worth $3 million annually.[35] After Du Pont and Sherman had finished consolidating their base and occupying much of the key terrain surrounding Port Royal harbor, the blockade was much stronger than before, and the Confederates now had to be ready for Union offensives deep in their territory.

Du Pont had demonstrated over the span of his lengthy career considerable abilities as a reformer, military intellectual, combat leader, planner, strategist, navigator, and seaman. However, an assessment of his leadership during this battle must take into consideration the fact that he was the first United States naval officer to command such a large force. With impressive assistance from Welles, Fox, Davis, and both Rodgerses, and his handpicked and, in most cases, excellent captains, Du Pont had been able to pull the expedition together in about six weeks' time, an impressive feat by any measure, and particularly so in the Civil War. The crushing gale and equipment loses would have completely disrupted many, perhaps most, Civil War leaders on land and sea, resulting in a delayed attack until they could round up their force and replace their losses. Du Pont, on the other hand, was willing to take a calculated risk by not waiting for the reassembly of his entire fleet at Port Royal, and he demonstrated impressive flexibility when he changed his plan not once but twice before execution on 7 November. The final plan was excellent; it addressed both the fortifications and the threat posed by the Confederate naval force and provided for follow-on landings of army troops to consolidate and expand their gains. Du Pont's performance during the battle was unimpeachable. Several reports cite Du Pont's orders directing the *Wabash* closer and closer to Fort Walker and the way he stood unperturbed on the quarterdeck as Confederate shells passed nearby.[36] He demonstrated considerable physical courage, and when his forces did not conform to his directions, he improvised enough to secure victory.

Still, either because he communicated his intent to his captains poorly or because he failed to explain the plan adequately, several of his subordinates did not follow instructions. Writing six months after the fact, Du Pont stated his belief that if the rest of the ships had followed the *Wabash* and *Susquehanna* as planned, "a second turn would have finished the forts in two hours instead of four."[37] The official record, Du Pont's personal correspondence, and the papers of eyewitnesses give no indication that he ever disciplined in writing the captains who failed to conform to the plan of battle or to respond to his signals during the engagement. Indeed, Du Pont's official report of the battle reads as if the plan proceeded as written and does not describe Godon's excursion out of the main battle line. Aside from his first comment about the *Wabash* doing all the work, he mentioned nothing else about the departure from his plan. Given his propensity for harboring a grudge, it seems likely that Du Pont was not very upset about the incident.[38]

The editor of Du Pont's papers, John D. Hayes, suggests that this reflected Du Pont's "determination not to open a futile controversy."[39] However, it is also likely that Du Pont wanted to support the captains—most of whom were his very close friends—and give them the benefit of the doubt; the first two captains to pull out of the main line of battle, Godon and John P. Gillis, were long-time friends of Du Pont. From General Drayton's report it seems clear that Godon's ship and those that followed him into enfilading positions did significant damage to Fort Walker. Godon may have simply used his initiative to place his ship in a position he believed would better serve Du Pont's overall intent. Indeed, in a letter to Sophie written six days after the battle, in his only written reference to Godon's deviation from his orders, Du Pont wrote that he changed the subject during a conversation on board the flagship that touched on the episode. "There was no want of courage anywhere, but . . . a want of head. I think Godon was hurt at something I said. . . . [But] [m]y remark involved a compliment, by saying he wanted a fight on his *own hook*—but he connected this with the other affair [pulling out of the line], but I hope he will get over it soon." Du Pont expressed confidence in his old friend by temporarily transferring his flag to the *Mohican* after the battle, and Godon ultimately rose to the rank of rear admiral. Nevertheless, Welles, writing in his diary after the war, claimed that Godon had been indignant when reprimanded by Du Pont: "At Port Royal, Godon placed his vessel . . . in a position where she enfiladed the

Rebel batteries and literally drove them from their guns. Du Pont, instead of thanking, he says, insulted him for it."[40]

Du Pont discouraged any further discussion of the incident. Indeed, his letter to Sophie indicates that he recognized Godon's actions as the result of individual initiative, not cowardice or disobedience. It seems probable that Du Pont issued only oral reprimands to these officers if he was concerned at all; the flag officer, after all, was never shy about voicing his opinions and judgments. Clearly, however, just as the credit should go to Du Pont for the victory, it is also the fate of all commanders to receive the blame for any failures on the part of subordinates. But in the excitement that followed the triumph and amid the innumerable tasks that Du Pont had to accomplish to consolidate the victory, disciplining subordinates was a low priority. In sum, the Port Royal victory was an impressive one indeed, and it immediately propelled Du Pont into the top echelon of Union military leaders.

The battle also had a significant operational impact on the Union leadership and public. The conventional wisdom before the naval actions at Cape Hatteras and Port Royal was that ships could not easily defeat shore fortifications. As Russell Weigley put it, "It was a military truism confirmed by generations of experience and as recently as the Crimean War of 1853–1855 that ships cannot defeat forts." Indeed, before Port Royal this truism was something with which Du Pont could readily agree, based on his own writings from ten years before, his study of similar attacks in the Crimean War, and his observations of the shelling of the Dagu forts in China.[41] Instead of witnessing a depressing affirmation of an accepted military axiom, the public in 1861 was treated to not just one but two examples of modern steam warships defeating shore fortifications and doing so with very little loss to the attacking force. Both the Union public and its leadership now anticipated similar successes whenever a United States Navy force challenged a Confederate fortification. Flag Officer David G. Farragut's successful running of the batteries protecting New Orleans in April 1862 provided a powerful exclamation point to the navy's earlier success. Public and official expectations were now clear: navy forces should be able to defeat enemy forts, period. The Navy Department learned another—and perhaps more dangerous—lesson from Port Royal and Cape Hatteras: the navy could do it alone. Welles and Fox now expected the navy to take and hold key coastal facilities without conducting joint operations with the army.

However, what Du Pont's superiors failed to realize was that the flag officer faced a much different and more difficult tactical challenge at both Port Royal and later at Charleston than Farragut had encountered. In these operations, Du Pont had few options available to him other than direct—and at times frontal—attack of the enemy forts. They had to be defeated before further operations could be considered.

The Confederates had a mixed reaction to the Union occupation of Port Royal. The first was despair. Southern diarist Mary Chesnut upon learning of the capture wrote: "I was sobbing to break my heart. . . . Utter defeat at Port Royal." Two days after the battle, the *Charleston Mercury* observed, "The tidings of the disaster to our arms at Port Royal cast a gloom over our city yesterday." Chesnut and many other civilians believed strongly that the newly arrived Union forces at Port Royal would soon move on Charleston or Savannah. Newspapers noted: "The Capture of Port Royal created great excitement and considerable apprehension in Savannah. Families commenced packing up, and large numbers of females and children were sent from the city to the up-country." On the same day that the *Wabash* opened fire on Fort Walker, General Robert E. Lee arrived in Charleston as Jefferson Davis's personal representative to observe and make recommendations on how to improve the South's coastal defenses. Having learned of the defeat, Lee wrote to Secretary of War Judah P. Benjamin that "the enemy, having complete possession of the water and inland navigation, commands all the islands on this coast, and threatens both Savannah and Charleston." The loss of Port Royal convinced him that the previous Southern strategy of trying to defend the entire coast was untenable, and he proceeded to fortify the most strategically valuable areas and abandoned attempts to defend the rest of the coast. On 21 November 1861, shortly after the loss of Port Royal, Lee wrote: "The guns from the less important points have been removed, and are strengthening those considered of greater consequence. The entrance to Cumberland Sound and Brunswick and the water approaches to Savannah and Charleston are the only points which it is proposed to defend."[42] Thus in the space of less than two weeks, the entire Confederate strategy for the defense of its coasts changed because of Du Pont's success at Port Royal.

The consequences of the "brilliant achievement" at Port Royal were profound. "The defeat at Port Royal had broken the people's confidence" and forced the Confederacy to assume a defensive posture, losing any advantage it might have had on the South Carolina coast.[43] The United States seized the initiative, both in strengthening the blockade and being poised to strike at any of a number of vital points up and down the southern coast from Charleston to Key West. In addition, the victory did much to boost Union morale after months of inaction, defeat, and disappointment, and it created widespread consternation throughout southern coastal areas for many months. Du Pont and his fleet also provided the catalyst for further joint operations in the East. By implementing the plan prepared by the Blockade Board, Du Pont essentially executed a campaign plan. In other words, he conducted a series of military operations linked in time and space leading to a clearly defined strategic objective: the tightening and improving of the blockade. Until Grant's Vicksburg campaign of 1863, no Union commander except Du Pont had planned and conducted a true campaign that successfully achieved a clearly defined strategic objective. Du Pont's "blockade improvement campaign" (as apt a title as any) and Grant's Vicksburg campaign were planned with a clearly defined strategic objective in mind. In both campaigns the commanders never lost sight of this objective, even if, in the navy's case, the civilian leaders did.

It did not take long for minor friction to develop between Sherman and Du Pont. After the army commander issued a proclamation to the population, Du Pont complained to Fox, "Ought Sherman to have issued a proclamation without my knowledge?" Also, Du Pont was eager to continue his campaign to strengthen the blockade and to facilitate future joint operations by seizing additional bases: "I am exceedingly anxious to get away to Fernandina. . . . if I can get through that and some other points perhaps St. Helena, I can come back here & make a station of it."[44] But he was not at all impressed by the army: "The mistake . . . is to consider these . . . volunteers an army." Du Pont accused the army of being largely comprised of an unruly, ill-disciplined, and looting rabble. Worse yet was that Sherman's force was too small to accomplish much beyond securing the Port Royal area; 13,000 troops were insufficient to take Charleston. Du Pont believed that "it would be wiser to prepare for a heavy movement of 50,000 men on Charleston."[45] Soon after he had consolidated his gains around Port Royal, Du Pont realized that most of the operations he wanted to conduct would be predominately naval despite his desire to use the army in large-scale assaults.

The seizure of Port Royal—that "magnificent acquisition"—was not only critical for morale purposes, but it also provided a deepwater port that became the home base for the South Atlantic Blockading Squadron for the rest of the war. Maintaining a secure blockade of the South placed extreme strain on both crew and ship. Steam vessels on blockade relied much more on their engines than did naval ships occupied with other duties; Du Pont was "painfully aware of the worthlessness of sailing vessels" for the blockade.[46] When he commanded the *Minnesota* on his long voyage to China, he used his engine sparingly to conserve precious coal, but also to reduce wear and tear on the machinery. Captains on the blockade had no such luxury. The effectiveness of the blockade depended on a patrolling ship's ability to maintain its station in all weather conditions, and only the heavy and almost constant use of a ship's engines could achieve this end. This wear and tear on the engines required continuous maintenance that usually meant frequent and extended trips to navy yards. Consequently, Du Pont was immediately faced with two immense logistical requirements: a reliable and adequate supply of coal and suitable maintenance facilities. He failed to prepare adequately for the former, and fuel shortages plagued the squadron for some time. As K. Jack Bauer has observed, this was probably an oversight due to his and his chief of staff's limited steam experience.[47] However, Du Pont immediately requested and established a series of floating machine shops at Port Royal that drastically reduced the time wasted by ships in traveling to navy yards hundreds of miles to the north. Du Pont had observed the operation of floating maintenance facilities while in China and adapted them with great success to his own situation. He described the kind of maintenance facility he needed in a letter to Fox written only five days after the battle: "I have just remembered that during the Crimean and China wars by England and France vessels fitted up as machine shops were used with remarkable advantage, and gunboats and large steamers were always undergoing repairs."[48] His blockading fleet needed many of the same maintenance facilities that they would enjoy at a navy yard. Du Pont understood that at the level of war on which he operated, logistics was the key to success.

Once the department responded to his request for these shops, Du Pont was able to maintain extremely high readiness rates among his ships and greatly increased their time on station, improving the overall effectiveness of the blockade.[49] For the ships' crews, however, the monotony of life on the blockade was now relieved less often by greatly anticipated trips to desirable liberty ports. A trip to Beaufort for an engine overhaul was simply not the same as a voyage to New York or Philadelphia for a tired and bored crew.

Along the coastline from Charleston to Florida, the most important strategic sites—all identified earlier by the Blockade Board—were Charleston, Stono Inlet, North Edisto, South Edisto, Saint Helena, Savannah, Fort Pulaski, Tybee Island, Wassaw Sound, Ossabaw Sound, New Brunswick, and Fernandina. "Three Cheers for Du Pont!" a northern newspaper exclaimed when the flag officer seized Fernandina, an objective identified as one of the most important on the east coast. By early spring Du Pont had either seized or rendered impotent every site on the list except Charleston and Savannah, culminating with the army's capture of Fort Pulaski on 11 April 1862. He was particularly delighted to establish a foothold in Georgia, the home of Senators Alfred Iverson and Robert Toombs. These were men Du Pont had "a special reason for disliking, in addition to their treachery and rebellion," for both had played prominent roles derailing the work of the Efficiency Board.[50]

In addition, Du Pont's fleet sank old rock-filled merchant hulks in channels approaching Charleston and Savannah. The tides and river action in these waterways soon scoured new navigable routes, and the sinking of the "Stone Fleet"—an operation, Du Pont complained, that "gave me much trouble"—obstructed many of the entrances favored by blockade-runners for only a few weeks.[51] He conducted some of these operations with army assistance, some with naval force alone, but all placed continuing pressure on the Confederates and facilitated the increased effectiveness of the blockade. Still, Du Pont and his army counterparts had yet to seize the two most coveted points in his area of operations: Charleston and Savannah.

"I will cork up Savannah like a bottle," Du Pont wrote to Sherman two weeks after the victory at Port Royal. Although Du Pont and Sherman effectively fulfilled what at the time must have seemed a boastful prediction, the flag officer has received much unwarranted criticism over his subsequent actions after Port Royal. Some historians have criticized Du Pont for failure to seize the initiative immediately after Port Royal to capture, attack, or at least directly threaten Charleston or Savannah or both.[52] Du Pont certainly wanted to adopt this course of action, and at least one of his captains believed that Savannah "could have been taken by a regiment within forty-eight hours after the Port Royal affair I have not the least doubt." Still, despite the navy's enthusiasm and aggressive attitude, it is doubtful that Sherman's force of 13,000 could have accomplished such an undertaking. Any attack on either city—Charleston being a much tougher objective—would have required considerable army augmentation. Savannah is nearly forty miles from Port Royal, and Charleston is over sixty miles away, making an attack overland very difficult. Furthermore, Lee began immediately to pull troops and guns away from indefensible areas and concentrate them at these two strategic points. Even with a carefully planned and executed joint operation including aggressive commanders from both services, success in such an endeavor would have been highly problematic. While admitting that land operations were "not my province," Du Pont nonetheless argued that the army's force at Port Royal "should be largely increased and a regular campaign in the South be commenced."[53] The army always considered these joint operations to be secondary efforts at best. At this time during the war, most military planners and commanders saw Richmond as the key to Union victory.

Less challenging would have been an attempt to cut the vitally important Charleston and Savannah Railroad, which ran only twenty miles from the base at Port Royal. However, a succession of Union army commanders suffering from a decided lack of aggressiveness (not unlike that plaguing Major General George B. McClellan) grossly overestimated the size of the enemy forces in the region. A halfhearted attempt to disrupt the railroad in October 1862 followed an abortive land operation against Charleston in June 1862. Finally, Du Pont was unable to persuade the army to do much of anything beyond routine occupation duties. Indeed, he could only suggest and try to bring indirect pressure to bear. This he did on numerous occasions, but until the short-lived command of Major General Ormsby Mac-Knight Mitchel in September 1862, Du Pont was beset with distinctly timid army counterparts. Still, the most important mission for Du Pont and his squadron was to establish a tight and effective blockade.

Despite the limitations within which he operated as commander of the South Atlantic Blockading Squadron when it came to the conduct of joint operations along the coast, Du Pont's primary mission after Port Royal was to apply ever-increasing and effective pressure against the rebels with his blockade. This task, Du Pont confided to Sophie, was "the most difficult part of my command . . . since I have got down here." The important but largely peripheral operations of "cruising, the reconnaissances, [and] the occupations go very well," but the flag officer grew frustrated over the running of his blockade by several Confederate steamers and the inattentiveness of some of his captains to their duty. Du Pont was particularly displeased with the exploits of Commander Gillis, whose inaction on the blockade allowed the rebel blockade-runner *Fingal* to escape and caused the flag officer to "lose my equanimity for the first time since I hoisted my flag in this ship." Another such performance, declared Du Pont, would force him to send "Gillis home under charges."[54]

Yet the conditions under which the blockading squadrons operated (especially along the Atlantic coastal regions) were trying at best. Shallow shoal waters, difficult tides, ships with limited endurance and range, and poor weather were just a few of the challenges facing blockading captains. Boredom, poor food, heat, limited leave opportunities, and blockade-runners that were invariably faster than their pursuers only added to their trials.[55] Percival Drayton, who served as one of Du Pont's captains until 1863, remarked somewhat defensively but accurately that "the difficulty in blockading is owing to the number of entrances for small vessels on this coast, many of which we have only found out lately and which even had we known of sooner it would have been next to impossible to close with the comparatively small number of vessels at the command of Du Pont."[56]

The area surrounding Charleston, the most porous region for blockade-runners in Du Pont's area of operations, was particularly difficult to shut down "owning to the great distances that the different entrances are apart." Indeed, wrote Drayton, "I am satisfied that ten vessels are scarcely sufficient . . . and we have scarcely been able to spare . . . more than two or three." Drayton's first lieutenant, Alfred Thayer Mahan, also observed that even with the newly captured base at Port Royal, lack of fuel and the limited range of the blockading fleet "constituted a very serious embarrassment on such duty as that of the South Carolina and Georgia coasts." Nevertheless, by late May 1862 Du Pont was able to reinforce the Charleston blockade, which often numbered over ten ships.[57]

As the work of the squadron progressed, Du Pont was able to observe and evaluate his senior officers. He lost confidence in some, such as John Gillis and John Missroon, but with the great majority, he found much to approve. Du Pont had chosen his subordinates well and had surrounded himself with highly competent officers—whom Gideon Welles would later dismissively refer to as Du Pont's "clique"[58]—most of whom would ultimately earn flag rank. Foremost among this group were Charles Henry Davis, C. R. P. Rodgers, Daniel Ammen, Percival Drayton, and John Rodgers. Some of his other officers viewed Du Pont's close relationship with many of his senior subordinates with resentment. Commander John B. Marchand of the *James Adger* and Lieutenant Daniel Ammen of the *Seneca* were particularly upset that Davis and the two Rodgerses had led several of the most daring, important, and visible expeditions in the months since Port Royal. The plum assignments handed to these "three favorites," wrote an annoyed Marchand, "has given me a most thorough disgust for Commodore Du Pont's administration of affairs here."[59]

Marchand was by no means the only junior officer who felt this way, but such jealousies are common in any military organization, as is the tendency for a commander to form close personal and professional bonds with his most trusted (and usually senior) subordinates. Marchand, however, was premature in his criticism, for Du Pont soon included the *James Adger* on several important missions, among them the expedition to seize Fernandina and Stono Inlet and command of the blockading ships outsider Charleston. Du Pont's confidence in Marchand was well founded as his bold action in crossing the bar at Stono Inlet revealed that Charleston was vulnerable to a land attack across James Island. However, the army bungled the subsequent Secessionville operation against Charleston in June 1862.[60]

Commanders also chafed at Du Pont's seeming unwillingness to share his plans with them. However, poor operational security had burned Du Pont before while chairman of the Blockade Board and during the Port Royal operation. His General Order Number 8, issued in February 1862, gives an indication of his obsession with security: "Nothing, in the suppression of this rebellion has been more difficult to contend with than information conveyed to the enemy of projected movements . . . by individuals hold-ing places of trust . . . not infrequently by the publication of personal let-ters. . . . I hereby enjoin it upon every officer and man of this fleet to avoid such a violation of military propriety. . . . Intended or not, the result of the practice is to give aid and comfort to the enemy."[61]

Thus from an operational standpoint, it was prudent for Du Pont to re-strict knowledge of his plans to his chief of staff and flag captain in most cases. The subsequent success achieved by these "favorites" and many oth-ers in the squadron make it clear that Du Pont's "clique" had more in com-mon with Admiral Horatio Nelson's "band of brothers" than with an obse-quious group of mindless sycophants as later alleged by Welles. In describing Du Pont's judgment in matters of personnel, one contemporary remarked: "Nearly all [of Du Pont's] commanding officers reached high rank. . . . Eleven of them attain[ed] the rank of rear admiral."[62] Subordinates de-scribed Du Pont's manner of leadership and discourse between fellow offi-cers as unfailingly courtly, polite, friendly, courteous, generous, kind, and gracious. The flag officer treated his officers with great respect and sensitiv-ity even when they probably did not deserve such conduct. His men were all given fair chances for distinction; those who succeeded gained the com-mander's trust and positions of greater authority and responsibility. Those who did not were given another chance, then reassigned to another squad-ron or given duties commensurate with their abilities.

Many of the naval officers who led the Union fleet at Port Royal faced another challenge in some ways more daunting than that posed by geogra-phy and the Confederates: the slavery issue. The realities of Southern plan-tation slavery challenged the preconceived beliefs of the officers and forced them to address matters such as the Union educational, occupational, and subsistence policy toward the ex-slaves. With the arrival of the Union fleet, the white population of the region deserted their plantations and fled inland or to Charleston and Savannah. Many attempted to escape with their slaves; some masters shot those who resisted, but most simply abandoned their bondsmen. Remarkably, to some observers, there was little visible property damage; the newly free slaves did not strike out at their ex-masters by de-stroying homes or property.[63]

A scant seven weeks after bombarding the forts—what the area's slaves would call "the day of the big-gun shoot"[64]—Du Pont wrote to Sophie, "My ideas have undergone great change as to the condition of the slaves since I came here and have been on the plantations." He went on to insist that he was still a constitutional conservative on the institution, but he had been wrong when he had argued in the past that slavery was "*patriarchal* in the

U.S. compared with the condition of the race in Africa." "God forgive me," Du Pont exclaimed. "I have seen nothing that has disgusted me more than the wretched physical wants of these poor people, who earn all the gold spent by their masters at Saratoga and Europe. No wonder they stand shooting down rather than go back to their owners."[65] Du Pont would never again defend slavery, and as he uncovered more of slavery's horrors, his attitude toward the South hardened even more.

As historian C. Vann Woodward noted, the 10,000 slaves left behind were at first uncertain whether the Union soldiers and sailors were "liberators or . . . a new set of masters," and the commanders were themselves unsure about the policy they should follow.[66] Neither Du Pont nor Sherman had received guidance from their service secretaries or the president on how they should treat the ex-slaves, nor had they developed any plan before the expedition to address the disposition of the ex-slaves. They probably believed that no plan was necessary because they assumed that rebel masters would simply carry off the slaves when they evacuated or that the slaves would flee on their own. This oversight contributed to much of the frustration experienced by ex-slaves and volunteer Northerners from benevolent organizations who flocked to the Port Royal area to aid them. Fortunately for the slaves freed by the arrival of the Du Pont's fleet, however, both commanders were sympathetic to their plight.

Soon after their arrival at Port Royal, Sherman and Du Pont assessed the situation of the ex-slaves and immediately took action to help alleviate their wretched condition. However, as winter arrived and the temperature dropped, the Union commanders quickly realized that the military alone could not care for the freedmen while conducting active combat operations. Virtually everything was needed: food, clothing, housing, medical care, and schooling. Du Pont and Sherman were finally forced to make an appeal to Northern charitable organizations for help. Their request for freedmen aid was widely circulated in the North, and soon it paid dividends. Many in the North desperately wanted the freed blacks not only to receive humanitarian aid but also to assist actively in the war effort. Such Washington notables as Charles Sumner, Salmon P. Chase, and William Seward all championed the ex-slaves at Port Royal and joined the plea for help. In February 1862 Du Pont happily exclaimed that "we have all kinds of agents out here—cotton collectors, statistic collectors, humanitarians, philanthropists, etc., the best among them the people of God, starting schools." Consequently, Du Pont threw his full support to the charitable organizations that set up in the Port Royal area to care for the needs of the ex-slaves. So supportive was he of the work of the benevolent groups in Port Royal to help the ex-slaves that in

June 1862 the newly formed National Freedman's Relief Association of New York passed a resolution of appreciation to Du Pont for his "evidences of personal care and kindness" shown to their workers.[67]

Although there would be some natural friction between the military men and the members of the benevolent organizations that flocked to Port Royal, in general the relations between the two groups were cordial and cooperative. Du Pont actively sought to employ freedmen in his machine shops and used them to fill out crew shortages in some of his vessels. He also supported the efforts by some of his captains to establish additional colonies where the ex-slaves could start their own farms and settle their families far away from the plantations that still evoked such bitter memories. As he learned more about the desperate plight of the region's black population and their treatment under the previous regime, Du Pont began to censure those who opposed emancipation, even good friends. When both Delaware senators voted against emancipation in the nation's capital, Du Pont was incensed, writing, "Mr. [Willard] Saulsbury and Mr. Bayard don't wish these men gradually freed; they must return to a pound of meal, one suit of very bad clothes, rarely meat, to whips with knots, to nails driven through the soft parts of their ears, and to the bloodhounds." This letter is particularly telling because James A. Bayard had been one of Du Pont's staunchest defenders during the Efficiency Board controversy. By April 1862 Du Pont was no longer a political conservative on slavery, and he proudly proclaimed to Sophie that "there is not a proslavery man" to be found among his officers.[68] When Sherman's replacement, General David Hunter, issued a general order in May 1862 purporting to free all the slaves in South Carolina, Georgia, and Florida, Du Pont was mildly offended that Hunter had not discussed his proclamation with him, but he did not question the message. Indeed, Du Pont was certain that slavery was ultimately doomed. "The death knell of slavery was sounded when that first gun was fired on Sumter," he declared. But he wondered if the government sanctioned Hunter's actions or if the general was motivated by political aspirations. To the great dismay of many of the benevolent societies at work in Port Royal, less than two weeks after it was issued, Lincoln rescinded the order as Du Pont predicted.[69]

One of Hunter's actions did receive Du Pont's approval: the drafting and organizing of black military units both to help relieve the burden on white troops for securing important logistics bases but also for the slaves' own defense. A reporter interviewed Du Pont as he watched one of Hunter's new regiments drill. Du Pont had arrived in the South "a thorough believer in the hopelessness of elevating the negro race," declared the correspondent, "but like Paul on the road to Damascus, he has seen a great light." Indeed,

Ex-slaves from the plantation of Confederate general Thomas F. Drayton freed by Du Pont and his fleet with the seizure of Port Royal, South Carolina. (Courtesy of the Massachusetts Commandery of the Military Order of the Loyal Legion of the United States and the United States Army Military History Institute)

the reporter went on, the admiral was "not ashamed to confess a total revolution of opinion in regard to the Negro question since he has been brought face to face with its realities." Although Hunter's project died that summer due to lack of funds to equip and pay the new soldiers, the experience paved the way for other successful ventures along the same lines. Du Pont wrote some months later that the ex-slaves he had seen "make excellent soldiers and are brave."[70]

Du Pont was a witness to an incident of extraordinary courage on 13 May 1862, when the Confederate armed steamer *Planter* surrendered to his blockading ships outside Charleston harbor. A crewman on the *Planter*, slave Robert Smalls, along with several other slaves and their families, had orchestrated the ship's daring capture and escape. After days of planning and waiting for just the right moment, Smalls and his gallant band of fifteen fellow slaves waited until the white crew had gone ashore for the evening and, knowing all of the Confederate recognition signals, were able to bluff their way past the formidable harbor defenses and out to the Union blockaders.

As the leader of this audacious act, Smalls was taken to Port Royal for an interview with Du Pont. Smalls's story delighted Du Pont, who proclaimed the now ex-slave "a hero." The detailed intelligence on Charleston's defenses provided by Smalls led directly to the capture of Stono Inlet and the subsequent—although ultimately unsuccessful—Union threat to Charleston's right flank. The *Planter* was immediately pressed into service by the squadron, and Smalls became a trusted pilot, leading an ironclad into battle a year later and eventually commanding his own ship. During Reconstruction he served several terms in the United States Congress. The *Planter* incident and other acts of individual and collective heroism convinced Du Pont that blacks could be effective soldiers.[71]

Du Pont was not the only member of the squadron who changed his views on slavery. None of the men who arrived at Port Royal were "prepared for what we have seen of the *institution*, and the Southern officers, of which this squadron has so many, seem more shocked than any others." South Carolina native Percival Drayton underwent a conversion similar to that of Du Pont, although he had long harbored a distrust of slavery. After serving in the area for a few weeks, Drayton recognized the basic humanity of the region's slaves. "My brother [Confederate general Thomas F. Drayton, the defender of Port Royal] . . . thinks that they [slaves] cannot be looked upon as persons, my answer to him was, that when a poor woman comes crying to me for the loss of her children or husband, but whom she could join by returning to a state of slavery, of which I have had many instances, I cannot but think that at least she has two of the distinctive attributes of the rest of the human race, love of liberty and offspring."[72]

Drayton completed his conversion to full-fledged abolitionist when, some months later, he wrote that "I must confess that after what I have seen here, of the horrors of the institution[,] I would be willing to do anything except to destroy the constitution" to force an end to slavery. With pre-war slavery beliefs similar to his commander's, Lieutenant Mahan also became a solid antislavery man after a short stay with the South Atlantic Blockading Squadron.[73] All of these men and many more—although few actually supported slavery before the war—underwent serious attitude modification after viewing the plight of the ex-slaves in the Port Royal area. Long-held beliefs in property rights, states' rights, white supremacy, black inhumanity, and other cherished but somewhat abstract concepts could not stand against the images of suffering and deprivation that these men witnessed firsthand. Most of them left Port Royal hating slavery and longing for its end, and many were convinced of the same basic humanity and equality of the ex-slaves to their white liberators.

It was one thing to become a staunch opponent of slavery as Du Pont and most of his officers had; it was another thing entirely to come up with a solution. As early as February 1862, Du Pont advocated immediate freedom for slaves in Confederate territory and, at war's end, compensated emancipation of slaves in the loyal border states. When Lincoln issued the preliminary Emancipation Proclamation in September, Du Pont thought it long overdue: "I thank my God we have the Proclamation." Two months later Du Pont tried to explain his radical change of heart in an emotional letter to Sophie. He had come to recognize, as had President Lincoln, that no reunion of North and South could possibly occur without the end of slavery. "Since I have seen slavery in its full . . . atrocities so far beyond anything I could have conceived, human beings treated like brutes, overworked, cruelly punished and starved to boot, I can hardly believe that a merciful God intended that we should come together again as before and that the power of the North should be added to that of the South in maintaining again and perpetuating such cruel destitution and misery to four millions of his people. . . . There is no gentleman in the North would keep his horse, cow, or pig as these creatures are kept."[74] In a year Du Pont had evolved from a tacit supporter of slavery to an advocate for the immediate abolition of slavery everywhere, including the border states. Although it is doubtful that Du Pont believed in full equality of the races, he did support the organizing of black regiments and, ultimately, full citizenship and suffrage. These antislavery views also led to his full embrace of the Republican Party.

Sophie, having had almost no firsthand experience with slavery, did not embrace her husband's change of heart and indeed wrote many times trying unsuccessfully to convince him that he was wrong: "You will have seen by some of my previous letters that I do not concur in all your opinions about slavery. I know it to be a great wrong and a great curse. But I do not think that justified us in doing wrong [taking slaves from their owners] to hasten its end." Despite his best efforts, Du Pont was never able to convince Sophie that slavery had to be destroyed and the ex-slaves be made citizens. Sophie countered that the abolitionists were to blame for any wrongs that Du Pont had witnessed and that the "contrabands" should not be freed outright. The government, Sophie argued, must take over their care until after the war when the "nation decides what to do with them."[75] Although Sophie would ultimately come out against slavery by the end of the war, this was one of the couple's very few areas of disagreement.

As offensive operations wound down, Du Pont devoted his full attention to the blockade. Coal shortages, the constant requirement for maintenance, and a shortage of ships continued to hamper his efforts to seal the Confederate coast throughout his tenure as commander of the South Atlantic Blockading Squadron. Although as many as five of six blockade-runners evaded the Union warships, Du Pont and Welles were convinced that they were having a considerable impact on the Confederate economy and war effort. Du Pont declared that "no blockade in the history of the world has ever been more effective, particularly when the extent and character of our coast in all its features are considered." "In no previous war," echoed Welles in December 1862, "had the ports of an enemy's country been so effectively closed by a naval force." Indeed, the South Atlantic Blockade Squadron under Du Pont captured sixty-nine blockade-running vessels worth a total of over $2.5 million. Du Pont and his officers and men profited from these captures through the time-honored tradition of awarding prize money. During his command Du Pont received a total of $75,000 for these captures, a considerable sum in those days.[76]

However, the effectiveness of the Union navy's blockade has been a contentious subject for historians for some time.[77] The two most persuasive and nuanced assessments belong to James M. McPherson and David G. Surdam. McPherson maintains that evasions of the blockade are almost irrelevant. "Rather," he argues, "one must ask how many ships carrying how much freight would have entered southern ports if there had been no blockade." Likewise, it mattered little how many blockade-runners were sunk; the important thing was how many regular merchant ships were kept in port. Surdam, echoing McPherson's thesis and taking it one step further, maintains that while the blockade had significant direct payoffs for the Union war effort, it was more important for its indirect effects on the Southern economy. Surdam claims that the blockade "severely reduced exports of staple products and curtailed Southern purchasing power" and it significantly "deranged interregional movement of goods."[78] In addition, the fleet's operations "depressed the prices of and revenues from staples such as cotton, tobacco, and sugar within the South while simultaneously raising the prices of imported products." The blockade also hampered and in many cases eliminated the ability of the Confederates to use their river and intercoastal transportation systems. Surdam concludes, and McPherson would certainly agree, that although he "hesitates to label the blockade a 'sufficient condition' for Union victory, one can think of it as a 'necessary' one."[79]

McPherson's logic coupled with Surdam's comprehensive analysis of the blockade's impact on the Southern economy and its role in the defeat of the Confederacy convincingly vindicates the product of Du Pont's strategic vision, planning, and campaign execution. The flexibility demonstrated by Du Pont and his staff during the blockade improvement campaign of October 1861 through April 1862 was excellent. The Port Royal expedition was but the first part of this campaign, followed by the seizure or isolation of other strategic points on the southern coast from Charleston to Key West. Often in cooperation with army forces but frequently going it alone, Du Pont and his squadron had tightened the blockade significantly, threatened invasion along multiple points, forced the Confederacy to change its defensive strategy, and set the conditions for future operations throughout the region. In addition, he gave his subordinate commanders numerous opportunities to participate in and lead independent operations. These challenges contributed to their personal and professional development; many of these men would rise to high flag rank and would lead the postwar navy. The relationships among these senior officers were congenial while they conducted the very challenging blockade mission. Du Pont had set a very positive command climate through his leadership, example, good humor, and tactical and technical competence. After the seizure of Fort Pulaski, however, Gideon Welles and Gustavus Fox pressured Du Pont to turn his attention to the biggest prize of all: Charleston.

8

The Objective Is Charleston

The fall of Satan's Kingdom.

— GUSTAVUS V. FOX

THE IMPORTANCE of the historic 9 March 1862 battle between the USS *Monitor* and CSS *Virginia* was not lost on Du Pont when he first heard the news while conducting the Fernandina expedition. His first reaction was one of shock at the large loss of life aboard the two Union wooden warships, *Cumberland* and *Congress*, sunk by the *Virginia* the day before. He noted that the timely arrival of the *Monitor* was "a special interposition of Providence." Several of Du Pont's friends and acquaintances were killed on the *Cumberland,* and his old Mexican War command, the *Congress,* was sunk. Du Pont's old friend Franklin Buchanan commanded the *Virginia.* Tossing restlessly throughout the night, Du Pont contemplated this momentous news and lamented that ships like his beautiful old command the *Minnesota* were now "dwarfed down to a thing like a mousetrap." Yet, Du Pont reflected, if the navy must transform itself to put down the rebellion, then it must do whatever was necessary. Du Pont rejoiced that the United States Navy was now in the lead technologically: "The *Monitor*, not the *Merrimack*, is the standard for all." [1]

Shortly after receiving this important news, Du Pont faced his own ironclad threat. News that the Confederates had begun converting the steamer *Fingal,* renamed *Atlanta,* into an ironclad at Savannah evoked a feeling of "*oppression*" in the flag officer. [2] An entirely different emotion predominated in the halls of the Navy Department after the battle. Both Secretary Welles and his assistant now turned their full attention to the capture of Charleston with the advent of the new wonder weapon.

In two ways Charleston was the biggest challenge Du Pont and his squadron faced: first, blockading the port but also, at the urging of both Gideon Welles and Gustavus Fox, capturing the city as well. As early as April 1862, after most of the squadron's coastal operations had concluded, Du Pont began to receive a series of messages directing him to turn his attention toward the seat of the rebellion itself. The *Monitor*'s dramatic victory at Hampton Roads in March emboldened the Navy Department in ways that would prove to be disastrous for both Du Pont and the service. Less than a month after the *Monitor*'s debut, and days before the fall of Fort Pulaski, Fox laid out his design for Du Pont's fleet. "Our summer's work must be Charleston by the navy. We can give you the *Monitor* and *Galena* [the Union's second ironclad], iron vessels, the former can go up to Charleston and return in perfect safety. . . . What do you say to it, and what should you require besides these vessels? I should like your views, and be enabled to give to you the crowning act of retribution."[3]

In a letter written the same day as Fox's remarkable communication, Du Pont outlined a much different concept, one that would require at least 5,000 army troops to achieve the same goal as that proposed by the assistant secretary.[4] (And as it turned out, his figure vastly underestimated the troops that would be required to take Charleston.) The two letters demonstrate a stark contrast in thinking between the Navy Department and its commander in the field. From the beginning Du Pont strongly advocated a joint operation with a robust army force operating in concert with a formidable naval fleet. Welles and Fox, however, wanted Du Pont to take Charleston with an all-navy force supplemented with the new miracle weapon: ironclads or, more specifically, monitors. This difference in outlook toward what was required to take Charleston would form the basis for a misunderstanding that prevented an adequate assessment of the navy's newly acquired technology.

The Union's 1863 Charleston operation is noteworthy for several reasons. First, it illustrates the tension that can exist between civilian and military leadership over the development and execution of theater strategy and operations. Close examination of this operation—the preparation, training, planning, and execution—sheds light on Du Pont's abilities as a high-level commander and the Navy Department's relationship with one of its top subordinates. Second, Du Pont's attack on Charleston in April 1863 marked the first time in history that an all-ironclad fleet was used in combat. The famous action between the USS *Monitor* and the CSS *Virginia* (formerly the *Merrimack*) was in reality only a brief, albeit important, tactical engagement. Du Pont's ironclad fleet at Charleston, however, marked the first integration of this revolutionary technology into the navy's larger organization. How the

United States Navy evaluated and integrated this new ironclad technology into the fleet and how the navy's line leadership received this equipment are fruitful lines of underexplored inquiry. In the end, the Navy Department's obsession with the monitor class of ironclad forced a relatively untried, flawed, and unsuitable weapon system on a field commander and his subordinates who recognized the ships' incompatibility with the mission they had to undertake.

Fox followed up his initial suggestion with more prodding, but this time with distinct emphasis on an all-navy operation: "We are ready to give you a force for Charleston. . . . If we give you the *Galena* and the *Monitor*, don't you think we can go squarely at it by the Channel, so as to make it *purely navy?* . . . If you can finish Charleston with the Navy, the Country will rejoice above all other victories."[5] Fox and Welles clearly wanted the navy to strike a major blow, not for any specific strategic or operational advantage but to bring attention to their service in a war in which the army was receiving the bulk of the credit.

For Du Pont, who had advocated close cooperation with the army since his *Report on the National Defences* and the Mexican War and had approached most of the operations in his area of responsibility with a joint perspective, this suggestion was jarring. The flag officer was as jealous of the navy's reputation as any officer on active duty, probably more than most, but he had witnessed the critical importance of army-navy cooperation since the Mexican War, and his experiences in command of the South Atlantic Blockading Squadron had only strengthened those convictions. The department's insistence on an all-navy operation against Charleston was not his only concern; after months during which Du Pont and his officers had looked for ways to get at Charleston, he was certain that Welles and Fox had grossly underestimated the strength of Charleston's defenses and the ability of ironclads to defeat them. Du Pont's reply to Fox's second letter clearly outlined his concerns: "Do not underrate the work; all the defenses for one year now have been *seaward*. . . . The middle ground is also fortified. . . . Then you know we go into a bag, no running past, for after we get up they can all play upon us."[6] A "bag" is an apt description. Any attacking ship that made it past Fort Sumter would be vulnerable to fire from several sides in a very constricted channel. Du Pont was reminding Fox that Charleston would not be a Port Royal or a New Orleans; there would be no simple running of the fortifications here. Indeed, Charleston's fortifications were much more formidable, and there was no clear channel into which the passing naval force could safely take refuge once they were past Fort Sumter. The only thing that awaited the attacking force once they passed Fort Sumter was additional fortifications.

When the first attempt by Union ironclad vessels to attack shore fortifications took place at Drewry's Bluff on the James River and was repulsed on 15 May 1862 with heavy casualties, it seemed to prove the prescience of Du Pont's cautioning note to Fox. Commander John Rodgers led a small flotilla including the *Monitor* and *Galena*—the two ships Welles and Fox thought sufficient to take Charleston—against Fort Darling, guarding the approaches to Richmond seven miles south of the Confederate capital. A combination of fierce gunfire and river obstructions defeated Rodgers's efforts. The *Monitor* once more proved that she could take a good deal of punishment, but the *Galena*—a completely different ironclad design—suffered terribly in the four-hour action. Upon learning of this defeat, Du Pont wrote that it "was a very ill-advised and incorrect operation to expose these gunboats before the Army could take the forts in the rear—but there is no use; our troops will not fight if gunboats are within their reach."[7] The flag officer knew that a well-sited, equipped, and manned shore fortification usually had a distinct advantage over ships no matter how effective their defensive armor. However, the decisive repulse of the *Monitor* and *Galena* at the hands of eight guns in an earthen fort did nothing to dampen Fox's and Welles's confidence in the monitor-type ironclad. In the eyes of the Navy Department, the monitor-class ironclad could do anything.

Du Pont may not have had the best luck with army-navy cooperation, nor did he have a particularly high opinion of army officers and troops, but he knew that little of significance on shore could be accomplished without them. Two days later he wrote Fox a letter in which, even though he had not seen a monitor, he identified the limitations of the design and urged caution and deliberation. Once again he laid out the flaws in the department's belief that Charleston—which Du Pont again described as a "'cul de sac' or bag"—could be taken by naval force alone: "I see with regret the want of success in the James River with the iron boat, showing more invulnerability on the part of the *Monitor* than power of aggression. Think coolly and dispassionately on the main object [Charleston]. . . . I merely allude to all this, that your own intelligent and brave mind may not be carried away by a superficial view of recent events."[8]

But the defeat at Drewry's Bluff and the admonition of their senior commander on the spot did nothing to dampen the enthusiasm of both Welles and Fox at the prospect of gaining the top prize. Fox in particular was undeterred. In his answer to Du Pont's cautionary note, Fox wrote: "I notice . . . your remarks about the Harbor at Charleston. It may be impossible, but the crowning act of this war ought to be by the navy. I feel that my duties are two fold; first, to beat our southern friends; second, to beat the Army." After this astonishing admission, Fox reemphasized his unqualified faith in the ironclad. "The *Monitor* can go all over the harbor and return with impunity. She is absolutely impregnable. . . . I pray you give us Charleston if possible, but in any event, the Dept relies upon your judgment . . . for the fall of Charleston is the fall of Satan's Kingdom." Not all of his captains shared Du Pont's sentiments. Daniel Ammen, yearning for action and venting his frustration with blockade duty outside Charleston, wrote that "we wait most impatiently for some of the iron clads and the prospect of an attack on this despicable hole." [9]

Du Pont was appalled by the department's attitude. He confided to Sophie that the department was "very quiet" about the failure of the ironclads at Drewry's Bluff; he dismissed Fox's faith in the virtues of the *Monitor* and repeated his call for a joint operation: "Fox thought the *Monitor*, and thinks yet, could play around, go up, and return—and she may—but, since the affairs at the Bluff in James River, her power of offense is not much, for an ordinary open fort hastily thrown up resisted all her efforts, and John Rodgers fought his ship magnificently but was knocked all to pieces. . . . Now Charleston *must fall* and will fall, but the time for coup de mains, naval or military, is all passed; it must be regularly approached." [10]

The challenge that Du Pont now faced in light of the department's increasing pressure on him to take Charleston was how aggressively he should push his own concept. Deeply concerned with his reputation, Du Pont failed to counter the expectations of his civilian masters forthrightly with his own proposals. Still, he felt that Welles and Fox had to see things his way since he was supplying the department with information that "will make them pause before any impulsive order." Preferring to pursue a conservative, indirect approach rather than direct confrontation, Du Pont forwarded to the assistant secretary in early July several letters from Percival Drayton—respected greatly by both Fox and Welles—advocating joint operations through James Island (forming the southern shore of Charleston harbor) as the only way to take the city. [11]

The disastrous Battle of Secessionville in June 1862 had done nothing to change Du Pont's mind about the vital importance of joint operations against Charleston. The escape of Robert Smalls in the *Planter* on 16 May 1862 was an intelligence coup of the first order for Du Pont and his army counterpart, General David Hunter. Smalls revealed that the Confederates had abandoned their positions guarding the seaward approaches to James Island. This left the back door to Charleston open from an attack across the island. Du Pont immediately recognized the opportunity for a coup de main joint operation that might just be able to seize Charleston itself. Consequently, Du Pont and Major General Hunter landed two divisions along with considerable naval support on James Island on 2 June. Instead of taking advantage of his excellent opportunity and pushing forward against very slight resistance, Hunter took counsel of his fears and believed he was heavily outnumbered. Leaving Brigadier General Henry W. Benham in command, Hunter directed him not to attack until ordered. For two weeks the Union forces dithered; Confederate commanders recognized the threat to Charleston's flank and reinforced the island. When Benham attacked rebel positions on 16 June near the town of Secessionville in direct violation of his orders, the Union troops were badly beaten with heavy losses. Hunter, fearing a Confederate counterattack, abandoned his forward positions and evacuated James Island. Like countless other occasions during the Civil War, it was a missed opportunity. Charleston might have been captured at relatively low cost. They would never have another chance like this one. Du Pont was disgusted: the joint operation on James Island was clearly, he wrote to Sophie, "the finest operation (I will say this to you) in its *promise* of results since the capture of the Port Royal forts." Upon reflection a few weeks later, he sarcastically complained to Fox about the military incompetence he had witnessed: "Oh those Soldiers I put them nearly on *top* of the house in Charleston, but I did not push them into the windows and they came back." Still, the Secessionville debacle only reinforced Du Pont's conviction about the vital importance of joint operations, provided they were properly conducted.[12]

Du Pont lost several opportunities to press his views. Sending the *Wabash* home to the Philadelphia Navy Yard in July for a much-needed refit and leave for the crew, he ordered his flag captain, C. R. P. Rodgers—also acting as de facto chief of staff after the reassignment of Charles Henry Davis—to confer with Fox and Welles on some issues he deemed critical. Chief among the topics discussed were promotions for deserving officers, vessel maintenance, and a request for additional ships better suited for blockade duty. During their meetings, however, Rodgers was unable to convince Welles and Fox that the proposed attack on Charleston must be a joint operation. Du Pont was shocked to receive a letter from Welles days after his meeting with Rodgers stating: "The Navy, ordinarily considered as incidental to land operations, has come to be considered as primary and principal. . . . Great success has brought great responsibility." Success had also brought great, and misguided, expectations. Sophie traveled to Philadelphia to speak to Rodgers and discovered to her horror that "the Department still intended you to do it [take Charleston from the sea]." She sadly exclaimed that Rodgers's revelation "affected me very much—knowing the almost impossibility of it."[13] Despite his disappointment in Rodgers's failure to sway Welles and Fox, Du Pont spent the summer believing that he had conveyed adequately his reservations about an all-navy attack on Charleston in his letters to Fox. He was wrong.

As the foundation for the Charleston misunderstanding was being laid, Du Pont reached the pinnacle of his profession. On 16 July 1862, having already received a resolution of thanks by Congress for his victory at Port Royal, Du Pont—along with the two more senior officers, Farragut and Goldsborough, as well as Foote—was promoted to the rank of rear admiral thanks to a recently passed navy act. These men were the first admirals in the history of the United States Navy. Two of Du Pont's former subordinates, Charles Henry Davis and James Lardner, were promoted to commodore. Du Pont happily told Sophie, "I am called 'Admiral' now by everybody— funny, is it not?" and asked, "Do you remember Mr. Jefferson's letter to Grandpa?" Forty-seven years before, Thomas Jefferson had secured midshipman and West Point cadet appointments for Du Pont. When Du Pont chose the navy, Jefferson wrote his grandfather that he hoped the young man would one day become one of the country's "high-Admirals." Now Du Pont had finally reached the position foretold by the third president.[14] It was a significant achievement by any measure, enhancing the reputation the thin-skinned Du Pont carefully protected.

The secretary and Fox, probably reacting to Du Pont's descriptions of the formidable Charleston defenses, proposed that the seagoing ironclad USS *New Ironsides,* then in the process of fitting out, be assigned to the South Atlantic Blockading Squadron along with the *Monitor* for an attack on the South Carolina port. The *New Ironsides* was the first of the true ocean-going ironclads in United States Navy service, but she was overshadowed by the Navy Department's monitor fever. Her design was closer to that of the European ironclad model of the HMS *Warrior.* Du Pont certainly would not turn down extra warships no matter what the type; the *Ironsides* would prove to be particularly useful to augment the existing blockading force patrolling the approaches to Charleston and to defend against rebel ironclads then rumored to be building in the port. "If it be possible to send the *Ironsides* to take up a position off that harbor," Du Pont wrote the secretary, "the efforts of the enemy" to deploy ironclads of their own to break the blockade "would be completely frustrated."[15] But he refused to accept the notion that the new ironclad technology could single-handedly take the city. "You know best about the *Ironsides,* I would like to have her," Du Pont assured Fox, and cautioned once again, "but she cannot take Charleston alone."[16]

Despite Du Pont's resistance to the pressures exerted by Welles and Fox,

Rear Admiral Du Pont during his trip to Washington for consultations with the Navy Department in October 1862. Photograph by F. Gutekunst. (Courtesy of the Hagley Museum and Library)

there is little doubt he understood the symbolic importance of Charleston that drove the secretary's enthusiasm for the operation. Still, he vowed he would not allow the department to push him into an untenable position by "impulsive nonsense," because although the capture of Charleston was important symbolically, its strategic importance was questionable. From the first meeting of the Blockade Board and throughout his command of the South Atlantic Blockading Squadron, Du Pont strongly believed that his most important strategic objective was to maintain and improve the integrity of the blockade. In addition, an attempted attack with inferior weapons surely invited the "mortification of defeat" that would inevitably lead to a "loss of prestige, and [a] baneful effect in Europe." Friend and now radical Republican congressman Henry Winter Davis encouraged Du Pont to stay the course: "You are plainly right in saying it ought to be a combined operation."[17]

His hope for an aggressive army commander who would cooperate in a joint operation against Charleston was fulfilled with the appointment of Major General Ormsby MacKnight Mitchel as the new commander of the Department of the South. Mitchel, a West Point classmate of Robert E. Lee and a world-famous astronomer, gained a measure of notoriety from his operations in Tennessee and Alabama as commander of the Second Division of the Army of the Ohio when he seized a large portion of the strategically important Memphis and Charleston Railroad and laid siege to Chattanooga itself in early 1862. Not until Sherman's campaign against Atlanta did a larger Union force venture deeper into the Confederacy.[18] Du Pont believed strongly that Mitchel's arrival and his own positive first impression of the general foreshadowed successful joint operations in the area. No sooner had Du Pont met Mitchel than the two men began to discuss future operations.

Before Du Pont and Mitchel could agree on any specific plans, Welles ordered the admiral to report to Washington for "the purpose of conferring with you upon matters pertaining to your squadron." Du Pont's loyal subordinate, C. R. P. Rodgers, sensing the admiral's frustration with the department's increasing pressure about Charleston and noting that an exhausted Du Pont needed leave, had written Fox without the admiral's knowledge asking that his chief be allowed to return home to "confer with the Navy Department concerning the wants and organization of his command . . . and a week at his home." In his last letter to Fox before departing Port Royal for home, Du Pont repeated once again that the department must not "go it half cocked about Charleston—it is a bigger job than Port Royal. . . . You & I planned the first . . . let us consult together again—Loss of life is nothing, but failure at Charleston is ten times the failure elsewhere."[19] For the first time since leaving Hampton Roads for Port Royal almost a year earlier, Du Pont had the opportunity to meet Welles and Fox in person and enjoy a short but much-needed rest.

Arriving home at Louviers on 30 September, Du Pont spent a pleasant few days with Sophie before reporting to the capital. At the same time, the ambitious chief of naval ordnance, Captain John A. Dahlgren, taking advantage of his close relationship with the president, sought to command the

Admiral and Mrs. Du Pont on the front porch of Upper Louviers. Photograph probably taken during Du Pont's brief visit home in October 1862. (Courtesy of Hagley Museum and Library)

force that was to take Charleston. On 3 October, Dahlgren confided to his journal, "I applied by letter to the Navy Department for command of the forces that are to attack Sumter and the other Charleston forts." When Welles broached the possibility to Du Pont, the proud admiral exploded in rage that Dahlgren was an officer who "chose one line in the walks of his profession [scientific ordnance work] while Foote and I chose another [sea duty]; he was licking cream while we were eating dirt. . . . Now he wants all the honors belonging to the other but without having encountered its joltings." Du Pont emphasized that most of his captains, and "above all Drayton," deserved promotion more than the ordnance expert.[20]

Du Pont argued that Dahlgren was qualified to command nothing larger than an ironclad in his squadron. Not wanting to upset either of his sensitive subordinates, Welles refused Dahlgren, diplomatically writing that "Rear Admiral Du Pont has been called to Washington to concert measures for this attack and the Department cannot consent to deprive him of the honor of leading and directing these forces. Your natural desire however to be present is appreciated and if you desire it, you can have orders to an iron-clad that will take part in the attack."[21] Du Pont saw Dahlgren's quest to join the squadron as nothing short of an attempted coup. This episode must have added to his anxiety over the upcoming Charleston mission and reinforced his decision not to push his apprehensions to the point of insubordination during his consultations with Welles and Fox.

Although he would later claim that he was mostly satisfied with the Washington meetings, it is obvious from Du Pont's correspondence that he was also very frustrated that he could not convince Welles and Fox that only a joint operation against Charleston could be successful. Welles wrote in his diary upon Du Pont's arrival in the capital that the admiral "looks hale and hearty" but once again criticized him for his propensity to build "naval clanship[s]" in his choice of his subordinates.[22] This oft-mentioned censure of the admiral for surrounding himself with highly qualified and loyal officers suggests that Welles was jealous of Du Pont's popularity within the officer corps.

While in Washington, Du Pont took the opportunity to have several photographs taken in his new rear admiral's uniform. These images show his new and enormous mustache. He had sported exaggerated sideburns for many years but had only starting growing a mustache since his arrival at Port Royal. The photographs of Du Pont taken in October 1862—in stark contrast to his pre–Port Royal images—reveal a very tired man whose hair is noticeably grayer than it was only two years earlier, a man burdened with responsibilities that dwarfed those ever faced by an American naval officer. He had been at sea for almost a year without a break, commanding the Union's most important and powerful naval force.

Du Pont made the social rounds in the capital, meeting with various officials and cabinet members including Lincoln; General Henry W. Halleck, whom he had transported on the *Cyane* several times during the Mexican War; Secretary of State William H. Seward; and Secretary of the Treasury Salmon P. Chase. The cabinet members all reminded Du Pont of the political importance of Charleston. In his meeting with the president on 16 October 1862, Du Pont "explained the general nature of our occupation off the seacoasts of three rebel states and the moral effect of this." Lincoln then criticized the army's failures at the "James Island affairs." The admiral was struck by Lincoln's frustration with Major General George McClellan and the Army of the Potomac. At one point in their conversation, Lincoln complained that McClellan was constantly badgering him for more troops; but, the commander in chief grumbled, "If you promise him those, he will call for ten thousand more." The hint was there for Du Pont to take: Lincoln was fed up with reluctant commanders. Perhaps because of Lincoln's unsolicited criticism of McClellan, Du Pont did not inform the president of his concerns over the monitors or his preference for a joint operation to take

Charleston.[23] The consummate military professional, Du Pont did not want to go over the heads of Fox and Welles, with whom he still had excellent relationships, and he likely believed that he had plenty of time to sway the two men without jumping the chain of command. In addition, the new *Passaic* monitors were still under construction; Du Pont was undoubtedly willing to give them the benefit of the doubt at this point. The fact that the president recognized and discussed with the admiral the army's dismal record near Charleston and elsewhere must have added to the pressure Du Pont felt.

During this trip he also had his first opportunity to inspect the *Monitor* and received a briefing on the new class of ironclad that the Navy Department hoped would improve on the original design; Welles earmarked at least two of the new vessels for his squadron and the Charleston operation. Du Pont was impressed with the defensive capabilities of the *Monitor* and exclaimed that the ship's design was "very extraordinary." Also striking were the XV-inch Dahlgren guns destined for mounting in the new *Passaic*-class monitors. After seeing a demonstration of these weapons, Du Pont began to feel more confident about the effectiveness of the ironclads, but he still voiced a cautionary note to Sophie: "With a sufficient number of these vessels so armed they would tear away, I believe, the walls of forts. My fear is that we shall be hurried on to our great work with very few."[24]

Du Pont still believed that an all-navy operation was folly. After his meetings with Welles and Fox, Du Pont wrote Sophie that nothing really had been resolved: "I leave under *no more plans* than the first day: a vague impression that Charleston must be taken—a marked appetite on the part of the government officials that it should be, and that very speedily, captured. . . . [They] talk of the 'grand attack' and all underrate the difficulties." Amplifying these remarks a few days later, Du Pont recounted a private conversation he had with Fox: "[I] posted him up in many things. I warned him against the undue influence of the political sentiment in hastening operations against Charleston. I told him it might be a joint movement of Army and Navy. He agreed so far as to have a force on James Island to take possession if we captured the city."[25]

Three days later Du Pont vented his frustrations to Henry Winter Davis: "In reference to the great matter of all, I could not induce an enlarged view of a joint expedition on such a scale as to ensure success. There is a marked appetite for the capture of the place, particularly among the members of the Cabinet, and when I mentioned this to Welles, he said 'Yes, they are like men with tapeworms.'" No minutes appear to exist of these meetings, so Du Pont's letters are the only accounts and thus must be used with caution. However, his letter to Henry Winter Davis suggests that Du Pont did raise his concerns to the secretary—indirectly to be sure—about the lack of a joint operation. Even if Fox had kept Welles in the dark about the admiral's worries up to this point—an extremely unlikely occurrence—there should have been no doubt by late October 1862 that Du Pont had serious reservations. With his extensive experience with the army and joint operations, Du Pont could not understand why "Fox's Navy feelings are so strong, and his prejudices or dislike of Army selfishness so great in their operations with our service, that he listens unwillingly to combined movements." But despite his disappointment over his inability to persuade Fox and Welles either to abandon or to expand the Charleston operation, he understood civilian control of the military and decided to salute and follow orders. "As you are aware," he reminded Davis, "it is not in my nature to press things . . . so I must trust in Providence, and do my duty whatever instruments and means are given me."[26] However, in the months remaining before the attack, Du Pont never hesitated to remind the department's leaders of the difficulties he faced.

Du Pont may not have succeeded in persuading Fox and Welles to see things his way, but Sophie was thrilled that he finally had the chance to express his concerns directly to his superiors: "I am glad, very glad of your having these days in Washington, and consequently the opportunity of full and free conversations with the heads of the Government . . . and giving them the information needed for them to estimate the difficulties you have to contend with."[27] Du Pont's letters to Sophie and Henry Winter Davis indicate that he presented his misgivings to his superiors. Du Pont clearly unburdened himself to Fox at length about his concerns, and it seems inconceivable that the assistant secretary did not keep Welles informed. This belies the claims later made by Welles that Du Pont never expressed reluctance or misgivings at any time before the attack on Charleston. Although disappointed that he was unable to change their minds at the conference, Du Pont felt certain that he had adequately explained the operation's considerable risk to his superiors.

The admiral's description and analysis of these meetings provide vital clues to the eventual failure of the Charleston expedition, the relationship between the commanders in the field and their civilian leaders, and the single-minded unwillingness of Fox and Welles to listen to any alternative to an all-navy attack to demonstrate and validate the efficacy of the new ironclads. Clearly Welles and Fox in coordination with Lincoln set the strategic stage for Du Pont, but they failed to take the opinion of their subordinate into account while they pushed him to execute operations for which he was not prepared.

Du Pont was very clear in his own mind and in his correspondence to Fox in particular before October 1862 that an all-navy attack on Charleston was unlikely to succeed and that only a large-scale joint operation would result in a satisfactory conclusion. But previous Du Pont biographers claim that he did not make these reservations known at his meetings in Washington. James Merrill writes that "Du Pont's silence deceived the Department into believing that his views coincided with their own" and that "Du Pont, admiral of the wooden Navy, the do-nothing Navy of the Mexican War, hemmed and hawed." K. Jack Bauer claims that during the meetings Du Pont "contented himself with recounting the difficulties he faced [and] the dangers of a premature move." In his biography of Welles, John Niven recognizes that Welles, the old Jacksonian Democrat, had developed a natural antipathy toward the wealthy Du Pont's aristocratic bearing. He also suggests that Du Pont was "too urbane, and too protective of himself, however, to offer any unsolicited opinion of the Charleston operation."[28] But it is clear that Du Pont not only voiced his opinion but also offered his judgment on numerous occasions from May 1862 through the conference and in the months to follow. Although there is no explicit evidence that Fox informed Welles of Du Pont's worries, the admiral had no reason to assume that the assistant secretary was not conveying his views in some fashion. The proposed Charleston operation was the biggest yet contemplated for the navy; it was the only game in town. What is clear is that Du Pont had dutifully given his civilian masters the benefit of his informed counsel. Welles and Fox ignored these warnings and admonitions and instead attributed Du Pont's reluctance to his disdain for new technology and his concern for his reputation if the audacious operation failed.

Character was vitally important to Du Pont, but there is no indication that concern for it prevented him from giving his best military advice. Although Du Pont himself recognized that "it is not in my nature to press things," he consistently advocated a joint operation and warned that no number of ships, even ironclads, could take Charleston alone. Fox then agreed to army cooperation but only for the purpose of occupying Charleston after the navy seized it. In their final conversation before Du Pont returned to Port Royal, the admiral cautioned Fox that his obsession with all-navy triumphs was unhealthy and did not serve the interests of the nation: "Undivided glory is very pleasant to contemplate, but our country is in a position where certainty of success in such an undertaking is of far more importance than what may accrue to different corps."[29] Du Pont understood better than any other senior Union leader in the Civil War except perhaps Grant and Porter that carefully coordinated joint operations provided the clearest path to final victory.

The relationship between Welles, Fox, and Du Pont was clearly a one-way street. The secretary and his assistant asked for Du Pont's thoughts on the operation, essentially ignored them, and instead tried to assuage his apprehensions with more ironclads. Du Pont understood and accepted the realities of civil-military relations in the United States, yet it is clear that the department ignored the military advice of one of its most experienced officers. This was a mistake. Du Pont was more than happy to accept reinforcements, and he consistently asked for more—if he had to execute this distasteful mission, then he wanted every ship he could get—but additional vessels did not create a joint operation. Before the October conference Du Pont wanted to use these reinforcements such as the *New Ironsides* to augment the blockade; after the conference it was clear that any ironclads earmarked for the South Atlantic Blockading Squadron were to be used for a Charleston attack. It was difficult, but even though he did not agree, Du Pont accepted the fundamental premise that political considerations such as the pressure to take Charleston must invariably drive military operations. That said, there is no evidence that Welles or Fox presented Du Pont's concerns or his request for a joint army and navy operation to the president. Indeed, the record suggests that they presented the Charleston mission to the president as an all-navy replay of Port Royal and New Orleans. When Du Pont aggressively voiced his unhappiness with the monitors starting in January 1863, and without the full story outlining the admiral's reluctance since May 1862, Lincoln came to regard Du Pont's reluctance before Charleston as comparable to McClellan's vacillation on numerous occasions. By the time of the Charleston attack, one thing Lincoln would not tolerate was a McClellan-like commander.

The theme that consistently weaves its way throughout the relationship between Welles, Fox, and Du Pont from May 1862 through June 1963 is the secretary's and Fox's total, almost obsessive, faith in the ability of the ironclad (especially the monitor design) to do almost anything. On the other hand, Du Pont recognized that the monitor-type vessel had great potential for certain missions but for not every task; this, along with the admiral's desire for an army and navy cooperative effort against Charleston, formed the basis for the conflict between Fox, Welles, and Du Pont. But "monitor fever" was gripping the Northern media, the public, and especially the Navy Department in the months after the battle at Hampton Roads.

The genesis of the *Monitor* came out of the actions of the navy's Ironclad Board that selected three competing designs in August and September 1861. The winning competitors included the *Monitor*, *New Ironsides*, and the ill-fated *Galena*. John Ericsson envisioned his design to be a relatively cheap ironclad vessel with extremely low freeboard and a revolving gun turret for use in the shallow eastern coastal waters of the United States against enemy ironclads. The victory of the *Monitor* over the *Virginia* at Hampton Roads in March 1862 caused an almost unprecedented public sensation. Quickly the *Monitor* and her class overshadowed all other designs, and to her and her sisters were attributed qualities they did not possess.[30] The contractors responsible for the construction of these ships capitalized on the press and public enthusiasm, and the Navy Department significantly expanded ironclad (particularly monitor) production. Fox in particular, an eyewitness to the battle at Hampton Roads and supported by Welles, became the foremost proponent of the monitor-type vessel and believed that their defensive strength made them capable of performing virtually any naval mission. Selection of the monitor as the technological paradigm for the Union navy in the Civil War was the direct result of the ship's victory at Hampton Roads combined with the observation of its dramatic success by a key decision maker, Fox. Du Pont found out to his dismay that once Fox saw the *Monitor* in action, it was almost impossible to change his mind about the class of vessel.[31]

In reality monitor ironclads were only suited to combat enemy ironclads or other shipping in relatively benign and protected coastal waters, something Du Pont recognized from the beginning. Nevertheless, as Robert Albion points out, the Navy Department and Congress "concentrate[d] upon a single device at the expense of a balanced force." Albion also observes that it would probably have been better for the United States Navy and the Union war effort if a ship of the *New Ironsides* class of ironclad had defeated the *Virginia* instead of the *Monitor*. If this had happened, the much more powerful and flexible "seagoing class of ironclad would have been built quicker and the monitors not forced down everyone's throat."[32] But the department selected the monitors, and the decision was final. Despite Du Pont's misgivings and his professional assessment that the monitors were unsuitable for attacking shore installations, Welles and Fox forced them and the Charleston operation upon Du Pont.

Introducing new technologies into the military—especially during wartime—presents significant challenges to leaders and adds levels of difficulty to what is already the most complex of human endeavors. Many variables affect the ease with which technologies are introduced, assimilated, and accepted by leaders and the rank and file. Wartime conditions naturally reduce training time on new weapons systems. Feedback from the field identifying and design flaws may be overlooked, testing ignored or short-changed, and quality control neglected as a new piece of equipment is rushed to the field. The requirement for the new technology may have been poorly defined, and thus the system might not really solve the problem for which it was designed and procured. Once the equipment is distributed to units in the field, commanders face additional challenges that are inherent in wartime: training on and maintaining the new technology and developing and testing new operational concepts, while sustaining ongoing combat operations. In addition, officers in the midst of a conflict are often reluctant, unwilling, or simply do not have the time to devote the resources necessary to field new technologies properly. These difficulties can aggravate the natural tendencies of many in the military to resist change. Du Pont and his captains and crews faced all of these challenges as they tried to field the new monitors, develop new tactics for their use, and, not least of their trials, maintain the vessels.[33]

William M. McBride notes that during the Civil War the gauge of effectiveness of the navy shifted from the quantitative measure of the number of warships to a "qualitative measure of naval power based on significant technological differences."[34] Du Pont also recognized this shift, albeit in a much different context, and indeed had advocated such a course of action as early as 1851 in his *Report on the National Defences* when he promoted the development and fielding of the most technologically advanced ships the navy could afford. Of course, Du Pont believed that these advanced ships had to fit into the navy's overall operational and strategic concept. After Hampton Roads, Welles and Fox felt no such restraint. The only real evaluation of the *Monitor*'s operational role was by Fox as he witnessed its victory over the *Virginia*. Other evidence, such as the Drewry's Bluff disaster, was discounted or ignored.

This engagement was the first practical demonstration of the new technology. However, a much more important and relevant test comes when the "first complete set of basic components [is] put into service."[35] For the Union navy in the Civil War, the first fully operational force was Du Pont's fleet of ironclads at Charleston. Yet the navy's first (and final) decision on the new technology's effectiveness was premature. With no operational concept with which to measure the performance of the monitor design, the navy's civilian leadership looked only to the *Monitor*'s uniqueness and initial success at Hampton Roads to advance the class. This decision came at the expense of a thoroughgoing analysis of the combat requirements of commanders at sea and of the capabilities and limitations of the new technology. Once the Navy Department embarked down the monitor path, getting it to reverse this trend proved impossible. The department stayed the course even after receiving clear evidence of the new vessels' limitations at Drewry's Bluff and Charleston.

Thus firmly in the grips of "technological inertia," the United States Navy remained committed to the monitor-type vessel until late in the nineteenth century. By late 1862 the monitor had become the sine qua non of the Union navy.[36] Welles and Fox were much more affected by public opinion and political pressure to achieve results than cost, capabilities, and effectiveness of the weapon system. In addition, their attitude toward the monitors reflected the "positive reinforcement of their preconceptions."[37] As a result, the navy and Du Pont became the victims of the *Monitor*'s early success.

New technology within a military organization can either flourish or founder depending on the ability of the organization's bureaucracy not only to champion the new technology but to test it thoroughly, to develop new tactics and doctrine for its dissemination and use within the fleet, and to provide logistics and maintenance. The United States Navy's nascent bureaucracy was unable to provide credible support mechanisms for the new vessels, including the testing and the development of a workable operational concept for their employment at sea. Du Pont and his captains (notably Drayton and John Rodgers) recognized these organizational shortcomings. Indeed, they based their criticisms of the monitors more on how the new ships were to be used and other organizational limitations than on the vessels' actual technical shortcomings. Du Pont's extensive experience as a commander and seaman in peace and in war and his long embrace of new technology suggest that his concerns over using the new vessels for a most difficult mission were based on tactical and operational reasons rather than the blind rejection of modern machines by an officer who was hopelessly ensconced in a "wooden age."[38]

Welles, Fox, newspaper reporters and editors, and the general public might extol the virtues—both real and imagined—of the monitors, but naval officers had to sail the warships, train their crews, and place them in harm's way. The monitors that the Navy Department earmarked for Du Pont's squadron for the Charleston attack were all second-generation improvements on the original monitor plan and all were designed (although not all constructed) by John Ericsson. These were the *Passaic*-class monitors, first proposed by Ericsson only days after the battle at Hampton Roads. The designer tried with the *Passaic* class to incorporate some of the lessons learned in that battle and to correct many of the shortcomings identified in the original *Monitor*.

The *Monitor* was extremely difficult to command from the low vantage point, only inches above the waterline, of the vulnerable pilothouse located on the forecastle. In addition, the captain could not communicate with his gunnery officer in the turret except by messenger. Other problems with the prototype included poor ventilation, excessive buildup of heat in the turret and crew spaces, leakage at the base of the turret in heavy weather, inadequate berthing areas, and low top speed. Ericsson was able to address some but not all of these shortcomings by incorporating some incremental improvements in the *Passaic* class. Unhappily for the navy, the exigencies of war and subsequent contractual problems led to poor quality control of the *Passaic* monitors. Kurt Hackemer observes that "the sheer magnitude and speed of the construction, as well as the technical challenges, overwhelmed the [government's] administrative mechanism." In addition, the *Passaic* contracts contained no "enforcement mechanisms" to ensure that changes and improvements occurred, nor were many of the captains' recommendations incorporated into the ships.[39] The result was incremental rather than substantive improvements over the original *Monitor*.

Aside from the fact that the new ships were larger than the original *Monitor*, the most significant and visible improvement to the *Passaic*-class vessels was the relocation of the pilothouse to the top of the turret. This position gave the captain and pilot 360-degree visibility, and they could easily communicate with the nearby gun crews, while the turret now had full range of motion. This enhancement had an important drawback, making the pilothouse even more vulnerable to enemy fire. Captains and pilots of these vessels soon learned that if their post suffered a direct hit, the bolts used in the pilothouse's construction would habitually shear and ricochet in all directions, often wounding the occupants. The inability of the *Monitor*'s XI-inch Dahlgren guns to penetrate the *Virginia*'s armor led to the decision to mount two mammoth XV-inch Dahlgrens, (the largest naval gun used in the war, in the *Passaic* class. Shortages of this gun soon forced a change in specifications calling for one XV-inch and one XI-inch gun per ship. Other changes included hydrodynamically superior underwater lines, larger boilers, better ventilation, a full smokestack, and thicker turret armor.[40]

Even with these modifications, the *Passaic* class retained some of the *Monitor*'s failings and added a few more. The new ships sluggishly answered helm instructions (a big problem in strong tidal or river currents) and were still quite slow despite navy specifications calling for sustained speeds of 9 knots and seven days' endurance; the *Passaic* class could only reach speeds of 7½ knots under very good conditions. The new ships' deeper draft (11½ to 12 feet compared with the *Monitor*'s 10 feet, still much less than most of the navy's larger wooden warships) limited the waters in which they could safely operate. The ships also leaked badly and were particularly tough to handle in anything other than perfect weather.

However, the XV-inch gun mount turned out to be the biggest problem

The monitor USS *Passaic*, with her extremely low freeboard and turret-mounted pilot-house clearly visible. Wash drawing by R. G. Skerrett, 1898. (Courtesy of the United States Naval Historical Center)

for the ships' commanders. Much to their dismay, the designers and the captains soon learned that the huge muzzle of the big Dahlgrens would not fit through the turret's gun ports; instead, it had to sit completely inside the turret. Obviously, this was unacceptable: the concussion from the huge gun in the enclosed turret could seriously injure the gun crew, and the accumulation of fumes could asphyxiate them. After attempting various fixes, Ericsson devised an ingenious but not altogether practical "smoke box" that attached the gun's muzzle to the turret's bulkhead, limiting the concussion and fumes within the turret to a barely acceptable level. Although this makeshift solution worked, the captains and crews were never happy with the arrangement. The gun had a notoriously slow rate of fire (one round every seven minutes, or fewer than nine rounds an hour), and the smoke box only aggravated it. Because the XV-inch gun with smoke box totally obscured its gun port, the crew had to aim the weapon from the port of the XI-inch gun; thus, the faster rate of fire of the XI-inch gun was reduced to that of its larger companion. Aiming was made even more difficult by the ship's imprecise turret controls that often forced the crews to make many time-consuming adjustments between rounds. Finally, since there were now two guns of different calibers, the ship's logistical requirements became more complex. After the battle at Charleston, Du Pont and his officers identified still more deficiencies.[41]

After the October conference the navy reassigned several of Du Pont's officers to command the new *Passaic*-class monitors then under construction.

Wartime photograph of the USS *Catskill*, showing the turret size and the location of the pilothouse on the *Passaic*-class monitors. The muzzles of both the XV-inch (*left gunport*) and XI-inch Dahlgren guns are also clearly visible. Note that the XV-inch gun is too large to extend beyond the turret wall. (Courtesy of the Massachusetts Commandery of the Military Order of the Loyal Legion of the United States and the United States Army Military History Institute)

These astute seamen immediately zeroed in on the monitors' shortcomings. Commander (and later rear admiral) Daniel Ammen, formerly of the *Seneca*, assumed command of the *Patapsco*. He was shocked by the weapons configuration in the *Patapsco*'s turret. Ammen noted with horror that Ericsson wanted to use brute force to make the XV-inch guns fit by the use of what the captain called a "stuffing box." This was ridiculous, argued Ammen, because "a state of war [is] a most unfavorable period for experiment." In a letter to ordnance chief Dahlgren, Ammen asked that since the larger gun was "incapable . . . of being quickly and closely sighted, would I not better have [an] XI-inch?" [42] Most of the captains of *Passaic*-class ships would ask similar questions in the months ahead.

The *Passaic*'s new captain, Commander Percival Drayton, was also concerned about his new ship and her contractor and designer, John Ericsson. The outspoken Drayton was appalled that the newspapers had been extolling the great virtues of the new monitors, when he had seen the vessels' many problems firsthand at the Brooklyn Navy Yard. Like Ammen, Drayton was particularly concerned with the turret and gun layout. The Swedish-born inventor had routinely ignored Drayton's recommendations on possible solutions. A frustrated Drayton wrote to a friend that Ericsson's abilities were overrated and that "from the first I have told him exactly what would occur, and have been invariably right and he wrong." Both Drayton and Dahlgren at one point recommended the obvious solution to the XV-inch gun problem of widening the gun port to accommodate the larger muzzle. This Ericsson refused to do because such a change would necessitate other modifications and could weaken the turret.[43]

Drayton also had other concerns: "The vessel will not go I am sure under any circumstances over seven knots, and there is no ventilation whatever, so far as I can see." Living aboard the monitors was uncomfortable under the best conditions. Drayton reported to Du Pont that living belowdecks felt more like being in a well, "such was the constant, drip, drip, drip."[44] Drayton, like many naval officers who had new technology forced on them, believed that the monitors could be greatly improved if only the department and contractors would allow the user more input into the design. He felt certain that if he was given a free hand, the *Passaic* would be a better ship, "if they will only give me a gun that can be fired."[45]

The ship's first cruise from New York to Hampton Roads in late November 1862 confirmed Drayton's fears. The seakeeping characteristics of the *Passaic* were dreadful, wrote Drayton. "The weather which was by no means bad, although the sea washed over the vessel like a log and completely flooded everything below, rendered things pretty uncomfortable." Worse yet, the boiler burst, forcing Drayton to return north to the Washington Navy Yard for repairs. While at the capital Drayton described to Du Pont how the *Passaic*'s performance fell far short of government specifications: "The fact is that he [Ericsson] has not kept to any promise of the contract. The speed is about five knots instead of nine, and the draft of water eleven feet six inches, which brings the rail only ten inches from the water."[46] Drayton was once again frustrated at the delays and because his suggestions and recommendations were ignored. Compounding Drayton's irritation were newspaper accounts that claimed for the monitors a "reputation [as] the most wonderful and complete invention of this or any other age." After completing a harrowing voyage to join Du Pont's squadron at Port Royal—in the teeth of a storm that sank the *Monitor*—Drayton summed up his thoughts on his new ship: "I cannot but think from my short experience that Ericsson's invention is about as much fitted to go to sea as a pleasure boat, and I only wish . . . that he could be persuaded to try a short voyage to judge from dear experience."[47]

As the *Passaic* limped into the Washington Navy Yard, Commander (later rear admiral) John Rodgers was waiting impatiently at the Brooklyn Navy Yard for the completion of another *Passaic*-class monitor, the *Weehawken*, which Du Pont had recommended that he receive. Of all the monitor captains, Rodgers was perhaps the most sanguine about the new ironclads. Even after his defeat at Drewry's Bluff, Rodgers believed that the new ironclads had great merit. With wide-ranging experience including command of a small flotilla that included the original *Monitor*, he was certain that the *Weehawken* and her sisters were much better ships. With the notable exception of the XV-inch gun arrangement, Rodgers wrote that he "like[d] the *Weehawken* very much."[48]

After attending to the time-consuming fitting out of his new vessel—a process that included an ignominious grounding and several breakdowns—Rodgers finally departed for Port Royal on 18 January 1863. In a feat of superb seamanship, he successfully sailed the *Weehawken* through a gale that forced many other ships into port, rivaling the storm that sank the *Monitor* and forced the *Passaic* to seek shelter. After the loss of the *Monitor* and all the negative reports coming out of the navy yards concerning the monitors, Fox and Welles understandably seized on Rodgers's exploit as proving the worth of the *Passaic*-class ships. When he heard the news of Rodgers's safe passage to Hampton Roads, Welles enthusiastically marked the event in his diary: "No man but John Rodgers would have pushed on his vessel in that terrific storm."[49] Fox seemed more concerned about how the *Weehawken*'s voyage would play in the press than the successful transit of a major combat asset. The assistant secretary wrote Du Pont that although the "loss of the *Monitor* brought up the 'I told you so' people, Rodgers' courage has extinguished them." To Rodgers, Fox wrote, "Your brave act has been of more use to us than a victory." Rodgers's own report was no less glowing an assessment of the monitor: "The behavior of the vessel [during the storm] was easy, buoyant and indicative of thorough safety, her movements filled me with admiration."[50]

Rodgers's account of the passage also described the result of plowing through thirty-foot waves: "A good deal of water came through the deck plates, and my cabin was overflowed." The monitor *Nahant* had also set sail for Hampton Roads but was forced by the gale to seek shelter near the Delaware River breakwater. Many like Welles and Fox praised the monitor for Rodgers's successful passage; others such as Commodore Charles Henry Davis had a more cynical view of the cruise. Davis argued that the *Weehawken* survived the gale in spite of, not because of, its inherent seaworthiness; Davis believed that only Rodgers's superior seamanship saved the ship, and indeed he was correct, for a year later high waves and faulty hatches combined to sink the *Weehawken* at her moorings, killing four officers and twenty-six sailors. Rodgers—virtually alone among the new monitor captains—may have been pleased with the seaworthiness of his new ship, but he would soon change his mind about her combat capabilities.[51]

As the captains of the monitors became familiar with their new commands, Du Pont returned from his brief Washington trip to the day-to-day concerns of administering the blockade and planning the attack on Charleston. The day before Du Pont's return, Major General Mitchel led 4,500 soldiers in an attempt to cut the Charleston and Savannah Railroad at Pocotaligo, South Carolina. Although well-fortified Confederate forces easily repulsed the Union troops, Mitchel proved he was more aggressive and audacious than most of the army commanders Du Pont had dealt with. But within days of Du Pont's return, Mitchel was dead of yellow fever; Du Pont served as one of his pallbearers. Intelligence reports also convinced Du Pont that Confederate ironclads then under construction at Charleston were now his greatest concern. Du Pont's only mention of ironclad reinforcements immediately upon his return to Port Royal was for the purpose of countering the Confederate ironclad threat. Clearly, the blockade's integrity and not Charleston was paramount to Du Pont.[52]

Since his time on the Blockade Board, Du Pont understood that his most important mission—the one that could lead directly to the strategic goal of strangling the South—was to continually improve the blockade. Seizing Charleston was not an important part of the blockade campaign. Indeed, Du Pont felt that the Navy Department's obsession with Charleston was nothing more than a peripheral operation that was draining resources and attention from what was strategically important: tightening the blockade. At this point in the war, Charleston was a luxury that the Union navy could not afford.

In early 1863 Charleston may indeed have been the most heavily fortified city in North America. Any naval force that hoped to get within cannon range of the city had to first negotiate the narrow ship channel that threaded precariously through dangerous shoals waters. When in full flood, the tides often exceeded four knots. A warship attempting to force its way into the harbor in the main channel first had to negotiate the guns at Fort Wagner on the northern tip of Morris Island. Next, the ship would come within range of Battery Gregg, then Fort Sumter, and Fort Moultrie on Sullivan's Island. If the vessel could handle the tides, currents, and guns, it now was faced with a line of obstructions covered by the fire from adjacent fortifications. Finally, if it got past the obstacles, it had to run a gauntlet of even more batteries and fortifications until finally it might arrive at the Charleston docks. Without a sizable amphibious force, even if the ironclads successfully passed Sumter, the obstacles, and the guns, the ships could threaten, they could inflict damage, but they could not take ground. Indeed, Charleston harbor was a "cul de sac" as Du Pont so fittingly described it.[53]

As the first reports concerning the status of the new monitors began to arrive, Du Pont was not unduly concerned. Drawing on his own experience as the commander of a new and technologically advanced ship, he believed that the right officers in charge accompanied by responsive contractors could solve most problems plaguing new vessels. In a 1 December 1862 letter to his friend Iowa senator James W. Grimes, a member of the Senate Naval Committee, Du Pont expressed optimism that the knowledge and experience of such capable officers as Drayton, John Worden (first captain of the *Monitor*), and John Rodgers would ensure that "some things [on the *Passaic*-class ships will] be remedied, which would have been fatal to their efficacy, and they are not quite remedied yet." Nevertheless, as the year ended, Du Pont shared his anxiety and concerns over the upcoming Charleston operation with Sophie: "It is a sentiment in the national heart that [Charleston] should be captured. . . . The attempt to be made soon, I presume, though we have not an iron vessel yet, is as complete an *experiment* as can be imagined." Furthermore, Du Pont complained, "I am satisfied that the power of aggression and even endurance of the ironclads are as much overrated by Mr. Fox and others as the extent and nature of the defenses of Charleston are underrated." This letter, like so many others that he wrote from November 1862 through March 1863, illustrates both the pressure he was feeling about the operation itself and his almost complete lack of confidence in the weapons he had to use. Still, Du Pont was very pleased with his captains. In this same letter Du Pont expressed gratitude that "the officers appointed to the ironclads [most based on his recommendations and requests] are on the whole the best that could be named—Drayton, Worden, John Rodgers . . . so that all that can be done with such craft will be."[54]

Du Pont was torn between his own view that the Charleston operation was an "experiment" using largely untried means (the technologically advanced monitors) and his duty to respond to the departmental, political, and public pressure to achieve a great military success. Consequently, in the wake of the Union army's disastrous battle of Fredericksburg, the admiral knew that he had to do his very best, so he asked the department to send him every ironclad it could spare for the upcoming attack. "Let there be no *stinting*," Du Pont urged Fox on 22 December, "for *we* must not fail." A delighted

Fox responded at once to Du Pont's request and its suggestion of newfound resolve: "We shall send you immediately the *New Ironsides*, the *Passaic*, the *Montauk*, the *Patapsco*, and the *Weehawken*. . . . The rebellion staggers to receive the final blow by your avenging arm, at Charleston and Savannah."[55]

The ironclads to which Fox referred were assigned originally to the North Atlantic Blockading Squadron to take Wilmington, North Carolina. The department canceled that mission after it determined that the water conditions in the Cape Fear River were unsuitable for ironclad operations. Finally, on 6 January 1863, after all the meetings and letters, Welles wrote Du Pont he could soon expect to see the ironclads *New Ironsides*, *Passaic*, *Montauk*, *Patapsco*, and *Weehawken* at Port Royal to reinforce his squadron "to enable you to enter the harbor of Charleston and demand the surrender of all its defenses or suffer the consequences of a refusal." Welles would later claim that the department never actually ordered Du Pont to take Charleston, but clearly this letter gave Du Pont his orders. The admiral's mission was now unmistakable. Welles went on to note that Major General David Hunter, the new commander of the army's Department of the South, would be given 10,000 troops to assist "as shall be deemed best," but that Charleston's capture "rests solely upon the success of the naval force."[56] It was now official: Du Pont had to conduct the mission with an all-naval force whether he wanted to or not, and in spite of his previous objections. Now all eyes and all the navy's resources were focused on Du Pont's command.

Union fortunes were bleak at best in January 1863. The Army of the Potomac had just been soundly defeated, once again, by Robert E. Lee's Army of Northern Virginia at Fredericksburg; the Union's first attempt to take Vicksburg had ended in defeat and withdrawal; Confederate general Braxton Bragg had only days before fought the Army of the Cumberland to a draw at Murfreesboro, Tennessee; and northern newspapers kept up a merciless drubbing of Welles and the department for the successes of numerous blockade-runners and what they saw as inaction on the part of the navy. Thus, the pressure was on Welles and, consequently, Du Pont.

Three rebel ironclads were now present in Du Pont's area of operations. By January 1863 the Confederates at Savannah had converted the blockade-runner *Fingal* into the ironclad ram *Atlanta*, and protecting Charleston were the ironclads *Palmetto State* and *Chicora*, among other ships and fortifications. Du Pont still viewed the blockade's integrity as a critical priority, indeed, his first priority. But with Welles's directive, priorities had to change; now receiving the new ironclads and integrating them into a viable attack plan against Charleston moved to the fore. Du Pont and his captains had been considering this thorny problem for some time. As early as October,

Du Pont had received a proposed attack plan from John Rodgers. Using experimental ordnance data from Europe, Rodgers believed that if a monitor fleet could stand off approximately 1,200 yards from the target (in this case Fort Sumter), its fire would have great effect on an enemy fortification, while "our ironclads will be secure" from significant damage. If the Confederate ironclads attempted to come out, Rodgers argued, the entire monitor force could defeat them quickly and then be redirected against the forts. In Rodgers's plan concentration was the key to success, and so he advocated defeating piecemeal each fort protecting Charleston harbor. Calling Rodgers's proposal "capital," Du Pont spent many hours pouring over charts of the harbor with his fleet captain, C. R. P. Rodgers, as he tried to fashion a workable plan.[57]

Expressing admiration for Rodgers's plan, Du Pont nevertheless restated his original and lasting opinion on the proper way to take Charleston: "I have never had but one opinion—that the capture of Charleston should be effected by a joint operation of Army and Navy . . . we should be willing to share the laurels." When Du Pont acknowledged Welles's 6 January order, he included a request for "additional ironclads, if possible, to those mentioned in your dispatch."[58] If Du Pont had to attack Charleston, he wanted every possible resource he could get. It was not going to be easy. Charleston, as Du Pont had argued many times, was not Port Royal, nor was it New Orleans, the scenes of the two most successful naval operations of the war. In early 1863 Charleston was the most heavily fortified port city in the South.

Also in his letter to Welles, for the first time, the admiral explicitly referred to his many previous messages to Fox outlining his reservations and recommendations about the Charleston operation. "The Department has been informed through my private letters to the Assistant Secretary of the general character and extent of the defenses of Charleston. I shall endeavor to execute its wishes with such force as it may deem necessary for this purpose."[59] If Welles was unaware of the voluminous stream of correspondence between Fox and Du Pont before, he now should have had no doubt that his commander was deeply concerned about the mission.

Du Pont's request for even more ironclads concerned the secretary. In his response Welles soothingly assured Du Pont that "the Department does not desire to urge an attack upon Charleston with inadequate means, and if after careful examination you deem the number of ironclads insufficient to render the capture of that port reasonably certain, it must be abandoned." Of course, Welles and Fox had been urging Du Pont to attack Charleston since May 1862. In the next paragraph, Welles once again pointed Du Pont in the desired direction, writing that because so many of the Union's best conventional warships were off chasing the Confederate raiders *Alabama* and *Florida*, the capture of Charleston was "imperative, and the Department will share the responsibility imposed upon the commanders who make the attempt."[60]

Welles's biographer John Niven writes that Du Pont's request for more ironclads "was totally unexpected." Welles, argues Niven, was unaware of Du Pont's concerns because the admiral had kept any differences of opinion between him and Fox from the secretary. Welles claimed in a letter to Du Pont on 14 May 1863 that he had had no prior knowledge of any misgivings the admiral may have had, for he had not "been advised of your opinions and views in regard to the feasibility or probable results of the demonstrations that were to be made." Indeed, Welles continued, Du Pont's post-attack letters were "the first intimation to the Department or the government that you, the admiral in command, entertained a doubt of either the propriety or expediency of the movement."[61] Welles's claim was simply wrong: at the very least, the Navy Department in the person of Fox had been kept abreast of Du Pont's misgivings all along the way. Du Pont was clearly more candid in writing with Fox than he was with the secretary; Du Pont and Fox were friends, and the assistant secretary had prior service as a naval officer. Du Pont made his opinions clear in the October 1862 conference in Washington, D.C., and in innumerable letters to Fox. Du Pont assumed that Fox would inform Welles of his opinion concerning a major naval operation, perhaps the most significant of the war to date. If Fox did not share these details with Welles, the department probably had decided to "put all their eggs" in the monitor basket, and the assistant secretary did not want any dispute over the ironclads' efficacy to become public. However, even if Fox did not inform Welles of his discussions and correspondence with Du Pont, the secretary had ample indicators of Du Pont's true opinion in several letters after late January. The burden was clearly on Fox, much more than on Du Pont, to keep his chief informed. The attack on Charleston was too important for misunderstandings.

Part of the dispute between Du Pont and the Navy Department grew out of the inability or the unwillingness of the navy's leaders to come to terms with the strength of Charleston's fortifications. Du Pont's increasingly frantic warnings that Charleston would be a very tough nut to crack, even with monitors, were met with reckless disregard. Ever since construction began on Fort Sumter in 1829, the city's gun emplacements had impressed observers. Besides the great fort, Charleston's defenses were formidable and arrayed in depth (as described earlier in this chapter). A succession of Confederate commanders had relentlessly improved the port's fortifications, ordnance, and manning since the war began in April 1861. Turning Charleston into an impregnable strongpoint became one of the Confederates' top priorities once they changed their coast defense strategy after the Union victory at Port Royal. Rebel leaders were confident they could withstand any seaward attack. Du Pont and his captains were painfully aware of these facts, but they were not the only ones who recognized the nature of the challenge.

British officers inspecting the fortifications thought them more impressive than those at Sevastopol in the Crimean War. Confederate general Pierre G. T. Beauregard also had developed special measures strictly for the monitors. He formed distinctive boat crews whose mission was to attack the monitors with torpedoes, grenades, and liquid fire. Beauregard also placed great reliance on underwater obstructions, reasoning that if the monitors were forced to slow down or, better yet, stop, his gunners would be that much more effective. Although most torpedoes were modest in size, the Confederates constructed at least one torpedo from an old boiler filled with black powder and electrically fired. This monster weighed in excess of 2,500 pounds and was capable of destroying any ship afloat. With the transfer of the monitors to Du Pont, Beauregard redoubled his efforts and reported in February 1863 that the installation of torpedoes throughout the main channel was proceeding in "every direction." Drayton described the torpedoes as "strewn about like autumn leaves." By early 1863 the Confederacy was able to equip its fortifications at Charleston with large-caliber guns with armor-piercing projectiles such as Brooke rifles. As one historian has observed, such defensive improvements would "no longer permit the [Union] such easy successes as those at Hatteras Inlet or Port Royal, as the U.S. Navy leaders would soon discover to their great discomfort."[62]

To their credit, Welles and Fox did their best to send every ironclad they could get their hands on to Du Pont. The first to arrive at Port Royal was the *New Ironsides* on 18 January 1863, followed the next day by the *Montauk* under the command of the *Monitor*'s first captain, Commander John Worden, and two days after that by Drayton's *Passaic*. The *Montauk*'s entry into Port Royal Sound caused a sensation throughout the squadron. Du Pont, who had never seen a monitor underway, described the scene: "Such a sight I have never seen. She was literally à fleur d'eau [level with the water]. In the relatively quiet waters of Port Royal harbor, the spray was flying over the deck; the crew huddled together under the lee of the turret looked like drowned rats."[63] Soon after, Du Pont dispatched Worden to Ossabaw Sound to guard against the escape of the *Atlanta* and the rebel privateer *Rattlesnake* (ex-*Nashville*).[64]

Du Pont was starting to feel the intense strain, and he confided his frustrations to Sophie, calling the proposed Charleston expedition a "chaotic conception" brought about by the "desire of the President and others '*to strike a blow*' somewhere." That was fine, he argued, but "one would suppose that somebody would sit down and study out how the blow was to be given."[65] Of course, he had already begun to study how to accomplish the mission, but the admiral undoubtedly was referring to the Navy Department's refusal to consider a joint operation. Du Pont had carefully considered the Rodgers proposal, but before he could decide on a course of action, he had to determine the actual operational capability of the ironclads. If the department refused to conduct full-scale trials of the monitors, Du Pont would. He decided to order the *Montauk* to engage the rebel strongpoint of Fort McAllister on the Ogeechee River south of Savannah. The results of this attack were mixed. Worden reported that although the rebel gunners hit the monitor "quite a number of times," it suffered little damage. After expending all his ammunition in a four-hour bombardment, Worden withdrew; the monitor in turn had inflicted little damage on the fort. To a friend, the admiral mused, "If one ironclad cannot take eight guns, how are five to take 147 guns in Charleston harbor?"[66]

The disgusted Du Pont dashed off a dispatch to Welles. He started off with the good news: "Considering it desirable to test in every way the efficiency of the ironclads that had arrived . . . I sent Commander Worden down to [Fort McAllister]. . . . [A]lthough the *Montauk* was struck thirteen (13) times, she received no injury." He then dropped the bad news: "My own previous impressions of these vessels, frequently expressed to Assistant Secretary Fox, have been confirmed, viz: that whatever degree of impenetrability they might have, there was no corresponding quality of aggression or destructiveness as against forts; the slowness of fire giving full time for the gunners in the forts to take shelter in the bombproofs. This experiment also convinces me of another impression, firmly held and often expressed, that in all such operations, to secure successes, troops are necessary." The *Montauk*'s sluggish rate of fire allowed the Confederate gunners to get off at least two shots for every one of the *Montauk*'s. Du Pont also described problems with the *New Ironsides*, such as extremely poor steering, and attempts to fix them. She was almost uncontrollable under many circumstances, not the least of which was when in shallow (her draft was very deep—15 feet 8 inches), fast-moving, and constricted waterways.[67] This was perhaps Du Pont's most forceful expression of his concerns that went directly to the secretary. At last Du Pont sent Welles two official dispatchs in one week, not a private letter to Fox which may or may not have been shared with the secretary.

As a commander, Du Pont never lost sight of his mission and caring for his men. However, the naval reformer and strategist in him recognized and appreciated the distinctiveness of the monitors. In a letter to a friend, the admiral paid tribute to the monitors' design, noting, "The conception is one of *genius*, and the mechanical contrivances to work such monster guns and turn the turrets are in keeping with this conception." But, he added, manning these ships was not easy. "I wish they had invented some cast-iron men and officers for them; their decks are awash in this harbor if the wind be fresh, and the crews look forlorn and sad."[68] The crews were also inexperienced. Very few officers and sailors had manned ironclad ships, especially such technologically advanced versions as the *Passaic*-class monitors. Their complexity and the idiosyncrasies inherent in any new ship made it very difficult for their captains and crews to figure out how to handle them and fight with these new vessels.

The *Montauk* tried again to destroy Fort McAllister on 1 and 15 February 1863 with similar results. The first success for the new ships occurred on 28 February when Worden attacked and destroyed the Confederate warship *Nashville*, renamed *Rattlesnake;* but the *Montauk* was damaged in this action by a torpedo, forcing Worden to run the ship aground.[69] Thinking that more monitors might make a difference and hoping to continue his evaluation and give the new ships and their crews every opportunity to train and to see some action, Du Pont ordered yet another attack on Fort McAllister on 3 March 1863, this time with *Passaic, Nahant,* and *Patapsco.* The outcome with three monitors was no better than the earlier attempts with one. An eyewitness to the 3 March attack observed, "It did not seem possible judging from our view of the fight, that the fort would be able to hold out long, and yet there was no perceptible slacking of fire on their part."[70]

This series of experiments was telling. Although the trials validated the defensive capabilities of the monitors, the attacks on Fort McAllister also demonstrated many shortcomings, including the vulnerability of the pilot-house, the extremely slow rate of fire, the susceptibility of the turrets to jamming, and the inability of the heavy ships to maneuver in a current. To Du Pont and his commanders, the Fort McAllister probes were proof that the monitors alone probably were incapable of taking Charleston. Du Pont was appalled at the performance of the monitors. If three of the most technologically advanced warships in the world could not destroy an earthen fort with a mere eight guns, how could they possibly take a port city surrounded by dozens of pieces of the most modern ordnance available to the rebels? To Gideon Welles, however, the experiments were a foolish waste of time that allowed the enemy to gauge the monitors' strengths and weaknesses. He chose not to answer Du Pont's Fort McAllister report and continued advocacy of a joint operation. In his diary the secretary wrote, "Du Pont has attacked Fort McAllister and satisfied himself that the turret vessels are strong and capable of great endurance, but at the same time he doubtless made the Rebels aware of these facts."[71] Apparently the secretary expected Du Pont to attack Charleston without training his crews or even determining the capabilities of his new and untried ships.

Delays plagued the squadron. The monitors were continually breaking down, a common occurrence with new and untried technology. Also, an embarrassing foray by Confederate ironclads against Du Pont's ships outside Charleston harbor in late January caused Beauregard to issue a proclamation claiming falsely that the blockade had been broken. Finally, the squadron awaited additional reinforcements. All of these setbacks contributed to the anxiety felt by everyone involved with the upcoming operation.[72]

In mid-February a meeting among the president, Secretary of War Edwin Stanton, Fox, and General John G. Foster, one of Hunter's subordinates, took place in the capital in which Foster discussed Du Pont's plans for Charleston, as he understood them. Foster laid out what was clearly a joint operation in which the army would besiege the city supported by Du Pont's fleet. It seems clear that Foster was speaking out of turn at the White House and had done no planning with Du Pont at all. He was likely trying to undermine the authority of General Hunter, with whom he had a running argument over who should be in overall command of the Department of the South. Du Pont hardly mentions Foster in his correspondence except to note the conflict between the two generals and to say that Foster was very familiar with the Charleston defenses. It is very unlikely that Du Pont, a stickler for rank and chain of command, would have actively planned operations with Foster while excluding Hunter.[73]

Lincoln was astonished, for Welles and Fox had assured him that the seat of rebellion would soon fall to an all-navy attack by a flotilla of invincible monitors. If the army was planning a large operation at this late date, more delays would inevitably follow. This was McClellanism all over again. Lincoln asked Fox to travel to Port Royal to get an assessment directly from Du Pont and to urge him to attack without further delay. Fox demurred, arguing that Du Pont's sensitive nature would take such a trip as a rebuke—he was probably right—but he assured the president that the naval attack was still on. Lincoln agreed, but from that point on he would never again hold a high opinion of Du Pont. Because the only information the president received on the Charleston attack came from Welles and Fox and because Du Pont had not informed the president of his misgivings in October, Lincoln's information was all one-sided. At the same time Welles was becoming more disillusioned with the admiral's want of "will and determination." While Du

Pont was right in expressing his opinion, Welles observed, "I deplore the signs of misgiving and doubt which have recently come over him—his shirking policy [and] getting in with the army."[74]

Welles and Lincoln gave Fox the task of bucking up the reluctant admiral. "The idea of a siege meets with such disfavor that the President wished me to go down and see you," Fox wrote to Du Pont. "Take your time, my dear admiral, we only say do it, but I beg you not to take these soldiers too closely into your counsels in a purely naval matter." Four days later Fox wrote again, promising two more monitors, telling the admiral not to attack until he was ready, and painting a glorious picture of Du Pont's certain victory: "You [will] arrive at the center of this wicked rebellion and there demand the surrender of the forts, or swift destruction. *The President and Mr. Welles are very much struck with this programme*. . . . I beg of you not to let the Army spoil it." Once again, it was made abundantly clear to the admiral that the department still did not understand how tough a nut Charleston would be to crack and that the army was to have nothing to do with this operation. Finally, evidence of Lincoln's growing impatience made its way back to Port Royal. Not only had Fox told Du Pont that to the president "the idea of a siege [and thus a joint operation] meets with . . . disfavor," but in early March a frustrated Lincoln had remarked to a White House visitor that "I fear he [Du Pont] does not appreciate at all the value of time."[75]

In response to Fox's notes and rumors of the president's concerns, Du Pont tried one more time to get the department to understand the complexity and difficulty of the Charleston attack. "The *Experiment* for it is nothing else (the trying of 200 guns with twenty) is too momentous to be trifled with," wrote Du Pont to Fox. "Excuse me but I could not but smile at your grand plan of sailing in silently on *our friends*," admonished the admiral. "There is no question what the result would be. . . . but my friend you have to *get there*—We'll do it if it can be done." He did appreciate Fox's efforts to send him every possible ironclad he could, but Du Pont wanted more. Fortunately for the squadron, Chief Engineer Alban Stimers, whom Du Pont called "Ericsson's high priest," witnessed the Fort McAllister experiments "and came to the same conclusion that I had long ago: that more vessels would be wanted, and [he] is going home to hurry out more." A resigned Du Pont declared, "He will enlighten them more at the Department than fifty letters from me would do."[76] The admiral would come to regret his faith in Stimers.

9

Charleston and Its Aftermath

We have failed as I felt sure we would.

—SAMUEL FRANCIS DU PONT

SOON THE Navy Department reinforced Du Pont's squadron with the *Keokuk*, an experimental ironclad with two XI-inch guns mounted in nonrotating barbettes, and two additional *Passaic*-class monitors, the *Catskill* and the *Nantucket.* By mid-March the attack force was set. The first all-iron fleet in history now consisted of nine ships: seven *Passaic*-class monitors, the oceangoing ironclad frigate *New Ironsides,* and the rather odd *Keokuk.* Also sent to Du Pont at this time was the *Alligator,* the Union submarine that owed its existence to the admiral's feasibility study and recommendation at the Philadelphia Navy Yard at the beginning of the war. But the craft never made it to Port Royal, foundering on the way south in a gale while under tow on 31 March 1863. No one died, but the only operational Union submarine was lost. It is very unlikely that the *Alligator* would have been of any use to Du Pont at Charleston.[1]

The fleet would be able to bring thirty-four guns to bear against enemy fortifications bristling with ordnance. The rest of March was consumed with preparation for the upcoming operation and correcting construction errors, design flaws, and shoddy workmanship in virtually every ship. As just one example, the attack on Fort McAllister demonstrated that the iron plates protecting the magazines were inadequate and needed reinforcement.[2] Only four of the ironclads had ever fired their guns in anger, most of the ships had been rushed through construction and hurried south to Port Royal with no trials or workups, and none had worked together as a team. The *Nantucket* fired her guns for the first time on 1 April, only five days before the attack.

After only two rounds her master reported that "all the nuts on the left of [the XV-inch] muzzle box was blown off." In a letter to friend and fellow squadron commander Rear Admiral David G. Farragut, Du Pont revealed what was probably his greatest misgiving about the operation: "All is new and untried."[3]

As Du Pont wrestled with hundreds of details, he found that his "mind is on a greater tension than it has been in my life before." The pressure was getting to the admiral. In the days before the attack, he once again poured out his misgivings to friends and family. To Sophie he complained of the difficult tides and shallow water in Charleston and that the XV-inch gun was a faulty weapon and that Dahlgren himself agreed. He feared it would have little effect on the Confederate earthworks. Du Pont wrote his old Crystal Palace friend William Whetten that monitors were great weapons against ships but there was "a *want* in these vessels where forts are concerned."[4] Even the most optimistic of his captains, John Rodgers, agreed with his chief and began having misgivings over the entire operation after the aborted attacks on Fort McAllister. Rodgers wrote: "I am less sanguine of taking Charleston than I was. The monitors have proved by practice at Fort McAllister . . . to be far less formidable in attack than was anticipated." On 3 April 1863 Rodgers echoed Du Pont when he wrote, "The experiment we are about to make is one of deep interest; no one can say before hand how the thing will turn out."[5]

While Du Pont and his key leaders were gloomy about their prospects against Charleston, the squadron's sailors were more optimistic about the outcome of the upcoming attack. A *Nahant* crewman was certain that his *Passaic*-class monitor would soon distinguish herself in "the greatest engagement that the world ever saw or heard of." Another sailor on the Charleston blockade wrote to his hometown newspaper and confidently declared that "your numerous readers may be prepared to hear the report of some loud Yankee thunder from this place. . . . All hands are wide awake and ready, and feel confident that a great and glorious victory will crown our efforts."[6] At least crew morale was not a problem.

One great concern, which Du Pont expressed in several letters, was that if he failed and lost an ironclad or two to the enemy, the Confederates could raise and repair them and break the blockade. Even officers who did not command ironclads and who would play a secondary role during the attack were apprehensive. Four days before the attack, the commander of the gunboat *Vermont* confided to his wife that "*we are not very sanguine* of the attack being successful, as the enemy has had such a long time at his command to make the most extraordinary preparations for defense in every conceivable shape." After Fort McAllister, the question of underwater obstructions had been at the forefront of Du Pont's worries. To Alexander D. Bache, Du Pont predicted that the future of coastal defense would not be "found in iron forts, iron towers—but in obstructions with iron vessels to guard them sufficiently to prevent their being removed."[7]

As the senior officer commanding the small monitor flotilla at Fort McAllister, Drayton agreed with Du Pont's assessment and wrote one of the most perceptive analyses of the challenges facing the fleet at Charleston. Drayton observed that guns and forts were tough enough, but the most problematic defenses for the monitors at Fort McAllister and especially at Charleston were the underwater obstacles and the torpedoes. Overcoming these obstacles under fire would be a very difficult task indeed. In a not-so-subtle swipe at the Navy Department, Drayton complained that "although all non-combatants think it is the easiest thing in the world to pull up piles and other encumbrances to a channel under fire, no one has yet been found anywhere at home or abroad, that can succeed in doing it, while shot are smashing your boats and killing your people."[8]

The difficulties inherent in breaching obstacles under fire were well known in army circles but had not often been faced by naval officers. The brilliant mind of John Ericsson created a possible solution for the torpedo problem. He devised a raft that when attached to the bow of a monitor and fitted with explosive charges and grapnels could, he supposed, clear any underwater obstacles without exposure of the crew to enemy fire. Although four of these devices were earmarked for Du Pont's squadron, only one survived the trip to Port Royal. Du Pont was not impressed. When he learned that three of the four rafts had been lost, he remarked, "It is a pity the fourth did not follow, for I have no more idea that we can use them than we can fly." The monitors' captains derisively dubbed the raft "John Ericsson's Deck Scraper." John Rodgers volunteered to test the invention and to use it at Charleston, but he steadfastly refused to employ the explosive charges. Rodgers feared that explosives dangling from a raft attached to the *Weehawken*'s bow would be more dangerous to his and other Union ships in the likely event of a collision in Charleston's constricted waters than to any underwater obstacle they might encounter. Ultimately, Du Pont chose the *Weehawken*, deck scraper attached but without explosives, to lead the attack.[9]

On 4 April 1863, after much consideration and debate, Du Pont issued his order for the attack on Charleston. The admiral outlined a plan that called for the ironclad flotilla to steam up the ship channel past the batteries on Morris Island and to "open fire on Fort Sumter when within easy range [from 600 to 800 yards]." The order admonished each ship's captain not to waste ammunition and to "render every assistance possible to vessels that may require it." After the flotilla finished with Fort Sumter, "it is probable that the next point of attack will be the batteries on Morris Island." The nine ironclads were to steam down the ship channel in the following order: *Weehawken*, Commander John Rodgers; *Passaic*, Commander Percival Drayton; *Montauk*, Commander John Worden; *Patapsco*, Commander Daniel Ammen; *New Ironsides*, Commander Thomas Turner, the flagship; *Catskill*, Commander George Rodgers; *Nantucket*, Commander Donald Fairfax; *Nahant*, Commander John Downes; and *Keokuk*, Lieutenant Commander A. C. Rhind.[10]

Notwithstanding Du Pont's usual penchant for attention to detail, and despite having a very capable fleet captain in C. R. P. Rodgers, the admiral's order issued to his captains was very poor indeed. The order provided little information to the commanders and offered no subsequent objectives once the fleet reduced Fort Sumter and "the batteries" on Morris Island. Du Pont did not appear to have considered the possibility of success or any other contingency. What happened if the underwater obstacles were not as formidable as Union intelligence had led him to believe? What course of action should the squadron pursue if the forts surrendered? Which ship or ships were to counter a possible attack by the Confederate ironclads *Chicora* and *Palmetto State*? How should the rest of the squadron's ships support the monitors' attack? Du Pont probably considered any direct support by his wooden warships as too hazardous, but his order did not say so, nor did it address any of the other questions.[11] The plan of attack probably would have been more comprehensive and well thought out had Du Pont had the benefit of Charles Henry Davis—the chief planner of the Port Royal expedition—as his chief of staff.

Perhaps Du Pont discussed these contingencies verbally with his captains, but the evidence does not support this. Apparently, Du Pont was so certain of failure, and probably early failure, that he thought detailed planning for possible sequels from the basic plan was a waste of time. Only days before the attack, Du Pont had learned of the death of a beloved cousin and sister-in-law. While his reaction to this sad news cannot excuse the poor planning, it might explain some of the admiral's apparent preoccupation, lethargy, and depression just before the attack. On the day he issued his attack plan, Du Pont wrote Sophie of his disgust over General Hunter's refusal to assist the attack in any meaningful way. "I think it well to mention these things," he told his wife, "for these operations and the capture of Charleston, or what is more probable the *failure* of its capture, will be a matter of historical discussion."[12] However, to the admiral's credit, he did entrust the role of leading the squadron into battle to John Rodgers, his able and most aggressive commander. Also, the captains of the first five ships in his line of battle were his very best.

As the captains prepared their ships and crews, a reporter filed a story and prophetically assessed the monitors: "The aggressive qualities of these seem much misconceived by the general public. Popular fancy, nurtured by journalistic ignorance and exaggeration, has enveloped them with a nimbus of irresistibility not at all warranted by their real merits. . . . They have marked deficiencies which render success not by any means absolutely certain." Upon viewing the formidable Charleston defenses through his telescope, an officer aboard the *Nahant* bitterly remarked, "This isn't going to be any such picnic as we had at Fort McAllister."[13]

History's first ironclad fleet crossed the Charleston bar on 6 April 1863 and prepared to attack the port city the next day. The fateful day was clear and calm with temperatures in the mid-60s. The idiosyncrasies of the new ships in the confining waters of Charleston harbor almost ensured that the day would not go smoothly. Rodgers on the *Weehawken* found it nearly impossible to maneuver with the antitorpedo raft attached. He ran into trouble early on 7 April when the raft fouled his anchor, preventing the departure of the fleet for over two hours.[14] The fleet finally got under way at noon. No one who witnessed the scene would ever forget it. Nine of the most advanced military machines the world had ever seen—true weapons systems, and the most complex that had ever been built—proceeded slowly and majestically toward Fort Sumter. It seemed to many observers that nothing could resist this inexorable procession of naval power.

Once underway, the crew of the *New Ironsides* lost control of the flagship twice in the swift current and shallow waters, forcing them to anchor both times to avoid drifting perilously close to the enemy shore. Both times the *Ironsides*'s control problems sent the line into confusion, causing the ship with the greatest number of guns to fall behind and preventing the admiral from being able to observe and closely supervise the action. Thus, Du Pont was unable to exercise any control over the battle almost from the moment the *New Ironsides* entered the harbor. A reporter on board the flagship wrote that "the *Ironsides* continued almost helpless at the mercy of the tide—now gaining a little, now backing, now striking bottom, now swinging to the right and left. Officers and crew grew restive. The enemy's guns were continually playing upon us. We had not yet returned a single shot."[15] The flagship, hit over ninety times and often out of control, became little more than a hindrance to the overall conduct of the battle.

At 2:00 P.M., Rodgers reported obstructions ahead. The battle began in earnest when the guns of Fort Moultrie opened fire at 3:00 P.M. Fort

Sumter's guns and those of the batteries on Morris Island followed quickly. As the Union fleet wallowed down the Charleston ship channel, the converging fire of several forts and batteries met it. In accordance with Du Pont's plan, the ironclads concentrated their fire on the great symbol of the Confederate rebellion, Fort Sumter.

With Du Pont's flagship falling behind the rest of the fleet, Rodgers as the lead captain made the key decision not to push through the obstructions and torpedoes clearly visible in the channel; the aggressive officer turned short of the desired attack position and opened fire. As one historian has observed, "This decision would doom any prospect of Union success." Rodgers pressed as close to the fort as he dared while keeping up as rapid a fire from his XV-inch and XI-inch guns as he could. The rest of the monitors followed suit and fired as best they could under a hail of Confederate shells. Because of the agonizingly slow rate of fire for the XV-inch guns, the monitors' crews were able to fire only fifty-five of the largest shells against the masonry walls of the fort. Of these, only thirty-four struck home. In stark contrast, the numerous Confederate batteries fired 2,209 rounds, hitting the Union ships over 400 times.[16] C. R. P. Rodgers wrote later that it seemed "as if the fires of hell were turned on the Union fleet. The air seemed full of heavy shot, and as they flew they could be seen as plainly as a baseball

Panoramic view of the first attack by an all-ironclad fleet in history against Charleston on 7 April 1863. Although this contemporary engraving distorts the distances, Du Pont and his officers and men clearly faced great difficulties as they tried to capture the

in one of our games." An account by the surgeon of the *Nahant* demonstrates the intensity of the fighting: "'My quartermaster is killed,' sang out our Captain, Downes. 'Pass him down and send up another! Mr. Clarke,'—to the ensign in charge of the 15-inch gun,—'you hav'n't hit anything yet!' 'We ain't near enough Captain Downes,' roared Clarke. 'Not near enough! God Damn It, I'll put you near enough! Starboard your helm, quartermaster!'"[17]

The *Nahant* closed to within 500 yards of Fort Sumter, nearer than any other Union ship. The *Nantucket* came within 700 yards, but her XV-inch gun was quickly disabled, and in almost three hours of combat, she was able to fire only fifteen shells. At approximately 5:00 P.M., with the ironclads making but little impression on the Confederate batteries and enduring relentless battering and with darkness swiftly approaching, Du Pont ordered the fleet to withdraw after an engagement lasting only an hour and forty-five minutes. The Confederate ironclads never even had to leave their moorings.[18] History's first all-iron fleet had been rebuffed. At the time of his order, the admiral fully intended to resume the attack the next day.[19]

At a conference that night with his captains, Du Pont learned that the damage to the Union vessels had been more severe than he first thought. The *Keokuk*, taking the brunt of the enemy fire, had been hit over ninety times. Her inferior armor had done little to protect her; she was able to re-

city from the sea. (From Paul F. Mottelay, ed., *The Soldier in Our Civil War: A Pictorial History of the Conflict, 1861–1865* [New York, 1884–85], 2:172. Photograph courtesy of the United States Naval Historical Center)

Charleston harbor and Du Pont's attack on the city, 7 April 1863

treat but sank early the next morning. The *Weehawken* was struck fifty-five times and sustained severe damage to her deck plates. *Passaic*, struck thirty-five times, had quickly lost the use of her turret and her XI-inch gun from a direct hit. Drayton was able to unjam the turret during the battle, but it never worked properly. Many of the captains learned of another monitor shortcoming during the battle: the turret invariably jammed when hit anywhere near the track on which it revolved. Hit forty-seven times, the *Patapsco* lost the use of her 8-inch rifle after firing only five shots. *Catskill* was hit only twenty times and reported no damage. *Nantucket* was struck fifty-one times and suffered a jammed turret and the breakdown of her XV-inch gun. The *Nahant* was hit thirty-six times, lost the use of her turret early in the fight, and "was badly mauled." Casualties on both sides of this revolutionary battle were very light. Only one Union sailor was killed during the battle: the quartermaster of the *Nahant* was struck down by a broken piece of iron after the ship's pilothouse sustained a direct hit; several other sailors were wounded. Confederate casualties included one killed and five wounded.[20] After hearing of the extensive damage to his ships, Du Pont decided not to renew the fight. The ironclad fleet had been soundly defeated.

"My precious Sophie," Du Pont wrote from Morris Island the day after the battle, "We have failed as I felt sure we would." This letter to Sophie marks the first time that Du Pont admitted that he felt that failure at Charleston was inevitable before the fact. Or it may simply be the immediate expression of a thoroughly depressed and discouraged commander who had just suffered an ignominious defeat. Still, Du Pont put forth to his wife the best face he could on the setback: "Do not be worried about this. I am quite calm and unruffled myself, knowing I have done all that was right and been mercifully protected by God, for had we got where we were going I believe we should have lost the whole fleet."[21]

Reflections of the battle's participants agree on most of the major aspects of the engagement. John Rodgers in his first account of the battle wrote his wife that "The fire was tremendous—and I do not believe the world has ever seen such a fire upon ships. . . . We were hit 55 times—this is wonderful accuracy since we were only about a foot above water and the turret is only 9 feet high. They say that the *Weehawken* was so enveloped in spray from the shot showered at her as to be completely invisible and people thought we had gone down." Rodgers was convinced that his turn away from the ship channel was a prudent decision although some accounts downplayed the actual number and extent of the torpedo threat. The future admiral also praised Du Pont's decision not to resume the battle, claiming that the damage to the ironclads "proved that the means were not reliable which he had at his dis-

Admiral Du Pont (*second from left*) and staff aboard his flagship, the USS *Wabash*, ca. 1863. Fleet Captain C. R. P. Rodgers is at the far left. The *Wabash*'s commander, Thomas G. Corbin, stands fifth from left. (Courtesy of Hagley Museum and Library)

posal . . . and this unreliability might have made a continuation of the fight the next day a disaster." Rodgers, the most optimistic of the captains before the battle, told his father-in-law that the shot sounded "like a swarm of bees," and he bitterly attacked Ericsson and the Navy Department for failing to conduct adequate tests at the Washington or Brooklyn Navy Yards instead of at Charleston.[22]

Drayton wrote a friend that after seeing Charleston's defenses close up, they were much more formidable than he had believed possible. If the Union ironclads had pushed forward, Drayton argued, Du Pont would have lost all his ships. The outspoken Drayton concluded his letter with a scathing indictment of those who pressured the squadron to attack Charleston: "All I have to say is, that if persons be found who believe that Charleston is to be taken by sea attack just send them down here to attempt it." Daniel Ammen agreed with his colleagues and later claimed that no amount of casualties would have dissuaded the captains from another assault if there had been a decent chance for success; he would always argue that the decision not to resume the attack was the correct one.[23]

Despite the loyal support of all his subordinate commanders, Du Pont's conduct of this battle was not impressive. Indeed, his planning and command of the attack pales in comparison with his efforts at Port Royal. First, Du Pont's battle plan was poor. Second, his choice of the *New Ironsides* as his flagship, knowing that ship's poor maneuvering qualities in constricted waters, was highly questionable. By placing himself and his staff aboard this ship, he ensured that he would not be able to get close enough to the forts to assess accurately the effectiveness of the Union fire. Also, he failed to plan for the underwater obstructions and torpedoes. He knew they were there; although he never conducted a thorough reconnaissance, he did have remarkably good intelligence through rebel deserters and contrabands. Yet, with the exception of the *Weehawken*'s antitorpedo raft (without the explosives), there were no contingencies to deal with the barriers. Finally, he did not recognize that their only realistic hope for success was a very aggressive attack that had to push through any obstacles and past the main rebel fortifications.

However, just as George Gordon Meade at Gettysburg placed his most aggressive subordinate, Major General John F. Reynolds, in a position to decide where and when to fight Lee's army, Du Pont placed his best commander, John Rodgers, in the lead. To Rodgers—the most assertive of Du Pont's elite group of captains—was given the responsibility either to turn away from the obstructions or to push on through. Rodgers undoubtedly made the right decision in this case. If the ironclads had hung up on the obstructions, they would have lost what little ability to maneuver they had, and more vessels would have been lost. The department had handed Du Pont an impossible task. Despite later claims by Welles, Du Pont did not sabotage the effort, but his heart was definitely not in the attack. He faced the worst of all possible circumstances for a military commander: Du Pont did not believe in his mission or the tools he had been given to accomplish his task. The result was almost preordained.

Du Pont's loyal crews and more junior subordinates were certain that the action would be renewed with increased vigor. One sailor wrote a few days after the battle that another attack was imminent, this time with army assistance; its absence had been the reason, he argued, for the failure of the first effort. As soon as preparations were made, he wrote, "it is expected that Admiral Du Pont will undertake the job he has got to do, and do it up in earnest." Apparently the officers in the squadron tried to convince their men that the repulse was really a success. "The late attack on Charleston is not looked upon as a defeat by our naval officers here," one observer wrote. "In one respect it is a victory, for Sumter was badly breached." The ironclads did inflict considerable damage on Fort Sumter, but the Confederates easily repaired it in a matter of days. The reporter was being optimistic when he reassured his readers that "the movement against Charleston is not abandoned, and the city will fall there is not the least doubt."[24] Many in the squadron and at home soon would be bitterly disappointed. Indeed, when Du Pont left the flagship, the *New Ironsides*, to return to the *Wabash* at Port Royal, the crew refused to cheer him.[25]

General Beauregard's account of the battle is remarkably similar to those of the Union commanders, with three exceptions. He stated that the ironclads fired the bulk of their rounds from a long range of approximately 1,300–1,400 yards and not the 600–800 claimed by several of the captains. On this point Beauregard was probably more accurate than the Union commanders, for during two years of uninterrupted defensive preparations, the Confederate gunners had carefully surveyed and placed range markers throughout the harbor. Also, General Beauregard wrote later that sixty-nine guns actually faced Du Pont's fleet; most other sources claim seventy-six Confederate guns engaged the Union ironclads on 7 April 1863. In addition, Beauregard later claimed that the Union commanders were incorrect when they noted that torpedoes were scattered throughout the channel. Beauregard claimed that although there were numerous underwater obstructions, in reality the number of torpedoes was small. As a result of the battle, the rebel commander concluded that the vaunted monitors were "not invulnerable nor invincible, and may be destroyed or defeated by heavy ordnance properly placed and skillfully handled." The rebel general would write many years later that "the spectacle of this singular combat between the fort and what appeared to be nine floating iron turrets—for the hulls of the monitors were almost wholly submerged—was, indeed, an impressive one, not to be easily forgotten."[26]

The battle resulted in numerous modifications and improvements to the monitors and the *New Ironsides*. The most significant improvement to the monitors was a sloped armor protective band between the turret and the turret ring; this modification reduced greatly the tendency of the turrets to jam after receiving a direct hit. The pilothouse of the *New Ironsides* was relocated in front of the smokestack. Although she would always suffer steering limitations, the *Ironsides* rendered good service throughout the rest of the war. It was arguably the Union's most useful ironclad design.

On 12 April 1863 Welles received the first accurate report of the defeat; Du Pont had sent Alexander C. Rhind, wounded commander of the ill-fated *Keokuk*, with his first dispatches. Lincoln and Welles had waited anxiously for results of the attack. But now Rhind briefed them on the disaster. At first, the secretary tried to put a positive spin on the attack, writing that "the monitor vessels have proved their resisting power, and but for the submarine obstructions, would have passed the forts and gone to the wharves of Charleston. This in itself is a great achievement."[27] It is hard to see how Welles could have reached this conclusion, except that he wanted to seize any opportunity he could to vindicate the monitors. Rhind's decidedly negative review of the ironclads' performance led Welles, who before the battle had a high opinion of Du Pont's envoy, to dismiss the commander's firsthand account because he had undoubtedly been "tutored" by the admiral. After Welles received Du Pont's first detailed report of the battle, in which Du Pont repeated, "I will only add that Charleston cannot be taken by a purely naval attack," he countered by claiming that the admiral had never informed him of any such misgivings.[28]

Yet for months, Du Pont had gone to great pains to inform both Fox and Welles of his reservations and concerns over the efficacy of the monitors and the difficulty of the mission. But to Welles, Fox, and Lincoln, Du Pont's defeat meant that his days as commander of the South Atlantic Blockading Squadron were numbered. For Fox and Welles, a change was essential because Du Pont would not support the monitors adequately, and the department had bet everything on these ironclads. When the time came for Welles to relieve Du Pont, Lincoln did not intervene on the admiral's behalf despite the urging of the influential congressman Henry Winter Davis and the favorable report of his own private secretary John Hay. The president had received two detailed letters that were highly sympathetic to Du Pont from Hay, who was with the squadron during and after the attack on Charleston.[29]

Hay wrote Lincoln that the officers and crews had acquitted themselves bravely and "as a whole they encountered the furious and concentrated fire of the enemy in a style for which even our own officers had scarcely dared to hope." The president's secretary also related a conversation he had with C. R. P. Rodgers, who stated that "although the attack had been unsuccessful and the failure would of course produce an unhappy effect upon the country, which had so far trusted implicitly in the invincibility of the Monitors, all the officers of the Navy, without exception, [were] united in the belief that what they attempted was impossible, and that we had reason for congratulation that what is merely a failure had not been converted into a terrible disaster." To his friend and fellow presidential secretary, John G. Nicolay, Hay argued that "I do not think Dupont is either a fool or a coward. I think there is a great deal of truth in his statement that while the fight in Charleston Harbor demonstrated the great defensive properties of the Monitors, it also proved that they could not be relied upon for aggressive operation." Despite these dispatches, Welles's and Fox's reports ensured that the president's opinion of Du Pont degenerated to the point where he seemed no better than McClellan. Lincoln had openly expressed his doubts about the admiral and the impending attack to Dahlgren a week before the attack.[30]

In the days after the defeat, Du Pont did not help his own cause by reacting too strongly to a telegram from an anxious and disappointed Lincoln directing the fleet to remain close to Charleston and a very negative account of his performance in the *Baltimore American*. In response to these perceived slights on his abilities, Du Pont, in typical fashion, dared Welles to relieve him: "I am . . . painfully struck by the tenor and tone of the President's order, which seems to imply a censure, and I have to request that the Department will not hesitate to relieve me by any officer who, in its opinion, is more able to execute that service in which I have had the misfortune to fail—the capture of Charleston."[31]

Soon after, Du Pont's captains composed an extraordinary joint statement in addition to their official reports, offering complete approval of Du Pont's decision not to renew the attack. They also included comprehensive criticism of the monitors. Signed by every captain except Worden—although fully supporting Du Pont, he had already left for home—the dispatch countered the *Baltimore American* account and expressed unreserved support for the admiral. The captains noted that they all believed that the fleet should have attempted an attack against Charleston, but "after the experience gained under the fire of the enemy, we were unanimously of opinion that a renewal of the attack would be unwise in the extreme." Welles dismissed the opinions of these captains, whom he discounted as being "schooled and trained" by the admiral. Welles was sure that Du Pont had put his officers up to writing the joint report, but a letter from Daniel Ammen to John Rodgers on 5 May 1863 suggests that the captains independently decided to write it. As he did throughout his career, Du Pont enjoyed the almost unanimous allegiance of his subordinates. A month after the battle, Rodgers wrote that "Admiral Du Pont did right." He went on to lament that the department had forced them to fight with the monitors without adequate trials and experimentation. He concluded, "Naturally we have much to learn in regard to them—it is expensive and humiliating to learn from the rebels."[32]

In an attempt to restore his damaged reputation, Du Pont called on Welles and Fox to release all of their correspondence to the press—especially the joint report signed by all of his captains—thinking this would vindicate him.[33] Welles and Fox refused to release the pertinent correspondence, probably because they did not want to bring even more attention to the failure of the monitors. The animosity between the department and Du Pont increased in the weeks after the attack.

Du Pont's close friend Congressman Henry Winter Davis felt strongly enough about Du Pont's predicament that he personally argued the admiral's case to Lincoln at the Executive Mansion on 2 May 1863. Davis wrote Du Pont that he told the president that "you had never thought the attack wise, had always said it must be a *joint* attack to be successful; that the Navy department knew of your views of the great danger of a purely naval attempt." Davis also presented Du Pont's views on the monitors and on the errors in the accounts of the *Baltimore American* and other newspapers. Davis was shocked to learn that this information "was *all new* to the President," but the congressman was encouraged by Lincoln's reassurance that Du Pont's position was in no danger because "his feelings of confidence and kindness [toward the admiral] are wholly unchanged." Davis ended the conference by urging the president to ask for all the pertinent reports from the Navy Department. Lincoln confessed that he had seen very few of Du Pont's messages and said that he wished Du Pont had mentioned his misgivings when they met in October 1862. Davis left the White House thinking Lincoln had agreed to look into the matter.[34]

Davis's assessment of Lincoln's reaction was too optimistic. Lincoln was preoccupied with the unfolding Chancellorsville campaign, and Du Pont's case was lost in the aftermath of that disastrous battle. Lincoln never intervened on the admiral's behalf. Also, Davis had been one of Lincoln's most vociferous critics, and the president probably was reluctant to give his opponent what some might view as a political victory. Clearly Lincoln had established a relatively hands-off attitude toward the navy, in stark contrast to his intimate involvement with the army on a day-to-day basis.[35] Lincoln was content to let Welles and Fox run the navy, and he seldom interfered. As a result, Welles and Fox felt comfortable with not informing the president of a senior commander's misgivings before a major operation. If Lincoln's supervisory microscope had been focused on the navy with the same intensity as it was on the army, the president surely would have been aware of all the issues surrounding the attack on Charleston. Finally, Lincoln's comment about his October visit with the admiral demonstrated an informal leadership style in which he wanted subordinates to be completely candid with him. Du Pont's rank consciousness probably ensured that the October meeting was merely a pleasant but unproductive social call.

The admiral also discovered that one of the sources for the *Baltimore American*'s article was Chief Engineer Alban C. Stimers. The outraged Du Pont demanded his court-martial. To the very sensitive admiral, it must have seemed like a replay of the Ritchie affair from the days of the Efficiency Board. Du Pont saw it as an unjust and unwarranted assault on his reputation while he had just been doing his duty. As in the Ritchie case seven years before, in the Stimers court of inquiry (Welles opted for the less burdensome and stigmatizing proceeding) the monitors were on trial more than the professional conduct of the chief engineer. And like the Ritchie trial, the Stimers court of inquiry did not turn out the way Du Pont had hoped. After several fitful sessions, the court found no reason to continue, giving Fox and Welles more ammunition against the admiral and for the monitors.[36] This was another slap in the face against Du Pont. He viewed Stimers's exoneration as another attempt by the department to undermine and discredit him, and he may have been right.

Welles and Fox had yet to receive the joint letter of the squadron's ironclad captains when they attempted to get one of these officers to turn against the admiral. They chose Rodgers; they chose the wrong man. Welles asked Rodgers to support the department's view toward the monitor. They obviously thought that his pre-Charleston optimism had survived the 7 April battle. Rodgers, to Welles's and Fox's chagrin, expressed complete support for Du Pont and offered constructive yet pointed criticism of the monitors.[37]

Around the time of the Davis-Lincoln meeting, Sophie started to sense that Du Pont had placed his career in real jeopardy. Correctly assuming that the reason he had not written her in some days was because he was instead writing official letters trying to clear his name, she begged him to stop. "I wish . . . when you are angry and worried, you would write to *me* more, and less to *others*, because it is *safer*, and after writing the first emotions to *me*, you are more likely to write calmly collectedly to others." When she heard of the Stimers affair, she gravely warned Du Pont that "I apprehend greatly your having taken a step you will regret." After thirty years of marriage, Sophie knew that in the circumstances Du Pont found himself after Charleston, he was his own worst enemy. After reviewing all of Du Pont's post attack correspondence with the Navy Department, Sophie reluctantly told Du Pont in late May 1863 that he had only himself to blame for his predicament. It seemed to her that "the Department did not *intend* to quarrel with you about the Charleston affair . . . but that the visit of Mr. Davis to the President, placing Fox in a vexatious position, roused his anger and hostility. . . . [H]is intervention has been an unfortunate one."[38]

Indeed, Sophie was probably correct. Had Du Pont swallowed his pride and continued to look for innovative ways to get at Charleston, he most certainly would have kept his job. His paramount concern for reputation overrode his common sense and prudence and led him to make ill-considered accusations and to write almost insubordinate letters to his civilian superiors. The fact that Du Pont was right does not change the reality that his judgment was lacking in the weeks and months after his defeat at Charleston. He should have listened to Sophie.

Du Pont's obsession with Stimers, his increasingly strident conflict with the department, and his reluctance to conduct any subsequent operations against Charleston gave Welles little choice but to relieve the admiral. But it is also clear that once Du Pont began to publicly criticize the ability of the monitors to take on fortifications publicly, he had to go. Welles and Fox could not allow a prominent admiral to threaten the weapon system on which the department had bet everything. Welles confided to his diary that "I fear he can be no longer useful in his present command, and am mortified and vexed that I did not earlier detect his vanity and weakness. They have lost us the opportunity to take Charleston, which a man of more daring energy, and who had not a distinguished name to nurse and take care of would have improved." This assessment contains some kernels of truth: Du Pont could be vain, and he was not aggressive or imaginative at Charleston. On the other hand, it turned out that the admiral's view of the operation was correct in almost every respect. Ironically, by late May, Welles, Lincoln, and Secretary of War Stanton decided that Du Pont was right: only a joint army and navy expedition could take Charleston.

In early May an exhausted and dispirited Du Pont sensed that his days in command of the South Atlantic Blockading Squadron were numbered. To Henry Winter Davis, Du Pont lamented that he probably would be sacrificed to the demands of the "ironclad plunderers." Resigned and just a bit self-pitying, he wrote that "I would like this cup [the struggle with the Navy Department] to pass by, for I have now been over two years and four months on ceaseless duty . . . and of the above period I have been nineteen months afloat; minus a brief period of ten days last October of recreation, I cannot call it rest."[39] He was tired and sick of heart. The long months at sea coupled with the pressures of command had taken a heavy toll. But despite the letter to Davis, Du Pont decided to continue to fight.

On 3 June 1863 Du Pont sent a very long letter to Welles repeating all of the familiar arguments and for the first time referring to his voluminous correspondence with Fox in the months leading to the April attack. It was too late. Less than a week later, the steamer *Circassian* dropped anchor at Port Royal. She was carrying official dispatches from home; one of them was an order from the secretary relieving Du Pont. Welles used Du Pont's own letter in reaction to the president's telegram as the final justification for Du Pont's relief: the admiral had literally asked for it. Although Du Pont surely expected it, the order struck him with the force of a sucker punch. "It is hard," he wrote Sophie, "after forty-seven years of service, and serving actively through the Mexican War and this from its inception, at great personal sacrifice and against some ill health, to be disposed of in this way." The only silver lining to the entire affair was that now he could rejoin Sophie at Louviers "where I long to be beyond description."[40]

Welles first designated Andrew Foote to replace Du Pont, but Du Pont's old friend died before he could take command. A reluctant Welles then selected Dahlgren—Lincoln's favorite but often at odds with the secretary—as the squadron's new commander. Days before Du Pont stepped down from his command, John Rodgers and the *Weehawken* gave the admiral a farewell present when they captured the feared Confederate ironclad *Atlanta*. Rodgers's victory added an exclamation point to Du Pont's long-held and often-voiced belief that the best mission for a monitor was to provide coastal defense and to fight other ironclads. One reporter noted that the great victory "has created the wildest excitement in the fleet, and has put new life into all hands."[41] Although Du Pont was very happy for his friend, the victory came too late to breath new life into his shattered career.

Dahlgren relieved Du Pont at Port Royal on 6 July 1863. When Dahlgren arrived in Port Royal, he reported that the squadron's morale was very poor.[42] Since the April disaster Du Pont had been obsessed with restoring his reputation at the expense of planning and conducting operations, the best cure for low morale. In his desire for complete and utter vindication for the Charleston debacle, Du Pont forfeited his career, tarnished his good name, and squandered the loyal support of many of his junior officers and men.

The energetic and ambitious Dahlgren attacked Charleston days after taking command. He tried a joint attack with General Quincy Adams Gillmore on 10 and 11 July that ended in disaster. Despite numerous other attempts over the next two years, Dahlgren and his army counterparts failed to take Charleston. The great birthplace of the rebellion would not fall until February 1865 when Union ground forces cut the city's supply lines, forcing the evacuation of the rebel garrison. Charleston fell with a whimper, not a bang. In a letter to the department written several months after the end of the war—a letter that was returned with a rebuke but without action—Dahlgren expressed almost unreserved support for Du Pont and his pre-attack assessments of the monitors and the chances for success of an all-navy assault on Charleston.[43]

It took only three days to travel from Port Royal to the Brandywine,[44] but with Du Pont alone with his thoughts, the trip must have been torture. Throughout his long years of service, Du Pont had always triumphantly returned to his family and home in robust health and the high spirits of an accomplished military professional. Indeed, his arrival was typically accompanied by the enthusiastic accolades of peers, superiors, and the press for his exploits at sea. This time was much different. This time his career and reputation were in tatters. Still, the exhausted admiral was determined to restore his good name. Sophie, however, was skeptical.

Upon his arrival at Louviers, Du Pont embarked on a protracted yet largely unsuccessful attempt to clear his name and restore his reputation with the help of his good friends and administration foes Congressman Davis and Senator Grimes. Taking their advice, Du Pont wrote an impertinent letter to Welles in October 1863 refuting charges that he did not use the monitors to best advantage, that he did not express his misgivings to the department before the battle, and that he failed to press the attack. Referring to Dahlgren's failed attempts to take the city, Du Pont wrote that "the recent operations before Charleston sufficiently vindicate my judgment." Welles was furious and responded to Du Pont with a lengthy list of his offenses:

> Your prompt abandonment of the harbor of Charleston after a brief attack—your disinclination to occupy the harbor—your declarations that the monitors could not remain there with safety—your doubts and misgivings in relation to those vessels—your opposition to a naval attack—your omission to suggest or advise any system of naval proceedings—your constant complaints—the distrust that painfully pervaded your correspondence—your distressing personal anxiety about yourself, that seemed to overshadow public duty—your assaults upon editors instead of assaults upon rebel batteries—your neglect of any reconnaissance of the harbor obstructions, or if such was ever made, your neglect to inform the Department of the fact—these, with your querulous and censorious charges which subsequently, during four months' leisure, have been garnered up and cherished.[45]

The battle was now truly joined. But despite the help of Du Pont's friends and family, Davis's and Grimes's attacks in Congress were blunted by Welles and Fox, and they skillfully controlled public perceptions of the monitors and the admiral.

Welles and Fox successfully turned the postattack debate into a question of Du Pont's ability to accept and handle new technology. Technological inertia ensured that the department would not deviate from its pre-Charleston support for the monitors. After Charleston, Welles noted in his diary that "the modern changes in naval warfare and in naval vessels are repugnant to [Du Pont]; and to the turret vessels he has a declared aversion. He has been active in schemes to retire officers; he is now at work to retire ironclads and impair confidence in them." Fox wrote John Ericsson, "Du Pont neither understands nor appreciates [ironclads], he is of a wooden age, eminent in that, but in any engineering one behind the times."[46] In these terms they attempted to depict the admiral, more or less successfully, to the public and to Congress.

Both these men were wrong. Du Pont was not against the monitor or the ironclad, but he did resist having to undertake a "forlorn hope" with tools of war that were ill suited to the mission. In his testimony in February 1864 before the Joint Committee on the Conduct of the War, Du Pont noted that he was not against the monitors, although he preferred the *New Ironsides* because it was the most versatile of the ironclad designs. He believed instead that "no one form or mode can be said to be superior to all others for *all* purposes; and as we should not confine ourselves to one kind of gun on shipboard, neither should we restrict ourselves to one class of ironclads." Du Pont's experience at Charleston did have a positive effect. As one historian has observed, after Charleston "public euphoria declined to the more practical, realistic view that Du Pont . . . had advocated" all along. Another historian argues that even though the proceedings sometimes were very partisan as in the case of Henry Winter Davis's overwrought defense of Du Pont in Congress, the "inefficiency and incompetence" in monitor design and construction "that were uncovered justified the investigation."[47]

The crowning indignity came when Welles replied to a congressional inquiry of February 1864. In his 11 April response, Welles masterfully twisted and misrepresented the facts of the Charleston operation. First, Welles quoted a letter written in May 1863 by General Hunter to Lincoln complaining about Du Pont's conduct during and after the battle; Hunter whined that he had not been included in the 7 April attack and that the admiral was not interested in further operations after the defeat. Welles implied that Du Pont had been ordered all along to "cooperate with the army" in any attempt to take Charleston; indeed, that he had disobeyed orders by not doing so. Yet Welles and Fox had insisted, almost from the time the smoke had cleared over the waters of Hampton Roads after the first battle of the ironclads, that any attempt on Charleston would be an all-navy show. Second, Welles wrote that "on no occasion, anywhere nor at any time, did Rear Admiral Du Pont protest to the department against making said attack.'" The secretary also declared that the department had never actually ordered Du Pont to make the attack.[48]

Welles was technically correct: there were no explicit orders directing an immediate attack on Charleston, and Du Pont never officially protested against making the attempt. But it had been clear to all involved—Welles, Fox, Lincoln, Du Pont, every one of his captains, and the public—that the success or failure of the admiral's command rested on seizing Charleston. If Du Pont did not conduct an all-navy attack on Charleston with the monitors, Welles would find someone who would. Du Pont had made his concerns and objections known to his superiors for months before the attack. To his credit, he did not appeal outside his chain of command to the president or the press. If he had, Welles would not have dared to write such a letter to Congress. Welles was misleading Congress to protect his department and its investment in the monitors.

In his report to Congress, Welles finally released all the documents and reports concerning ironclads. However, he did not include the numerous letters between Du Pont and Fox outlining the admiral's concerns and his recommendations for joint operations and Fox's (and Welles's) desire for an all-navy operation. Also not released were any minutes of the meetings among the key individuals during Du Pont's October 1862 Washington visit. Finally, Welles failed to make public a report signed by all of Du Pont's monitor commanders in May 1863 outlining the shortcomings of their ships. The captains had agreed with Du Pont's assessment that while the monitors were not useful in the open ocean or against forts, "when employed against vessels of any class known to us, in smooth harbors, they will hardly fail to be in the highest degree effective." The captains also seconded Du Pont's belief that "possessing the advantage of a secure harbor, and choosing the time of exit, these vessels can, in our opinion, greatly harass a blockading force."[49]

Henry Winter Davis wanted Du Pont to release all of his private correspondence with Fox to counter the navy's case, but Sophie flatly refused. Sophie had been furious when Fox released to the press one of the private letters—a favorable one—Du Pont had written after Port Royal; she had no intention of allowing her husband to stoop to Fox's level now. "*Their* doing so, does not exonerate him [Du Pont] for doing the same thing, a thing which he disapproves *in them*."[50]

At Sophie's urging, Du Pont reluctantly gave up the struggle against the department after the secretary published his report. It was over. Welles and Fox had won. They succeeded in maintaining the primacy of the monitors at the expense of Du Pont's career and reputation. This was a crushing disappointment; for the first time in almost five decades, his beloved service had turned its back on him.

Epilogue

DU PONT technically remained on active duty after giving up the South Atlantic Blockading Squadron and began to serve on various boards and commissions. In June 1864, after Du Pont had given up his struggle against the department, he received a letter from his old friend Charles Henry Davis, now head of the Bureau of Navigation in Washington, D.C. Davis wrote that Fox had asked him to contact Du Pont about accepting command of the Pacific Squadron. Davis noted that "Mr. Fox seemed to fear that you, or your friends [Congressman Davis and Senator Grimes], might take the offer unkindly: though if his language meant anything, it is just the other way."[1] The letter gives no indication whether this was a legitimate offer with Welles's approval, or if the assistant secretary was merely trying to reestablish his old friendship with the admiral. Davis urged his old friend and boss to accept the new assignment, but Du Pont would have none of it.

Command of a tiny force composed of three to five ships was unacceptable to the admiral who had commanded the largest combat fleet in United States history, at times reaching seventy ships. Such an offer was downright insulting, thought Du Pont. Sophie agreed. Du Pont wrote his old chief of staff that "there is certainly nothing to be gratified with in the command of the Pacific station—it is service during war but not war service." Although he had ceased to challenge the department actively, the residual bitterness was still there. "I can receive nothing as a favor until the Department has withdrawn its insults."[2]

With Sophie at their beloved Louviers, Du Pont anxiously followed the fortunes of Union arms during the bloody summer of 1864. As Grant's offensive against Lee ground to a halt outside Petersburg and Confederate general Jubal Early threatened the capital, Union war weariness reached its zenith. By the middle of August, Du Pont had come to the same conclusion as his friend Henry Winter Davis, who wrote that Lincoln "is a defeated man *now*. . . . unless something happen[s], i.e., a victory." In his despair Du Pont believed that Lincoln should step aside for a new Republican nominee, because although he admired Democratic presidential candidate General George B. McClellan, he did not like his peace platform.[3]

As the momentous election of 1864 approached, Du Pont and Sophie embarked on a pleasant trip together to New York, Newport, and Boston. There he met with friends including his old chief, George Bancroft; John Jacob Astor; and Alexander Dallas Bache, then suffering from the debilitating stroke that led to his death three years later. Lincoln's reelection relieved Du Pont, but at this point his attitude toward the president was lukewarm at best, probably as the result of his relationship with radical Republican Henry Winter Davis. Before this trip undetermined health problems cropped up, probably related to complications from diabetes. Du Pont had to watch his diet for several years. Recently, he had been losing weight, particularly in the wake of his relief from command, and had grown progressively weaker. Although the trip north invigorated him, upon his return to Louviers in late November 1864, he consulted with a team of doctors in a vain attempt to regain weight and strength. Like many patients before and after, he complained about their advice: "I have long and improved lists of what I am to eat and drink and what to avoid . . . but this is not easy. The most recent English work on corpulency says bread and *sugar* are the most fattening of any substance eaten—now these are specially *interdicted* in my case." Although his doctors also recommended that he and Sophie spend some time resting in the south of France, Du Pont refused to leave the country during wartime.[4]

As his health continued to decline, Du Pont uncharacteristically began to criticize naval colleagues, including old friends like Vice Admiral Farragut and Rear Admiral David D. Porter who had achieved great victories. He still smarted from his relief and his battle with the department and viewed the popularity of these officers both in the public and within the department with great jealousy. Only three short years before, Du Pont was the toast of the naval community. Now he was virtually forgotten.

He achieved some small measure of professional vindication in February 1865 when he heard that Southern troops had evacuated Charleston and Union forces had then occupied the city and its forts. As Du Pont had predicted, an army force finally severed Charleston's lines of communication and caused its downfall. Writing to Henry Winter Davis, Du Pont wistfully declared that "I should be grateful for many reasons, for none more than the justification it gives to the confidence of those friends who have clung by me. I presume none but the latter however will think of the capture in this connection."[5]

Two more opportunities to contribute to the navy presented themselves. In early 1865 he helped Henry Winter Davis draft a bill that would have established a board of senior officers—based in part on the Blockade Board of 1861—which would act as the de facto planning staff for the Navy Department. Such an organization would have been unprecedented in the American military establishment and would have greatly enhanced the capabilities and effectiveness of naval operations. But the bill submitted and promoted by Davis, one of the most controversial congressmen in the House, had little chance of passage. In their last symbolic shot against Davis and Du Pont, Welles and Fox successfully fought against the bill and its implied criticism of their handling of the war. This failed effort would be Du Pont's last attempt to initiate naval reform.[6]

But one final chance for Du Pont to play an important role presented itself in February 1865. For the first time Congress directed the navy to convene a Board on Promotions that would consider senior officers for advancement. Admiral Farragut, the president of the board, insisted to Fox and Welles that Du Pont be a member. Farragut's prestige trumped the department's objections, and Du Pont soon received orders to attend. Farragut understood that many men who had served honorably in the South Atlantic Blockading Squadron would be ignored if their former commander was not on the board to speak on their behalf. This was personnel reform of the kind that Du Pont had always advocated: a mechanism to promote deserving officers who had performed well in the most rigorous and hazardous service. This was his chance to take care of his loyal subordinates. On 5 March 1865, despite his frail health, Du Pont reported to Admiral Farragut in Washington, D.C., for duty on the board. The members were Farragut, Du Pont, Goldsborough, Porter, and Charles Henry Davis. Although frustrated with his colleagues at times, Du Pont was able to secure promotions for Percival Drayton and C. R. P. Rodgers, among others. It seems fitting that Du Pont's last official duty was to ensure the promotion by merit of some of his most deserving captains.[7]

With the exception of his trip to Washington, D.C., Du Pont spent his time quietly at Louviers with Sophie at his side. Sophie would recall that the couple whiled away many pleasant days sitting together in the admiral's study at Louviers overlooking his beloved dogwood trees and flower garden, as Du Pont worked on his correspondence and Sophie on her needlework. However, while in Washington for the promotion board, Du Pont caught a severe cold that brought on what was almost certainly a series of acute and life-threatening bronchial asthma attacks. One such attack in March 1865 terrified Sophie, who woke up to find Du Pont struggling to breathe. She was sure he was about to die and asked him if he was ready to meet God. "I'm ready," he gasped. In late March he wrote Henry Winter Davis that "I have been very near the dark valley, indeed I had one foot well over the threshold." He described the heroic measures used by his sister-in-law to bring him back from the brink: "Four full tumblers of mustard and hot water caused the spasm of my lungs to relax, and I was instantly relieved." A distraught Sophie wrote Davis that "the sojourn to Washington was very unfavorable to his health and he lost rapidly what he had seemed to have gained in the two previous months."[8] He recovered from that attack, but others followed, although with less frequency and severity.

When spring arrived and Du Pont's dogwoods began to bloom around Louviers, his health appeared to improve slightly, although he was stricken with two more attacks. As the war wound down to its inevitable conclusion, the couple even spoke of finally taking their doctors' advice, and they began to plan a visit to Europe. Du Pont and Sophie, like the rest of the North, rejoiced at Grant's victory at Appomattox. "My sickroom, as you may suppose," he wrote to Thomas Turner, "has been cheered like the whole country by the good news from Virginia, especially by the surrender of Lee and his army which foreshadows the blessings of an early peace."[9] It was now only a matter of days before the war was over.

The celebration quickly turned to mourning along the Brandywine when they learned that Lincoln had been assassinated. Du Pont was shocked and outraged: "After the first idea of pain and horror at such a tragedy . . . had passed off, I felt as if our national fame had received a great blot."[10] Although he often disagreed with Lincoln's policies, Du Pont always respected the president, liked him as a person, and certainly saw him as the best man available.

In late June, Du Pont felt fit enough to travel, and the couple prepared to make a short trip to Philadelphia. Despite his fragile health, Du Pont retained his sense of humor. On 18 June he wrote Henry Winter Davis that he was faithfully following his doctor's orders. "I am, I *think*, a great deal better—have gotten back to the whisky and, lest I should get overfond of it, I suppose, take it twice a day in cod-liver oil! To console myself for this ordeal, I take a little *without* the oil."[11]

Sophie and Du Pont checked into the La Pierre House Hotel on 22 June

1865. From his hotel room Du Pont wrote a pleasant, chatty letter to his old friend and comrade Percival Drayton. He wrote of old navy friends and acquaintances, the upcoming trip to Europe, and the status of the freedmen on Hilton Head. Du Pont signed the letter, "Believe me yours affectionately, S. F. Du Pont." [12] In the middle of the night, Du Pont was stricken by another massive attack. A doctor was called, but this time there was no reprieve. The admiral died with Sophie at his side at 4:45 A.M. on 23 June 1865, four days short of their thirty-second anniversary and three months shy of his sixty-second birthday. Newspaper accounts of Du Pont's death called his illness "a disease of the throat," but Sophie's description of the symptoms suggest severe asthma or chronic bronchitis brought on by his March cold. [13]

Sophie was devastated but remarkably composed. She must have sensed that his time on earth was running out. They had shared triumphs, tragedies, illness, injury, a love of God, and long, tedious, and often terrifying separations. Their relationship had grown and evolved as they all do, but by almost any standard the Du Pont marriage was a great success and brought happiness and fulfillment to both Sophie and Frank.

Henry Winter Davis was heartbroken. "My loss," he wrote, "is irreparable not merely in the loss of my best friend but of the only advisor whose judgment I was willing to take against my own." [14] Although most obituaries touched on the Charleston debacle, nearly all were exceptionally laudatory. Du Pont himself probably would have been surprised that many of the accounts of his life emphasized his exceptionally humane treatment of the ex-slaves of Port Royal. In a moving, and witty, eulogy, Henry Winter Davis praised his friend as an "earnest advocate of emancipation" who "declared that the war could never end till slavery was destroyed." Moreover, Davis continued, "He never cast a democratic vote." [15]

Du Pont had served his country for forty-nine years, fought in two wars, and endured years of separation from his family. Although Gideon Welles directed all navy installations to commemorate the admiral's funeral with flags at half-staff and salutes, no official representatives attended the ceremony aside from an honor guard consisting of 200 marines from Du Pont's last peacetime command, the Philadelphia Navy Yard. The senior pallbearer was Major General George Gordon Meade, the hero of Gettysburg and a friend since Du Pont's days with the Lighthouse Board. Also in the official party was Commodore Thomas Turner, the captain of the *New Ironsides* on that fateful April day at Charleston, and Commodore James Lardner, who as commander of the *Susquehanna* stood by Du Pont's flagship as rebel shells peppered the Union fleet at Port Royal. Du Pont's closest relatives and

friends—those whose unwavering support after Charleston helped to assuage somewhat the sting of national disgrace—mourned him in a solemn
ceremony and comforted a grieving Sophie. After a brief but moving service
in Christ Church—the place of worship Du Pont did so much to establish
and nurture—and surrounded by members of his personal and professional
families, the admiral's flag-draped coffin was drawn slowly down a tree-lined
lane to the private du Pont family plot in Greenville, Delaware, adjacent to
the original gunpowder works, across the Brandywine from Louviers. Du
Pont's grave is marked only with his name, rank, dates, and "US Navy."[16]
Sophie would join him twenty-three years later, but only after a tireless effort to restore her husband's name. She also embarked on a successful campaign to gather and arrange his voluminous collection of personal papers.

Samuel Francis Du Pont's story is one of the most heartbreaking of the
Civil War. For over twenty years Du Pont was one of the most important
figures in the United States Navy. Although he was recognized as an extremely competent seaman and leader well before the Mexican War, that
conflict thrust him into prominence in the service while he was still a relatively junior commander. In a war that provided few opportunities for the
United States Navy to shine, Du Pont's successful exploits in the Pacific bur-
nished his reputation within and outside of the service. Thus by the early
1850s Du Pont found himself in a uniquely powerful position to influence
naval and military policy and strategy, and he was able to advance successfully his own notions of naval reform through a labyrinth of department and
congressional barriers after overcoming considerable bureaucratic inertia.

The secretary of war's request that Du Pont provide his assessment of the
nation's defense policy in 1851 gave him the opportunity to produce and dis-
seminate to key decision makers his vision for the future direction of the
United States Navy. In a well-reasoned and thoroughly supported document, Du Pont advocated a strategy similar to that later advanced by America's great naval strategist Alfred Thayer Mahan. Du Pont also not only recognized the importance of the navy's experiments with steam and propeller
technology but recommended an acceleration of that effort with an aim toward deploying the most technologically advanced warship in the world.
This report marked him as having one of the navy's premier minds.

He was also a dedicated reformer who was willing to risk his career and
his most important possession, his reputation, in an unwavering quest to
make the navy a more efficient branch of the armed forces. The many positive results of the 1855 Efficiency Board were due almost solely to his efforts.
Du Pont's defense strategy—one of its products being the development and
fielding of state-of-the-art steam warships—coupled with the elimination of

incompetent officers and the promotion of many deserving men meant enhanced navy readiness as the service entered a decade of immense challenge.

Du Pont was intelligent, charismatic, refined, and polite, extremely well read and, among naval officers of the day, well educated. Du Pont's personality and social skills easily allowed him to act as an effective, albeit reluctant, diplomat. The department sensibly chose him for such sensitive missions as the voyage of the USS *Minnesota* to China and as chief of the escort mission for the first Japanese embassy to the United States. He was also much respected as an excellent leader and seaman. His personal wealth, self-confidence, and personality ensured that he could be frank with peers and superiors without fear of retribution. Du Pont was an excellent administrator, judge of subordinates, strategist, and reformer. Subordinates respected and admired him for his ability to delegate and the value he placed on his officers' opinions and initiative. He was also well liked for his loyalty toward his friends, former subordinates, and shipmates.

Du Pont's technical and professional expertise and extensive seagoing experience made him the obvious choice to lead the Blockade Board at the start of the Civil War; the board formulated a plan for the effective blockade of the Confederacy. Du Pont's leadership and guidance throughout this process produced the operational concept for blockade and key joint operations—arguably the navy's most important missions—followed by the Union navy throughout the war. The Blockade Board's plan proved to be the only coherent and long-range strategic plan fashioned by either side early in the war. The Union navy operated from Du Pont's plan throughout the conflict, an unequaled accomplishment in the Civil War.

After his great victory at Port Royal during which he led the largest United States fleet up to that point, Du Pont became the country's most famous naval officer since the War of 1812. His rapid fall from grace only seventeen months later marks him as the most tragic naval figure of the war. He was personally courageous as evidenced by his deeds in the Mexican War and at Port Royal; but at Charleston his demoralized performance was lackluster, and he demonstrated little aggressiveness. Given the limitations under which he operated, the Charleston attack demanded the utmost in imagination and audacity. The admiral's plan and his conduct of the battle demonstrated neither trait. There was no plan for follow-on operations and no plan in the event something went wrong; in short, there were no alternatives except retreat should the ships fail to destroy or pass Fort Sumter. In contrast, his performance had been excellent for the first eight months he was in command of the blockading squadron, culminating in the seizure of Fort Pulaski. This is not to say that success at Charleston was possible. Indeed, Du Pont's and his successor's difficulties make it clear that Charleston could not have been seized by warships alone, nor could anything other than a major joint operation using substantial ground forces have succeeded. Du Pont's characterization of the Charleston attack as a "forlorn hope" is correct. But Welles and Fox, chafing under intense newspaper criticism, were determined to reprise the great victories at New Orleans and Port Royal and insisted over Du Pont's objections that he stage a purely naval attack with a fleet of seemingly invincible monitors. When the inevitable failure validated Du Pont's preattack warnings and concerns and threatened to expose the department's overreliance on monitor-class vessels, the admiral became expendable. Despite support for Du Pont throughout the service, Welles and Fox painted him as antimonitor, antitechnology, and an officer who disregarded orders.

Welles and Fox were wrong. On the contrary, Du Pont embraced technology, as illustrated by his advocacy of the new propeller frigates in the 1850s, his work at the Crystal Palace, his sponsorship of the submarine study at the Philadelphia Navy Yard, his recommendation before the war that the department conduct ironclad experiments, his own experimentation with his monitors, and his acknowledgment of the importance of ironclads in general. Indeed, Du Pont's assessment of the new technology was highly nuanced and demonstrated a professional analysis of the monitors based on long naval experience. He recognized that the monitors were not suitable for all naval missions, nor were they sufficient to guarantee success at Charleston. The *Passaic*-class monitors that comprised the majority of his ironclad fleet did not have the offensive firepower, the speed, and the maneuverability to take on the multilayered Charleston defenses, run through the underwater obstructions, and seize the city itself. Du Pont knew this, had known it for some time, and his inadequate attack plan reflects his pessimism. His captains, most of them handpicked by the admiral, were perhaps the most talented group of United States naval officers in the nineteenth century. Whether or not his pessimism infected them, they shared their commander's concerns before the battle and fully supported his actions after it. But Du Pont could not fight the power of the department. His relief was probably preordained the moment he identified the monitors' shortcomings.

Improved communications between Washington, D.C., and the field could have prevented disagreements such as those between Du Pont and the Navy Department. But all parties were at fault. Although Du Pont made his reservations known on numerous occasions, he should have been much more adamant. He should have made sure that Fox passed along his concerns to Welles.[17] He also should have sought from the president, and he would have almost surely received, army support for a planned joint operation against Charleston. After having exhausted his attempts to stave off disaster, Du Pont should have bowed to the obvious political exigencies driving Welles, Fox, and Lincoln that demanded an attack on Charleston. Once he was committed, he should have done his very best, but he did not. In military affairs—as in most human endeavors—personalities are everything. Under most circumstances Du Pont's personal relationships between superiors, peers, and subordinates were excellent. However, as the admiral grew frustrated with his inability to convince Welles and Fox of the inadvisability of attacking Charleston with monitors, he became almost fatalistic about the outcome. His resignation—coupled with his respect for the traditional chain of command—meant that he would not go over Fox and Welles to the president. The department head and his assistant were wrong to advocate an all-navy operation, and they improperly forced the operation on Du Pont because of their misplaced faith in the monitors and because of a destructive interservice rivalry.[18] Fox and Welles had allowed themselves to become as obsessed with Charleston as Union army commanders had been with Richmond, all to the detriment of the blockade.

Perhaps the position for which Du Pont was best suited was a post that did not exist in the United States Navy in 1863: naval chief of staff or admiral in chief of the Union navy. Du Pont would have been able to provide much of the navy's operational and strategic direction, allowing Welles and Fox to concentrate on administrative and logistical requirements. As one of the navy's most admired figures, Du Pont would have commanded the respect of fellow officers. With his considerable experience in the halls of Congress and the workings of Washington's complex bureaucracy, he would have been a natural at the job. Or, Du Pont could have acted as a combination of a chief of staff like Major General Henry W. Halleck and a general in chief like Grant, setting strategic priorities, recommending allocation of resources, and serving as a buffer between commanders on station and their civilian masters. He would have been suited to this sort of position where his thin skin would not have been easily bruised. But the department never contemplated something along these lines.

Despite the abrupt end to his otherwise superlative career, Du Pont's efforts were critical to the success and the domination of the Union navy in the Civil War. His strategic writings in 1851, the strengthening of the officer corps in 1855, his strategic direction of the Union blockade, and his command of the South Atlantic Blockading Squadron all served to enhance the competence and effectiveness of the navy. Although he could never have anticipated the coming of the Civil War, Du Pont struggled to improve the readiness of the navy in any way he could; he was always striving to improve the navy's "efficiency."

Du Pont was a warrior, a diplomat, a thoughtful strategist, a confirmed reformer, and an experienced and supremely competent seaman. As accomplished as he was professionally, he was much more than that. He was also a loving, attentive, and affectionate husband, a steadfast and loyal friend and colleague, and, on occasion, an implacable foe. Situated less than half a mile from the site of their beloved home and only about 300 yards from the Brandywine, Sophie and Frank rest together in the du Pont family cemetery shaded by stately trees that witnessed the building of the first powder mills along the river. One modest obelisk rises slightly higher than the headstones marking the resting places of other du Ponts. No epitaph is inscribed on the admiral's stone, but the words of his trusted old subordinate C. R. P. Rodgers could admirably serve that purpose: "Few commanders-in-chief have had the good fortune to inspire the same admiration, affection, and trust that the officers who came in contact with Admiral Du Pont felt for him." [19]

Du Pont always enjoyed the wholehearted support of his family, his fellow officers, and the navy writ large. Congress authorized $20,000 for a large statue of the admiral, which was erected in the center of Washington's Dupont Circle and dedicated by President Chester A. Arthur and other dignitaries in December 1884.[20] The statue has since been replaced by a fountain and moved to Delaware, not far from the site of Louviers. Three navy ships have been named after the admiral: a torpedo boat and two destroyers; the last USS *Du Pont* was scrapped in 1993. Another ship, a modern cruiser, still bears the name of Du Pont's greatest victory, the USS *Port Royal*. Perhaps it is time for the navy to name another ship for an officer who gave so much to his service and his country.

Notes

Abbreviations

ARSN   U.S. Congress, Senate Executive Documents, *Annual Report of the Secretary of the Navy*

Du Pont, *Letters*   Samuel F. Du Pont, *Samuel Francis Du Pont: A Selection from His Civil War Letters*, ed. John D. Hayes (Ithaca, N.Y., 1969)

HML   Hagley Museum and Library, Greenville, Del.

Naval Records   Naval Records Collection of the Office of Naval Records and Library, Record Group 45, National Archives, Washington, D.C.

ORA   Department of War, *Official Records of the Union and Confederate Armies in the War of the Rebellion*, 128 vols. (Washington, D.C., 1898)

ORN   Department of the Navy, *Official Records of the Union and Confederate Navies in the War of the Rebellion*, 30 vols. (Washington, D.C., 1927)

SFDP   Samuel Francis Du Pont

SMDP   Sophie Madeline Du Pont

USNA   Special Collections and Archives Division, U.S. Naval Academy, Annapolis, Md.

Introduction

1. Dahlgren, *Memoir of John A. Dahlgren*, 6 July 1863 diary entry, 397; SFDP to Percival Drayton, 29 July 1863, in Du Pont, *Letters* 3:205–9; Browning, *Success Is All That Was Expected*, 215; Schneller, *Quest for Glory*, 254; *New York Times*, 15 July 1863; log of the U.S. Steam Frigate *Wabash*, 6 July 1863, Bureau of Naval Personnel, Ships' Logs, Stations, and Miscellaneous, RG 24, National Archives.

1. The Early Years

1. See Duke, *Portrait of a Dynasty*, 50–85; Dutton, *Du Pont*, 3–42; Ferrari, *Du Pont*. See also Hayes, "Introduction," in Du Pont, *Letters* 1:xlvii–l; Merrill, *Du Pont*, 1–4; Du Pont, *Du Pont*, 3–7; Bauer, "Samuel Francis Du Pont," 142–43.

2. Undated manuscript, W9-18504, SFDP Papers, HML; McKee, *A Gentlemanly and Honorable Profession*, 92–95.

3. Merrill, *Du Pont*, 4–6; Hayes, "Introduction," in Du Pont, *Letters* 1:li–lii; Bauer, "Samuel Francis Du Pont," 143; Du Pont, *Du Pont*, 6–7; M. Constant to Victor du Pont, 1 Feb. 1814, W3-2805, Victor M. du Pont Papers, HML.

4. Merrill, "The First Cruise of a Delaware Midshipman," 256–57; SFDP to Benjamin W. Crowninshield, 1 Jan. 1816, W9-9, SFDP Papers, HML.

5. Undated manuscript, W8-31982, Henry A. du Pont Papers, HML.

6. SFDP to Alfred du Pont, 29 Apr. 1821, W9-116, SFDP Papers, HML.

7. SFDP to "My Dear Parents," 1 Nov. 1817, W9-46, to Charles du Pont, 11 Nov. 1817, W9-49, to his parents, 24 Feb., 3 June 1818, W9-57, W9-63, ibid.; SFDP, Journal of the USS *Franklin* and *Erie*, USNA.

8. Merrill, "The First Cruise of a Delaware Midshipman," 256–68; undated description of Du Pont's first cruise, W9-40142, SFDP Papers, HML. For Du Pont's description of himself, see SFDP to John Forsyth, 21 Sept. 1840, W9-627, ibid.

9. SFDP to Garrett Pendergrast, 3 Feb., 7 May 1820, W9-95, W9-102, SFDP Papers, HML; Merrill, "Midshipman Du Pont and the Cruise of *North Carolina*, 1825–1827," 220–21; SFDP to Victor du Pont, 1 Dec. 1824, quoted ibid., 212–13.

10. Merrill, "Midshipman Du Pont and the Cruise of *North Carolina*, 1825–1827," 219; SFDP to Victorine du Pont, 25 Mar. 1825, W9-175, SFDP Papers, HML.

11. SFDP to Garrett Pendergrast, 13 June 1829, W9-212, to Victorine du Pont, 10 May 1830, W9-235, SFDP Papers, HML.

12. SFDP to John S. Wily, 23 Jan. 1831, W9-248, ibid.

13. Low and Kinsley, *Sophie Du Pont*, 18–19, 13.

14. SMDP to Henry du Pont, 2 Aug. 1832, W9-21241, and SMDP diary entry, 6 May 1832, W9-40376, SMDP Papers, HML.

15. SMDP to Henry du Pont, 26 Aug. 1832, W9-21245, ibid.

16. Low and Kinsley, *Sophie Du Pont*, 171; SMDP to Henry du Pont, 4 Mar. 1833, W9-21272, SMDP Papers, HML; Wilmington, Del., *News Journal*, 18 June 2000.

17. SMDP to Henry du Pont, 18 Mar. 1833, W9-21274, to Clementina B. Smith, 20 Mar. 1833, W9-21275, and SMDP diary entries, 6, 9 Feb. 1832, W9-40375, SMDP Papers, HML.

18. SMDP to SFDP, 21 Mar. 1833, W9-21276, ibid.

19. SFDP to Garrett Pendergrast, 17 Apr. 1833, W9-295, SFDP Papers, HML; SMDP to SFDP, 23 Apr. 1833, W9-21282, SMDP Papers, HML.

20. SFDP to Garrett Pendergrast, 11 July 1833, W9-309, to Charles H. Davis, 29 Sept. 1833, W9-311, SFDP Papers, HML. See also Sophie's brief undated account of the wedding, W9-40141, SMDP Papers, HML. On their use of "Du Pont," see Hayes, "Introduction," in Du Pont, *Letters* 1:xlviii n. Upper Louviers was demolished in the early 1990s to make way for an expansion of the Du Pont Country Club.

21. Low and Kinsley, *Sophie Du Pont*, 172–73.

22. SMDP to SFDP, 24 Dec. 1833, W9-21294, to Evelina du Pont Bidermann, Jan. 1834, W9-21296, SMDP Papers, HML.

23. SFDP to Charles H. Davis, 7 May 1834, W9-325, to SMDP, 8 Mar. 1839, W9-534, SFDP Papers, HML. See also Low and Kinsley, *Sophie Du Pont*, 171–74.

24. SFDP to Charles H. Davis, 27 Aug. 1835, W9-369, SFDP Papers, HML. The first suggestion of his change of heart occurred in a letter to Garrett Pendergrast on 28 Aug. 1834, W9-334, ibid.

25. SFDP to Garrett Pendergrast, 19 Nov. 1835, W9-380, to Henry du Pont, 2 May 1836, W9-426, to SMDP, 18 June, 19 June 1836, W9-435, W9-436, to Commodore Alexander J. Dallas, 27 July 1836, W9-443, to Alexander S. Mackenzie, 8 Feb. 1837, W9-463, ibid.

26. Langley, *Social Reform in the United States Navy*, 25–26; Howarth, *To Shining Sea*, 145; Todorich, "Franklin Buchanan," 93–94; Huntington, *Soldier and the State*, 217.

27. SFDP to Joseph Smith, 29 Jan. 1839, W9-528, SFDP Papers, HML.

28. Du Pont, *Du Pont*, 19–42; Merrill, *Du Pont*, 97–128; Bauer, "Samuel Francis Du Pont," 145; SFDP to Charles Henry Davis, 26 June 1840, W9-623, SFDP Papers, HML.

29. SFDP to SMDP, 3 Feb., 8 Mar. 1839, W9-530, W9-534, SFDP Papers, HML; SMDP to SFDP, 24 Nov. 1838, W9-21344, SMDP Papers, HML. Sophie's important influence on Du Pont's professional life reflects the upper-class gender roles in the early nineteenth century described by Allgor, *Parlor Politics*, 240–41.

2. The Mexican War

1. SFDP to Garrett Pendergrast, 6 Sept. 1840, W9-626, SFDP Papers, HML.

2. SFDP to Charles H. Davis, 31 May 1838, W9-491, to Garrett Pendergrast, 7 Jan. 1837, W9-480, ibid.; Christman, *Naval Innovators*, 61–66; Bauer, "Samuel Francis Du Pont," 145.

3. SFDP to Garrett Pendergrast, 8 July 1842, W9-719, to SMDP, 24 July 1842, W9-721, SFDP Papers, HML. For the Wilkes exploring expedition, see Philbrick, *Sea of Glory*.

4. Philbrick, *Sea of Glory*, 309–13; Merrill, *Du Pont*, 149–52.

5. Bauer, "Samuel Francis Du Pont," 145; SFDP to Alexander Slidell Mackenzie, 9 Jan. 1843, W9-768, to Matthew C. Perry, 10, 13, 14, 16, 21, 23 Jan. 1843, W9-769, W9-770, W9-771, W9-773, W9-774, W9-775, SFDP Papers, HML.

6. SFDP to Alexander Slidell Mackenzie, 10 May 1844, W9-894, to Charles H. Davis, 20 May 1844, W9-896, SFDP Papers, HML.

7. SFDP to Alexander Slidell Mackenzie, 24 Aug. 1845, W9-932, to Garrett Pendergrast, 26 Aug. 1845, W9-933, ibid.

8. Smith, "An Uncertain Passage," 86–88.

9. For Bancroft's founding of the Naval Academy, see Todorich, *Spirited Years*, 5–18. See also SFDP to SMDP, 1 Oct. 1849, W9-1139, SFDP Papers, HML.

10. See esp. Bauer, *Mexican War*.

11. SFDP to Garrett Pendergrast, 8 Nov. 1844, W9-911, SFDP Papers, HML; SMDP to Clementina B. Smith, 22 Aug. 1845, W9-21584, SMDP Papers, HML.

12. SFDP to SMDP, 13 Nov. 1845, W9-970, SFDP Papers, HML.

13. Bauer, *Mexican War*, 174; Van Denburgh, *My Voyage in the United States Frigate Congress*, 73–74.

14. SFDP to SMDP, 22 Feb. 1846, W9-989, SFDP Papers, HML; Van Denburgh, *My Voyage in the United States Frigate* Congress, 167.

15. Colton, *Deck and Port*, 24 July 1846 journal entry, 394.

16. SFDP to SMDP, 23 July 1846, W9-1000, SFDP Papers, HML; Merrill, *Du Pont*, 169–81; Du Pont, *Du Pont*, 45; Bauer, "Samuel Francis Du Pont," 146; Hayes, "Introduction," in Du Pont, *Letters* 1:lx.

17. Bauer, *Mexican War*, 174; Bauer, *Surfboats and Horse Marines*, 170–84; Amero, "The

Mexican-American War in Baja California," 51; Pourade, *Silver Dons*, 78–79; Frémont, *Memoirs of My Life* 1:563. See also SFDP to Richard Stockton, 23 Sept. 1846, W9-1011, SFDP Papers, HML.

18. Bauer, *Mexican War*, 189–91. See also Bauer, *Surf Boats and Horse Marines*, 170–238; Merrill, *Du Pont*, 181–98; Du Pont, *Du Pont*, 46–56; Bauer, "Samuel Francis Du Pont," 146; Hayes, "Introduction," in Du Pont, *Letters* 1:lxi. For Stockton's praise of Du Pont's performance in a letter to the secretary of the navy, see Robert F. Stockton to George Bancroft, 23 Nov. 1846, in Bauer, *New American State Papers* 5:243–46.

19. SFDP to SMDP, 19 Jan. 1847, W9-1022, to Garrett Pendergrast, 23 Jan. 1847, W9-1025, SFDP Papers, HML.

20. SFDP to Alexander Slidell Mackenzie, 17 Mar. 1847, W9-1032, ibid.

21. Bauer, *Mexican War*, 344–45; Bauer, *Surfboats and Horse Marines*, 207–9; Amero, "Mexican-American War in Baja California," 51–52.

22. Amero, "Mexican-American War in Baja California," 54–58; "Synopsis of the Cruise of the U.S. Ship *Cyane* during the Years of 1845, '46, '47, and '48," n.d., in Du Pont's hand, W9-1100, SFDP Papers, HML.

23. Amero, "Mexican-American War in Baja California," 54–58; "Synopsis of the Cruise of the U.S. Ship *Cyane*," n.d., in Du Pont's hand, W9-1100, SFDP Papers, HML.

24. SFDP to William B. Shubrick, 16 Feb. 1848, W9-1065, SFDP Papers, HML. See also Amero, "Mexican-American War in Baja California," 54–58; Journal of a Cruise of the USS *Cyane*, 15 Feb. 1848, USNA.

25. SFDP to SMDP, 5 Mar., 21 Feb. 1848, W9-1066, W9-1062, SFDP Papers, HML; SMDP to SFDP, 2 Apr. 1848, W9-21757, SMDP Papers, HML; Journal of a Cruise of the USS *Cyane*, 15 Feb. 1848, USNA.

26. "Synopsis of the Cruise of the U.S. Ship *Cyane* during the Years of 1845, '46, '47, and '48," n.d., in Du Pont's hand, W9-1100, SFDP Papers, HML; Journal of a Cruise of the USS *Cyane*, 15 Feb. 1848, USNA.

27. SMDP to SFDP, 11 Oct. 1848, W9-21779, to Clementina B. Smith, 24 Oct. 1848, W9-21783, SMDP Papers, HML.

28. SFDP to SMDP, 6 Oct., 8 Oct. 1850, W9-1201, W9-1202, SFDP Papers, HML.

29. SMDP to SFDP, 15 Mar. 1846, W9-21634, SMDP Papers, HML.

30. See Smith, "An Uncertain Passage," 88–89; Langley, *Social Reform in the United States Navy*, 131–206; Glenn, *Campaigns against Corporal Punishment*, 103–26; Buker, "Captain's Mast," 143–45; Merrill, *Du Pont*, 200–201.

31. SFDP to William A. Graham, 27 Sept. 1851, W9-1255, SFDP Papers, HML.

32. SFDP to Charles Henry Davis, 14 May 1850, W9-1176, ibid.

33. SFDP to SMDP, 4 Jan. 1852, W9-1281, Henry Winter Davis to SFDP, 16 Feb. 1851, W9-6038, ibid.; Langley, *Social Reform in the United States Navy*, 174–75, 196–203; Merrill, *Du Pont*, 200–201; Litten, "Navy Flogging," 145–65.

34. William A. Graham to SFDP, 14 Apr. 1851, SFDP to Graham, 16 Apr. 1851, Commanders' Letters, M147, roll 42, Naval Records. For the board's membership, see Du Pont notes, 12 May 1851, W9-1226, SFDP Papers, HML; Du Pont, *Du Pont*, 58–59; Merrill, *Du Pont*, 202–4. For the state of the lighthouses on the East Coast, see Samuel Lockwood to SFDP, 15 May 1851, W9-6103, SFDP Papers, HML.

35. SFDP to SMDP, 23 May 1851, W9-1229, SFDP Papers, HML.

3. A Strategy for a Modern Navy

1. Clary, *Fortress America*, 37–39.

2. Weigley, *American Way of War*, 60; Clary, *Fortress America*, 39–40.

3. Monroe quoted in Howarth, *To Shining Sea*, 133. For the navy's technological experiments and the actions of Perry and Stockton, see Weigley, *American Way of War*, 62–63. For the steam frigate, see Canney, "The *Fulton II*," 193–201. For the 1842 shipbuilding fiasco, see Howarth, *To Shining Sea*, 147. Nathan Miller states that the legacy of the War of 1812 lasted well into the middle of the century (*U.S. Navy*, 85). For Upshur's actions to improve the navy, see Howarth, *To Shining Sea*, 146–48; Albion, *Makers of Naval Policy*, 70–71, 188–94. See also Bauer, "George Bancroft," 217–29; Langley, "William Alexander Graham," 257–67.

4. Canney, *Old Steam Navy* 1:3–5.

5. See Hagan, *This People's Navy*, 122–23; Tucker, "U.S. Navy Steam Sloop *Princeton*," 96–113.

6. SFDP to Garrett Pendergrast, 20 May 1844, W9-895, SFDP Papers, HML; Tucker, "U.S. Navy Steam Sloop *Princeton*," 111.

7. For the unproductive nature of American naval strategic thought after the Mexican War, see Sprout and Sprout, *Rise of American Naval Power*, 115, 135–38. For the Navy Lyceum, see Schroeder, "Matthew Calbraith Perry," 8; see also Langley, *Social Reform in the United States Navy*, 25–26. Samuel Huntington cites the Navy Lyceum as part of the intellectual renaissance (*Soldier and the State*, 217–18).

8. Sprout and Sprout, *Rise of American Naval Power*, 138.

9. Langley, "William A. Graham," 257–66; John P. Gillis to SFDP, 11 Jan. 1851, W9-6005, John S. Missroon to SFDP, 14 Jan. 1851, W9-6009, Franklin Buchanan to SFDP, 27 Jan. 1851, W9-6018, Samuel Lockwood to SFDP, 28 Jan. 1851, W9-6019, SFDP to Charles H. Davis, 7 Feb. 1851, W9-1212, Henry A. Adams to SFDP, 14 Feb. 1851, W9-6035, SFDP Papers, HML.

10. Clary, *Fortress America*, 45–46.

11. *Journal of the House of Representatives of the United States, 1850–1851*, 31st Cong., 2d sess., 3 Mar. 1851, 397.

12. C. M. Conrad to William A. Graham, 17 June 1851, Letters Received by the Secretary of the Navy from the President and Executive Agencies, M517, roll 8, Naval Records.

13. William A. Graham to SFDP et al., 23 June 1851, Letters Sent by the Secretary of the Navy to Officers, 1798–1868, M149, roll 47, ibid.

14. Du Pont, *Du Pont*, 59; Merrill, *Du Pont*, 204–5; SFDP to SMDP, 19, 20, 28, 29 June, 3, 6 July 1851, W9-1238, W9-1239, W9-1240, W9-1241, W9-1247, to Charles H. Davis, 16 July 1851, W9-1247, SFDP Papers, HML.

15. Louis M. Goldsborough to SFDP, 13 Aug. 1851, W9-6150, SFDP Papers, HML. As far as the U.S. Navy is concerned, Samuel Huntington is incorrect to say that the "American Military Enlightenment" that began in 1832 had ended by 1846 (*Soldier and the State*, 217–18). See Hayes, "Introduction," in Du Pont, *Letters* 1:lxii; Merrill, *Du Pont*, 205–7; Hackemer, *U.S. Navy and the Origins of the Military-Industrial Complex*, 16–17.

16. Morris, "Report of Commodore Morris," *Papers on the Subject of National Defences*, 3–6. For Commodore Charles Morris's brilliant career, see Schneller, *Quest for Glory*, 107–8.

17. Perry, "Report of Commodore M. C. Perry," *Papers on the Subject of National Defences*, 7–12. For Perry's naval career, see Schroeder, "Matthew C. Perry," 3–25; Morison, *"Old Bruin"*; Schroeder, *Matthew Calbraith Perry*. For Perry's thoughts on the role of the U.S. Navy in general, see Smith, "An Uncertain Passage," 95–97.

18. Matthew Fontaine Maury to SFDP (with Du Pont's marginal notes), n.d. but probably Sept. or Oct. 1851, W9-1253, SFDP Papers, HML.

19. Maury, "Report of Lieutenant M. F. Maury," *Papers on the Subject of National Defences*, 32–65. See also Stanton, "Matthew Fontaine Maury," 46–63; Christman, *Naval Innovators*, 111–16.

20. Thornton Jenkins to SFDP, 15 Aug. 1851, W9-6151, SFDP Papers, HML.

21. See Allison, "John A. Dahlgren," 33–34. See also Schneller, *Quest for Glory*; Christman, *Naval Innovators*, 103–8.

22. "Report of Lieutenant John A. Dahlgren," *Papers on the Subject of National Defences*, 65–90.

23. Du Pont, *Report on the National Defences*, 3.

24. SFDP to Charles H. Davis, 18 Sept. 1851, W9-1253, SFDP Papers, HML.

25. Du Pont, *Report on the National Defences*, 4. For a general discussion of Du Pont's report, see Merrill, *Du Pont*, 205–7; Hayes, "Introduction," in Du Pont, *Letters* 1:lxii.

26. Du Pont, *Report on the National Defences*, 6, 7, 8. For a discussion of Cass's report, see Clary, *Fortress America*, 41–42.

27. Du Pont, *Report on the National Defences*, 8, 10, 9.

28. See Clausewitz, *On War*, 89, 479–82; Paret, "Clausewitz," in Paret, *Makers of Modern Strategy*, 201; Handel, *Masters of War*, 65–75.

29. Du Pont, *Report on the National Defences*, 9–11, 18–19.

30. Ibid., 14.

31. Ibid., 19–20.

32. Sprout, "Mahan," 415–45. See also Crowl, "Alfred Thayer Mahan," in Paret, *Makers of Modern Strategy*, 450–51; Millett and Maslowski, *For the Common Defense*, 260; Weigley, *American Way of War*, 173–78; Brodie, "Technological Change, Strategic Doctrine, and Political Outcomes," 277–78; Sumida, *Inventing Grand Strategy and Teaching Command*, 41.

33. Alfred Thayer Mahan as quoted in Gooch, "The Weary Titan," 278.

34. Du Pont, *Report on the National Defences*, 21–22.

35. Millett and Maslowski, *For the Common Defense*, 124–25; Weigley, *American Way of War*, 62–64; Albion, *Makers of Naval Policy*, 190–91.

36. Du Pont, *Report on the National Defences*, 22.

37. Ibid. For the "dreadnought" theory, see Goldrick, "The Problems of Modern Naval History," 15.

38. Du Pont, *Report on the National Defences*, 24–28.

39. Millett and Maslowski, *For the Common Defense*, 124; Calvert, *Mechanical Engineer in America*, 253. For the technology and relative sophistication of nineteenth-century navies, see Goldrick, "The Problems of Naval History," 12–13.

40. Du Pont, *Report on the National Defences*, 28, 17.

41. SFDP to Charles H. Davis, 10 Sept., 17 Oct. 1851, W9-1252, W9-1256, Davis to SFDP, 25 Oct. 1851, W9-6189, SFDP Papers, HML.

42. SFDP to Charles H. Davis, 8 Nov., 14 Dec. 1851, W9-1261, W9-1272, ibid.

43. Conrad, *Report of the Secretary of War on the Subject of Fortifications*, 5–7. For

Du Pont's assessment of Conrad's report, see SFDP to Charles H. Davis, 14 Dec. 1851, W9-1272, SFDP Papers, HML.

44. *Report of General J. G. Totten, Chief Engineer, on the Subject of National Defences*, 76–78.

45. SFDP to SMDP, 15 Jan. 1852, W9-1284, 15 Jan. 1852, W9-1291, Isaac I. Stevens to SFDP, 10 Feb. 1852, W9-6283, Henry Winter Davis to SFDP, 23 Feb. 1852, W9-6289, SFDP Papers, HML.

46. SMDP to SFDP, 16 Jan. 1851, W9-21968, SMDP Papers, HML.

47. SFDP to SMDP, 20 Feb. 1852, W9-1291, Henry H. Lewis to SFDP, 6 Mar. 1852, W9-6296, Thomas O. Selfridge to SFDP, 15 Mar. 1852, W9-6300, Franklin Buchanan to SFDP, 5 Apr. 1852, W9-6327, SFDP to Charles H. Davis, 20 Mar. 1852, W9-1308, Samuel Breck to SFDP, 10 Apr. 1852, W9-6324, SFDP Papers, HML.

48. According to Samuel Huntington, the nineteenth-century military officer believed that "the rights of an officer to speak and act politically were no different . . . than those of any other American citizen" (*Soldier and the State*, 207–8).

49. See Smith, "An Uncertain Passage," 100–101.

50. See Canney, *Lincoln's Navy*, 63–67. For assessments of the *Merrimack*s as too slow and conservative in design, see Sprout and Sprout, *Rise of American Naval Power*, 145; Smith, "An Uncertain Passage," 101–2. See also Vlahos, "The Making of an American Style, 1797–1887," 9–10; Paullin, *Paullin's History of Naval Administration*, 219–20. For more convincing arguments for the superiority of this class of ship, see Tomblin, "From Sail to Steam," 216–18; Hackemer, *U.S. Navy and the Origins of the Military-Industrial Complex*, 6–7.

51. Weigley, *American Way of War*, 64.

52. SFDP to Henry W. Davis, 2 Sept. 1852, W9-1323, SFDP Papers, HML. For the reforms recommended by the Lighthouse Board, see Bauer, "Samuel Francis Du Pont," 146–47; Merrill, *Du Pont*, 208; Hayes, "Introduction," in Du Pont, *Letters* 1:lxiii. See also SFDP to SMDP, 11 Feb. 1852, W9-1287, William B. Shubrick to SFDP, 1 June 1852, W9-6376, SFDP to SMDP, 1 June 1852, W9-1306, SFDP Papers, HML.

53. Theodore Sedgwick to SFDP, 6 Aug. 1852, W9-6421, SFDP Papers, HML; Hirschfeld, "America on Exhibition," 101–16; Burrows and Wallace, *Gotham*, 669; Hayes, "Introduction," in Du Pont, *Letters* 1:lxiii; Merrill, *Du Pont*, 209–10. For the formation of the Crystal Palace Association, see Post, "New York Crystal Palace Exhibition," 337–38; Coleman, "The Exhibition in the Palace," 459–60.

54. See Post, "New York Crystal Palace Exhibition," 337–41; Coleman, "The Exhibition in the Palace," 459–62; Burrows and Wallace, *Gotham*, 669–70.

55. For the pay raise campaign, see Henry W. Morris to SFDP, 3 Dec. 1852, W9-6538, Thompson D. Shaw to SFDP, 12 Dec. 1852, W9-6548, SFDP Papers, HML; SFDP to John P. Kennedy, 15 Dec. 1852, Commanders' Letters, M147, roll 44, Naval Records.

56. Theodore Sedgwick to SFDP, 20, 29 Dec. 1852, W9-6552, W9-6561, Alfred Pell to SFDP, 7 Jan. 1853, W9-6589, SFDP Papers, HML.

57. For the navy's final permission that allowed Du Pont to accept the position, see John P. Kennedy to SFDP, 22 Feb. 1853, W9-6649, ibid.

58. SFDP to SMDP, 11 Feb. 1853, W9-1390, ibid.

59. SMDP to Victorina and Eleuthera du Pont, 11 May, 14, 15 July 1853, W9-22092, W9-22136, W9-22138, to Henry Winter Davis, 12 May 1853, W9-22094, SMDP Papers, HML.

60. SFDP to Henry Winter Davis, 15 June 1853, W9-1434, Sedgwick to SFDP, 25 June 1853, W9-6747, Detmold to SFDP, 9 July 1853, W9-6750, SFDP to SMDP, 14 July 1853, W9-1437, SFDP Papers, HML. For Pierce's appearance, see Steen, "America's First World's Fair," 265–67.

61. *Daily Alton [Ill.] Telegraph*, 11 Aug. 1853.

62. SFDP to Henry Winter Davis, 31 Aug. 1853, W9-1444, to SMDP, 6 Sept. 1853, W9-1446, to Charles H. Davis, 1 Oct. 1853, W9-1451, SFDP and Davis to Theodore Sedgwick, 15 Oct. 1853, W9-1456, SFDP to William Whetten, 15 Mar. 1854, W9-1510, SFDP Papers, HML; Davis, *Life of Charles Henry Davis*, 94; Merrill, *Du Pont*, 215–16.

4. The Efficiency Board of 1855

1. Huntington, *Soldier and the State*, 206–7.

2. Slagle, *Ironclad Captain*, 76. See also Langley, *Social Reform in the United States Navy*, 20–25; Smith, "An Uncertain Passage," 89.

3. Tucker, *Andrew Foote*, 78. Du Pont provided a similar analysis of the deadwood in the officer system to Mallory; see Mallory, *Report of the Committee on Naval Affairs*, SR 271, 33d Cong., 1st sess., 18 May 1854, 1:194–96.

4. Slagle, *Ironclad Captain*, 74–75.

5. Tucker, *Andrew Foote*, 23; John S. Missroon to SFDP, 27 Jan. 1855, W9-7221, SFDP Papers, HML.

6. See Chisholm, *Waiting for Dead Men's Shoes*. Cf. Westwood, "Reform in the United States Navy," 107–18; Blume, "'Concessions Where Concessions Could Be Made,'" 147–59.

7. Chisholm, *Waiting for Dead Men's Shoes*, 216–17; Langley, *Social Reform in the United States Navy*; Langley, "James Cochran Dobbin," 285–86; Smith, "An Uncertain Passage," 100–101; Sprout and Sprout, *Rise of American Naval Power*, 141–45.

8. Merrill, *Du Pont*, 217; Bauer, *New American State Papers*, 189–97; Hayes and Smith, *Politics of Naval Innovation*, 14; *ARSN*, 5 Dec. 1853, 312.

9. SFDP to Charles H. Davis, 13 July 1854, W9-1524, SFDP Papers, HML; Mallory, *Report of the Committee on Naval Affairs*, 189–97. For discussion of the circular letter, see Thomas O. Selfridge to SFDP, 7 Mar. 1854, W9-6978, Andrew A. Harwood to SFDP, 22 Apr. 1854, W9-6998, George W. Harrison to SFDP, 15 July 1854, W9-7056, ibid. George A. Magruder, in a letter to SFDP, 22 July 1854, W9-7063, ibid., noted that the secretary had "favorably received" the circular letter. See also Durkin, *Stephen R. Mallory*, 64–66.

10. *ARSN*, 4 Dec. 1854, 394.

11. Bauer, "Samuel Francis Du Pont," 147; SFDP to SMDP, 12, 14 Jan. 1855, W9-1562, W9-1563, SFDP Papers, HML; SFDP to Dobbin, 16 Jan. 1855, Commanders' Letters, M147, roll 48, Naval Records.

12. See Chisholm, *Waiting for Dead Men's Shoes*, 226–34.

13. SFDP to SMDP, 14 Jan. 1855, W9-1563, SFDP Papers, HML.

14. SFDP to James C. Dobbin, 16 Jan. 1855, Commanders' Letters, M147, roll 48, Naval Records.

15. Ibid.

16. SFDP to George A. Magruder, 1 Feb. 1855, W9-1570, SFDP Papers, HML; Chisholm, *Waiting for Dead Men's Shoes*, 234.

17. SFDP to Charles H. Davis, 6 Feb. 1855, W9-1571, Jonathan M. Foltz to SFDP,

7 Feb. 1855, W9-7231, Edward W. Carpender to SFDP, 9 Feb. 1855, W9-7236, SFDP to SMDP, 10 Feb. 1855, W9-1573, William L. Hudson to SFDP, 12 Feb. 1855, W9-7238, SFDP Papers, HML.

18. SFDP to SMDP, 12 Feb. 1855, W9-1575, to SMDP (telegram), 13 Feb. 1855, W9-1576, ibid.; SMDP to SFDP, 13 Feb. 1855, W9-22264, SMDP Papers, HML; Albion, *Makers of Naval Policy*, 189–94.

19. For the text of the Efficiency Act, see Chisholm, *Waiting for Dead Men's Shoes*, 235–36.

20. SFDP to SMDP, 14, 17 Feb. 1855, W9-1576, W9-1579, Charles H. Davis to SFDP, 16 Feb. 1855, W9-7247, Henry Winter Davis to SFDP, 18 Feb. 1855, W9-7253, Louis M. Goldsborough to SFDP, 28 Feb. 1855, W9-7264, George W. Harrison to SFDP, 27 Feb. 1855, W9-7262, SFDP Papers, HML.

21. Thomas Turner to SFDP, 14 Feb. 1855, W9-7246, Charles H. Davis to SFDP, 16 Feb., 4 Mar. 1855, W9-7247, W9-7276, John S. Missroon to SFDP, 16, 22 Feb. 1855, W9-7250, W9-7257, Louis M. Goldsborough to SFDP, 27 Feb. 1855, W9-7264, SFDP to Charles H. Davis, 27 Feb. 1855, W9-1581, ibid.

22. Merrill, *Du Pont*, 218; Chisholm, *Waiting for Dead Men's Shoes*, 237. For Du Pont's assessment of his fellow members, see SFDP to Charles H. Davis, 24 June 1855, W9-1613, SFDP Papers, HML.

23. Schroeder, "Matthew Calbraith Perry," 22. See also Schroeder, *Matthew Calbraith Perry*.

24. Langley, "James Cochrane Dobbin," 291; George A. Magruder to SFDP, 28 Feb. 1855, W9-7263, SFDP to Charles H. Davis, 3 Apr. 1855, W9-1588, to Garrett Pendergrast, 7 Apr. 1855, W9-1589, SFDP Papers, HML.

25. SFDP to Charles H. Davis, 3 Apr. 1855, W9-1588, SFDP Papers, HML.

26. SFDP to Andrew Foote, 15 Apr. 1855, W9-1596, to Charles H. Davis, 3 Apr. 1855, W9-1588, ibid.

27. SFDP to William Whetten, 28 May 1855, W9-1605, Dobbin to Commodore William B. Shubrick et al., 20 June 1855, W9-7379, W9-1614, ibid.

28. Dobbin to Commodore William B. Shubrick et al., 20 June 1855, W9-7379, W9-1614, SFDP manuscript, n.d., n.p., May 1855, W9-1606, James C. Dobbin to SFDP, 5 June 1855, W9-7379, ibid.

29. Langley, "James C. Dobbin," 293.

30. At the time the nation assumed that the board examined every officer closely, and many historians have made the same assumption, including James Merrill, Spencer Tucker, K. Jack Bauer, Frank L. Williams, Dudley Cornish Taylor, and John H. Schroeder.

31. SFDP Board Notes, n.d., W9-18475, SFDP Papers, HML.

32. SFDP to SMDP, 20 June 1855, W9-1609, to Henry Winter Davis, 21 June 1855, W9-1610, SFDP memorandum describing board procedures, n.d., W9-1617, ibid.; Merrill, *Du Pont*, 219–20; Du Pont, *Du Pont*, 63–84; Chisholm, *Waiting for Dead Men's Shoes*, 238–39; Todorich, "Franklin Buchanan," 102; Tucker, *Andrew Foote*, 79–80; Bauer, "Samuel Francis Du Pont," 147–48; Taylor and Laas, *Lincoln's Lee*, 78. For the recap of results, see SFDP Efficiency Board Notes, n.d., W9-18475, SFDP Papers, HML: Captains: seventeen placed on leave; fifteen furloughed; three dropped; thirty-five total. Commanders: twenty-one on leave; twelve furloughed; six dropped; thirty-nine total. Lieutenants: eighteen on leave; forty-eight furloughs; nineteen dropped; eighty-five total. Promotable Masters: one leave; zero furlough; nine dropped; ten total. Passed Midshipmen: zero leave;

two furlough; thirteen dropped; fifteen total. Masters: fourteen leave; three furlough; zero dropped; seventeen total.

33. James M. McIntosh to SFDP, 30 June 1855, W9-7403, Henry A. Steele to SFDP, 3 July 1855, W9-7412, SFDP Papers, HML; Dahlgren, *Memoir of John A. Dahlgren*, 173; Lt. John A. Dahlgren to Andrew Foote, 27 June 1855, Dahlgren Papers, Library of Congress.

34. SFDP to SMDP, 23 June 1855, W9-6312, to Henry Du Pont, 11 July 1855, W9-1624, to James C. Dobbin, 20 July 1855, W9-1631, SFDP Papers, HML.

35. SFDP Efficiency Board Notes, W9-18475, SFDP to James S. Biddle, 29 Nov. 1855, W9-1676, ibid.

36. "Case of Lt. Matthew C. Perry, Jr., New York," 184–90, SFDP Efficiency Board Notes, W9-18475, ibid.

37. "Case of Lieutenant James M. Watson, Virginia," 47–48, "Case of Commander James Glynn, Pennsylvania," 242–43, "Case of Foxhall A. Parker, New York," 208–10, ibid.

38. "Case of Lieutenant William D. Porter," 55–56, ibid.

39. "Case of Commander John I. Young, New York," 230–31, "Case of Lieutenant James S. Palmer, New Jersey," 64–65, "Case of Commander Edward W. Carpender," 237–38, ibid.

40. "Case of Lieutenant Raphael Semmes, Missouri," 70–71, ibid.

41. "Case of Lieutenant Matthew Fontaine Maury," 62–64, ibid.; Stanton, "Matthew Fontaine Maury," 46–63.

42. "Case of Lieutenant John A. Dahlgren, Pennsylvania," 73–76, SFDP Efficiency Board Notes, W9-18475, SFDP Papers, HML.

43. SFDP to Dobbin, 20 July 1855, W9-1631, ibid.

44. SFDP to Andrew Foote, 7 Aug. 1855, W9-1637, John S. Missroon to SFDP, 30 Aug. 1855, W9-7471, Foote to SFDP, 4 Aug. 1855, W9-7448, ibid.

45. SFDP to Henry Winter Davis, 2 Aug. 1855, W9-1635, ibid.

46. SFDP to Andrew Foote, 7 Aug. 1855, W9-1637, ibid.

47. SFDP to SMDP, 7 Sept. 1855, W9-1644, Henry Winter Davis, 10 Sept. 1855, W9-1645, ibid.; James C. Dobbin to President Franklin Pierce, 5 Sept. 1855, Pierce to Dobbin, 12 Sept. 1855, both letters printed in the *Daily National Intelligencer*, 13, 14, 25 Sept., 1 Oct. 1855.

48. The *New York Courier*, *New York Herald*, and *Philadelphia Inquirer* were particularly vocal in their criticism early after the release of the board's report. See SFDP to James S. Biddle, 17 Sept. 1855, W9-1646, SFDP Papers, HML.

49. *New York Herald*, 16 Sept. 1855; Henry A. Adams to SFDP, 12 Sept. 1855, W9-7486, SFDP Papers, HML.

50. For a small sample of the many letters Dobbin received, see L. C. Simonds to James C. Dobbin, 18 Sept. 1855, P. Page to Dobbin, 18 Sept. 1855, D. Geisinger to Dobbin, 18 Sept. 1855, Henry W. Ogden to Dobbin, 19 Sept. 1855, John H. Graham to Dobbin, 20 Sept. 1855, Thomas Pettigru to Dobbin, 22 Sept. 1855, Edward W. Carpender to Dobbin, 22 Sept. 1855, Cadwalader Ringgold to Dobbin, 29 Sept. 1855, William M. Armstrong to Dobbin, 28 Sept. 1855, Commanders' Letters, M147, roll 49, Naval Records.

51. George S. Blake to SFDP, 18 Sept. 1855, W9-7499, SFDP Papers, HML. See also Schroeder, *Matthew Calbraith Perry*, 253.

52. John S. Nicholas to SFDP, 18 Sept. 1855, W9-3619, and "Case of Commander John S. Nicholas," 247, SFDP Efficiency Board Notes, W9-18475, SFDP Papers, HML;

Matthew Fontaine Maury to James C. Dobbin, 20 Sept. 1855, as quoted in Lewis, *Matthew Fontaine Maury*, 108–9. See also Maury to William B. Blackford, 23 Sept. 1855, Maury Papers, Library of Congress; Maury to SFDP, 8 Nov. 1855, W9-7580, SFDP Papers, HML.

53. SFDP to James S. Biddle, 11 Oct. 1855, W9-1646, SFDP Papers, HML. At the same time, after thirty-eight years of naval service, Du Pont received his new captain's commission to date from 14 Sept. 1855 (SFDP to James C. Dobbin, 11 Oct. 1855, Captains' Letters, M125, roll 354, Naval Records).

54. Durkin, *Stephen R. Mallory*, 70–73.

55. Charles H. Davis to Harriet Davis, 10 Mar. 1856, Davis, *Life of Charles Henry Davis*, 99; Bauer, "Samuel Francis Du Pont," 148.

56. Matthew Fontaine Maury to Frank Minor, 9 Oct. 1855, Maury Papers, Library of Congress. See also Maury to John Rodgers, 5, 18 Oct., 17 Nov., 22 Dec. 1855, John Rodgers Family Papers, ibid.

57. Matthew Fontaine Maury to Frank Minor, 16 Oct. 1855, Maury Papers, ibid.

58. The average time spent on officers' cases during modern military promotion and selection boards is from an electronic mail communication with Col. Michael Colpo, U.S. Army personnel officer, U.S. Army Personnel Command, Alexandria, Va., 31 Aug. 2001

59. Matthew Fontaine Maury to William Blackford, 17 Oct. 1855, Maury Papers, Library of Congress; analysis from SFDP Efficiency Board Notes, W9-18475, SFDP Papers, HML.

60. Matthew Fontaine Maury to Frank Minor, 31 Oct. 1855, Maury Papers, Library of Congress.

61. See Matthew Fontaine Maury's handwritten note on a letter from Sylvanus Godon to Maury, 13 Nov. 1855, and Maury to Frank Minor, 28 Nov. 1855, ibid.

62. John S. Missroon to SFDP, 31 Dec. 1855, W9-7634, and SFDP Efficiency Board Notes, W9-18475, SFDP Papers, HML. The sectional equity also holds by category: Lieutenants: thirty-nine removed from the South (ten dropped, seven leave, twenty-two furlough); forty-three removed from the North (six dropped, ten leave, twenty-seven furlough). Commanders: nineteen removed from the South (three dropped, ten leave, six furlough); eighteen removed from the North (three dropped, eleven leave, four furlough). The navy list for 1855 reveals the following sectional breakdown of the total force: Northern officers: 56 percent of the total; Southern officers: 44 percent (State Department, *Register of Officers and Agents*).

63. *ARSN*, 3 Dec. 1855, 10–11.

64. SFDP to Charles H. Davis, 21 Nov. 1855, W9-1669, Louis M. Goldsborough to SFDP, 19 Dec. 1855, W9-7624, SFDP Papers, HML. *ARSN*, 3 Dec. 1855, 12. For press support of Maury, see Lewis, *Matthew Fontaine Maury*, 112–13; Williams, *Matthew Fontaine Maury*, 278–83. For Dobbin's attempt to find a way to restore Maury, see ibid., 283. The only historian who mildly criticizes Dobbin for failure to exercise dynamic leadership in preparing the navy and public for the process is Langley, "James C. Dobbin," 293.

65. *New York Daily Times*, 22 Jan. 1856; *Delaware State Reporter*, 8 Feb. 1856; SFDP to Garrett J. Pendergrast, 25 Oct. 1855, W9-1658, "Case of Commander Robert Ritchie," 246–47, SFDP Efficiency Board Notes, W9-18475, SFDP to SMDP, 21 Jan. 1856, W9-1698, SFDP Papers, HML.

66. SFDP to James C. Dobbin, 14 Dec. 1855, Letters Received by the Secretary of the Navy, M147, roll 49, Naval Records; SFDP to Charles H. Davis, 26 Jan. 1856, W9-1707, to Andrew Foote, 28 Jan. 1856, W9-1708, to Henry Winter Davis, 28 Jan. 1856, W9-1709,

"Copy of Minutes of Court-Martial Held at U.S. Navy Yard, Philadelphia, 18 Jan–1 Feb 1856," with Dobbin's endorsement attached, W9-7713, SFDP Papers, HML; Hayes, "Introduction," in Du Pont, *Letters* 1:lxiii. Most historians have misread Dobbin's review as essentially finding Ritchie innocent. It did not; indeed, Dobbin believed that the court had been too easy on Ritchie, but again, he did nothing to remedy the situation.

67. Langley, "James Cochrane Dobbin," 297.

68. SMDP to SFDP, 15 Jan., 5, 25 Feb. 1856, W9-22329, W9-22342/22350, SMDP Papers, HML.

69. U.S. Congress, *Congressional Globe*, 34th Cong., 1st sess., 11 Mar. 1856, 173; Bauer, "Samuel Francis Du Pont," 165.

70. Merrill, *Du Pont*, 22–25; Chisholm, *Waiting for Dead Men's Shoes*, 241–62; Lewis, *Matthew Fontaine Maury*, 113–14; Smith, "An Uncertain Passage," 89–90; Bauer, "Samuel Francis Du Pont," 148; Durkin, *Stephen R. Mallory*, 70–83; Williams, *Matthew Fontaine Maury*, 284–93. For Du Pont's opposition to the courts of inquiry and his unsuccessful effort to convince Dobbin to appoint younger officers to the courts of inquiry, see SFDP to James S. Biddle, 29 July 1856, W9-1809, to SMDP, 31 Jan. 1857, W9-1853, to George S. Blake, 8 Feb. 1857, W9-1860, SFDP Papers, HML.

71. SFDP to Samuel Mercer, 4 July 1859, W9-2054, SFDP Papers, HML.

72. Phelps to Elizabeth Phelps, 14 Mar. 1859, to Elisha Whittlesey, 2 May 1859, both quoted in Slagle, *Ironclad Captain*, 102–4.

73. Chisholm, *Waiting for Dead Men's Shoes*, 263; Smith, "An Uncertain Passage," 89; Todorich, "Franklin Buchanan," 102.

74. Smith, "An Uncertain Passage," 90.

75. Louis M. Goldsborough to SFDP, 16 Sept., 3 Oct. 1855, W9-7497, W9-7534, Thomas Turner to SFDP, 25 Sept. 1855, W9-7522, SFDP Papers, HML; Charles H. Davis to James C. Dobbin, 22 Sept. 1855, Commanders' Letters, M147, roll 49, Naval Records; Seth Ledyard Phelps to Alfred Phelps, 14 Sept. 1855, quoted in Slagle, *Ironclad Captain*, 77–78; Mahan, *From Sail to Steam*, 23.

76. Durkin, *Stephen R. Mallory*, 83.

5. From China to the Philadelphia Navy Yard

1. George S. Blake to SFDP, 23 July 1856, W9-7972, SFDP Papers, HML. See also John S. Missroon to SFDP, 19 July 1855, W9-7964, Franklin Buchanan to SFDP, 4 Aug. 1856, W9-7992, ibid.

2. SFDP to James C. Dobbin, 22 Aug. 1856, W9-1814, ibid. Du Pont specifically asked for one of the new *Merrimacks*: "Understanding the *Roanoke* is nearly ready to be placed in commission, I respectfully . . . ask to be considered an applicant for the command of that steamer" (SFDP to Dobbin, 30 Dec. 1856, Captains' Letters, M125, roll 356, Naval Records).

3. Hagan, *This People's Navy*, 151; Merrill, *Du Pont*, 228–29.

4. SFDP to SMDP, 7 Mar. 1857, W9-1873, SFDP Papers, HML.

5. Langley, "James C. Dobbin," 297.

6. SFDP to Garrett Pendergrast, 12 Apr. 1857, W9-1889, SFDP Papers, HML.

7. SFDP to George S. Blake, 10, 11 Apr. 1857, W9-1886, W9-1888, ibid.; SFDP to Isaac Toucey, 11 Apr. 1857, Captains' Letters, M125, roll 357, Naval Records.

8. Merrill, *Du Pont*, 229–30; SFDP to SMDP, 16, 18 Apr. 1857, W9-1892, W9-1893,

to George S. Blake, 19 Apr. 1857, W9-1895, to Charles H. Davis, 4 May 1857, W9-2104, SFDP Papers, HML; SMDP to SFDP, 20 Apr. 1857, W9-22454, SMDP Papers, HML. See also SFDP to Isaac Toucey, 15 May 1857, Captains' Letters, M125, roll 357, Naval Records.

9. Canney, *Lincoln's Navy*, 66.

10. Mahan, *From Sail to Steam*, 33. For the British response to the new frigates, see Canney, *Lincoln's Navy*, 66.

11. Merrill, *Du Pont*, 230; SFDP to SMDP, 29 May 1857, W9-1913, SFDP Papers, HML; SFDP to Isaac Toucey, 1 June 1857, Captains' Letters, M125, roll 357, Naval Records.

12. SFDP, manuscript detailing the voyage entitled "U.S. Steam Frigate *Minnesota*," n.d., W9-2084, SFDP Papers, HML.

13. SMDP to SFDP, 1 July 1857, W9-22475, SMDP Papers, HML; SFDP to James S. Biddle, 1 July 1857, W9-1924, SFDP Papers, HML.

14. SFDP to SMDP, 4 Sept. 1857, W9-1929, SFDP Papers, HML.

15. SFDP, "U.S. Steam Frigate *Minnesota*," W9-2084, ibid.; Merrill, *Du Pont*, 231–32; Hayes, "Introduction," in Du Pont, *Letters* 1:lxiv.

16. SFDP, "U.S. Steam Frigate *Minnesota*," W9-2084, SFDP to James S. Biddle, 15 Dec. 1857, W9-1957, SFDP Papers, HML; Merrill, *Du Pont*, 231–32; Hayes, "Introduction," in Du Pont, *Letters* 1:lxiv; Du Pont, *Du Pont*, 89–90; log of the USS *Minnesota*, 31 Oct. 1857, USNA.

17. Quoted in Merrill, *Du Pont*, 231.

18. SFDP, "U.S. Steam Frigate *Minnesota*," W9-2084, SFDP Papers, HML; Hayes, "Introduction," in Du Pont, *Letters* 1:lxiv; Merrill, *Du Pont*, 232–33.

19. SMDP to SFDP, 5 Jan. 1858, W9-22539, James Bayard to SMDP, 6 Jan. 1858, W9-22543, Thornton Jenkins to SMDP, 8 Jan. 1858, W9-22543, SMDP Papers, HML.

20. William K. Mayo to Louis M. Goldsborough, 15 June 1859, Louis M. Goldsborough Papers, Library of Congress.

21. SFDP to SMDP, Journal Letter no. 17, 28 Apr. 1858, W9-1968, Journal Letter no. 19, 21 May 1858, W9-1972, SFDP Papers, HML. See also Boot, *Savage Wars of Peace*, 53–54.

22. Bauer, "Samuel Francis Du Pont," 148; Merrill, *Du Pont*, 237–40; Hayes, "Introduction," in Du Pont, *Letters* 1:lxiv; SFDP, "U.S. Steam Frigate *Minnesota*," W9-2084, SFDP to Benjamin B. Gerhard, 22 May 1858, W9-1973, SFDP Papers, HML. Both Merrill and Bauer conclude that Du Pont's observations had convinced him that modern warships could defeat forts.

23. SFDP to Benjamin B. Gerhard, 22 May 1858, W9-1973, to SMDP, Journal Letter no. 20, 26 May 1858, W9-1974, SFDP Papers, HML. In his letter to Sophie, he spoke of the Chinese equipping their forts with "worthless gun[s]." That Du Pont made no specific mention of the "ships versus fort" debate in any of his letters written during the voyage of the *Minnesota* suggests that he did not believe the allied seizure of the Dagu forts to be the extraordinary event that Bauer and Merrill claim he believed they were.

24. SFDP, "US Steam Frigate *Minnesota*," W9-2084, ibid.; Merrill, *Du Pont*, 240; Hayes, "Introduction," in Du Pont, *Letters* 1:lxiv. For the treaty text, see "Treaty of Tientsin, June 1858," accessed 22 Apr. 2002 at http://web.jjay.cuny.edu/~jobrien/reference/ob27.html.

25. Long, *Gold Braid and Foreign Relations*.

26. SFDP, "US Steam Frigate *Minnesota*," W9-2084, SFDP Papers, HML; Long, *Gold*

Braid and Foreign Relations, 240–45; Du Pont, *Du Pont,* 96–97; Hayes, "Introduction," in Du Pont, *Letters* 1:lxvi; Bauer, "Samuel Francis Du Pont," 148; SFDP to SMDP, Journal Letter no. 36, 19 Jan. 1859, W9-2019, SFDP Papers, HML.

27. SFDP to John A. Dahlgren, 16 Aug. 1859, Dahlgren Papers, Library of Congress; SFDP to Alexander D. Bache, 17 June 1859, W9-2046, to Samuel Mercer, 4 July 1859, W9-2054, SFDP Papers, HML.

28. SFDP to James S. Biddle, 23 July 1859, W9-2057, SFDP Papers, HML.

29. SFDP to Alexander Slidell Mackenzie Jr., 17 June 1859, W9-2047, ibid.; Hayes, "Introduction," in Du Pont, *Letters* 1:cxiii.

30. Quoted from an undated, unsigned, and probably unsent letter in Du Pont's hand written immediately after Brown's trial to a British acquaintance named Ellen (SFDP, "Memorandum for Ellen," W9-2088, SFDP Papers, HML).

31. SFDP to Garrett Pendergrast, 4 May 1860, W9-2133, ibid.

32. Ibid.

33. Merrill, *Du Pont,* 248–49; SFDP to John S. Missroon, 5 May 1860, W9-2134, to Alexander D. Bache, 15 May 1860, W9-2140, SFDP Papers, HML.

34. Awaji-No-Kami, *Diary of the First Japanese Embassy to the United States,* 68, 194–95, 208–9; Bush, *77 Samurai: Japan's First Embassy to America,* 149–226.

35. SFDP to SMDP, 14 May 1860, W9-2139, SFDP Papers, HML; Awaji-No-Kami, *Diary of the First Japanese Embassy to the United States,* 73.

36. SFDP to SMDP, 17 May 1860, W9-2143, SFDP Papers, HML; Merrill, *Du Pont,* 250; Awaji-No-Kami, *Diary of the First Japanese Embassy to the United States,* 73–77, 79; Yanaga, "The First Japanese Embassy to the United States," 124.

37. SFDP to Lewis Cass, 30 May 1860, W9-2150, SFDP Papers, HML. Du Pont was outraged that the senator had referred to Lieutenant Porter as a "subaltern" instead of his naval rank; this Du Pont felt was an intolerable insult. For just one of many examples of Du Pont's help in dealing with American customs, see Awaji-No-Kami, *Diary of the First Japanese Embassy to the United States,* 88.

38. SFDP to SMDP, 6 June 1861, W9-2153, SFDP Papers, HML.

39. *New York Times,* 18 June 1860. For the activities of the Japanese Embassy during its stay in the United States, see Awaji-No-Kami, *Diary of the First Japanese Embassy to the United States,* 99–130; Yanaga, "The First Japanese Embassy to the United States," 125–38. See also Miyoshi, *As We Saw Them,* 136.

40. SFDP to Henry Winter Davis, 12 July 1860, W9-2183, SFDP Papers, HML.

41. Miyoshi, *As We Saw Them,* 174.

42. Yanaga, "The First Japanese Embassy to the United States," 138; Miyoshi, *As We Saw Them,* 182.

43. SFDP to SMDP, 26 Nov. 1860, W9-2227, to James S. Biddle, 9 Nov. 1860, W9-2213, SFDP Papers, HML.

44. SFDP to SMDP, 29 Nov. 1860, W9-2220, ibid.; SFDP to Louis M. Goldsborough, 14 Dec. 1860, in Du Pont, *Letters* 1:10.

45. SFDP to Isaac Toucey, 8 Dec. 1860, Captains' Letters, M125, roll 366, Naval Records; SFDP to Henry Winter Davis, 30 Dec. 1860, in Du Pont, *Letters* 1:15. For the suggestion that the president gave Du Pont the Philadelphia position, see Merrill, *Du Pont,* 254; Du Pont, *Letters* 1:16. See also SFDP to Toucey, 21 Dec. 1860, Captains' Letters, M125, roll 366, Naval Records.

46. Dorwart, *Philadelphia Navy Yard*, 81; SFDP to Henry Winter Davis, 16 Nov. 1860, W9-2214, SFDP Papers, HML.

47. SFDP to Andrew Foote, 25 Jan. 1861, in Du Pont, *Letters* 1:28; SFDP to Hiram Paulding, 1 May 1861, Captains' Letters, M125, roll 368, Naval Records

48. SFDP to Franklin Buchanan, 26 May 1861, Buchanan to SFDP, 9 July 1861, in Du Pont, *Letters* 1:72, 94–100; Symonds, *Confederate Admiral*, 137–40; Todorich, "Franklin Buchanan," 102–3.

49. SFDP to William Whetten, 1 Mar. 1861, in Du Pont, *Letters* 1:38–39.

50. SFDP to Samuel Mercer, 13 Mar. 1861, to Henry Winter Davis, 22 Mar. 1861, ibid., 42–44.

51. SMDP to Henry A. du Pont, 28 Apr. 1861, W9-22915, SMDP Papers, HML.

52. Dorwart, *Philadelphia Navy Yard*, 81–84; Merrill, *Du Pont*, 254–58; Du Pont, *Du Pont*, 104–5; Percival Drayton to Lydig M. Hoyt, 19 Aug. 1861, Drayton, *Naval Letters*, 5.

53. Du Pont, *Du Pont*, 105; Bauer, "Samuel Francis Du Pont," 148–49.

54. According to Dorwart, the building of the *Tuscarora* between 26 June and 24 Aug. 1861 was a fifty-nine-day record that "revived the spirits of local communities shaken by the outbreak of the war" (*Philadelphia Navy Yard*, 84).

55. John Lenthall to SFDP, 3 Feb. 1861, SFDP to Lenthall, 5, 16 Feb. 1861, in Du Pont, *Letters* 1:30–31 and nn. See also Tomblin, "From Sail to Steam," 250.

56. Stories quoted in Ragan, *Union and Confederate Submarine Warfare in the Civil War*, 7–11.

57. Commanders Henry R. Hoff and Charles Steedman and Chief Engineer Robert Danby to SFDP, 7 July 1861, "Claim against the U.S. Government by a Frenchman Named de Villeroi for the Construction of a Submarine (*Alligator*)," Navy Subject File AV, Miscellaneous, box 119, Naval Records.

58. Ibid.

59. Ragan, *Union and Confederate Submarine Warfare in the Civil War*, 10–11, 21–23, 44–47, 53–56, 64–69, 72–74, 78–84; Commodore Joseph Smith to Brutus de Villeroi, 1 Nov. 1861, Navy Subject File AV, and Villeroi to Abraham Lincoln, 4 Sept. 1862, Letters Received by the Secretary of the Navy: Miscellaneous Letters, 1801–4, M124, roll 382, Naval Records; Selfridge, *Memoirs*, 68–71. Raimondo Luraghi claims that Du Pont commissioned Villeroi to build the submarine specifically to "destroy the feared ironclad *Virginia*" (*A History of the Confederate Navy*, 251, 430). There is no evidence to support this claim. Du Pont recognized the strange vessel's potential, and he directed his officers to make a thorough evaluation well before the *Virginia*'s threat. The evaluation with Du Pont's endorsement led the Navy Department to construct a larger version. It was only later that Navy Department officials saw the submarine as a possible counter to the *Virginia*.

6. The Blockade Board of 1861 and Union Naval Strategy

1. Lincoln, "Proclamation of Blockade," 19, 27 Apr. 1861, in Lincoln, *Collected Works* 4:338–39, 346; SFDP to William Whetten, 3 May 1861, W9-2283, SFDP Papers, HML. On the challenges faced by the U.S. Navy in the early days of the Civil War and in particular the blockade, see McPherson, *Battle Cry of Freedom*, 313–14, 369; Browning, *From Cape Charles to Cape Fear*, 1; Welles, *ARSN*, Dec. 1861, 9–12.

2. Historians have often erroneously referred to this panel as the Strategy Board. Sec-

retary of the Navy Gideon Welles called it a "Commission of Conference" or "Mixed Conference," and the board members themselves variously referred to their undertaking as a "board," "conference," "Commission of Conference," and "Blockade Board" (Gideon Welles to Charles Henry Davis, 26, 29 June 1861, Navy Subject File On, Strategy and Tactics, box 453, Naval Records; SFDP to Alexander D. Bache and Charles H. Davis, 2 Oct. 1861, Correspondence of A. D. Bache, Superintendent of the Coast and Geodetic Survey, 1843–1865, M642, roll 243, Records of the Coast and Geodetic Survey, RG 23, National Archives).

3. Anderson, *By Sea and by River*, 34–35.

4. Welles, *ARSN*, 2 Dec. 1861, 9–11.

5. Welles to SFDP, 21 Apr. 1861, in Du Pont, *Letters* 1:56.

6. Alexander D. Bache to Welles, 27 Apr. 1861, Gideon Welles Papers, Library of Congress; Bache, *Annual Report of the Superintendent of the U.S. Coast Survey*, 5 Nov. 1861, 1–2.

7. Northern yards began to build the *Unadilla* gunboats within a month of Fort Sumter. They were 158 feet long, 700 tons, with only a 10-foot draft. These ships were typically armed with one large gun (usually a XI-inch Dahlgren smoothbore or a 100-pound Parrott rifle). Although not very fast at 10 knots, they served admirably throughout the war (Canney, *Lincoln's Navy*, 58–59).

8. Browning, *From Cape Charles to Cape Fear*, 6–7.

9. McPherson, *Battle Cry of Freedom*, 369.

10. Stringham bitterly complained that he needed more ships for the Hatteras operation in August 1861 (Browning, *From Cape Charles to Cape Fear*, 7).

11. Gideon Welles to Mary Welles, 14 Apr. 1861, Gideon Welles Papers, Library of Congress.

12. For months the Navy and the War Departments flooded Bache and the Coast Survey with requests for charts and maps. See Bache to Abraham Lincoln, 26 Apr. 1861, Correspondence of A. D. Bache, Superintendent of the Coast and Geodetic Survey, 1843–1865, M642, roll 243, RG 23, National Archives; Bache, *Annual Report of the Superintendent of the U.S. Coast Survey*, 5 Nov. 1861, 1–2.

13. A. D. Bache to Charles O. Boutelle, 3 Jan. 1861, in Bruce, *Launching of American Science*, 298.

14. Gustavus V. Fox to SFDP, 22 May 1861, W9-10864, SFDP Papers, HML.

15. SFDP to A. D. Bache, 30 May 1861, W9-2293, to Henry Winter Davis, 1 June 1861, W9-2294, ibid.

16. SFDP to SMDP, 28, 30 June 1861, W9-2309, W9-2311, ibid.; A. D. Bache to Wolcott Gibbs, 26 Sept. 1863, in Bruce, *Launching of American Science*, 299.

17. Commander Davis was appointed to the board on 25 June 1861 and Major Barnard on 26 June 1861. Bache was officially released by Secretary of the Treasury Salmon P. Chase for duty on the board on 24 June 1861 (Welles to S. P. Chase, 24 June 1861, to Charles Henry Davis, 25 June 1861, Correspondence of the Secretary of the Navy, RG 45, National Archives; Welles to John G. Barnard, 26 June 1861, *ORN*, ser. 1, 12:195.

18. SFDP to William Whetten, 23 June 1861, W9-2304, SFDP Papers, HML.

19. Du Pont, *Du Pont*; Merrill, *Du Pont*. See also Riggs, *A Guide to the Manuscripts in the Eleutherian Mills Historical Society*, 379–86; Hayes, "Introduction," in Du Pont, *Letters* 1:xlv–lxix. For Du Pont's strategic ideas, see Du Pont, *Report on the National Defences*, 4.

20. Reingold, "Alexander Dallas Bache," 165.

21. Davis, *Life of Charles Henry Davis*, 86–87, 121; SFDP to A. D. Bache, 30 May 1861, W9-2293, SFDP Papers, HML.

22. Warner, *Generals in Blue*, 19–20; SFDP to SMDP, 28 June 1861, W9-2309, SFDP Papers, HML; John G. Barnard to A. D. Bache, 1, 16, 17, 27, 30 May 1861, Correspondence of A. D. Bache, Superintendent of the Coast and Geodetic Survey, 1843–1865, RG 23, National Archives; Cooling, *Symbol, Sword, and Shield*, 37, 57–62. Barnard wrote extensively on many subjects, but he was at his best when writing on coastal defenses; see Barnard, *Notes on Sea-Coast Defence*. Rowena Reed claims that Barnard was the personal representative of General McClellan to the Blockade Board (*Combined Operations in the Civil War*, 39), but there is no evidence that Barnard was anything other than an engineer who was an expert on coastal defenses.

23. Welles to SFDP, A. D. Bache, Charles Henry Davis, and John G. Barnard, 25 June 1861, Confidential Letter Book of the Secretary of the Navy, Correspondence of the Secretary of the Navy, Naval Records.

24. Charles Henry Davis, Minutes of the Strategy Board, 27 June 1861, Navy Subject File ON, Strategy and Tactics, box 453, Naval Records; SFDP to SMDP, 28 June 1861, W9-2309, SFDP Papers, HML.

25. Davis, Minutes of the Strategy Board, 27, 29 June, 15 July 1861, Navy Subject File ON, Strategy and Tactics, box 453, Naval Records; SFDP to SMDP, 4 July 1861, W9-2317, SFDP Papers, HML.

26. Unsigned and undated topic outline, Navy Subject File ON, Strategy and Tactics, box 453, Naval Records.

27. *ORN*, ser. 1, vol. 12:196.

28. Ibid., 195–98; *ORA*, ser. 1, 53:67–73. The board's reports are located in several locations in both the *ORN* and *ORA*. In the *ORN*, ser. 1, vol. 12, the third report is incorrectly listed as the second report. The second report is located in the *ORA*.

29. *ORN*, ser. 1, 12:198–206.

30. Lincoln, "Memoranda of Military Policy Suggested by the Bull Run Defeat, 23 July 1861," in Lincoln, *Collected Works* 4:457; SFDP to SMDP, 26 July 1861, W9-2332, SFDP Papers, HML.

31. Davis to Mrs. Davis, 27 July 1861, in Davis, *Life of Charles Henry Davis*, 127; SFDP to SMDP, 26 July 1861, W9-2332, SFDP Papers, HML.

32. *ORN*, ser. 1, 16:618–30.

33. Welles to SFDP, 3 Aug. 1861, ibid., 12:207.

34. Welles, *ARSN*, Dec. 1861, 7; SFDP to SMDP, 4 Aug. 1861, W9-2340, to Henry Winter Davis, 5 Aug. 1861, W9-2341, SFDP Papers, HML.

35. Welles, *Diary*, 23 Aug. 1864 entry, 2:117–18.

36. *ORN*, ser. 1, 16:651–55, 680–81; SFDP to Fox, 27 Sept. 1861, in Fox, *Confidential Correspondence*, 51–52.

37. SFDP and Charles Henry Davis to A. D. Bache, 2 Oct. 1861, Bache to Davis and SFDP, 16 Oct. 1861, to John G. Barnard, 16 Oct. 1861, Correspondence of A. D. Bache, Superintendent of the Coast and Geodetic Survey, 1843–1865, RG 23, National Archives.

38. Silas H. Stringham to Welles, 16 Sept. 1861, Welles to Stringham, 18 Sept. 1861, to Louis M. Goldsborough, 18 Sept. 1861, to SFDP, 18 Sept. 1861, *ORN*, ser. 1, 6:216, 232, 233, 12:208.

39. Clausewitz, *On War*, 88–89.

40. For the strategic importance of bases of operations, see Jomini, *Art of War*, 77–84.

41. Corbett, *Some Principles of Maritime Strategy*. For an analysis of Corbett's ideas that contrasts them with those of Mahan and Clausewitz, see Jablonsky, *Roots of Strategy* 4:17–19, 153–60; Handel, *Masters of War*, 277–98.

7. *The Great Southern Expedition*

1. SFDP to Louis M. Goldsborough, 25 Aug. 1861, Goldsborough Papers, Library of Congress.

2. SFDP to Henry Winter Davis, 4 Sept. 1861, to George S. Blake, 27 Sept. 1861, in Du Pont, *Letters* 1:141–42, 153–54. For this first joint operation of the Civil War, see Reed, *Combined Operations in the Civil War*, 11–16; Weigley, *A Great Civil War*, 73–74; Merrill, "The Hatteras Expedition, August 1861," 204–19.

3. SFDP et al. to Gideon Welles, 16 July 1861, *ORN*, ser. 1, 12:200–201; McPherson, *Battle Cry of Freedom*, 370. Dana Wegner claims that Du Pont wanted Stringham to set up a logistical base at Hatteras ("The Union Navy, 1861–1865," 114), but this was Stringham's and Butler's decision; Du Pont wanted the inlets blocked and the sounds controlled.

4. SFDP et al. to Welles, 13 July 1861, *ORA*, ser. 1, 53:71, 73.

5. SFDP to SMDP, 22 Aug. 1861, W9-2351, SFDP Papers, HML; Welles to SFDP, 18 Sept. 1861, *ORN*, ser. 1, 12:208; SFDP to SMDP, 18 Sept. 1861, in Du Pont, *Letters* 1:150–51. See also *ARSN*, Dec. 1861.

6. SMDP to SFDP, 16 Oct. 1861, W9-23015, SMDP Papers, HML.

7. Welles to SFDP, 12 Oct. 1861, *ORN*, ser. 1, 12:214–15; SFDP to SMDP, 17 Oct. 1861, in Du Pont, *Letters* 1:169–71. .

8. Welles, *Selected Essays*, 120–22; Bauer, "Samuel Francis Du Pont," 150; Merrill, *Du Pont*, 264. Robert Erwin Johnson believes that Du Pont selected Port Royal himself and would have done so with no further prodding by Fox (*Rear Admiral John Rodgers*, 171). See also SFDP to Gustavus V. Fox, 24 Oct. 1861, in which Du Pont speaks of a conference on the *Wabash* between himself and the generals about "the *big* place," which Fox noted in the letter's margin was "Port Royal that I insisted upon" (Fox, *Confidential Correspondence* 1:58).

9. SFDP to SMDP, 24, 26 Oct. 1861, in Du Pont, *Letters* 1:181–89; SFDP to Fox, 27 Oct. 1861, in Fox, *Confidential Correspondence* 1:60.

10. SFDP to A. D. Bache, 20 Oct. 1861, W9-2385, SFDP Papers, HML; Luraghi, *History of the Confederate Navy*, 183.

11. SFDP to Fox, 29 Oct. 1861, in Fox, *Confidential Correspondence* 1:64; Louis M. Goldsborough to Lizzy Goldsborough, 28 Oct. 1861, Goldsborough Papers, Library of Congress.

12. Lincoln, "General Order," 4 Oct. 1861, Welles to SFDP, 12 Oct. 1861, *ORN*, ser. 1, 6:293, 12:215. Winfield Scott sent a like message to General Sherman on 14 Oct. 1861 (ibid., 220).

13. Judah P. Benjamin to Francis W. Pickens, 1 Nov. 1861, *ORA*, ser. 1, 6:306. Other contemporary accounts indicate that most newspapers believed that Charleston was the fleet's destination; see Osbon, *A Sailor of Fortune*, 133. See also the *New York Tribune*, 8 Nov. 1861; *New York Herald*, 6 Nov. 1861.

14. Bright, "Confederate Coast Defense," 89–92; Drayton, "Report of Brig. Gen. Thomas F. Drayton, C.S. Army, of the Bombardment of Forts Walker and Beauregard," 24 Nov. 1861, *ORA*, ser. 1, 6:6–13; Browning, *Two If by Sea*, 117–18; Lowe, "Big Gun

Bombardment of Port Royal," 1–4; Guinn, "Coastal Defense of the Confederate Atlantic Seaboard States, 1861–1862," 211–12; Ammen, "Du Pont and the Port Royal Expedition," 677; Luraghi, *A History of the Confederate Navy*, 190–91.

15. Steedman, *Memoir*, 294; Porter, *Naval History of the Civil War*, 57.

16. Sharps, "Reynolds' Regrets," 27–29; Gibson and Gibson, *Assault and Logistics*, 16–17; log of the U.S. Steam Frigate *Wabash*, 29 Oct.–4 Nov. 1861, Bureau of Naval Personnel, Ships' Logs, Stations, and Miscellaneous, RG 24, National Archives; Roswell H. Lamson to Flora Lamson, 4 Nov. 1861, in Lamson, *Lamson of the* Gettysburg, 40; Robert Gould Shaw to Sarah Shaw, 5 Nov. 1861, in Shaw, *Blue-Eyed Child of Fortune*, 158.

17. Thomas W. Sherman to "The Adjutant General," 8 Nov. 1861, *ORA*, ser. 1, 6:4; SFDP to SMDP, 4, 5 Nov. 1861, in Du Pont, *Letters* 1:212–15. For the fleet's departure and harrowing voyage south to Port Royal, see Page, *Ships versus Shore*, 110–12; Porter, *Naval History of the Civil War*, 53–55; Ammen, *Old Navy and the New*, 346–47; Bauer, "Samuel Francis Du Pont," 150–51; Reed, *Combined Operations in the Civil War*, 27–28; Merrill, *Du Pont*, 265–66; Ammen, *Atlantic Coast*, 17–18; Steedman, *Memoir*, 288–89; Johnson, *John Rodgers*, 173–74; SFDP to Welles, 6 Nov. 1861, *ORN*, ser. 1, 12:258–61.

18. SFDP to Welles, 6 Nov. 1861, *ORN*, ser. 1, 12:258–61.

19. SFDP to SMDP, 5 May 1862, in Du Pont, *Letters* 2:31–36; Davis, *Life of Charles Henry Davis*, 164–65, 182.

20. For Du Pont's plan and the disposition of his forces, see *ORN*, ser. 1, 12:262–65.

21. Welles, *Diary*, 30 Sept. 1867 entry, 3:216–17.

22. SFDP to Welles, 11 Nov. 1861, *ORN*, ser. 1, 12:262.

23. Bauer, "Samuel Francis Du Pont," 151.

24. SFDP to SMDP, 7 Nov. 1861, in Du Pont, *Letters* 1:222–23. See also Levin, "A Marylander's Eyewitness Account of the Battle of Port Royal, South Carolina, 7 November 1861," 181–82. John P. Gillis, commander of the gunboat *Seminole*, sent excerpts of his ship's log to President Lincoln (J. P. Gillis to Abraham Lincoln, 7 Nov. 1861, Lincoln Papers, Library of Congress), but the log does not address the fact that the *Seminole*, following close behind Godon's *Mohican*, failed to follow Du Pont's prebattle instructions.

25. Steedman, *Memoirs*, 292.

26. Du Pont, *Letters* 1:223n. Commander John P. Gillis, commanding the gunboat *Seminole*, wrote that Du Pont ordered "cease firing" at 2:45 P.M. and that the U.S. flag was raised over Fort Walker at 3:03 P.M. (John P. Gillis to Abraham Lincoln, 7 Nov. 1861, Lincoln Papers, Library of Congress). It is unclear why there is a fifty-minute time discrepancy between Du Pont's and Gillis's accounts.

27. Roswell H. Lamson to Flora Lamson, 8 Nov. 1861, in Lamson, *Lamson of the* Gettysburg, 42–43 log of the U.S. Steam Frigate *Wabash*, 7 Nov. 1861, Bureau of Naval Personnel, Ships' Logs, Stations, and Miscellaneous, RG 24, National Archives.

28. *Hartford Courant*, 16 Nov. 1861.

29. Mahan, *From Sail to Steam*, 163–64. Lt. Alfred Thayer Mahan, a young officer and recent Naval Academy graduate, was on board the *Pocahontas* that day. His brief combat experience at Port Royal would be the first and last of his long career (ibid.; Seager, *Alfred Thayer Mahan*, 36).

30. Most accounts of the battle list twenty-three Union wounded; however, Du Pont sent a supplemental casualty report to Secretary Welles listing five additional wounded who had been overlooked (SFDP to Welles, 21 Nov. 1861, *ORN*, ser. 1, 12:266; log of the U.S. Steam Frigate *Wabash*, 7 Nov. 1861, Bureau of Naval Personnel, Ships' Logs, Stations, and

Miscellaneous, RG 24, National Archives). Also, the Confederate number was probably higher, for Sherman reported seeing twenty bodies near Fort Walker alone (Thomas W. Sherman to Adjutant General, 8 Nov. 1861, *ORA*, ser. 1, 6:4).

31. *New York Herald*, 14 Nov. 1861; *New York Tribune*, 9 Nov. 1861; *New York Times*, 14 Nov. 1861; *ARSN*, 2 Dec. 1861, 7.

32. Herman Melville, *Battle-Pieces and Aspects of War* (New York, 1866) Project Gutenberg's E-Book Project no. 12384 (19 May 2004), http://www.gutenberg.net/dirs/1/2/3/8/12384/12384-h/12384-h.htm Internet.

33. SFDP, "General Order No. 2," 8 Nov. 1861, *ORN*, ser. 1, 12:286.

34. SFDP to J. L. Lardner, 9 Nov. 1861, ibid.; Courtemanche, *No Need of Glory*, 35.

35. Vail, *Three Years on the Blockade*, 80–81; Merrill, *Rebel Shore*, 32–33.

36. Osbon, *A Sailor of Fortune*, 143–44.

37. SFDP to SMDP, 5 May 1862, in Du Pont, *Letters* 2:31–36.

38. Ibid.; SFDP to Welles, 11 Nov. 1861, *ORN*, ser. 1, 12:262–65.

39. Du Pont, *Letters* 1:223n. For criticism of Du Pont's performance at Port Royal, see Bauer, "Samuel Francis Du Pont," 151.

40. Thomas F. Drayton to Assistant Adjutant General, 24 Nov. 1861, *ORA*, ser. 1, 6:4; SFDP to SMDP, 13 Nov. 1861, in Du Pont, *Letters* 1:238–39; Welles, *Diary*, 30 Sept. 1867 entry, 3:216–17.

41. Weigley, *A Great Civil War*, 73–74; SFDP to SMDP, "Journal Letter No. 54," 5 May 1862, in Du Pont, *Letters* 2:31–36.

42. Chesnut, *Mary Chesnut's Civil War*, 8 Nov. 1861 diary entry, 230; *Charleston Mercury*, 9, 11 Nov. 1861; Robert E. Lee to Judah P. Benjamin, 9 Nov. 1861, to Samuel Cooper, 21 Nov. 1861, *ORA*, ser. 1, 6:312, 327; Bright, "Confederate Coast Defense," 92; Luraghi, *A History of the Confederate Navy*, 187; Guinn, "Coastal Defense of the Confederate Atlantic Seaboard States, 1861–1862," 363–67.

43. Bright, "Confederate Coast Defense," 96.

44. SFDP to Fox, 15, 11 Nov. 1861, in Fox, *Confidential Correspondence*, 72–73, 68–69.

45. SFDP to SMDP, 1 Dec. 1861, in Du Pont, *Letters* 1:263–66.

46. Nicolay and Hay, *Abraham Lincoln* 5:18–20; SFDP to Fox, 11 Nov. 1861, in Fox, *Confidential Correspondence*, 68.

47. Bauer, "Samuel Francis Du Pont," 152.

48. SFDP to Fox, 12 Nov. 1861, *ORN*, ser. 1, 12:341.

49. Browning, *Success Is All That Was Expected*, 109–10; Johnson, "Investment by Sea," 54.

50. *Barnstable Patriot*, 25 Mar. 1862; SFDP to James Wilson Grimes, 2 Dec. 1861, in Du Pont, *Letters* 1:268; Woodman, "The Stone Fleet," 233–55.

51. SFDP to Charles I. du Pont, 20 Feb. 1862, in Du Pont, *Letters* 1:335. Britain and France bitterly protested the navy's "stone fleet" tactics, with little effect (Bauer, "Samuel Francis Du Pont," 152; Hayes, "Introduction," in Du Pont, *Letters* 1:lxxiii; Davis, *Charles Henry Davis*, 196–200; Ammen, *Atlantic Coast*, 41–42).

52. SFDP to Thomas Sherman, 23 Nov. 1861, *ORN*, ser. 1, 12:324–25. For criticism of Du Pont, Sherman, and the latter's replacement, Maj. Gen. David Hunter, see Merrill, *Du Pont*, 270–73; Merrill, *Rebel Shore*, 40–49; Bright, "Confederate Coast Defense," 166–68; Bauer, "Samuel Francis Du Pont," 153.

53. Percival Drayton to Edwin Hoyt, 30 Nov. 1861, 18 Jan. 1862, in Drayton, *Naval Letters*, 8–9, 12; SFDP to James Wilson Grimes, 2 Dec. 1861, in Du Pont, *Letters* 1:269.

54. SFDP to SMDP, 24 Dec. 1861, in Du Pont, *Letters* 1:286–87.

55. Merrill, "Men, Monotony, and Mouldy Beans," 49–59.

56. Percival Drayton to Edwin Hoyt, 22 Apr. 1862, in Drayton, *Naval Letters*, 17.

57. Ibid.; Mahan, *From Sail to Steam*, 163–64.

58. Welles, *Diary*, 2 Oct. 1862 entry, 1:160.

59. Marchand, *Charleston Blockade*, 24 Jan. 1862 journal entry, 85.

60. John B. Marchand to SFDP, 5 Feb. 1862, ibid., 113; see also ibid., 112, 129, 154–65; Symonds, *Historical Atlas of the U.S. Navy*, 96.

61. SFDP, General Order No. 8, South Atlantic Blockading Squadron, 13 Feb. 1862, John Rodgers Family Papers, Library of Congress.

62. Porter, *Naval History of the Civil War*, 78–79.

63. Percival Drayton to Edwin Hoyt, 30 Nov. 1861, in Drayton, *Naval Letters*, 9; Rose, *Rehearsal for Reconstruction*, 107–8.

64. Rose, *Rehearsal for Reconstruction*, 11.

65. SFDP to SMDP, 30 Dec. 1861, in Du Pont, *Letters* 1:294.

66. Rose, *Rehearsal for Reconstruction*, xii.

67. Ibid., 20–23, 41; SFDP to Henry Winter Davis, 25 Feb., 8 July 1862, in Du Pont, *Letters* 1:412n, 2:156 and n.

68. SFDP to SMDP, 10 Apr. 1862, "Journal Letter No. 56," 13 May 1862, "Journal Letter No. 58," 24 May 1862, in Du Pont, *Letters* 1:412–13, 2:51–52, 70–71.

69. Rose, *Rehearsal for Reconstruction*, 144–49, 150–51; SFDP to SMDP, 11 May 1862, to Benjamin Gerhard, 27 May 1862, in Du Pont, *Letters* 2:44–46, 75.

70. *Grand Traverse [Mich.] Herald*, 8 Aug. 1862; Rose, *Rehearsal for Reconstruction*, 146–49, 189–90; SFDP to Titus Coan, 8 Feb. 1863, in Du Pont, *Letters* 2:423.

71. Quarles, "The Abduction of the *Planter*," 5–10; SFDP to SMDP, "Journal Letter No. 56," 13 May 1862, "Journal Letter No. 70," 4 July 1862, in Du Pont, *Letters* 2:51, 150–51; Browning, *Success Is All That Was Expected*, 96–97.

72. SFDP to Charles I. du Pont, 20 Feb. 1862, in Du Pont, *Letters* 1:337; Percival Drayton to Edwin Hoyt, 18 Jan. 1862, in Drayton, *Naval Letters*, 11.

73. Percival Drayton to Edwin Hoyt, 24 Mar. 1862, in Drayton, *Naval Letters*, 14–15; Seager, *Mahan Letters*, 37.

74. SFDP to Charles I. du Pont, 20 Feb. 1862, to William Whetten, 8 Oct., 14 Nov. 1862, in Du Pont, *Letters* 1:337–38, 2:244–45, 282; SFDP to SMDP, 10 Nov. 1862, W9-2730, SFDP Papers, HML.

75. SMDP to SFDP, 29 Apr. 16 Feb. 1862, W9-23145, W9-23113, SMDP Papers, HML.

76. SFDP to Welles, 23 Apr. 1862, *ORN*, ser. 1, 12:772; *ARSN*, 1 Dec. 1862, 3; Hayes, "Introduction," in Du Pont, *Letters* 1:lxxvi.

77. See Anderson, *By Sea and by River*, 232; Roland, *Confederacy*, 137; Owsley and Owsley, *King Cotton Diplomacy*, 229–67; Price, "Ships That Tested the Blockade of the Carolina Ports, 1861–1865," 196–241; Price, "Ships That Tested the Blockade of the Gulf Ports, 1861–1865," 262–97; Price, "Ships That Tested the Blockade of the Georgia and East Florida Ports, 1861–1865," 97–132; Vandiver, *Confederate Blockade Running through Bermuda, 1861–1865*, xli; Still, "A Naval Sieve," 44; Wise, *Lifeline of the Confederacy*, 226; Beringer, Hattaway, Jones, and Still, *Why the South Lost the Civil War*, 139, 201; Luraghi, *Rise and Fall of the Plantation South*, 137.

78. McPherson, *Battle Cry of Freedom*, 380–83; Surdam, "The Union Navy's Blockade Reconsidered," 85.

79. McPherson, *Battle Cry of Freedom*, 86, 382; Surdam, *Northern Naval Superiority and the Economics of the American Civil War*, 53, 207.

8. The Objective Is Charleston

1. SFDP to SMDP, "Journal Letter No. 40," 19 Mar. 1862, "Journal Letter No. 51," 29 Apr. 1862, in Du Pont, *Letters* 1:370–72, 2:21.

2. SFDP to SMDP, 24 Mar. 1862, "Journal Letter No. 43," 30 Mar. 1862, ibid., 385n, 393–94. See also Welles, *Diary*, 10 Aug. 1862 entry, 1:72. The *Atlanta* made her first trial voyage on 31 July 1862; a monitor in Du Pont's squadron, the *Weehawken*, ultimately captured her on 17 June 1863.

3. Gustavus V. Fox to SFDP, 3 Apr. 1862, in Fox, *Confidential Correspondence*, 114–15. Gideon Welles sent a like letter to Du Pont on 13 May 1862 (Du Pont, *Letters* 2:55). For descriptions of these ships, see Canney, *Lincoln's Navy*, 73–74.

4. SFDP to Fox, 3 Apr. 1862, in Fox, *Confidential Correspondence*, 115–18; SFDP to SMDP, "Journal Letter No. 44," 5 Apr. 1862, in Du Pont, *Letters* 1:403.

5. Fox to SFDP, 12 May 1862, in Fox, *Confidential Correspondence*, 119–20.

6. SFDP to Fox, 25 May 1862, ibid., 120–21.

7. SFDP to SMDP, "Journal Letter No. 60," 29 May 1862, in Du Pont, *Letters* 2:79.

8. SFDP to Fox, 31 May 1862, in Fox, *Confidential Correspondence*, 122–23. See also Tomblin, "From Sail to Steam," 315–16.

9. Fox to SFDP, 3 June 1862, in Fox, *Confidential Correspondence*, 126–28; Daniel Ammen to John Dahlgren, 25 June 1862, Dahlgren Papers, Library of Congress.

10. SFDP to SMDP, "Journal Letter No. 65," 22 June 1862, in Du Pont, *Letters* 2:129.

11. Ibid.; SFDP to Fox, 9 July 1862, in Fox, *Confidential Correspondence*, 133–37; Percival Drayton to SFDP, 30 June, 2 July 1862, in Du Pont, *Letters* 2:150n.

12. Browning, *Success Is All That Was Expected*, 97–103; SFDP to SMDP, 4 July 1862, in Du Pont, *Letters* 2:151; SFDP to Fox, 15 Aug. 1862, in Fox, *Confidential Correspondence* 149.

13. C. R. P. Rodgers to SFDP, 18, 19 July 1862, SFDP to SMDP, "Journal Letter No. 78," 27 July 1862, Welles to SFDP, 28 July 1862, in Du Pont, *Letters* 2:162–68, 174–75; SMDP to SFDP, 2 Aug. 1862, W9-23205, SMDP Papers, HML.

14. Tucker, *Andrew Foote*, 199; SFDP to SMDP, "Journal Letter No. 80," 7 Aug. 1862, in Du Pont, *Letters* 2:183; Hayes, "Introduction," ibid., 1:lii.

15. Canney, *Lincoln's Navy*, 73; Roberts, *USS* New Ironsides *in the Civil War*, 29–39; Canney, *Old Steam Navy* 2:15–20; Fox to SFDP, 5 Aug. 1862, in Fox, *Confidential Correspondence*, 143–44; SFDP to Welles, 5 Sept. 1862, in Du Pont, *Letters* 2:216.

16. SFDP to Fox, 15 Aug. 1862, in Fox, *Confidential Correspondence*, 148–49.

17. SFDP to SMDP, "Journal Letter No. 91," 12 Sept. 1862, Henry Winter Davis to SFDP, 2–3 Sept. 1862, in Du Pont, *Letters* 2:229 and n.

18. See Mitchel, *Ormsby MacKnight Mitchel*.

19. Welles to SFDP, 26 Sept. 1862, C. R. P. Rodgers to Fox, 3 Sept. 1862, in Du Pont, *Letters* 2:236, 213–14n; SFDP to Fox, 20 Sept. 1862, Fox, *Confidential Correspondence*, 155–56.

20. Dahlgren, *Memoir of John A. Dahlgren*, 381; Schneller, *Quest for Glory*, 231–32; SFDP to Fox, 8 Oct. 1862, in Du Pont, *Letters* 2:243–44. See also Tucker, *Andrew Foote*, 235.

21. Welles to John A. Dahlgren, 8 Oct. 1862, Dahlgren Papers, Library of Congress. See also Welles, *Diary*, 1 Oct. 1862 entry, 1:158.

22. Welles, *Diary*, 2 Oct. 1862 entry, 1:160.

23. SFDP to SMDP, "Journal Letter No. 1, New Series," 21 Oct. 1862, in Du Pont, *Letters* 2:252–53.

24. Ibid., 22 Oct. 1862, 258.

25. SFDP to SMDP, 18 Oct. 1862, "Journal Letter No. 1, New Series," 22 Oct. 1862, ibid., 248–49, 259.

26. SFDP to Henry Winter Davis, 25 Oct. 1862, W9-2711, SFDP Papers, HML.

27. SMDP to SFDP, 18, 23 Oct. 1862, W9-23269, W9-23271, SMDP Papers, HML.

28. Merrill, *Rebel Shore*, 137–38; Bauer, "Samuel Francis Du Pont," 154; Niven, *Gideon Welles*, 427. William Roberts also concludes that Du Pont did not explicitly outline the difficulties he would face at Charleston (*Civil War Ironclads*, 92–93).

29. SFDP to SMDP, "Journal Letter No. 1, New Series," 22 Oct. 1862, in Du Pont, *Letters* 2:259.

30. See Canney, *Lincoln's Navy*, 26–27, 72, 202. See also Roberts, *Civil War Ironclads*, 22–23; Hackemer, *U.S. Navy and the Origins of the Military-Industrial Complex*, 75–85; Allard, "Naval Technology during the American Civil War," 116.

31. Roberts, *Civil War Ironclads*, 5, 22–23; Morison, *Men, Machines, and Modern Times*, 36–38.

32. Albion, *Makers of Naval Policy*, 198. See also Roberts, *Civil War Ironclads*, 3.

33. For the challenges inherent in wartime innovation, see Rosen, *Winning the Next War*, 22–23. See also McBride, *Technological Change and the United States Navy*, 4.

34. McBride, *Technological Change and the United States Navy*, 8.

35. Lautenschlager, "Technology and the Evolution of Naval Warfare," 174–75.

36. Rosen, *Winning the Next War*, 38–39, 110. For the concept of technological inertia in warfare, see Roland, *Technological Fix*, 7, 16.

37. Beyerchen, "From Radio to Radar," 270.

38. Smith, *Military Enterprise and Technological Change*, 23. William McBride argues that Welles was a visionary who successfully fought against such old line officers such as Du Pont who were hopelessly lost in the past (*Technological Change and the United States Navy*, 14–15). See also Murray, "Innovation," 326.

39. Hackemer, *U.S. Navy and the Origins of the Military-Industrial Complex*, 96–97, 109–10. See also Roberts, *Civil War Ironclads*, 33.

40. Canney, *Old Steam Navy* 2:75–77. Only three of the *Passaic* monitors ever received their second XV-inch gun, and then just weeks before the end of the war.

41. Ibid., 78–79. See also MacBride, *Civil War Ironclads*, 23–25; Tomblin, "From Sail to Steam," 291–93. For the problems caused by the *Passaics*' XV-inch guns, see Canfield, "Guns for the Monitors," 48–55; Roberts, *Civil War Ironclads*, 43. See also Allison, "John A. Dahlgren," 37–38; Schneller, *Quest for Glory*, 218–23.

42. Daniel Ammen to John A. Dahlgren, 9 Nov. 1862, Dahlgren Papers, Library of Congress. Ammen's *Patapsco* was unique among the *Passaic* class monitors in Du Pont's fleet because her armament included one XV-inch Dahlgren gun and an 8-inch, 150-pound Parrott rifle ("Statistical Data of Ships," *ORN*, ser. 2, 1:170; Canfield, "Guns for the Monitors," 50).

43. Percival Drayton to Edwin Hoyt, 16 Nov. 1862, in Drayton, *Naval Letters*, 19–20; Schneller, *Quest for Glory*, 221.

44. Percival Drayton to SFDP, 24 Nov. 1862, in Du Pont, *Letters* 2:292–93; Drayton to Alexander Hamilton, 5 Dec. 1862, in Drayton, *Naval Letters*, 21.

45. Percival Drayton to John A. Dahlgren, 23 Nov. 1862, Dahlgren Papers, Library of Congress.

46. Percival Drayton to Alexander Hamilton, 5 Dec. 1862, in Drayton, *Naval Letters*, 20; Drayton to SFDP, 20 Dec. 1862, in Du Pont, *Letters* 2:305; Roberts, *Civil War Ironclads*, 85.

47. Percival Drayton to Alexander Hamilton, 16 Dec. 1862, to Edwin Hoyt, 5 Jan. 1863, in Drayton, *Naval Letters*, 22–23, 24.

48. Johnson, "John Rodgers," 264–66; SFDP to Fox, 19 Nov. 1862, in Fox, *Confidential Correspondence*, 168; John Rodgers to Anne Rodgers, 9 Dec. 1862, 4, 15, 18 Jan. 1863, Rodgers Family Papers, Library of Congress.

49. Taylor and Laas, *Lincoln's Lee*, 118; Johnson, "John Rodgers," 265–66; Welles, *Diary*, 22 Jan. 1863 entry, 1:226. For Rodgers's experiences during the final construction and fitting out of the *Weehawken*, see Johnson, *John Rodgers*, 223–32; John Rodgers to Anne Rodgers, 5, 8 Jan. 1863, SFDP to John Rodgers, 6 Jan. 1863, Rodgers Family Papers, Library of Congress.

50. Fox to SFDP, 23 Jan. 1863, in Fox, *Confidential Correspondence*, 175–76; *ORN*, ser. 1, 13:373–75; Fox to John Rodgers, 23 Jan. 1863, John Rodgers to Anne Rodgers, 22, 24 Jan. 1863, Rodgers Family Papers, Library of Congress. See also Heitzman, "The Ironclad *Weehawken* in the Civil War," 193–94.

51. John Rodgers to Anne Rodgers, 22 Jan. 1863, Hiram Paulding to John Rodgers, 24 Jan. 1863, Alban C. Stimers to John Rodgers, 25 Jan. 1863, Charles Henry Davis to John Rodgers, 25 Jan. 1863, Rodgers Family Papers, Library of Congress.

52. SFDP to SMDP, "Journal Letter No. 1, New Series," 23 Oct. 1862, "Journal Letter No. 5," 1 Nov. 1862, "Journal Letter No. 11," 16 Nov. 1862, SFDP to Welles, 25 Oct. 1862, in Du Pont, *Letters* 2:262, 271, 284–85, 266–67. See also Mitchel, *Ormsby MacKnight Mitchel*.

53. SFDP to Fox, 31 May 1862, in Du Pont, *Letters* 2:92.

54. SFDP to James W. Grimes, 1 Dec. 1862, W9-2750, SFDP Papers, HML; Percival Drayton to SFDP, 8 Nov. 1862, SFDP to SMDP, "Journal Letter No. 22," 27 Dec. 1862, in Du Pont, *Letters* 2:281, 324. See also SFDP to John Rodgers, 6 Jan. 1863, Rodgers Family Papers, Library of Congress.

55. SFDP to Fox, 22 Dec. 1862, Fox to SFDP, 6 Jan. 1863, in Fox, *Confidential Correspondence*, 172, 173.

56. Welles to SFDP, 6 Jan. 1863, *ORN*, ser. 1, 13:503; Welles, *Diary*, 5 Jan. 1863 entry, 1:216.

57. John Rodgers to SFDP, 29 Oct. 1862, *ORN*, ser. 1, 13:421–23; SFDP to SMDP, 12 Dec. 1862, in Du Pont, *Letters* 2:324n; John Rodgers to Anne Rodgers, 15 Jan. 1863, Rodgers Family Papers, Library of Congress.

58. SFDP to John Rodgers, 6 Jan. 1863, Rodgers Family Papers, Library of Congress; SFDP to Welles, 24 Jan. 1863, *ORN*, ser. 1, 13:535. In his letter to Welles, Du Pont mistakenly referred to Welles's order of "15 January," but he meant 6 January.

59. SFDP to Welles, 24 Jan. 1863, in Du Pont, *Letters* 2:377.

60. Welles to SFDP, 31 Jan. 1863, ibid., 399–400.

61. Nevin, *Gideon Welles*, 428–49; Welles to SFDP, 14 May 1863, in Du Pont, *Letters* 3:113–14.

62. Bauer, "Samuel Francis Du Pont," 154–55; Bright, "Confederate Coast Defense," 176–78, 183–88; Percival Drayton to Edwin Hoyt, 28 Feb. 1863, in Drayton, *Naval Letters*, 29–30; Merrill, *Rebel Shore*, 137–38; Tomblin, "From Sail to Steam," 317–21; Burton, *Siege of Charleston*, 135–36; Page, *Ship versus Shore*, 132–33; Luraghi, *A History of the Confederate Navy*, 195–96.

63. SFDP to SMDP, "Journal Letter No. 29," 19 Jan. 1863, in Du Pont, *Letters* 2:368.

64. SFDP to SMDP, "Journal Letter No. 29," 18, 19, 20, 21, 22, 24 Jan. 1863, ibid., 2:365–74.

65. SFDP to SMDP, "Journal Letter No. 30," 25 Jan. 1863, ibid., 365–74, 378–79.

66. John Worden to SFDP, 27 Jan. 1863, *ORN*, ser. 1, 13:544–45; SFDP to Benjamin Gerhard, 30 Jan. 1863, in Du Pont, *Letters* 2:394. See also Roberts, *Civil War Ironclads*, 86–87.

67. SFDP to Welles, 28 Jan. 1863, in Du Pont, *Letters* 2:543–44. See also Rodgers, "Du Pont's Attack at Charleston," 4:5; Canney, *Old Steam Navy*, 15–19; Roberts, *USS* New Ironsides *in the Civil War*, 30–32.

68. SFDP to Benjamin Gerhard, 30 Jan. 1863, in Du Pont, *Letters* 2:394.

69. Osbon, *A Sailor of Fortune*, 239–44; Morris, *"Nashville,"* 38–45. The destruction of the *Nashville* (renamed *Rattlesnake*) was a great relief to Du Pont and the department; see Ammen, *Atlantic Coast*, 87; SFDP to SMDP, "Journal Letter No. 38," 1 Mar. 1863, in Du Pont, *Letters* 2:458.

70. Merrill, *Du Pont*, 286–87; Du Pont, *Du Pont*, 153–58; Rodgers, "Du Pont's Attack at Charleston," 33–34; Porter, *Naval History of the Civil War*, 371–72; Ammen, *Atlantic Coast*, 83–89; Vail, *Three Years on the Blockade*, 105–7; Bauer, "Samuel Francis Du Pont," 155–56; Canfield, "Guns for the Monitors," 50–51.

71. Welles, *Diary*, 17 Mar. 1863 entry, 1:249; see also Welles to SFDP, 4 Nov. 1863, in U.S. Department of the Navy, *Report of the Secretary of the Navy in Relation to Armored Vessels*, 267.

72. Browning, *Success Is All That Was Expected*, 138, 140–42; *Boston Herald*, 19 Feb. 1863.

73. SFDP to SMDP, "Journal Letter No. 34," 11 Feb. 1863, Fox to Du Pont, 16 Feb. 1863, Du Pont to Fox, 2 Mar. 1863, in Du Pont, *Letters* 2:430, 443–45, 463–64; Welles, *Diary*, 16 Feb. 1863 entry, 1:236.

74. Nicolay and Hay, *Abraham Lincoln* 7:59–61; Nevin, *Gideon Welles*, 431–32; Welles, *Diary*, 16 Feb. 1863 entry, 1:236–37.

75. Fox to SFDP, 16, 20 Feb. 1863, in Fox, *Confidential Correspondence*, 179–82; Richardson, *Secret Service*, 323.

76. SFDP to Fox, 25 Feb., 2 Mar. 1863, in Fox, *Confidential Correspondence*, 182, 187; SFDP to SMDP, "Journal Letter No. 39," 4 Mar. 1863, in Du Pont, *Letters* 2:466–67.

9. Charleston and Its Aftermath

1. For the *Keokuk*, see Canney, *Lincoln's Navy*, 73–74, 194. For the *Alligator*, see Ragan, *Union and Confederate Submarine Warfare in the Civil War*, 99–105.

2. John Rodgers to Anne Rodgers, 24 Mar. 1863, Rodgers Family Papers, Library of Congress.

3. William H. Maies, 1 Apr. 1863 journal entry, William H. Maies Papers, Minnesota Historical Society; SFDP to David G. Farragut, 9 Mar. 1863, in Du Pont, *Letters* 2:475.

4. SFDP to William Whetten, 17 Mar. 1863, in Du Pont, *Letters* 2:489. Other letters outlining Du Pont's concerns include SFDP to SMDP, "Journal Letter No. 39," 7 Mar. 1863, to Charles Henry Davis, 31 Mar. 1863, ibid., 471–74, 530–32; John A. Dahlgren to SFDP, 12 Mar. 1863, in Dahlgren, *Memoir of John A. Dahlgren*, 286.

5. John Rodgers to unknown correspondent, 10 Mar. 1863, to William L. Hodge, 3 Apr. 1863, Rodgers Family Papers, Library of Congress.

6. *Chelsea [Mass.] Telegraph and Pioneer*, 21 Mar. 1863; *Boston Herald*, 17 Mar. 1863.

7. Charles Steedman to Sarah Steedman, 3 Apr. 1863, in Steedman, *Memoir*, 366–67; SFDP to Alexander D. Bache, 13 Mar. 1863, in Du Pont, *Letters* 2:499n. See also Roberts, *Civil War Ironclads*, 89.

8. Drayton to Edwin Hoyt, 4 Mar. 1863, in Drayton, *Naval Letters*, 31–32.

9. SFDP to SMDP, "Journal Letter No. 45," 17 Feb. 1863, in Du Pont, *Letters* 2:439. For the antiobstacle raft, see Canfield, "Guns for the Monitors," 52–53; Johnson, "John Rodgers," 266; John Rodgers to Anne Rodgers, 6 Mar. 1863, Rodgers Family Papers, Library of Congress. A second "deck scraper" appears to have been issued to the *Nantucket*, but she did not practice with the device, nor did she use it in combat (William H. Maies, 18 Mar. 1863 journal entry, William H. Maies Papers, Minnesota Historical Society).

10. "Order of Battle and Plan of Attack," SFDP to South Atlantic Blockading Squadron Captains, 4 Apr. 1863, *ORN*, ser. 1, 14:8–9. Note that Du Pont's letter-book transcript reads "*Weehawken*—with raft" (Du Pont, *Letters* 2:542n).

11. Villard, *Memoirs* 2:31.

12. SMDP to SFDP, 9 Apr. 1863, W9-23388, SMDP Papers, HML; SFDP to SMDP, "Journal Letter No. 50," 4 Apr. 1863, in Du Pont, *Letters* 2:544.

13. *New York Tribune*, 5 Apr. 1863; Villard, *Memoirs* 2:31–2; Hunter, *A Year on a Monitor and the Destruction of Fort Sumter*, 46.

14. Alban Stimers to Gideon Welles, 14 Apr. 1863, John Rodgers to SFDP, 20 Apr. 1863, *ORN*, ser. 1, 14:41–45; log of the U.S. Steam Frigate *Wabash*, 7 Apr. 1863, Bureau of Naval Personnel, Ships' Logs, Stations, and Miscellaneous, RG 24, National Archives.

15. Villard, *Memoirs* 2:42.

16. Browning, *Success Is All That Was Expected*, 174. Beauregard later wrote that Confederate gunners hit the Union ships 520 times; see Beauregard, "The Defense of Charleston," 14.

17. Belknap, "Reminiscence of the Siege of Charleston," 169.

18. Hunter, *A Year on a Monitor*, 50–51. For Charleston's Confederate ironclads *Chicora* and *Palmetto State*, see Lockhart, "The Confederate Naval Squadron at Charleston and the Failure of Naval Harbor Defense," 257–75; Still, *Iron Afloat*, 112–27.

19. Rodgers, "Du Pont's Attack at Charleston," 32–47; Beauregard, "The Defense of Charleston," 1–23; Merrill, *Du Pont*, 290–94; Hayes, "Introduction," in Du Pont, *Letters* 1:lxxxiii–lxxxiv; Bauer, "Samuel Francis Du Pont," 156; Henig, "Du Pont, the Navy Department, and the Attack on Charleston," 68–77; Bright, "Confederate Coast Defense," 188–90; Fowler, *Under Two Flags*, 254–55; Ammen, *Old Navy and the New*, 372–74; Page, *Ship versus Shore*, 132–34; Anderson, *By Sea and by River*, 157–68; Burton, *Siege of Charleston*, 136–45; Roberts, *USS New Ironsides in the Civil War*, 50–56; Belknap, "Reminiscence of the Siege of Charleston," 163–71; Jones, *Siege of Charleston and the Operations on the South Atlantic Coast*, 168–83; Johnson, *John Rodgers*, 242–48; Heitzmann, "The *Weehawken* in the Civil War," 196–97. See also William H. Maies, 7 Apr. 1863 journal entry, William H. Maies Papers, Minnesota Historical Society. Accounts by Du Pont essentially mirror those of the other participants. See SFDP to SMDP, "Journal Letter No. 53," 8 Apr. 1863, to Welles, 8 Apr., 15 Apr. 1863, to David Hunter, 8 Apr. 1863, to Henry Winter Davis, 8 Apr. 1863, to SMDP, "Journal Letter No. 55," 10 Apr. 1863, in Du Pont, *Letters* 3:3–36.

20. Rodgers, "Du Pont's Attack at Charleston," 32–47; Beauregard, "The Defense of Charleston," 1–23; Merrill, *Du Pont*, 290–94; Hayes, "Introduction," in Du Pont, *Letters* 1:lxxxiii–lxxxiv; Bauer, "Samuel Francis Du Pont," 156; Henig, "Du Pont, the Navy De-

partment, and the Attack on Charleston," 68–77; Bright, "Confederate Coast Defense," 188–90; Ammen, *Old Navy and the New,* 372–74; Page, *Ship versus Shore,* 132–34; Anderson, *By Sea and by River,* 157–68; Burton, *Siege of Charleston,* 136–45; Roberts, *USS* New Ironsides *in the Civil War,* 50–56; Belknap, "Reminiscence of the Siege of Charleston," 163–71; Jones, *Siege of Charleston and the Operations on the South Atlantic Coast,* 168–83; Johnson, *John Rodgers,* 242–48; Heitzmann, "*Weehawken* in the Civil War," 196–97.

21. SFDP to SMDP, 8 Apr. 1863, in Du Pont, *Letters* 3:3–5.

22. John Rodgers to Anne Rodgers, 13 Apr. 1863, to William L. Hodge, Apr. 1863, Rodgers Family Papers, Library of Congress. For the obstacles in Charleston harbor on 7 Apr. 1863, see Du Pont, *Letters* 3:13n.

23. Drayton to Alexander Hamilton, 15 Apr. 1863, in Drayton, *Naval Letters,* 32–33; Ammen, *Atlantic Coast,* 102–3.

24. *Boston Herald,* 16 Apr., 2 May 1863.

25. SFDP to Thomas Turner, 14 May 1864, in Du Pont, *Letters* 3:341–43.

26. Beauregard Official Report, *ORA,* ser. 1, 14:242. Beauregard, "The Defense of Charleston," 1–23. Milton Perry argues that a good number of torpedoes blocked the main ship channel off the northern face of Fort Sumter. One of the huge "boiler" torpedoes failed to detonate when the *Ironsides* anchored directly over it (*Infernal Machines,* 50–53).

27. Welles, *Diary,* 12 Apr. 1863 entry, 1:267.

28. SFDP to Welles, 8 Apr. 1863, *ORN,* ser. 1, 14:3–4; Welles, *Diary,* 21 Apr. 1863 entry, 1:277.

29. Niven, *Gideon Welles,* 437–39; Henig, "Du Pont, the Navy Department, and the Attack on Charleston," 74–75.

30. John Hay to Abraham Lincoln, 8, 10 Apr. 1863, John Hay Papers, Brown University Library; John Hay to John G. Nicolay, 23 Apr. 1863, Hay, *At Lincoln's Side,* 37. For Lincoln's expression of doubt, see West, "Lincoln's Hand in Naval Matters," 175.

31. Lincoln telegram to SFDP, 13 Apr. 1863, SFDP to Welles, 16 Apr. 1863, in Du Pont, *Letters* 3:25, 37–39; Charles D. Fulton telegram to the *Baltimore American,* 13 Apr. 1863, Lincoln Papers, Library of Congress. See also Nevin, *Gideon Welles,* 436–37.

32. Percival Drayton, John Rodgers, Daniel Ammen, George Rodgers, D. M. Fairfax, and John Downes to Welles, 24 Apr. 1863, *ORN,* ser. 1, 14:45–48; Welles, *Diary,* 8 May 1863 entry, 1:295; Daniel Ammen to John Rodgers, 5 May 1863, John Rodgers to Anne Rodgers, 2 May 1863, Rodgers Family Papers, Library of Congress. John A. Dahlgren, Du Pont's eventual replacement, also noted that Du Pont's captains were unanimous in support of the admiral (Dahlgren, *Memoir of John A. Dahlgren,* 6 May 1863 journal entry, 391).

33. SFDP to Welles, 22 Apr., 27 May 1863, Welles to SFDP, 15 May 1863, in Du Pont *Letters* 3:50–56, 145–58, 115–18.

34. Henry Winter Davis to SFDP, 3 May 1863, SFDP to Davis, 11 May 1863, in Du Pont, *Letters* 3:79–83, 102–4; Henry Winter Davis to Abraham Lincoln, 4 May 1863, Lincoln Papers, Library of Congress. See also Henig, *Henry Winter Davis,* 179–80.

35. For Lincoln as an activist commander in chief, see Cohen, *Supreme Command,* 15–51.

36. Roberts, *Civil War Ironclads,* 99–100.

37. Rodgers to Welles, 2 May 1863, quoted in Hayes, "Introduction," in Du Pont, *Letters* 1:lxxxvii–xc.

38. SMDP to SFDP, 7, 16, 30 May 1863, W9-23409, W9-23416, W9-23427, SMDP Papers, HML.

39. SFDP to Henry Winter Davis, 3 May 1862, in Du Pont, *Letters* 3:75.

40. Welles, *Diary*, 30 Apr. 1863 entry, 1:288; SFDP to Welles, 3 June 1863, Welles to SFDP, 3 June 1863, SFDP to SMDP, 9 June 1863, "Journal Letter No. 70," in Du Pont, *Letters* 3:152–60, 167–68.

41. John Rodgers to Anne Rodgers, 17, 18 June 1863, SFDP to John Rodgers, 18, 21 June 1863, Rodgers Family Papers, Library of Congress; Still, *Iron Afloat*, 128–38; Bruce, *Lincoln and the Tools of War*, 240; *Boston Herald*, 25 June 1863.

42. Dahlgren, *Memoir of John A. Dahlgren*, 4–6 July 1863 journal entry, 396–97; Allison, "John A. Dahlgren," 39–40.

43. Weigley, *A Great Civil War*, 420; journal entry, 10–11 July 1863, and Dahlgren letter, 8 Nov. 1865, in Dahlgren, *Memoir of John A. Dahlgren*, 398–400, 551.

44. SFDP to Welles, 10 July 1863, in Du Pont, *Letters* 3:199.

45. SFDP to Welles, 22 Oct. 1863, Welles to SFDP, 4 Nov. 1863, ibid., 257–71; Hayes, "Introduction," ibid., 1:xci.

46. Welles, *Diary*, 25 May 1863 entry, 1:311–12; Gustavus V. Fox to John Ericsson, 27 Feb. 1864, in Du Pont, *Letters* 3:314n.

47. U.S. Congress, *Report on the Committee on the Conduct of the War, 1865* 2:95–96; Hess, "Northern Response to the Ironclad," 134; Tap, *Over Lincoln's Shoulder*, 233. See also Du Pont, *Du Pont*, 266–67; Henig, *Henry Winter Davis*, 178–80; Reid, "Historians and the Joint Committee on the Conduct of the War," 319–41.

48. David Hunter to Abraham Lincoln, 22 May 1863, *ORN*, ser. 1, 14:32–35; Welles to Schuyler Colfax, 11 Apr. 1864, in U.S. Department of the Navy, *Report of the Secretary of the Navy in Relation to Armored Vessels*, i–v. For a pro-Welles and Fox account of the controversy, see Bennett, *Steam Navy of the United States*, 403–19.

49. Welles, *Diary*, 9 Apr. 1864 entry, 2:7; John Rodgers, Daniel Ammen, George Rodgers, John Downes, and D. M. Fairfax to Welles, 25 May 1863, *ORN*, ser. 1, 14:214–16.

50. SMDP to SFDP, 15 Nov. 1861, W9-23044, to Henry Winter Davis, 21 Apr. 1864, W9-23558, SMDP Papers, HML.

Epilogue

1. Charles Henry Davis to SFDP, 5 June 1864, in Du Pont, *Letters* 3:253.

2. SFDP to Charles Henry Davis, 11 June 1864, to William Whetten, 15 Aug. 1864, ibid., 354–56, 367.

3. Henry Winter Davis to SFDP, 18 Aug. 1864, ibid., 369.

4. Ibid., 1:47; SFDP to Henry Winter Davis, 2 Nov., 5 Dec. 1864, ibid., 3:410–15. For Du Pont watching his diet, see ibid., 1:47.

5. SFDP to Henry Winter Davis, 22 Feb. 1865, ibid., 3:450.

6. Bauer, "Samuel Francis Du Pont," 157–58; SFDP to Henry Winter Davis, 4 Feb. 1865, in Du Pont, *Letters* 3:430–5; Hayes, "Introduction," ibid., 1:xcii; Henig, *Henry Winter Davis*, 235–37.

7. Percival Drayton to SFDP, 21 Jan. 1865, SFDP to Henry Winter Davis, 4 Feb. 1865, to Percival Drayton, 17 Feb. 1865, to SMDP, 9, 11 Mar. 1865, in Du Pont, *Letters* 3:429–35, 444–46, 454–55. See also Hayes, "Introduction," ibid., 1:xciii.

8. SMDP to "My Dear Friend," 1865, W9-39901, SMDP Papers, HML; SFDP to Henry Winter Davis, 31 Mar. 1865, SMDP to Henry Winter Davis, 31 Mar. 1865, in Du Pont, *Letters* 3:461 and n.

9. SFDP to Thomas Turner, 14 Apr. 1865, in Du Pont, *Letters* 3:463–64.

10. SFDP to Henry Winter Davis, 19 Apr. 1865, ibid., 464–65.

11. Ibid., 18 June 1865, 475.

12. SFDP to Percival Drayton, 22 June 1865, ibid., 479–82.

13. Newspaper accounts of Du Pont's death, W9-18494, SMDP Papers, HML; *New York Times*, 24 June, 5 July 1865; discussion with Dr. Michael Oplinger, 16 Apr. 2004.

14. Quoted from Henig, *Henry Winter Davis*, 245.

15. Eulogy by Henry Winter Davis, 25 June 1865, W9-18415, SMDP Papers, HML.

16. Ibid.; Duke, *Du Ponts*, 177–78; *Hagerstown [Md.] Herald and Torch*, 5 July 1865. See also Cleaves, *Meade of Gettysburg*, 48.

17. Browning, *Success Is All That Was Expected*, 210–12.

18. Roberts, "'The Name of Ericsson,'" 842–43.

19. Rodgers, "Du Pont's Attack at Charleston," 33.

20. *Hagerstown [Md.] Herald and Torch*, 25 Dec. 1884.

Bibliography

PRIMARY SOURCES

Manuscript Collections

Hagley Library and Museum, Greenville, Del.
    Samuel Francis Du Pont Papers
    Sophie Madeline Du Pont Papers
    Victor M. du Pont Papers
John Hay Library, Brown University, Providence, R.I.
    John Hay Papers
Manuscript Division, Library of Congress, Washington, D.C.
    John A. Dahlgren Papers
    Andrew H. Foote Papers
    Louis Goldsborough Papers
    Samuel Phillips Lee Papers
    Abraham Lincoln Papers
    Matthew Fontaine Maury Papers
    Matthew C. Perry Papers
    Rodgers Family Papers
    Gideon Welles Papers
    John L. Worden Papers
Minnesota Historical Society, Saint Paul
    William H. Maies Papers
National Archives, Washington, D.C.
    Record Group 23, Records of the Coast and Geodetic Survey
        Correspondence of A. D. Bache, Superintendent of the Coast and Geodetic Survey
    Record Group 24, Bureau of Naval Personnel
        Ships' Logs, Stations, and Miscellaneous
            Log of the U.S. Steam Frigate *Wabash*
    Record Group 45, Naval Records Collection of the Office of Naval Records and
        Library
        Confidential Letter Book of the Secretary of the Navy
        Letters Sent by the Secretary of the Navy to Officers,
            1798–1868

Letters Received by the Secretary of the Navy:
   Miscellaneous Letters, 1801–84
Letters Received by the Secretary of the Navy from the
   President and Executive Agencies
Captains' Letters
Commanders' Letters
Navy Subject Files
   AV Miscellaneous
   ON Strategy and Tactics
Special Collections and Archives Division, Nimitz Library, United States
   Naval Academy
Samuel Francis Du Pont, Journal of the USS *Franklin* and USS *Erie*, 1817–19
Log of the USS *Minnesota*, 21 May 1857–20 May 1859
Journal of the Cruise of the USS *Cyane*, 24 July 1846–7 August 1848

Public Documents

United States. Congress. *Congressional Globe.* 34th Cong., 1st sess., 11 March 1856.
———.———. House. Executive Document No. 1. *Annual Report of the Secretary of the Navy.* 37th Cong., 3d sess., vol. 3, ser. 1158, 1 Dec. 1862, 3–46.
———.———.———. Executive Document No. 1. *Annual Report of the Secretary of the Navy.* 38th Cong., 1st sess., vol. 4, ser. 1183, 7 Dec. 1863, iii-xxxv.
———.———. *Journal of the House of Representatives of the United States, 1850–1851.* 31st Cong., 2d sess..
———.———. Senate. Executive Document No. 1. *Annual Report of the Secretary of the Navy.* 33d Cong., 1st sess., vol. 3, ser. 692, 5 Dec. 1853, 297–319.
———.———.———. Executive Document No. 1. *Annual Report of the Secretary of the Navy.* 33d Cong., 2d sess., vol. 2, ser. 747, 4 Dec. 1854, 383–403.
———.———.———. Executive Document No. 1. *Annual Report of the Secretary of the Navy.* 34th Cong., 1st sess., vol. 3, ser. 812, 3 Dec. 1855, 3–18.
———.———.———. Executive Document No. 1. *Annual Report of the Secretary of the Navy.* 37th Cong., 2d sess., vol. 3, ser. 1119, 2 Dec. 1861, 3–23.
———.———.———. Executive Documents. *Annual Report of the Superintendent of the U.S. Coastal Survey.* 37th Cong., 2nd sess., 5 Nov. 1861.
———.———.———. Miscellaneous Document No. 23. *The Appointment of a Committee to Investigate the Proceedings of the Late Naval Board.* 34th Cong., 1st sess., vol. 1, ser. 835, 29 Feb. 1856.
———.———.———. Miscellaneous Document No. 24. *A Copy of the Charges, etc., upon Which the Officers of the Navy Were Removed and Disrated by the Action of the Late Naval Board.* 34th Cong., 1st sess., vol. 1, ser. 835, 29 Feb. 1856.
———. Department of the Navy. *Official Records of the Union and Confederate Navies in the War of the Rebellion.* 30 vols. Washington, D.C., 1927.
———.———. *Report of the Secretary of the Navy in Relation to Armored Vessels.* Washington, D.C., 1864.
———. Department of State. *Register of Officers and Agents, Civil, Military, and Naval, in the Service of the United States on the Thirteenth of September 1855.* Washington, D.C., 1855.

——.——. "Treaty of Tientsin, June 1858," accessed 22 Apr. 2002 at http://web.jjay.cuny
    .edu/~jobrien/reference/ob27.html.
——. Department of War. *Official Records of the Union and Confederate Armies in the War of
    the Rebellion.* 128 vols., Washington, D.C., 1898.

Newspapers

Barnstable [Mass.] Patriot
Boston Herald
Charleston [S.C.] Mercury
Chelsea [Mass.] Telegraph and Pioneer
Daily Alton [Ill.] Telegraph
Delaware State Reporter, Dover
Grand Traverse [Mich.] Herald
Hagerstown [Md.] Herald and Torch
Hartford Courant
National Intelligencer, Washington, D.C.
News Journal, Wilmington, Del.
New York Courier
New York Daily Times
New York Herald
New York Tribune
New York Times
Philadelphia Inquirer

Books and Chapters

Ammen, Daniel. *The Atlantic Coast.* New York, 1883.
——. "Du Pont and the Port Royal Expedition." In *Battles and Leaders of the Civil War,*
    vol. 1, ed. Robert Underwood Johnson and Clarence Clough Buel, 671–91. New
    York, 1887.
——. *The Old Navy and the New.* Philadelphia, 1891.
Awaji-No-Kami, Muragaki. *Kokai Nikki [Wonder Land]: The Diary of the First Japanese Em-
    bassy to the United States of America.* Tokyo, 1958.
Barnard, John G. *Notes on Sea-Coast Defence: Consisting of Sea-Coast Fortification, the Fifteen-
    Inch Gun, and Casement Embrasures.* New York, 1861.
Bauer, K. Jack, ed. *The New American State Papers, Naval Affairs.* 10 vols. Wilmington, Del.,
    1981.
Beauregard, P. G. T. "The Defense of Charleston." In *Battles and Leaders of the Civil War,*
    vol. 4, ed. Robert Underwood Johnson and Clarence Clough Buel, 1–23. New
    York, 1887.
Belknap, George E. "Reminiscence of the Siege of Charleston." *Papers of the Military His-
    torical Society of Massachusetts* 12 (1912): 155–207.
Chesnut, Mary Boykin. *Mary Chesnut's Civil War.* Ed. C. Vann Woodward. New Haven,
    1981.
Colton, Walter. *Deck and Port: or Incidents of a Cruise in the United States Frigate* Congress *to
    California.* New York, 1850.

Conrad, Charles M. *Report of the Secretary of War on the Subject of Fortifications and Floating Defences.* Washington, D.C., 1851.

Dahlgren, John A. "Report of Lieutenant J. A. Dahlgren." Pp. 65–90 in *Papers on the Subject of National Defences, in Reply to a Communication from the Secretary of War.* Washington, D.C., 1851.

Dahlgren, Madeline V. *Memoir of John A. Dahlgren, Rear Admiral of the United States Navy.* New York, 1887.

Davis, Charles Henry. *Life of Charles Henry Davis, Rear Admiral, United States Navy, 1807–1877.* Boston, 1899.

Drayton, Percival. *Naval Letters of Captain Percival Drayton, 1861–1865.* New York, 1906.

Du Pont, Samuel F. *Report on the National Defences.* Washington, D.C., 1852.

——. *Samuel Francis Du Pont: A Selection from His Civil War Letters.* Ed. John D. Hayes. Ithaca, N.Y., 1969.

Fox, Gustavus Vasa. *Confidential Correspondence of Gustavus Vasa Fox, Assistant Secretary of the Navy, 1861–1865.* Ed. Robert M. Thompson and Richard Wainwright. 2 vols. New York, 1918.

Frémont, John Charles. *Memoirs of My Life.* Chicago, 1887.

Hay, John. *At Lincoln's Side: John Hay's Civil War Correspondence and Selected Writings.* Ed. Michael Burlingame. Carbondale, Ill., 2000.

Hunter, Alvah F. *A Year on a Monitor and the Destruction of Fort Sumter.* Ed. Craig Symonds. Columbia, S.C., 1987.

Lamson, Roswell H. *Lamson of the* Gettysburg: *The Civil War Letters of Lieutenant Roswell H. Lamson, U.S. Navy.* Ed. James M. McPherson and Patricia R. McPherson. New York, 1997.

Lincoln, Abraham. *Collected Works.* Ed. Roy P. Bassler. New Brunswick, N.J., 1953–55.

Mahan, Alfred Thayer. *From Sail to Steam: Recollections of Naval Life.* New York, 1907.

Marchand, John B. *Charleston Blockade: The Journals of John B. Marchand, US Navy, 1861–1862.* Ed. Craig L. Symonds. Newport, R.I., 1976.

Maury, Matthew Fontaine. "Report of Lieutenant M. F. Maury." Pp. 32–65 in *Papers on the Subject of National Defences, in Reply to a Communication from the Secretary of War.* Washington, D.C., 1851.

Morris, Charles. "Report of Commodore Morris." Pp. 3–6 in *Papers on the Subject of National Defences, in Reply to a Communication from the Secretary of War.* Washington, D.C., 1851.

Nicolay, John C., and John Hay. *Abraham Lincoln: A History.* 10 vols. New York, 1909.

Osbon, Bradley S. *A Sailor of Fortune: Personal Memoirs of Captain Bradley S. Osbon.* Ed. Albert B. Paine. New York, 1906.

Perry, Matthew C. "Report of Commodore M. C. Perry." Pp. 7–12 in *Papers on the Subject of National Defences, in Reply to a Communication from the Secretary of War.* Washington, D.C., 1851.

Porter, David Dixon. *The Naval History of the Civil War.* New York, 1886.

Richardson, Albert D. *The Secret Service.* Hartford, 1865.

Rodgers, C. R. P. "Du Pont's Attack at Charleston." In *Battles and Leaders of the Civil War,* vol. 4, ed. Robert Underwood Johnson and Clarence Clough Buel, 32–47. New York, 1888.

Selfridge, Thomas O., Jr. *Memoirs of Thomas O. Selfridge, Jr., Rear Admiral, U.S.N.* New York, 1924.

Shaw, Robert Gould. *Blue-Eyed Child of Fortune: The Civil War Letters of Colonel Robert Gould Shaw.* Ed. Russell Duncan. Athens, Ga., 1992.

Steedman, Charles. *Memoir and Correspondence of Charles Steedman, Rear Admiral, United States Navy.* Ed. Amos L. Mason. Cambridge, Mass., 1912.

Totten, John G. *Report of General J. G. Totten, Chief Engineer, on the Subject of National Defences.* Washington, D.C., 1851.

Vail, Israel Everett. *Three Years on the Blockade: A Naval Experience.* New York, 1902.

Van Denburgh, Elizabeth Douglas. *My Voyage in the United States Frigate* Congress. New York, 1913.

Viele, Egbert L. "Avenging First Bull Run: The Port Royal Expedition." In *Battles and Leaders of the Civil War*, vol. 5, ed. Peter Cozzens, 91–102. Champaign, Ill., 2002.

Villard, Henry. *Memoirs of Henry Villard: Journalist and Financier, 1835–1900.* New York, 1904.

Welles, Gideon. *Diary of Gideon Welles, Secretary of the Navy under Lincoln and Johnson.* Ed. Howard K. Beale. 3 vols. New York, 1960.

——. *Selected Essays by Gideon Welles: Civil War and Reconstruction.* Ed. Frank Mordell. 2 vols. New York, 1959.

Secondary Sources

Books

Albion, Robert G. *Makers of Naval Policy, 1798–1947.* Ed. Rowena Reed. Annapolis, 1980.

Allgor, Catherine. *Parlor Politics: In Which the Ladies of Washington Help Build a City and a Government.* Charlottesville, Va., 2000.

Anderson, Bern. *By Sea and by River: The Naval History of the Civil War.* New York, 1962.

Bauer, K. Jack. *The Mexican War, 1846–1848.* New York, 1974.

——. *Surfboats and Horse Marines: U.S. Naval Operations in the Mexican War, 1846–48.* Annapolis, 1969.

Bennett, Frank M. *The Steam Navy of the United States.* Pittsburgh, 1896.

Beringer, Richard E., Herman Hattaway, Archer Jones, and William N. Still, Jr. *Why the South Lost the Civil War.* Athens, Ga., 1986.

Boot, Max. *The Savage Wars of Peace: Small Wars and the Rise of American Power.* New York, 2002.

Bradford, James C., ed. *Captains of the Old Steam Navy: Makers of the American Naval Tradition, 1840–1880.* Annapolis, 1986.

Bright, Samuel R., Jr. "Confederate Coast Defense." Ph.D. diss., Duke Univ., 1961.

Browning, Robert M., Jr. *From Cape Charles to Cape Fear: The North Atlantic Blockading Squadron during the Civil War.* Tuscaloosa, Ala., 1993.

——. *Success Is All That Was Expected: The South Atlantic Blockading Squadron during the Civil War.* Washington, D.C., 2002.

Browning, Robert S., III. *Two If by Sea: The Development of American Coastal Defense Policy.* Westport, Conn., 1983.

Bruce, Robert V. *The Launching of American Science, 1846–1876.* New York, 1987.

——. *Lincoln and the Tools of War.* Urbana, Ill., 1989.

Burrows, Edwin G., and Mike Wallace. *Gotham: A History of New York City to 1898.* New York, 1999.

Bush, Lewis. *77 Samurai: Japan's First Embassy to America.* Tokyo, 1968.

Canney, Donald L. *Lincoln's Navy: The Ships, Men, and Organization, 1861–65.* Annapolis, 1998.

——. *The Old Steam Navy.* Vol. 2. *The Ironclads, 1842–1885.* Annapolis, 1993.

Chisholm, Donald. *Waiting for Dead Men's Shoes: Origins and Development of the U.S. Navy's Officer Personnel System, 1793–1941.* Palo Alto, Calif., 2001.

Clary, David A. *Fortress America: The Corps of Engineers, Hampton Roads, and United States Coastal Defense.* Charlottesville, Va., 1990.

Clausewitz, Carl von. *On War.* Ed. and trans. Michael Howard and Peter Paret. Princeton, N.J., 1984.

Cleaves, Freeman. *Meade of Gettysburg.* Norman, Okla., 1960.

Cohen, Eliot A. *Supreme Command: Soldiers, Statesmen, and Leadership in Wartime.* New York, 2002.

Coletta, Paolo E., ed. *American Secretaries of the Navy.* 2 vols. Annapolis, 1980.

Cooling, Benjamin Franklin, III. *Symbol, Sword, and Shield: Defending Washington during the Civil War.* 2d ed. Shippensburg, Pa., 1991.

Corbett, Julian S. *Some Principles of Maritime Strategy.* Introduction and notes by Eric J. Grove. Annapolis, 1988.

Cornish, Dudley Taylor, and Virginia Jean Laas. *Lincoln's Lee: The Life of Samuel Phillips Lee, United States Navy, 1812–1897.* Lawrence, Kans., 1986.

Courtemanche, Regis A. *No Need of Glory: The British Navy in American Waters, 1860–1864.* Annapolis, 1977.

Dorwart, Jeffery M. *The Philadelphia Navy Yard: From the Birth of the U.S. Navy to the Nuclear Age.* Philadelphia, 2000.

Du Pont, Henry Algernon. *Rear Admiral Samuel Frances Du Pont.* New York, 1926.

Dupree, A. Hunter. *Science in the Federal Government: A History of Policies and Activities to 1940.* Cambridge, Mass., 1957.

Durkin, Joseph T. *Confederate Navy Chief: Stephen R. Mallory.* Columbia, S.C., 1987.

Dutton, William Sherman. *Du Pont: One Hundred and Forty Years.* New York, 1942.

Ferrari, Michelle. *Du Pont: 200 Years of an American Family.* New York, 2000.

Fowler, William M., Jr., *Under Two Flags: The American Navy in the Civil War.* New York, 1990.

Gibson, Charles D., and E. Kay Gibson. *Assault and Logistics: Union Army Coastal and River Operations, 1861–1866.* Camden, N.J., 1995.

Glenn, Myra C. *Campaigns against Corporal Punishment: Prisoners, Sailors, Women, and Children in Antebellum America.* Albany, 1984.

Guinn, Gilbert Sumter. "Coastal Defense of the Confederate Atlantic Seaboard States, 1861–1862: A Study in Political and Military Mobilization." Ph.D. diss., Univ. of South Carolina, 1973.

Hackemer, Hurt Henry. *The U.S. Navy and the Origins of the Military-Industrial Complex, 1847–1883.* Annapolis, 2001.

Hagan, Kenneth J., ed. *In Peace and War: Interpretations of American Naval History,* Westport, Conn., 1984.

——. *This People's Navy: The Making of American Sea Power,* New York, 1991.

Handel, Michael I. *Masters of War: Classical Strategic Thought.* 3d ed. Portland, Oreg., 2001.

Hattendorf, John B., ed. *Doing Naval History: Essays for Improvement.* Newport, R.I., 1995.

Hayes, Bradd C., and Douglas V. Smith, eds. *The Politics of Naval Innovation.* Newport, R.I., 1994.

Henig, Gerald S. *Henry Winter Davis: Antebellum and Civil War Congressman from Maryland.* New York, 1973.

Howard, Michael, and John F. Guilmartin Jr. *Two Historians in Technology and War.* Carlisle, Pa., 1994.

Howarth, Stephen. *To Shining Sea: A History of the United States Navy, 1775–1991.* New York, 1991.

Huntington, Samuel P. *The Soldier and the State: The Theory and Politics of Civil-Military Relations.* Cambridge, Mass., 1957.

Jablonsky, David, ed. *Roots of Strategy.* Book 4. Mechanicsburg, Pa., 1999.

Johnson, Robert Erwin. *Rear Admiral John Rodgers, 1812–1882.* Annapolis, 1967.

Jomini, Antoine Henri de. *The Art of War.* Novato, Calif., 1992.

Langley, Harold D. *Social Reform in the United States Navy, 1789–1862.* Urbana, Ill., 1967.

Lewis, Charles Lee. *Matthew Fontaine Maury: The Pathfinder of the Seas.* Annapolis, 1927.

Long, David F. *Gold Braid and Foreign Relations: Diplomatic Activities of U.S. Naval Officers, 1798–1883.* Annapolis, 1988.

Low, Betty-Bright P., and Jacqueline Kinsley. *Sophie Du Pont, a Young Lady in America.* New York, 1987.

Luraghi, Raimondo. *A History of the Confederate Navy.* Trans. Paolo E. Coletta. Annapolis, 1996.

——. *The Rise and Fall of the Plantation South.* New York, 1978.

MacBride, Robert. *Civil War Ironclads: The Dawn of Naval Armor.* Philadelphia, 1962.

McBride, William M. *Technological Change and the United States Navy, 1865–1945.* Baltimore, 2000.

McKee, Christopher. *A Gentlemanly and Honorable Profession: The Creation of the U.S. Naval Officer Corps, 1794–1815.* Annapolis, 1991.

McPherson, James M. *Battle Cry of Freedom: The Civil War Era.* New York, 1988.

Melville, Herman. *Battle-Pieces and Aspects of War* (New York, 1866) Project Gutenberg's E-Book Project no. 12384 (19 May 2004), http://www.gutenberg.net/dirs/1/2/3/8/12384/12384-h/12384-h.htm Internet.

Merrill, James M. *Du Pont: The Making of an Admiral.* New York, 1986.

——. *The Rebel Shore: The Story of Union Sea Power in the Civil War.* Boston, 1957.

Milby, Burton E. *The Siege of Charleston, 1861–1865.* Columbia, S.C., 1970.

Miller, Nathan. *The United States Navy.* 3d ed. Annapolis, 1997.

Mitchel, Frederick A. *Ormsby MacKnight Mitchel: Astronomer and General.* New York, 1887.

Miyoshi, Masao. *As We Saw Them: The First Japanese Embassy to the United States (1860).* Berkeley, Calif., 1979.

Morison, Samuel E. *"Old Bruin": Commodore Matthew C. Perry, 1794–1858.* Boston, 1967.

Munden, Kenneth W., and Henry Putney Beers. *The Union: A Guide to Federal Archives Relating to the Civil War.* Washington, D.C., 1998.

Murray, Williamson, and Allan R. Millett, eds. *Military Innovation in the Interwar Period.* New York, 1996.

Naval History Division. *Civil War Naval Chronology, 1861–1865.* 6 vols. Washington, D.C., 1961–66.

Niven, John. *Gideon Welles: Lincoln's Secretary of the Navy.* New York, 1973.

Odgers, Merle M. *Alexander Dallas Bache, Scientist and Inventor.* Philadelphia, 1947.

Owsley, Frank L., and Harriet C. Owsley. *King Cotton Diplomacy: Foreign Relations of the Confederate States of America.* Chicago, 1959.

Page, David. *Ships versus Shore: Civil War Engagements along Southern Shores and Rivers.* Nashville, 1994.

Paullin, Charles Oscar. *Paullin's History of Naval Administration, 1775–1911.* Annapolis, 1968.

Perry, Milton F. *Infernal Machines: The Story of Confederate Submarine and Mine Warfare.* Alexandria, Va., 1985.

Philbrick, Nathaniel. *Sea of Glory: America's Voyage of Discovery, the U.S. Exploring Expedition, 1838–1842.* New York, 2003.

Pourade, Richard F. *The Silver Dons: The History of San Diego.* San Diego, Calif., 1965.

Ragan, Mark K. *Union and Confederate Submarine Warfare in the Civil War.* Mason City, Iowa, 1999.

Reed, Rowena. *Combined Operations in the Civil War.* Annapolis, 1978.

Riggs, John Beverly. *A Guide to the Manuscripts in the Eleutherian Mills Historical Society.* Greenville, Del., 1970.

Roberts, William H. *Civil War Ironclads: The U.S. Navy and Industrial Mobilization.* Baltimore, 2002.

——. *USS* New Ironsides *in the Civil War.* Annapolis, 1999.

Roland, Alex. *The Technological Fix: Weapons and the Cost of War.* Carlisle, Pa., 1995.

Roland, Charles P. *The Confederacy.* Chicago, 1960.

Rose, Willie Lee. *Rehearsal for Reconstruction.* New York, 1964.

Rosen, Stephen Peter. *Winning the Next War: Innovation and the Modern Military.* Ithaca, N.Y., 1991.

Salter, William. *The Life of James W. Grimes.* New York, 1876.

Schneller, Robert J., Jr. *A Quest for Glory: A Biography of Rear Admiral John A. Dahlgren.* Annapolis, 1996.

Schroeder, John H. *Matthew Calbraith Perry: Antebellum Sailor and Diplomat.* Annapolis, 2001.

Seager, Robert. *Alfred Thayer Mahan: The Man and His Letters.* Annapolis, 1977.

Slagle, Jay. *Ironclad Captain: Seth Ledyard Phelps and the United States Navy, 1841–1864.* Kent, Ohio, 1996.

Sprout, Harold H., and Margaret T. Sprout, eds. *The Rise of American Naval Power, 1776–1918.* Princeton, N.J., 1966.

Sumida, Jon T. *Inventing Grand Strategy and Teaching Command.* Baltimore, 1997.

Surdam, David G. *Northern Naval Superiority and the Economics of the American Civil War.* Columbia, S.C., 2001.

Symonds, Craig L. *Confederate Admiral: The Life and Wars of Franklin Buchanan.* Annapolis, 1999.

——. *The Naval Institute Historical Atlas of the U.S. Navy.* Annapolis, 1995.

Tap, Bruce. *Over Lincoln's Shoulder: The Committee on the Conduct of the War.* Lawrence, Kans., 1998.

Todorich, Charles M. *The Spirited Years: A History of the Antebellum Naval Academy.* Annapolis, 1984.

Tomblin, Barbara B. "From Sail to Steam: The Development of Steam Technology in the United States Navy, 1838–1865." Ph.D. diss., Rutgers Univ., 1988.

Tucker, Spencer C. *Andrew Foote: Civil War Admiral on Western Waters*. Annapolis, 2000.

Vandiver, Frank E., ed. *Confederate Blockade Running through Bermuda, 1861–1865: Letters and Cargo Manifests*. Austin, Tex., 1947.

Warner, Ezra. *Generals in Blue: Lives of the Union Commanders*. Baton Rouge, La., 1964.

Weigley, Russell F. *The American Way of War: A History of United States Military Strategy and Policy*. New York, 1973.

——. *A Great Civil War: A Military and Political History, 1861–1865*. Bloomington, Ill., 2000.

Williams, Frank L. *Matthew Fontaine Maury: Scientist of the Sea*. New Brunswick, N.J., 1963.

Wise, Stephen R. *Gate of Hell: Campaign for Charleston Harbor, 1863*. Columbia, S.C., 1994.

——. *Lifeline of the Confederacy: Blockade Running during the Civil War*. Columbia, S.C., 1988.

Articles and Chapters

Allard, Dean C. "Naval Technology during the American Civil War." *American Neptune* 49:2 (1989): 114–22.

Allison, Davis K. "John A. Dahlgren: Innovator in Uniform." In *Captains of the Old Steam Navy: Makers of the American Naval Tradition, 1840–1880*, ed. James C. Bradford, 26–45. Annapolis, 1986.

Amero, Richard W. "The Mexican-American War in Baja California." *Journal of San Diego History* 30:1 (1984): 49–64.

Bauer, K. Jack. "George Bancroft, 11 March 1845–9 September 1846." In *American Secretaries of the Navy*, ed. Paolo E. Coletta, 1:217–29. Annapolis, 1980.

——. "Samuel Francis Du Pont: Aristocratic Professional." In *Captains of the Old Steam Navy*, ed. James C. Bradford, 142–65. Annapolis, 1986.

Beyerchen, Alan. "From Radio to Radar: Interwar Military Adaptation to Technological Change in Germany, the United Kingdom, and the United States." In *Military Innovation in the Interwar Period*, ed. Williamson Murray and Allan R. Millett, 265–99. New York, 1996.

Blume, Kenneth J. "'Concessions Where Concessions Could Be Made': The Naval Efficiency Boards of 1855–1857." In *New Interpretations in Naval History: Selected Papers from the Fourteenth Naval History Symposium*, ed. Randy C. Balano and Craig L. Symonds, 147–59. Annapolis, 2001.

Brodie, Bernard. "Technological Change, Strategic Doctrine, and Political Outcomes." In *Historical Dimensions of National Security Problems*, ed. Klaus Knorr, 263–306. Lawrence, Kans., 1994.

Buker, George E. "Captain's Mast: Conservatism vs. Liberalism." *American Neptune* 30:4 (1970): 136–46.

Canfield, Eugene B. "Guns for the Monitors." *Naval History* 14:1 (2000): 48–55.

Canney, Donald L. "The *Fulton II* and the Beginnings of the American Steam Navy." Ed. Jack Sweetman. *New Interpretations in Naval History*. Annapolis, 1993, 193–201.

Coleman, Earle E. "The Exhibition in the Palace: A Bibliographical Essay." *Bulletin of the New York Public Library* 64:9 (1960): 459–77.

Crowl, Philip A. "Alfred Thayer Mahan: The Naval Historian." In *Makers of Modern Strategy from Machiavelli to the Nuclear Age*, ed. Peter Paret, 444–77. Princeton, N.J., 1986.

Gallagher, Gary W. "Blueprint for Victory: Northern Strategy and Military Policy," In

Writing the Civil War: The Quest to Understand, ed. James M. McPherson and William J. Cooper Jr., 8–35. Columbia, S.C., 1998.

Goldrick, James. "The Problems of Modern Naval History." In *Doing Naval History: Essays for Improvement,* ed. John B. Hattendorf, 11–23. Newport, R.I., 1995.

Gooch, John. "The Weary Titan: Strategy and Policy in Great Britain, 1890–1918." In *The Making of Strategy: Rulers, States, and War,* ed. Williamson Murray, MacGregor Knox, and Alvin Bernstein, 278–306. New York, 1999.

Hattendorf, John B. "Introduction." In *Doing Naval History: Essays for Improvement,* ed. Hattendorf, 1–8. Newport, R.I., 1995.

Heitzman, William Ray. "The Ironclad *Weehawken* in the Civil War." *American Neptune* 42:7 (1982): 193–202.

Henig, Gerald S. "Admiral Samuel Francis Du Pont, the Navy Department, and the Attack on Charleston, April 1863." *Naval War College Review* 31:2 (1979): 68–77.

Hess, Earl J. "Northern Response to the Ironclad: A Prospect for the Study of Military Technology." *Civil War History* 31:2 (1985): 126–43.

Hirschfeld, Charles. "America on Exhibition: The New York Crystal Palace." *American Quarterly* 9:2 (1957): 101–16.

Johnson, Robert E. "Investment by Sea: The Civil War Blockade." *American Neptune* 32:6 (1972): 45–57.

——. "John Rodgers: The Quintessential Nineteenth Century Naval Officer." In *Captains of the Old Steam Navy,* ed. James C. Bradford, 253–74. Annapolis, 1986.

Langley, Harold D. "James Cochrane Dobbin, 8 March 1853–6 March 1857." In *American Secretaries of the Navy,* ed. Paolo E. Coletta, 12:279–300. Annapolis, 1980.

——. "William Alexander Graham, 2 August 1850–30 June 1852." In *American Secretaries of the Navy,* ed. Paolo E. Coletta, 1:257–67. Annapolis, 1980.

Lautenschlager, Karl, "Technology and the Evolution of Naval Warfare." In *Naval Strategy and National Security,* ed. Steven E. Miller and Stephen Van Evera, 173–221. Princeton, N.J., 1988.

Levin, Alexandria Lee. "A Marylander's Eyewitness Account of the Battle of Port Royal, South Carolina, 7 November 1861." *Maryland Historical Magazine* 85:2 (1990): 179–83.

Litten, Jane. "Navy Flogging: Captain Samuel Francis Du Pont and Tradition." *American Neptune* 58:2 (1998): 145–65.

Lockhart, Paul D. "The Confederate Naval Squadron at Charleston and the Failure of Naval Harbor Defense." *American Neptune* 44:3 (1984): 257–75.

Lowe, William C. "Big Gun Bombardment of Port Royal." *America's Civil War* 13:6 (2001): 30–41.

Merrill, James M. "The First Cruise of a Delaware Midshipman: Samuel Francis Du Pont and the *Franklin.*" *Delaware History* 20:4 (1983): 256–68.

——. "The Hatteras Expedition, August, 1861." *North Carolina Historical Review* 6:1 (1952): 204–19.

——. "Men, Monotony, and Mouldy Beans: Life on Board Civil War Blockaders." *American Neptune* 16:1 (1956): 49–59.

——. "Midshipman Du Pont and the Cruise of the *North Carolina,* 1825–1827." *American Neptune* 40:3 (1980): 211–25.

Morris, H. Jerry. "*Nashville.*" *Civil War Times Illustrated* 25:1 (1986): 38–45.

Murray, Williamson. "Innovation: Past and Future." In *Military Innovation in the Interwar Period,* ed. Williamson Murray and Allan R. Millett, 300–368. New York, 1996.

Paret, Peter. "Clausewitz." In *Makers of Modern Strategy from Machiavelli to the Nuclear Age*, ed. Peter Paret, 186–213. Princeton, N.J., 1986.

Post, Robert C. "Reflections of American Science and Technology at the New York Crystal Palace Exhibition." *Journal of American Studies* 17:3 (1983): 337–56.

Price, Marcus W. "Ships That Tested the Blockade of the Carolina Ports, 1861–1865." *American Neptune* 8:7 (1948): 196–241.

——. "Ships That Tested the Blockade of the Georgia and East Florida Ports, 1861–1865." *American Neptune* 15:1 (1955): 97–132.

——. "Ships That Tested the Blockade of the Gulf Ports, 1861–1865." *American Neptune* 2:1 (1951): 262–90.

Quarles, Benjamin. "The Abduction of the *Planter*." *Civil War History* 4:1 (1958): 5–10.

Reid, Brian Holden. "Historians and the Joint Committee on the Conduct of the War, 1861–1865." *Civil War History* 38:4 (1992): 319–41.

Reingold, Nathan. "Alexander Dallas Bache: Science and Technology in the American Idiom." *Technology and Culture* 11:2 (1970): 163–77.

Roberts, William H. "'The Name of Ericsson': Political Engineering in the Union Ironclad Program, 1861–1863." *Journal of Military History* 63:4 (1999): 823–44.

Schroeder, John H. "Matthew Calbraith Perry: Antebellum Precursor of the Steam Navy." In *Captains of the Old Steam Navy: Makers of the American Naval Tradition, 1840–1880*, ed. James C. Bradford, 3–25. Annapolis, 1986.

Sharp, Arthur G. "Reynolds' Regrets." *Civil War Times Illustrated* 16:8 (1977): 22–33.

Smith, Geoffrey S. "An Uncertain Passage: The Bureaus Run the Navy, 1842–1861." In *In Peace and War: Interpretations of American Naval History, 1775–1984*, ed. Kenneth J. Hagan, 79–106. Westport, Conn., 1984.

Smith, Merritt Roe, "Introduction." In *Military Enterprise and Technological Change: Perspectives on the American Experience*, ed. Smith, 1–37. Cambridge, Mass., 1988.

Sprout, Margaret T. "Mahan: Evangelist of Sea Power." In *Makers of Modern Strategy: Military Thought from Machiavelli to Hitler*, ed. Edward Meade Earle, 415–45. Princeton, N.J., 1944.

Stanton, William. "Matthew Fontaine Maury: Navy Science for the World." In *Captains of the Old Steam Navy: Makers of the American Naval Tradition, 1840–1880*, ed. James C. Bradford, 46–63. Annapolis, 1986.

Steen, Ivan D. "America's First World's Fair: The Exhibition of the Industry of All Nations at New York's Crystal Palace, 1853–1854." *New York Historical Society Quarterly* 47:3 (1963): 257–87.

Still, William N., Jr. "A Naval Sieve: The Union Blockade in the Civil War." *U.S. Naval War College Review* 36:3 (1983): 38–45.

Surdam, David G. "The Union Navy's Blockade Reconsidered." *Naval War College Review* 51:4 (1998): 85–107.

Todorich, Charles M. "Franklin Buchanan: Symbol for Two Navies." In *Captains of the Old Steam Navy: Makers of the American Naval Tradition, 1840–1880*, ed. James C. Bradford, 87–112. Annapolis, 1986.

Tucker, Spencer C. "U.S. Navy Steam Sloop *Princeton*." *American Neptune* 49:2 (1989): 96–113.

Vlahos, Michael E. "The Making of an American Style." In *Naval Engineering and America Sea Power*, Ed. Randolph W. King, 3–29. Baltimore, 1989.

Weddle, Kevin J. "The Blockade Board of 1861 and Union Naval Strategy." *Civil War History* 48:2 (2002): 123–42.

——. "'The Magic Touch of Reform': Samuel Francis Du Pont and the Efficiency Board of 1855." *Journal of Military History* 68:2 (2004): 471–504.

Wegner, Dana. "The Union Navy, 1861–1865." In *In Peace and War: Interpretations of American Naval History, 1775–1984*, ed. Kenneth J. Hagan, 107–25. Westport, Conn., 1984.

West, Richard S., Jr. "Lincoln's Hand in Naval Matters." *Civil War History* 4:2 (1958): 175–83.

Westwood, Howard C. "Reform in the United States Navy: The 'Plucking' of Officers in the Latter 1850s." *American Neptune* 50:2 (1990): 107–18.

Woodman, John E., Jr. "The Stone Fleet." *American Neptune* 21:4 (1961): 233–55.

Yanaga, Chitoshi. "The First Japanese Embassy to the United States." *Pacific Historical Review* 9:2 (1940): 113–38.

Index

A Nation Divided:
New Studies in Civil War History